Modern-Day Bolivia:

Legacy of the Revolution
and
Prospects for the Future

Contributors

Robert J. Alexander, Professor of Economics and Political Science, Rutgers University

Sylvia Borzutsky, Department of Political Science, University of Pittsburgh.

Juan L. Cariaga, Professor of Economics, San Andres University

L. Enrique García-Rodríguez, Sub-Secretary, Bolivian Ministry of Planning and Coordination and Professor of Economics, The Catholic University of Bolivia

Ray Henkel, Assistant Professor of Geography, Arizona State University

E. James Holland, Dean of the College of Liberal and Fine Arts and Professor of Government, Angelo State University

Herbert S. Klein, Professor of History, Columbia University

Jerry R. Ladman, Director, Center for Latin American Studies and Associate Professor of Economics, Arizona State University

James M. Malloy, Professor of Political Science, University of Pittsburgh

Juan Antonio Morales, Professor of Economics and Statistics and Director of Social and Economic Research Institute, The Catholic University of Bolivia

Salvador Romero Pittari, Vice Rector and Professor of Sociology, The Catholic University of Bolivia

José Isaac Torrico, Chairman, Department of Statistics, The Catholic University of Bolivia, and the United States Agency for International Development, La Paz

E. Boyd Wennergren, Director, Consortium for International Development, La Paz, and Professor of Economics, Utah State University

Morris D. Whitaker, Associate Professor of Economics, Utah State University

James W. Wilke, Professor of History, University of California at Los Angeles

Cornelius H. Zondag, Adjunct Professor, Center for Latin American Studies, Arizona State University

---

[1]Positions listed are those current at the time of the March 1978 conference.

Modern-Day Bolivia:

Legacy of the Revolution
and
Prospects for the Future

Jerry R. Ladman

Editor

Published by
Center for Latin American Studies
Arizona State University
Tempe, Arizona

Library of Congress Cataloging in Publication Data

Modern Day Bolivia.

   Chiefly papers from a conference which was held Mar. 15-18, 1978
on the campus of Arizona State University and which was sponsored
by its Center for Latin American Studies.
   Includes index.
   1. Bolivia--Politics and government--1952-   --Congresses.
2. Bolivia--Economic conditions--1952-   --Congresses. I.
Ladman, Jerry R., 1935-   . II. Arizona State University,
Center for Latin American Studies.
F3326.M55 1982   984'.052   82-22070
ISBN 0-87918-052-8

Published in the United States of America.

Typing by Lynnette Winkelman

Printed by Affiliated Lithographers, Inc.

Bookbinding by Roswell Bookbinding

Bureau of Publications • 12164

TO

ALL MY BOLIVIAN FRIENDS

Table of Contents

Figures

Tables

Appendices

Preface

Since 1976 I have visited Bolivia several times a year on a research project dealing with rural financial markets. In the process I had the opportunity to continually observe at close hand the important events and changes in that country, including three elections and several changes of government. In my early visits I was impressed by the growing economy that had been led by the petroleum and agricultural booms in the eastern tropical plains. These favorable economic conditions engendered considerable optimism for the future of this country, which by any measure was considered one of the poorest in Latin America. I was surprised to learn, however, that scholars had directed relatively little attention to the events of Bolivia during the times of four successive military governments in the late 1960s and 1970s, and in particular had not studied the government of General Hugo Banzer Suarez who was president from 1971 to 1978. In sharp contrast there had been a plethora of works written on the 1952 revolution, undertaken by the National Revolutionary Movement Party (MNR), and how that revolution had succeeded or failed until 1964 when the MNR was overthrown in a military coup led by General René Barrientos.

It was because of this hiatus that the idea to hold the conference, "Modern-Day Bolivia: Legacy of the Past and Perspectives for the Future," was born. The purpose of the conference was to assemble both Bolivian and North American experts to present papers and discuss Bolivian economic, social, and political events since the fall of the MNR in 1964, but with emphasis on the Banzer period and the outlook for the future. The conference was sponsored by the Center for Latin American Studies of Arizona State University. It was held on March 15-18, 1978, on the university campus in Tempe, Arizona.

The papers contained in the volume, with the exception of the final three chapters, were presented at that conference and deal with an analysis of the economic, political, and social changes between 1964 and early 1978. In some of the papers there is reference to the elections, scheduled for July 1978, that were supposed to return Bolivia to a democratic government. There was a strong feeling among the conferees that the new government would inherit a healthy economy and they were generally optimistic about Bolivia's future. Yet, at the time of the conference the key events of the 1978 elections had not yet begun to unfold, or at least to be understood fully. Nor was there a grasp of the true state of the problems with the economy. Consequently, I attempted to provide a prospective for these in Chapter XV, which was written about one year after the conference.

Meanwhile, the failure of the 1978 elections to establish a democratically elected government combined with a rapidly deteriorating economy set into motion a series of forces that created considerable problems as Bolivia continued its quest for a democratic government over the next two years. Finally, after two more general elections and five different governments, the attempt came to its conclusion when the military took power by force in July 1980 under the leadership of General Luis García Meza.

Unforeseen delays in the publication of the volume in the year and one-half after the conference virtually dictated that I include yet another chapter, XVI, to cover the events of this two-year period. Undoubtedly, the events and problems experienced by Bolivia in this two-year period had an important influence on both the content and tone of the final chapter that deals with the future of Bolivia following the García Meza coup in 1980. Were the final chapter to have been written immediately following the conference the outlook would have been considerably more optimistic, but less realistic as more recent events have demonstrated. Just prior to publication a brief epilogue was added to capsulize the additional changes of government taking place up to October, 1982.

There were a number of persons who played important roles in the planning stages of the conference. Deep appreciation is expressed to the then Bolivian ambassador to the United States, Alberto Crespo, and the then United States ambassador to Bolivia, William Steadman, for their support of the idea. Many persons provided invaluable advice in recommending conference participants, but particular gratitude should be expressed to Juan Cariaga, Robert Pace, and John Scafe. Fellow Bolivianists at Arizona State University — Ray Henkel, Lewis Tambs, and Cornelius Zondag — provided valuable input in the formulation of the program and speakers.

In addition to those persons who presented papers at the conference a special note of thanks goes to those who chaired the several sessions: Oscar Ayala, Melvin Burke, Mario Cortéz, Michael Meyer, Shoshana Tancer, and David Toyryla. We were especially pleased that Carlos Iturralde Ballivian, the then recently appointed Bolivian ambassador to the United States, was able to be with us to address the group at the evening banquet.

With respect to the book, appreciation is expressed to the authors, many of whom had to practice considerable forebearance as they suffered through revisions of their papers at the request of the editor. Special recognition goes to Deborah Baldwin and Lee Dowling, who provided editorial assistance at various stages of the manuscript and to Heidi Donlan Osselaer, who did the final editing and assisted in the preparation of the index. The Center office staff typed and retyped many manuscripts in preparation for the final typing which was very ably done by Lynnette Winkelman.

Tempe, Arizona   October, 1982

Chapter I

Introduction and Overview
Jerry R. Ladman

The 1952 revolution was a turning point in Bolivian history. The revolution resulted from an amalgamation of converging forces brought about by the economic crisis of the world-wide depression and the ignominious loss of considerable territory to Paraguay in the Chaco War, both in the 1930s. Much has been written about this revolution undertaken by the National Revolutionary Movement Party (MNR), especially about how it lost its momentum, culminating in the overthrow of the MNR in 1964 by the military.[1] In contrast, relatively little has been written about the post-1964 period when, except for brief periods, Bolivia was under military rule. In particular there has been scant analysis of the government of General Hugo Banzer Suarez who was president for the remarkably long period, by Bolivian standards, from 1971 to 1978.[2] The intent of this volume is to begin to fill this void with a series of papers on "modern-day" Bolivia, defined as the period after the fall of the MNR in 1964 but with emphasis on the Banzer period and the subsequent attempt of Bolivia to redemocratize. The papers, prepared by both Bolivian and North American scholars, treat different aspects of Bolivian politics, society, and economy.

Most of the papers were prepared in early 1978, prior to the July elections of that year that were supposed to allow the democratic process to choose Banzer's successor. However, the elections were nullified for reasons of fraud and within days the would-be president General Juan Pereda Asbún took control of the government by force. The next two years witnessed two more elections and a series of six military or civilian governments as Bolivia attempted to return to democracy. The attempt failed when General Luis García Meza led a successful military coup on July 17, 1980, to prevent the apparent winner of the 1980 election, Hernán Siles Zuazo, from taking office. Consequently, in order to not lose the value of these events in making predictions about Bolivia's future, another paper that provides a brief overview and analysis of the two-year period is included.

The volume is divided into six separate but interrelated parts: (a) The Legacy of the Past, (b) Political Development, (c) Foreign Influence and Foreign Relations, (d) Economic Development, (e) Social and Economic Change, and (f) The End of an Era and Prospects for the Future. The following sections briefly summarize each chapter. Each chapter is written so that it can be read independently of others. Some authors may differ over their interpretation of events, and the editor has respected their differences. The book is designed in a chronological sequence and presents an overall view when read in its entirety.

THE LEGACY OF THE PAST

In Chapter II Herbert Klein provides an overview of Bolivian history up to the 1952 revolution. Emphasis is placed on the economic and political factors of the nineteenth and twentieth centuries that led to the revolution. To understand modern-day Bolivia it is necessary to have knowledge of its past. It is striking that, in many ways, contemporary Bolivia is very similar to that of times long past.

In Chapter III Cornelius Zondag examines the revolution and, in particular, the very important role of U.S. support for the cause, introducing the role of personalities in ensuring that support. He examines the factors leading to the downfall of the MNR government as it became less responsive to populist elements and leaned towards a state-capitalist mode of governance.

POLITICAL DEVELOPMENTS

Populism vs. State Capitalism

In Chapter IV James Malloy and Silvia Borzutsky elaborate on this theme by showing how the Bolivian experience with populism and state capitalism fits within a general pattern of political economy followed in many Latin American export-based economies after the depression of the 1930s. They then show how the Bolivian populist movement failed and the state-capitalist model of the middle class emerged at the expense of organized labor and the peasants. When the MNR became incapable of effectively leading the country the military stepped in but maintained the same state-capitalist framework for the economy. Factions within the military prevented a unified military rule and, indeed, have caused rapid turnovers of governments. Successful and long-enduring presidents such as Banzer had to develop a highly personalized, authoritarian style of leadership based on clientelistic manipulation of civilian and military elites and suppression of organized opposition. The rapid economic growth of the *Oriente*, or the eastern lowlands, in this period is a complicating factor as it shifts regional balances of power. The authors conclude that the underlying political instability still exists and has become more complex. They predict that the state-capitalist mode of government will continue in the future under leadership provided by the military. The ability of any regime to remain in power will be determined by its deftness in manipulating the clientelistic factions within the elite. Unfortunately, this does not bode well for Bolivia's popular classes.

Organized Labor

In Chapter V Robert Alexander chronicles and analyzes the role of organized labor, Bolivia's most powerful populist element since the 1952 revolution. He examines changes in the organizational structure and leadership of the trade unions in the context of the different presidential regimes, but emphasizes the role that labor played in the political economy in each period. During the early years of the revolution organized labor was an important element in the MNR government but then began to lose its influence as the peasants and the military ascended in importance. After 1964, during the period of the military governments, labor was viewed not only as a force to be reckoned with, but also as a threat to stability and, consequently, was constantly repressed and marginated in the political structure when possible. The chapter concludes with an analysis of how the Banzer administration coped with this situation.

FOREIGN INFLUENCE AND FOREIGN RELATIONS

The United States

In Chapter VI James Wilkie analyzes Bolivia's relations with the United States by examining the patterns of the very considerable U.S. foreign assistance to the relatively small republic. He reports that U.S. aid was extremely important to the new revolutionary government in financing socioeconomic projects. After 1964, however, increasingly large amounts and proportions of total U.S. aid were directed to military purposes, an important factor in the build-up of the armed forces. Given the favorable growth of the Bolivian economy, U.S. aid has become progressively less important when measured as a percent of gross domestic product. Wilkie concludes that although on balance U.S. aid to Bolivia likely has been beneficial to the country, it is now time to make important cutbacks in the program. He argues his case on the grounds that Bolivia is no longer financially dependent on the United States and that much of the aid is going to support the military regime. The chapter has a useful statistical appendix containing data on Bolivia.

The Claim for an Outlet to the Sea

There are perhaps few issues as dear to the hearts of Bolivians as their perceived right for a territorial outlet to the Pacific which has been denied them since the loss of their littoral to Chile in the War of the Pacific, 1879-1883. This issue is at the nexus of Bolivia's relations with Chile and Peru. E. James Holland provides an overview of the history of the issue and then examines in detail the relations between the three countries during the Banzer regime and their impact on domestic Bolivian politics. He concludes that the lack of success of Banzer in striking a satisfactory accord with Chile was a significant factor in his downfall. The success of future governments in negotiating a solution will depend upon many factors, but perhaps most important will be that the government have the necessary legitimacy to come to a settlement that may cost Bolivia some territory. It is doubtful whether a military government would ever be in this position.

ECONOMIC DEVELOPMENT

Diagnostic Overview

In Chapter VIII Juan L. Cariaga provides a concise overview of the Bolivian economy since 1964 in the context of the heritage of the 1952 revolution, emphasizing agriculture in the postland reform period, mining in the postnationalization period, the Petroleum Code, and education. Although acknowledging that the rate of economic growth has been quite favorable since that year, he stresses that there are major problems in the Bolivian economy that may prove to be severe bottlenecks toward future progress. The heavy Bolivian dependence on foreign trade leaves the nation very vulnerable to world price fluctuations. Furthermore, this dependence leaves the government exposed to variations in tax revenues, created by a tax structure that heavily relies upon duties on imports and exports.

Another bottleneck is the rigidity of production in agriculture and mining. Although there was rapid growth of commercial agriculture in the *Oriente*, there was little progress in raising production in the traditional farming areas where the large bulk of the rural population resides.

Mining suffers from low revenues and the high costs of inefficient operations. This is particularly true for the large State Mining Company, COMIBOL. An inadequate tax system and politically motivated factors such as the maintenance of an undervalued currency and the high costs of labor, including fringe benefits, are important elements in causing the problems of COMIBOL.

Petroleum development, originally stimulated by the MNR government, offered promise to Bolivia, but, unfortunately, not as much has been discovered as was expected. It has been an important source of export revenue in recent years, but the rapid increases in domestic consumption, in part spurred by highly subsidized prices, suggest that Bolivia may indeed import petroleum in the not-too-distant future.

Although the revolution created major changes in the Bolivian economy, there are many deficiencies in the postrevolution economy, many of which emanate from the acts and philosophy of the revolution itself. Cariaga concludes that the future of the Bolivian economy will depend upon the ability of its future governments to correct many of these deficiencies. In the short run it will require a devaluation and more realistic pricing policies. In the long run it will be determined by adhering to rational development plans.

Structural Change and Planning

In Chapter IX L. Enrique García-Rodríguez elaborates on the patterns of structural change discussed in the previous chapter. Given the instability and high inflation rates of the 1950s, it was not until the 1960s that the economy began to grow in real terms. Domestic savings and investment increased as the economy grew, particularly after 1964. The sectoral composition of investment changed. Whereas mining and hydrocarbons received a large majority of the investment in the period of the MNR, after 1964 very notable increases in investment in agriculture, manufacturing, and services were observed. Although Bolivia is one of the least-developed Latin American economies and income distribution is quite unequal, social indicators show that there have been notable increases in the levels of literacy, nutrition, and life expectancy since the revolution.

A major change in the Bolivian economy was the rapid growth of the public sector. In 1976 it accounted for 33 percent of GDP, and was composed of two hundred institutions. Particularly important was the growth of public enterprises involved in a wide array of activities such as mining, hydrocarbons, cement, sugar, milk, transportation, and financial intermediation. García-Rodríguez criticizes many of these activities for being inefficient, and having little favorable impact on employment and income distribution due to their capital-intensive nature.

Against this background of the changes in the economy, García-Rodríguez presents a detailed analysis of government development policy since 1960. Bolivia's first attempt at a long-term development program came with the *1962-1971 Ten-Year Plan*, a primitive effort listing broad goals but with scant attention given to implementing policies. The Barrientos government minimized planning and advocated an economic system based on free enterprise. However, this government placed great emphasis on social and economic infrastructure projects. Ovando Candia resurrected the planning process and developed the *Social and Economic Strategy* for the twenty-year period, 1971-1991. This plan emphasized an increased role for the public sector, export promotion, and import substitution and placed less emphasis on infrastructural projects.

When Banzer came to power the immediacy of short-run problems did not allow the government to give much priority to long-range planning. This changed in 1974 when an elaborate infrastructure for planning was established that included the establishment of a Ministry of Planning and Coordination. In 1975 a *National Plan for Economic and Social Development* was presented for the 1975-1980 five-year period. In contrast to previous documents, the *Plan* concentrated not only on broad goals but also sectoral and regional targets that were supported by specific investment projects. Moreover, the *Plan* gave careful consideration to financing the projects.

In conclusion, García-Rodríguez states that although there have been many improvements in the economy as well as the levels of living since the revolution, much remains to be done, especially for the rural poor. He believes that planning, such as that undertaken since 1974, is the right way to correct this situation. He cautions that a development strategy which relies heavily on the public enterprises, as presently structured and operated, will not lead to efficiency, equity or financial stability.

Foreign Sector

The central importance of Bolivia's dependence upon foreign trade is emphasized by both Cariaga and García-Rodríguez. In Chapter X Juan Antonio Morales analyzes in detail Bolivia's foreign trade, balance of payments, trade policies, and participation in the Latin American Free Trade Association (LAFTA) and the Andean Group.

Historically Bolivia has used the export of primary products as an engine of growth and as the wherewithal to acquire imports of both consumer and productive goods. When the MNR government came to power it began to look more inward for a means to solve the nation's economic problems. After 1964, the military governments gave more emphasis to expanding exports. The fact that the respective values of exports and imports were equivalent to 22 and 25 percent of GDP from 1965 to 1972 demonstrates the importance of trade to the country.

Tin has been a predominant Bolivian export, but beginning in 1967 hydrocarbons became increasingly important. Since 1964 agricultural goods have gained in importance and there is a perceptible increase in exports of manufactured goods. Capital goods have been the principal import followed by intermediate and consumer goods. Much foreign trade is not counted due to high volume of contraband activity.

Bolivia regularly has a positive balance of trade but the costly debt service on its large foreign debt leaves a deficit in the current account of the balance of payments. Fortunately, with the generally robust economy since 1964, it has been able to attract foreign capital to offset the deficit. Moreover, with the exception of 1972, the inflows of foreign capital have allowed the government the flexibility to avoid the unpopular measure of devaluation. Morales points out, however, that the continued inflow of foreign capital could create a debt servicing crisis in the future.

Bolivia's policies to favor exports have centered on stabilizing prices for its principal exports. It has participated in the International Tin Agreement. It is not a member of OPEC but benefits from the high world prices that organization has brought about and has entered into an agreement for selling natural gas to Argentina at an established price. In 1977 the government instituted the Law of Fiscal Incentives for Non-Traditional Exports that employs various subsidies to encourage more exports of these products.

The expansion of exports, the fortuitously high prices for oil and tin, and the concomitant inflow of foreign capital since 1964 have been key elements in explaining Bolivia's growth. Morales points out, however, that the contribution to growth and development was not as important as could have been expected. Much of the foreign exchange was used to import costly consumption goods and much of the foreign investment went into projects of dubious value compared to alternative uses of funds. He concludes that prospects for continued expansion of primary product exports are dim unless more investment is oriented towards exportation of minerals and hydrocarbons.

Agriculture

In an overview of the agricultural sector in Chapter XI, Morris D. Whitaker and E. Boyd Wennergren show the dichotomy between the recently developed commercial agriculture in the lowlands of the *Oriente* and the much more traditional agriculture practiced in the *Altiplano* and Mountain Valley regions. Bolivian agriculture is characterized as underdeveloped. Only 12 percent of the cultivable land is planted to annual crops, the level of technology employed is low, modern product and input markets are lacking, and government support for the sector is insufficient.

Underdevelopment is reflected in the poor performance of the sector since 1960, although there was some improvement in the early 1970s with the boom in the *Oriente*. Production of basic foodstuffs has lagged behind population growth causing food prices to rise, increases in imports, and undernourishment. The authors argue that the relative neglect of the sector by the government in combination with ad hoc, uncoordinated foreign assistance have been major factors in keeping the sector from developing the infrastructure of human capital, viable institutions, and policies that are essential to provide the basis for development of the sector.

Whitaker and Wennergren conclude that although Bolivia has a natural resource base that is well-suited for agriculture, the prognosis for significantly improving the country's agricultural sector over the next two decades is pessimistic. They reach this conclusion by projecting the experience of the recent past to the future. They do not see that the government will develop the necessary programs and policies. Moreover, any efforts that are made will be hampered by the lack of trained professionals to undertake the necessary research, extension, and policy making. Even if these problems were corrected it would still take at least five to ten years to make significant improvements in the performance of the sector.

Public Policy for Agriculture

In Chapter XII José Isaac Torrico explores the role of the public sector in Bolivian agriculture. The number of government institutions serving agriculture increased sharply in the 1970s, resulting in a corresponding increase in the federal budget appropriated for the sector. This growth has been concentrated in decentralized agencies rather than within the Ministry of Peasant Affairs and Agriculture. Especially important was the growth of the regional development corporations and the agro-industries of the Bolivian Development Corporation (CBF). The development of institutions, however, is not sufficient to foster agricultural development. Many of the institutions lack an adequate budget and sufficient numbers of well-trained professionals to carry out their tasks. Moreover, the overall lack of a coherent, coordinated government policy for the sector has hampered their effectiveness.

Torrico examines several major components of public policy for agriculture in the 1970s. Much policy was designed for non-agricultural objectives such as import substitution, export promotion, and low urban wages. The latter has resulted in artificially low prices for basic foodstuffs grown largely by the peasants of the *Altiplano* and Mountain Valley regions. Thus, these farmers have less incentive to grow these products and have not had the opportunity for economic advancement had prices been allowed to rise with market forces. Agricultural credit was mostly channeled to commercial agriculture in the *Oriente* to the benefit of the middle- and large-sized farmers of that region and to the neglect of the peasants in the traditional areas of the nation. Torrico concludes that the policies have not benefited the large majority of the rural population but rather have favored mostly the commercial farmers of the *Oriente*.

SOCIAL AND ECONOMIC CHANGE

Migration and Colonization in the *Oriente*

In Chapter XIII Ray Henkel examines an important new phenomenon in Bolivia since the 1952 revolution, the settlement of the rural *Oriente* by migration and colonization. Once the mountainous highway from La Paz and Cochabamba was completed to Santa Cruz, considerable migration established a new era for Bolivia with the development of petroleum and agricultural-based natural resources. Spontaneous colonization by persons from the interior was followed shortly by government-directed colonization projects. Many of these projects were considerably less successful than planned. Henkel attributes this to poor access roads, insufficient planning, absence of capital, and excessive control over the colonists.

The impact of colonization on the environment is examined. It is shown to have caused severe soil erosion, seasonal flooding, loss of wildlife habitat, and destruction of valuable genetic material. Henkel concludes that in the future, it is virtually certain that Bolivia's next frontier will be the northeastern states of the Beni and Pando. The successes and failures of the *Oriente* experience should provide invaluable insight into the measures needed to plan for and cope with the migrations to these new areas.

Role of the State

In Chapter XIV Salvador Romero Pittari examines the role of the state in the rural-urban configuration of Bolivia. He argues that since the 1952 revolution the role of the state increased and widened tremendously, especially in the decade of the seventies, such that it penetrated almost all aspects of the social and economic structure. Therefore, in this new authoritarian-bureaucratic framework, the state has become the arena where social conflicts are expressed and attempts are made at their resolution.

The peasant society was brought under the heavy influence of the state since the government controls their markets, credit, public services, and infrastructure. As such, the state establishes the limits to the social-cultural participation by the peasant. Simultaneously, as the country has become increasingly urbanized, the state has become more involved in providing urban services.

Government policy in both rural and urban areas has benefited certain regions, especially those along the La Paz, Cochabamba, and Santa Cruz axis. The inequality of growth and competition for government resources has bred considerable inter-regional conflict. Moreover, the impact in the favored regions has mostly benefited the middle- and upper-level income groups. Thus the increasingly authoritarian-bureaucratic role of the state has led to regional and class conflicts under which the peasant and urban working classes have been the losers. Romero sees little prospect for change unless future governments incorporate the peasants and working classes into the ruling political coalitions.

THE END OF AN ERA

The "Economic Miracle"

In Chapter XV Jerry R. Ladman examines the "economic miracle" of the Banzer years. He contends that the "miracle" was indeed not a miracle, but rather a myth based on unfounded prospects for petroleum and fortuitous events in the international petroleum and minerals markets. This chapter describes how Banzer came to power in 1971 and was able to remain as president for seven years, a very long time by modern-day Bolivian standards.

One key to Banzer's long tenure was a temporarily strong economy based in the development of export-oriented agricultural and petroleum production in the *Oriente*. This situation enabled the government to rapidly expand its role in society and build a large coterie of public employees loyal to the president. The private sector benefited from the high level of economic activity and favorable government policies. Another key was Banzer's effectiveness in marginating the opposition by repressive measures that virtually eliminated political parties and organized labor. The result was an authoritarian-bureaucratic government based on a coalition between the military and the conservative private sector.

When it became apparent the economic miracle was indeed a myth and harsh unpopular measures would be necessary to correct this situation, it was clear the government would need a popular mandate to effectively deal with these problems as well as with the thorny question with Chile over Bolivia's outlet to the sea. Elections were called for 1978 and most thought that Banzer would try to succeed himself. However, when the government was forced to lift some of the repressive measures to allow the opposition to participate in the elections, considerable opposition to the president surfaced. Banzer decided not to run and picked Air Force General Juan Pereda Asbún as the official candidate. The main opposition was former president and MNR leader Hernán Siles Zuazo who headed a left-of-center coalition, the Democratic Popular Coalition (UDP). The election outcome was very close, but when it became apparent that excessive fraud at the polls had taken place, the elections were annulled. Uncertain about his future as a presidential candidate, Pereda took over the government in a coup in late July. Thus the Banzer era came to an ignominious end.

Further Attempts to Redemocratize

The Pereda coup did not untrack the attempt to return to democracy. Indeed, for the next two years Bolivia was immersed in what was almost a singular goal: to obtain a democratically elected government. In this period, which culminated in the military coup of July 1980 led by General Luis García Meza, Bolivia was constantly in a state of crisis as it confronted the difficult economic and political legacies of the Banzer years while simultaneously trying to elect a government. In the process the country experienced six governments and two more elections. Briefly, the sequence of events is that Pereda, who proved to be ineffective as a president was overthrown in November 1979 in a military coup led by General David Padilla Arancibia. Padilla was committed to a return to democracy and led the country to general elections in July 1980. However, the results of the presidential elections were inconclusive and congress named an interim government headed by the president of the senate, Walter Guevara Arce. In November 1980 Guevara, unable to manage the country for lack of a power base, was toppled in a military coup led by Colonel Natusch Busch. Popular resistance left many dead and wounded, making it clear that Natusch had to be replaced. Sixteen days after the coup started, congress, labor, and the military agreed upon another compromise interim president, Lydia Gueiler, president of the Chamber of Deputies, the nation's first female president. Gueiler served until another general election was held in June 1980. Shortly thereafter General García Meza assumed power to prevent the apparent winners of the election, Siles Zuazo and the leftist UDP, from assuming power.

In Chapter XVI Ladman provides an overview of these events and an analysis of why the attempt at redemocratization failed. During this two-year period, the country emerged from the repression of the previous military governments. For the first time in many years, organized labor, political parties, and an elected congress played important roles alongside the military in determining the course of events. Simultaneously the military went through a time of evaluating its place in society as younger, liberal officers began to exert influence. The United States also played an important role by lending its power to support the elections as part of its human rights policy.

From the outset it was clear that harsh measures were necessary to correct the worsening economy. However, until Gueiler, the successive governments were unable to take these measures because they did not have the sufficiently broad power base necessary to deal with the protests and disturbances certain to arise among organized labor and the popular classes. Nor did these governments have the strength to prevent the conservative elements of the military from stepping in to give order and assume power once unrest had broken out. Thus, the successive governments postponed the necessary measures until an elected government with a popular mandate could come to power. Meanwhile, the economy continued to deteriorate, instability heightened, and the required measures became increasingly more severe.

Simultaneously, the regrouping of political parties and organized labor gave more strength to the popular classes and leftist elements. Labor had clearly demonstrated its strength in organizing resistance to the Natusch Busch rebellion, and Siles Zuazo and the left-leaning UDP coalition had shown its vote-getting power in the 1978 and 1979 elections. This trend was of considerable concern to rightist elements in the private sector and military who feared that Siles might win the 1980 election.

General García Meza assumed the leadership of the highly motivated and divided military in the attempt to guard against the leftist trend.

Unsuccessful in provoking a cause for a coup prior to the election, he acted following the election to prevent the UDP from coming to power. In but a short time his government nullified the opposition and established a regimen that was intolerant of dissension. Bolivia was again firmly in the hands of the conservative military and prospects for another attempt at returning to a popularly elected government in the next few years were very dim.

PROSPECTS FOR THE FUTURE

In Chapter XVII Ladman argues that the future of Bolivia is inextricably tied to the economy. The short-term performance of the economy and the longer-term patterns of economic growth and the associated distributions of income and wealth will have an important impact not only on economic progress, but also the degree of political stability and the success of future governments.

Bolivia's extreme dependence on the external sector will make it subject to periodic economic fluctuations that can be destabilizing in the shorter run. The best means to counter this is to strengthen the domestic economy. However, it has been demonstrated historically that the export of nonrenewable resources, such as minerals and petroleum, has not led to widespread domestic development. Therefore, Bolivia must look inward to the growth of the domestic economy to provide for long-term economic development.

With a preponderance of the population in rural areas and the small domestic market, the appropriate development strategy must target on rural areas and small-scale industry, especially in the *Altiplano* and Mountain Valley Regions where the bulk of the population is concentrated. Another impetus for growth can come from the continued development of the *Oriente*, especially in the Beni, and the Chapare. Simultaneously, Bolivia will need to rely on the export of traditional products, and try to seek alternate exports among agricultural products in order to finance development and to service foreign debt. If the domestic development strategy is not pursued, Bolivia will eventually come upon a time of reckoning when its ability to export traditional products declines. At that time it would be much more difficult to launch a domestic development strategy and to experience long-run economic development.

Economic progress will depend upon the capabilities of future governments to cope with the periodic crises and long-term development. To do so will require major reforms and changes in economic policies on many fronts, many of which will have a populist bias as they will favor workers and peasants and redistribute economic programs from some of the richer to poorer regions of the country.

It is doubtful whether the conservative military style government will make these changes. The increased polarization of political movements, as manifested in the recent decline in the center and the strengthening of the left and right, has reinforced their resolve to counter the left and will likely cause them to resist directing resources to programs to benefit the popular sectors. Moreover, the conservative private sector and state capitalism constituents of their coalition would likely be harmed by the changes. Given the legacy of the well-entrenched internal political economy of government decision making it is unlikely that the military would take major action that would run counter to the interests of their coalition. Nor, for the same reasons, are they likely to allow an election to take place under which the left is likely to win.

The lack of action will, however, only lead to increasing instability, particularly as the populist forces become more disaffected. To counter this trend the likely outcome is that the moderate military forces will gather increasing influence and assume control of the government. This leadership would be more responsive to populists, undertake economic programs that lead the desired economic development, and eventually turn the government over to elected officials. If however, the conservatives remain in power and follow the above-described behavior patterns, Bolivia likely will neither experience long-term widespread economic development nor political stability. The result could be another internal uprising that would try to provide the populists with the benefits they failed to receive from the 1952 revolution.

ENDNOTES FOR INTRODUCTION AND OVERVIEW

1. See for example: Robert J. Alexander, *The Bolivian National Revolution* (New Brunswick, N.J.: Rutgers University Press, 1958); James M. Malloy, *Bolivia: The Uncompleted Revolution* (Pittsburgh: University of Pittsburgh Press, 1970); and James M. Malloy and Richard Thorn, eds., *Beyond The Revolution: Bolivia Since 1952* (Pittsburgh: University of Pittsburgh Press, 1971); Christopher Mitchell, *The Legacy of Populism in Bolivia: From the MNR to Military Rule* (New York: Praeger, 1977); James W. Wilkie, *The Bolivian Revolution and U.S. Aid Since 1952* (Los Angeles: Latin American Center, University of California at Los Angeles, 1969); and Cornelius H. Zondag, *The Bolivian Economy, 1952-65: The Revolution and Its Aftermath* (New York: Praeger, 1966).

2. A notable exception is Mitchell, op. cit., who analyzes the Banzer regime through 1976.

Part One

The Legacy of the Past

Chapter II

Bolivia Prior to the
1952 Revolution [1]
Herbert S. Klein

THE GEOGRAPHICAL SETTING

The historical development of Bolivian society has been significantly influenced by its rather unique geographical setting. With its heartland in one of the world's highest permanently settled intermountain valleys, the *Altiplano*, Bolivia has been defined by altitude and ecological environment. Though located within the world's tropical zone, the concentration of the population of Bolivia on the *Altiplano* has meant that national development has occurred in a relatively cold and hostile physical environment.

To supplement the deficiencies of this highland region, the *Altiplano* populations have had recourse to a series of associated lower altitude semi-tropical and temperate valleys in the eastern Andean mountain chain. These extensive and varied valleys have given the highland populations access to all the traditional crops available to pre-Columbian and post-contact Amerindian populations and have provided a crucial supplement of the main diet on the *Altiplano*. Together, these *sub-puna* valleys, *Yungas*, and the *Altiplano* comprise only two-fifths of the national territory even as measured by the reduced area of today, yet still contain after years of emigration four-fifths of the population. Thus Bolivia through most of its recorded history can be defined as a core heartland of plateau and associated valleys, intimately tied to similar systems north of Lake Titicaca, and only loosely connected to the vast lowland and coastal territories over which it claimed sovereignty.

THE PRE-COLUMBIAN INDIAN CIVILIZATIONS

Isolated from extensive contact with the coast to the East, the *Altiplano* has formed a region of continuous culture with southern Peru and has shared much of the culture of this common highland area for most of its historical development. Thus from the earliest evidence of human existence in this region, which is currently estimated to date from 21,000 years ago, the highland has developed at a different rate from the Pacific coastal zones. While the coastal Peruvian valleys saw the early development of village agriculture, the highlands did not have settled village agriculturalists until 2,500 B.C. By about 1,500 B.C. the unique concentration of highland peoples in metal development made this an important speciality of the zone, with copper being one of the first metals to be worked.

By 100 B.C. the highlands were experiencing a tremendous spurt of cultural advancement with the Wari-Tiahuanaco complex in the Lake Titicaca area slowly coming to dominate first the highlands and finally most of the coastal and Andean regions of Peru. At this point the full development of the region's advanced technology occurred, including the introduction of bronze and the final domestication of the region's traditional plants and animals. By 100 A.D. the Tiahuanaco religious center was becoming well known and the cultural aspects developed on the highlands soon spread throughout the entire Andean area. The dominant and imperial influence of the Wari-Tiahuanaco lasted until the middle of the twelfth century A.D. when it was destroyed and was replaced by regional florescent states.

In the Bolivian highlands the collapse of Tiahuanaco influence led to the rise of the Aymara regional kingdoms around Lake Titicaca and in all the important *sub-puna* and *Yungas* valleys. These highland weaving and herding societies maintained *Altiplano* colonists in all the major *sub-puna* valleys as well as on the Pacific coast, and thus were able to produce fish, maize, coca and tropical fruits along with potatoes and other highland root crops.

This whole system of vertical integration of micro-ecological zones, producing different crops and integrated into a non-market economy through an elaborate system of kinship and exchange, was fundamental in maintaining a powerful and economically vital system of Aymara states on the *Altiplano*. Thus the major states of the Colla, Lupaga, Pacajes and the Omasuyo formed an important challenge in wealth and population to the emerging Quechua-speaking state developing at Cuzco in the same period.

Along with the Aymara and Quechua, the other major linguistic group in the southern Andean highlands were the Urus. By historic times, that is by the period following the collapse of Tiahuanaco, the Uru were a poor and subservient group whose *ayllus* were distributed throughout the highlands and valleys in association and seeming dependence upon the Aymara communities. Largely fishermen and landless laborers, they were nevertheless treated with unusual cultural deference by the Aymara and may in fact have preceded them in this region.

The arrival of the Incas in the second half of the fifteenth century changed little of the social, economic and political organization of the Aymara kingdoms. Retaining the traditional rulers and contenting themselves with extracting surpluses through tribute payments, the *Cuzqueños* did little to disturb the fabric of Aymara life. This wealthy region was so important that it became one of the four administrative areas of the empire and was known as Kollasuyo. Nevertheless, integration was not peaceful and in 1470 there was a major revolt against the Incas among several of the Aymara kingdoms. The result was that the two kingdoms of Omasuyo and Pacajes were thoroughly subjugated and Quechua-speaking colonists were established in all of their areas, especially in the valley of Cochabamba and the southern valleys. It was, in fact, this last revolt and associated wars which were to determine the final linguistic composition of Bolivia from the fifteenth century until today.

So rich, powerful and populous were the Aymara kingdoms, that even in subjugation they retained an autonomy unique by Incan standards. Moreover, even the continued quechuaization of the Andean populations by the Spanish missionaries after the Conquest in the sixteenth century, had little impact on the Aymara and Uru speakers.

THE COLONIAL PERIOD

The importance of the Bolivian highlands within Peruvian society was recognized almost immediately after the Spanish Conquest in the late 1530s. Like the rest of the highland Peruvian region it had a dense, settled population of village agriculturalists who could easily be exploited. It also proved to be the center of silver mining in Spanish South America and thus was to become one of the two most important centers of the New World colonial empire. When Potosí was discovered in 1545, the rich deposits of silver in the famous *Cerro Rico* represented the largest concentration of silver then available in the Western world. Almost immediately Spanish capital poured into the Bolivian highlands to develop this enormous resource and create a complex of urban centers. To the mining towns of Potosí and Oruro, were added such cities as Sucre, Cochabamba, and La Paz, which both serviced the mines and dominated the best zones of Amerindian agriculture.

The emphasis of Spanish colonial rule in Bolivia, or Upper Peru as it was then called, was exploitation of the rich mineral deposits through the use of forced Indian labor, wage and contract labor, and even some slaves, and the exploitation of peasant agriculture. Both the highlands and the surrounding valleys of Peru and Bolivia became labor pools and supply centers for the mines. Silver mining was of such importance that, by the middle of the seventeenth century, the arid plateau town of Potosí had the largest population of any city in the entire hemisphere, with over one hundred thousand persons.

By the middle of the seventeenth century, however, a major secular decline began within the Upper Peruvian society as a result of the decline in silver production and the continuing demographic crises. The impact of new European diseases and the systematic exploitation of native population through the forced labor system of the *mita* had produced a negative growth rate in the Amerindian population by the last quarter of the sixteenth century, and it would take almost a century for population to begin to recover its positive growth. Equally, the first rich veins of silver were soon exhausted in the Potosí mines, and the consequent necessity of going into deep shaft mining and seeking new sources of silver was both highly expensive and time consuming. It was only with the help of positive government incentives in the middle of the eighteenth century that the mining industry again revived and succeeded in achieving impressive growth rates.

The late eighteenth century economic boom was a precarious one, however, based on heavy government subsidization of mining. With the collapse of the Spanish empire beginning with the Napoleonic wars and lasting until 1825 in Upper Peru, the entire mining industry went into a long secular decline which was not reversed until the middle decades of the nineteenth century. Whereas there were forty refineries smelting ore in Potosí in 1803, by 1825 there were only fifteen, and production had declined by more than 80 percent. By the time of the first Bolivian national census in 1846, it was estimated that there were some ten thousand abandoned mines in the republic.

1825-1880: ECONOMIC STAGNATION, RETRENCHMENT AND LOSS OF NATIONAL TERRITORY

In 1825 Bolivia obtained its independence from Spain. Incapable of exporting its silver at the levels of colonial production, the new republic rapidly lost its advanced economic standing within Spanish America.

Already by the end of the colonial period such marginal areas as the Río de la Plata and Chile were forging ahead on the basis of meat and cereal production. Bolivia, however, was a net importer of basic foods, even those which were exclusively consumed by its Indian population. In addition, none of its other mineral resources were of sufficient value to overcome the high transportation costs involved in getting the minerals to the coast. With little taxable trade and few exportable resources beyond its very modest precious metals production, Bolivia was forced to rely on the direct taxation of its Indian peasant masses.

In the nineteenth century, Indians constituted over two thirds of the national population and were primarily engaged in barter markets and subsistence agriculture. Heavily taxed with corvée labor obligations, all Indians who were members of the free peasant communities—a majority until the beginning of the twentieth century—were also required to pay a head tax called a *tributo*, and even a consumption tax on the uniquely Indian-consumed product of coca. Thus the poorest elements in the society were regressively taxed in the heaviest manner possible. Until well into the last quarter of the nineteenth century, this Indian taxation was the largest source of the national government's revenues. With the more progressive nations relying almost exclusively on the import and export taxes of a constantly expanding international commerce, it is easy to see why Bolivia rapidly lost its prominent position within the continent and began to be classified as one of the most backward of the new republics.

This economic stagnation and decline, however, initially had little impact on the political life of the republic. Both Antonio José de Sucre and Andrés de Santa Cruz reorganized the Bolivian economy and state finances in the 1820s and 1830s, so that Santa Cruz was finally able to unify Bolivia with Peru into a government known as the Confederation. But Chilean opposition destroyed the Confederation attempt, and Bolivia quickly turned in upon itself and, thenceforth, abandoned all attempts at international expansion. Rather, its efforts for the next half century would be primarily to integrate its far-flung borders into a coherent relationship with the core of the republic, the *Altiplano*, and the eastern Andean valleys. But this attempt was doomed to failure as Bolivia lacked the population and resources to exploit either its Amazon or Pacific frontiers. Despite the enormous wealth in nitrates and guano available on the Bolivian Pacific coast, the nation was incapable of exploiting them even on a joint basis with foreign capital. What little capital was available within Bolivia's upper class was totally committed to *Altiplano* mining. Rather, it was the Peruvians, Chileans, North Americans, and Englishmen who exploited these resources, and soon the flag was following trade. Between the Chilean War with the Confederation in 1838-1839 and the outbreak of the War of the Pacific in 1879, Chile constantly and successfully expanded its claims against Bolivian sovereignty in the Pacific, and, finally, in the War of the Pacific it took the entire Atacama coast.

1880-1930: NEW POLITICAL PARTIES, THE DECLINE OF SILVER AND THE RISE OF TIN

The fall of the Pacific litoral to Chile during the War of the Pacific was in many ways a blessing in disguise for Bolivia, for it marked a major turning point in national history. From the fall of the Confederation to the War of the Pacific, Bolivia had gone through one of the worst periods of *caudillo* rule experienced by any country in Latin America during the nineteenth century. However, silver mining had revived in the decades of the 1850s and 1860s under the impact of new capital inputs from Chile and England. By the time of the War of the Pacific international market conditions for silver and the introduction of new technology and capital had greatly revived the national mining industry. It was the War of the Pacific which enabled the new mining entrepreneurs to capture political control of the nation and definitively to break the hold of the now discredited military officers on national political life.

Starting in 1880 Bolivia moved into an era of a limited-participation civilian government, with the national upper class dividing into Liberal and Conservative parties which then proceeded to share power. This intraclass political party system finally brought Bolivia the stability needed for economic development. Though the parties were split on personality and anticlerical issues, they were identical in their desire to promote economic growth. From 1880 to 1899 the nation was ruled by the Conservatives, whose principal function was to encourage the mining industry through the development of an international rail network. It was the transportation to the coast which had traditionally been the heaviest cost item in Bolivian mining. Railroad construction to the Pacific ports of Antofagasta and Arica finally reduced that cost to a reasonable level and permitted much larger bulk shipments of other previously unexploited ores as well.

It was this renaissance in silver mining which also brought about major changes in the Bolivian social structure. With the revival of the mining centers and the steady growth of one or two major urban centers, the demand for food grew. The creation of a railroad and highway network connecting the urban and mining centers with previously isolated areas was the impetus for an important expansion in commercial agriculture. Though no reliable statistics are available for the nineteenth century on the production of foodstuffs, the rapid expansion of the *latifundia* system attests to the growth of this sector.

Whereas in 1846 over 63 percent of the Indians were still members of free landowning communities, by 1900 this percentage had declined to only 27 percent, reflecting a major growth in *latifundias*. At the same time the development of mining and the general increase in commerce finally saw the Indian head tax, which from 1825 to 1860 had been the primary source of government revenues, become an increasingly less significant item in government finance.

Simultaneously, there was a percentage decline of the Indian population and an increase of the *mestizo,* or *cholo* population, which by 1900 represented 27 percent of the national total. Forming a crucial middle cultural and economic layer between the whites and the Indians, the *cholos* greatly modified the bipolarity of traditional Bolivian society. They also formed the basic elements in the growth of the urban populations.

It was thus an economically expanding and socially developing nation which the Liberals inherited when they seized power from the Conservatives in the so-called Federal Revolution of 1899. Supposedly fought over the permanent placing of national institutions in the cities of Sucre or La Paz, the federal revolt was primarily a power struggle between the two parties themselves. Unfortunately for the Conservatives, their strength was too closely tied to the traditional Sucre-Chuquisaca elite, much of which was synonymous with the silver mining class. The Liberals, however, had the bulk of their strength in La Paz, which by this period was three times the size of Sucre and the largest urban center in the nation.

The Liberal victory was also closely associated with a basic shift in the mining economy. As the world silver market began to collapse in the 1880s and early 1890s, there began a major shift to tin mining on the Bolivian *Altiplano.* Long found in association with silver, tin did not become an important product until the end of the nineteenth century, when the demand suddenly soared in all the major industrialized countries. Thus, by 1900 tin had completely superceded silver as Bolivia's primary export, accounting for over 50 percent of the value of its national exports.

The shift to tin mining not only occurred at the same time as the Liberal revolt and was closely associated with the new party, but it also brought about a basic change within the capitalist class in Bolivia. Whereas the silver mining elite had been almost exclusively Bolivian, the new tin miners were more cosmopolitan and included in the early years both foreigners and some new Bolivian entrepreneurs. Tin mining now absorbed far more capital and produced considerably more wealth than the old silver mining industry, and the new companies which emerged became complex international ventures directed by professional managers.

Given this new economic complexity and the political stability already achieved by the Conservatives and perpetuated by the Liberals, the tin mining elite found it profitable to withdraw from direct involvement in national political life. Whereas almost all the Bolivian presidents under conservative rule had been either silver magnates or partners in silver mining ventures, the Liberal leaders and subsequent presidents of the twentieth century were largely outside the mining elite. No tin magnate actively participated in a leadership position within the political system. Rather, they were now to rely on a far more effective system of pressure group politics, which in Bolivian terms came to be known vulgarly as the *Rosca*, a term used to designate the oligarchy and the groups of lawyers and others supporting them.

A primary task of the Liberal politicians who ruled Bolivia from 1899–1920 was to settle Bolivia's chronic border problems. In 1899, Brazilian settlers forced the secession of the Eastern Bolivian province of Acre. In 1903 the Bolivian government recognized the annexation of this territory by Brazil. Later, in 1904 a treaty was signed to officially cede Bolivia's former territory on the Pacific Coast to Chile in return for indemnization. Secondly, the Liberals continued to expand the communications network initiated under the Conservatives. Bolivia was able to finance a great railroad construction era with large sums received from Chile for the Pacific coast territory and a large indemnity from Brazil for the loss of Amazon territory. By 1920 most of the major cities were tied together by rails, La Paz was connected to two international Pacific ports, a new line was started to Lake Titicaca and the Peruvian border, and one had been built to Tarija and the Argentine frontier. The Liberals also concentrated on school construction and modern urban development, primarily in La Paz. The result of all their efforts was a major expansion of the vital communications infrastructure initiated under the Conservatives.

The period of Liberal rule was also the most quiescent in Bolivian political history. The Liberal party, dominated by the figure of Ismael Montes, easily destroyed the federalists who had supported the party during the revolution. Their success led to the total collapse of the Conservative party. It was not until 1914 that an effective two-party system was again established, when many of the political "outs" along with a large number of new and younger elements finally organized the Republican party. Like its two predecessors the Republican party was composed of the white upper and middle classes with a fundamental belief in the liberal and positivist ideologies held by their predecessors.

Thus the period from 1880 to approximately 1932 can be seen as a coherent political era in which a two-party system alternated power in roughly ten to twenty-year periods of activity. While there were many *golpes de estado* even in this period, these were traditionally civilian led affairs most often involving limited violence with rather mild repression following the failure or success of the revolt. Equally the violence, except for the 1899 Federal Revolution, was confined to *cholos* and whites with the Indians being deliberately kept out of the fighting and also denied access to arms. For although the parliamentary and presidential system which the Conservatives, Liberals and Republicans had constructed was not amenable to peaceful transitions of presidential candidates, it was nevertheless based on an upper-class white consensus. Since the Indians were known to revolt frequently, the whites and *cholos* deliberately isolated them even from the moderate violence needed to keep the system functioning. So successful were politicians of all persuasions in this effort that few arms ever reached the hands of the Indians in the nineteenth and most of the twentieth centuries. Almost all of the famous Indian revolts, or *guerras de casta*, were fought with farm implements, with the whites and *cholos* having a virtual monopoly of firearms. However, it would be the progressive deterioration of elite consensus which in the late 1920s and 1930s finally broke this political isolation of the Aymara and Quechua peasants.

The deterioration of the elite consensus was preceded by fundamental changes in the national economy in the decade of the 1920s. While in the early years of this decade the Bolivian tin industry had experienced a brilliant post-war recovery and the achievement in 1929 of its highest production figure ever, the national economy was undergoing serious change. Long term price declines for tin had already begun by the middle years of the decade, and by 1930 the international tin market was in a state of near collapse as consumption declined throughout the world as a result of the Great Depression. The impact on Bolivia was profound, with production declining and the mining industry reducing its workforce and its contribution to the national economy. While the crisis of the depression would last only until the mid 1930s, long-term structural changes had taken place within the tin industry which would have important effects on national growth.

The decade of the twenties saw the final consolidation of the tin industry into the Big Three companies—those of Patiño, Hochschild and Aramayo—and the end of massive foreign investments. Moreover a progressive decline in the tin content of the ores and the end of new capital inputs meant the progressive decapitalization and declining productivity of the tin mines in the following decades. These structural changes in the major export sector of the national economy would soon have their effect on the national political system.

THE 1930s: THE DEPRESSION, CHACO WAR
AND RADICAL MILITARY RULE

By the 1920s, the Republican Party had replaced the Liberals, and in turn had split into several personalistic factions. By 1930 the most conservative of these factions, led by Daniel Salamanca, carried out a coup d'état against the regime and came to power. But the impact of the Great Depression on the national economy created severe political strains which the new government was incapable of handling. The end result was that a national political crisis was created which provided the excuse for Daniel Salamanca to provoke a long standing frontier dispute with Paraguay into a full scale international war which began in 1932.

The Chaco War was a long and costly disaster for Bolivia. The three years of bitter fighting on the southeastern frontiers left 100,000 Bolivian men dead, wounded, deserted, or captured. It also lost far more territory than Paraguay had claimed even in its most extreme demands. The fact that Bolivia entered the war with a better-equipped and supposedly far better-trained army only aggravated the sense of frustration at the disaster among the literate elite of the nation.

Previously wedded to the traditional elite and party system, the young veterans of the middle- and upper-class families now refused to support their rule. Suddenly the Bolivian political spectrum was filled with a host of small parties and groups that had not existed in the prewar period. Although some socialist and communist groups had been formed in Bolivia in the late 1920s, they had been destroyed by Salamanca during the war. Virtually no contract had existed between these extremely marginal groups (which were even poorly represented in the labor movement) and the traditional prewar parties. From 1935 on, however, this vacuum was filled by a host of competing groups all of which sapped the strength of the traditional parties on the right and encouraged the expansion of the extreme parties on the left.

The result of this new postwar political growth among the literate white and *cholo* elements in Bolivian society initially led to the inability of any one leader or party to gain control of the government. Thus in early 1936 the army seized power in a coup supported by a large number of the new moderate socialist groups. This was the army's first return to a governing situation since 1880.

But this new politicization of the army reflected the new currents of what everyone was beginning to call the Chaco generation. Thus the military regimes which ruled Bolivia from 1936 to 1939 were led by the junior officer veterans and declared themselves socialist. The results of this rule of the so-called "military socialists" were a fervent reformist activity in national society which saw the first serious social legislation ever enacted in Bolivia, and a major restructuring of the national political structure. The radical military officers carried out Bolivia's first labor code, wrote a totally new national constitution in 1938 which declared private property a right dependent upon social utility, and proposed the active intervention of the state in promoting welfare and social change. The Standard Oil Company holdings in Bolivia were nationalized, and finally the government promoted unionization of workers and supported the proliferation of a host of radical new parties to challenge the power of the old oligarchic entities.

1943-1952: THE RETURN TO CIVILIAN RULE AND THE DEVELOPMENT OF CIVILIAN REVOLUTIONARY PARTIES

But the radicalism of the junior officers frightened the more traditional elements in the Army. When President Germán Busch committed suicide in 1939, the senior officers reasserted control, and invited the traditional oligarchic parties back into power. Thus began the attempt, from 1939 to 1952, to reverse the political forces unleashed by the Chaco War and the radical regimes of the younger officers led by David Toro and Germán Busch. Forgetting historic conflicts, the traditional parties found themselves forced to band together in a united front against the rising strength of the new political forces in the nation. At first they were committed to a traditional presidential and parliamentary system but by the last years of the period they would abandon all efforts to govern democratically, and turn towards the Army as the only guarantor of their political, economic and social interests. This return to conservative military rule was doomed to failure, however, given the political mobilization which had already begun, and which the traditional elite found itself incapable of halting even by force.

At all levels, after 1936, there occurred a mobilization and incorporation of groups and classes previously isolated from national political life. In the late thirties and early forties the Bolivian tin miners were finally organized into powerful unions. This immediately led to a series of bloody, violent strikes and government massacres, the most famous being the Catavi mine massacre at the Patiño Company works in December of 1942. Along with the miners, factory workers and other urban elements also unionized. There were also the beginnings of syndicalization efforts among peasants, with the Quechua peasants of the Cochabamba valley being the first to organize formally and demand political and economic rights.

By the early 1940s these efforts toward mobilization on the part of peasants and workers were matched by a progressive political radicalization among the white and *cholo* literate population. These groups now began organizing radical Marxist parties of all types, most of which demanded nationalization of the basic resources and a modification of the capitalist economy in Bolivia. Eventually to emerge from this active polit icalization were three radical parties: the Trotskyite Revolutionary Workers' Party (POR), with close links to the unionized miners; the Marxist Revolutionary Party of the Left (PIR), with powerful support among the middle class; and the National Revolutionary Movement Party (MNR), an amalgam of socialist and fascist elements which equally claimed important middle class and later union support.

Though the POR, PIR and MNR were all pro-labor, their respective international sympathies prevented their initial coalition into a revolutionary force. The result of these divisions was the preservation of the traditional government for another decade, despite the basic weakness of the traditional parties and despite the continued division within the army between the radical and conservative elements.

THE PREEMINENCE OF THE MNR PRIOR TO
THE REVOLUTION OF 1952

This intra-Army feud again erupted in 1943 when a lodge of fascist officers seized the government, named Major Gualberto Villarroel president, and brought the MNR to power as its major civilian ally. While the MNR succeeded in organizing the first national federation of mine workers and also held the first national Indian congress of peasant representatives its pro-Axis politics and its internal support of violence alienated the powerful PIR as well as the traditional parties, all of whom—with strong U.S. backing—formed an anti-fascist coalition and overthrew the MNR-military regime in July of 1946. In allying with the PIR, the traditional parties indicated their own inability to control even the limited literate electorate of Bolivia, which had now become extremely radicalized. But in its turn the PIR would find its support eroded away in the six years of conservative rule as it found itself in alliance with governments determined to depoliticize the working classes and remove all radical elements from the middle class. The end result of all this activity was the rise of the MNR to preeminent position. Removing its more pro-fascist elements, and absorbing the most important labor supporters of the POR, the MNR now became a powerful middle-class and worker-class movement of socialist reform, and the leading opponent of the rule of the traditional elite. By mid-1949 the MNR was able to lead a powerful revolt that almost succeeded in overthrowing the government. In the presidential elections of 1951 the party emerged victorious, only to have the military out in jugue to prevent its installation. Thus the stage was set for a full-scale assault on the national government by the party, which was to occur on April 9, 1952.

On that day the MNR seized the armories of La Paz and distributed arms to the civilian population. Concurrently the miners rose in revolt. From the 9th to the 11th a bitter civil war was fought whose end results were the total defeat of the Bolivian national army by the miners and civilians and accession to power by the MNR. Víctor Paz Estenssoro, the principal MNR leader, returned from exile to assume the presidency.

The Revolution is Conditioned by Links to the Past

In viewing the political, social and economic developments which led up to the National Revolution of 1952 from a retrospective position it is evident that certain basic trends of the post-1952 period should have been anticipated. The previous six-year period, for example, had forced the MNR into a position of open alliance with the mine workers and engendered as well a sympathetic stance toward the agrarian question. Thus co-government, nationalization of the mines, support of organized labor, and active support for land reform were the expected results of both the pro-grammatic development of MNR political ideology and the reality of its political support.

Nevertheless, the fact that the MNR was essentially a middle-class movement whose leadership was systematically anti-Marxist would ulti-mately influence the MNR in its refusal to go to a full-scale redistribution of income and a destruction of the class system in Bolivia. Largely through the accident of a massive inflation, the middle class was severely tested in the post-1952 period. Nevertheless, the MNR both accepted North American aid—with all its conditions—and systematically channeled much of that aid into the development of the private sector of the economy. Except in the area of tin, private mining quickly came to dominate most mineral production, while an entirely new large-scale commercial agricul-tural economy was developed in Santa Cruz. Thus while the MNR shattered many of the traditional institutions of Bolivia and ended the feudal aspects of its rural economy, the party essentially moved Bolivia into the era of capitalist, and not socialist, development.

Corruption of party members and the government quickly became established. Given the ambivalence of party aims after nationalization of the Big Three mining companies, added to the crises of the economy and the expansion of the bureaucracy to meet social demands, this was almost inevitable. This corruption in turn created new alliances as the MNR found support among the new or traditional economic elites benefiting from increased government expenditure. This in turn enabled the party to operate without the unqualified support of organized labor. The con-servative support of the now landed rural peasantry gave the regime the crucial power base to oppose the increasingly embittered organized labor movement. The result was the famous alliance of party and peasants against workers, to which Paz Estenssoro finally added a revitalized mili-tary. It was this policy of divide and rule among the recently mobilized popular classes which finally corrupted the social revolution which the MNR had so brilliantly initiated in April of 1952.

ENDNOTE FOR CHAPTER II

1. This essay is based on a wide range of sources and books. For the interested reader wishing to pursue some of these themes, the following works are suggested. The standard source on the geography of Bolivia is Jorge Muñoz Reyes, *Geografía de Bolivia* (La Paz: Academia Nacional de Ciencias de Bolivia, 1977). Luis G. Lumbreras, *The Peoples and Cultures of Ancient Peru* (Washington, D.C.: Smithsonian Institution Press, 1974) and Edward P. Lanning, *Peru Before the Incas* (Englewood Cliffs, New Jersey: Prentice-Hall, 1967), provide good introductions to the pre-Columbian period. For the colonial period see Josep M. Barnadas, *Charcas, 1535-1565. Orígenes históricos de una sociedad colonial* (La Paz: Centro de Investigación y Promoción de Campesinado, 1973); Nicolás Sánchez-Albornoz, *Indios y Tributos en Alto Perú* (Lima: Instituto de Estudios Peruanos, 1978); and Lewis Hanke, *The Imperial City of Potosí* (The Hague: Nijhoff, 1956).

   In dealing with the developments of 19th century society, the older surveys of Alcides Arguedas, *Historia general de Bolivia (el proceso de la nacionalidad), 1809 1921* (La Paz: Arnó hermanos, 1922), Enrique Finot, *Nueva historia de Bolivia (ensayo de interpretación sociologica)* (2d. ed.; La Paz: Editorial Gisbert, 1954) and Jorge Basadre, *Chile, Perú y Bolivia independientes* (Barcelona: Salvat, 1948) are still quite useful. For the late nineteenth and first half of the twentieth century see Herbert S. Klein, *Parties and Political Change in Bolivia, 1880-1952* (London: Cambridge University Press, 1969). The multiple volume histories of Arguedas covering the period from the wars of independence to 1920 are followed by a similar style series done by Porfirio Díaz Machicado, starting with his study of Saavedra (La Paz: A. Tejerina, 1945) and ending with Peñaranda (La Paz: A. Tejerina, 1958) and given the generic title of *Historia de Bolivia*.

   The period of the Chaco War is well surveyed in Roberto Querejazo Calvo, *Masamaclay. Historia política, diplomática y militar de la Guerra del Chaco* (3rd ed., La Paz: Editorial Los Amigos del Libro, 1975). The turbulent era of the 1930s and 1940s is analyzed in great detail by Augusto Céspedes, *El dictador suicida* (Santiago de Chile: Editorial Universitaria, 1956) and his *El presidente colgado* (La Paz: Editorial J. Alvarez, 1971), and also by Luis Peñaloza, *Historia del movimiento nacionalista revolucionario, 1941-1952* (La Paz: Editorial Librería, 1963).

   The economic history of the nineteenth and twentieth centuries is surveyed by Casto Rojas, *Historia financiera de Bolivia* (2d ed.; La Paz: Editorial Universitaria, Universidad Mayor de San Andrés, 1977); Luis Peñaloza, *Historia económica de Bolivia* (2 vols.; La Paz: no publisher noted, 1953-1954) and by CEPAL, *El desarrollo económico de Bolivia* (México: CEPAL, 1958). The labor movement is the subject of an impressive survey by Guillermo Lora, *Historia del movimiento obrero* (3 vols.; La Paz: Editorial Los Amigos del Libro, 1967-1970; English edition with Cambridge University Press, 1977). Unfortunately no broad surveys are yet available for the social, ethnic and rural history of Bolivia in its period of independence.

Chapter III

Bolivia's 1952 Revolution: Initial Impact and U.S. Involvement
Cornelius H. Zondag

INTRODUCTION

In some respects, Bolivia's social revolution of 1952—the second such revolution in Latin America—has been very much underrated. Much has been written about both its initial and long-term impact, as reflected in expressions such as "the uncompleted revolution," "the revolution that lost its way" and the "restrained revolution"; but little wonder has been expressed that the revolution should have succeeded at all.

In retrospect, it can be seen that it did succeed owing to a combination of favorable circumstances, of which some were clearly beyond the control of the original revolutionaries, while others were created at least in part by their intelligent and persistent efforts.

UNITED STATES SUPPORT FOR THE REVOLUTION

In contrast to the cases of Russia, Mexico and Guatemala where the revolutionaries were immediately faced with American opposition, Bolivia's 1952 revolutionaries suffered no such fate, in spite of the fact that the party which undertook the revolution, the National Revolutionary Movement Party (MNR), had experienced very poor relations with the United States during the previous decade. For instance when the MNR government first assumed power in 1943 under the direction of President Gualberto Villarroel, the United States could not bring itself to recognize the regime for some six months.

From the beginning, personality factors played an important role in getting support of the United States government for the revolution. For instance, it was a fortunate circumstance that shortly after the MNR took over in 1952, the new American president sent his brother, Dr. Milton Eisenhower, to Latin America on a fact-finding mission. President Eisenhower had earnestly hoped to visit all American republics in the early months of his administration because he firmly believed that a dependable hemispheric partnership was essential to mutual freedom. Unfortunately, however, recurrent crises in general East-West relations prevented these proposed visits.

Insofar as Bolivia was concerned, Milton Eisenhower proved to be an excellent choice. First he was clearly sympathetic to the revolution. As an educator and agriculturalist, he was fascinated with Bolivia's land reform. Second, as an objective observer he was able to put the revolution in a proper perspective during this time when there was an American obsession against communism. As he put it, "We should not confuse each move in Latin America toward socialization with Marxism, land reform with communism, or even anti-yankeeism with pro-Sovietism."[1] Thus, Dr. Eisenhower played an important role in the granting of U.S. emergency assistance to Bolivia which was formalized in an exchange of letters between Presidents Paz Estenssoro and Eisenhower on October 1st and October 14th, 1953, respectively. In these letters the U.S. president authorized the following measures for emergency assistance:

(1) To make available 5 million dollars in agricultural products from Commodity Credit Corporation Stocks under the Famine Relief Act.

(2) To provide 4 million dollars from Mutual Security Act funds for other essential commodities.

(3) To more than double the technical assistance program.

Another favorable factor was that at the time of the revolution Dr. Carter Goodrich, an American, was the Special Representative of the United Nations Mission of Technical Assistance to Bolivia. As a sympathetic American and a tactful negotiator, he played an important role in the improvement of U.S.-Bolivian relations.

Another fortunate circumstance was that, being situated at some 12,000 feet above sea level, Bolivia was to some extent immune to U.S. political appointments. As a hardship post carrying a 25 percent salary differential, it only rated a career ambassador, a factor that turned out to be another blessing in establishing good relations between the new regime and the United States. Both Ambassador Edward Sparks and U.S. Technical Assistance Mission Director Oscar Powell were able to lay the foundations at an early date for a good and close working relationship between the two countries.

Another important personality was the colorful, guitar-playing Bolivian Ambassador in Washington, Víctor Andrade, whose role on the Washington scene was often crucial. Andrade, a veteran of the Chaco War who had worked in the tin mining industry, had been a visiting professor at the New School for Social Research in New York and a former employee of Nelson Rockefeller's Basic Economy Corporation in Ecuador. Quick to detect where the power centers were located, he was often able to make a direct pitch to the right people. Apart from that, he had become a personal friend of President Eisenhower and had easy access to him.

As Andrade points out, luck also played a role. This was the case in 1953 when death took the ex-Senator and Democratic Majority Leader Millard Tydings who, as a paid spokesman for the nationalized Big Three tin mining companies, had been a strong opponent of the Bolivian revolution.[2]

Nelson Rockefeller's early support of the Bolivian course was an additional plus, along with other more peripheral factors such as the fact-finding missions by Assistant Secretary of State for Latin American Affairs Henry Holland, Senator Capehart and others, each of whom turned in a positive report. Luck again entered the picture when Senator Bourke Hickenlooper, greatly angered because the wrong arrangements had been made by the Bolivians during his 1954 visit to the Santa Cruz area, was pacified when he caught a thirty-four pound trout in Lake Titicaca.

In a more serious vein, it would seem that the human rights issue tended to evoke additional sympathy for Bolivia in the United States. In a country mired in feudalism and beset by the exploitation of the majority of its people by either the Big Three mine owners or the landlords, the image of the Tin Barons, the only ones financially capable of mounting the anti-MNR public relations campaign, was definitely not good.

The State Department's obsession with communism during the John Foster Dulles-Joseph McCarthy era contributed another circumstance cleverly exploited by the Bolivians. Keeping Bolivia from going communist was obviously of high priority to the United States. In return for enough foreign aid to keep the revolution afloat, the MNR leaders could steer a course which would avoid extremes. Even opponents of the regime could live with the thought that the MNR, which in its early days seemed to have something for everybody, represented merely a nationalistic or Bolivia first movement.

Moreover, the quality of the MNR leadership was impressive and its goals seemed respectable. Early protagonists of the revolution such as President Víctor Paz Estenssoro, Vice President Hernán Siles Zuazo, Foreign Minister Walter Guevara Arce, Head of the Bolivian Development Corporation Alfonso Gumucio, and Eduardo Hinojosa, the American-trained petroleum engineer who brought about the early successes of the Bolivian State Petroleum Company (YPFB), impressed the Americans with their complete dedication and often eighteen-hour-a-day work schedules. Besides, they seemed to have a plan even if most of it was based on a design for economic diversification drawn up by former U.S. Ambassador Mervin Bohan some ten years earlier. Some of the components of this plan, such as the development of the Santa Cruz area, fascinated many American agricultural advisors. Sympathy for the objectives of the revolution as well as concern for the plight of the peasants generated support for the cause of the MNR. Most people seemed to overlook, however, that the MNR government in its early days was not undertaking planning but was merely practicing crisis management in an effort to try to satisfy all the interest groups within its party which, ironically, provided it with an image of broad popular support.

A number of crucial issues were also factors in bringing the United States and Bolivia together. On the American side was the question of geo-politics, i.e., the control of the high plateau in the heart of South America. There was perhaps some guilt over U.S. policy of trying to keep tin prices down just prior to the revolution which, incidentally, may well have been a factor in its success. There was also the fact that Paz Estenssoro had obtained a plurality in the elections of 1951, which seemed to vest the regime in a measure of legitimacy.

Even more important was the fact that the MNR government was able to present the expropriation of the Big Three mining companies as a special case which did not affect Bolivia's basically favorable attitude towards private investment. This was evidenced by the country's non-interference in the mining properties owned by W. R. Grace and Company as well as by its decision in the early 1950s to welcome Texas financier and mining promotor Glenn McCarthy to the Bolivian scene.

On the Bolivian side there was the all important consideration that the MNR had nowhere to go but the United States, other than perhaps Argentina, which could not provide much effective help. In the rest of Latin America, particularly Bolivia's neighbor Peru, the Bolivian revolution was virtually greeted with a big yawn. As a matter of fact some people felt at the time that the fate of the revolution could have been decided in a matter of weeks by simply blocking some of Bolivia's major international roads and railways. Thus the fact remains that the initial achievement of the revolution—the MNR staying in power—was largely due to

United States support for it plus a number of factors which can be sum-
med up in the one statement that without luck nobody fares well.

The twelve-year period following the 1952 revolution constituted a
remarkable if not unique period for Bolivia in terms of political stability,
social change and human suffering. It can be divided into three stages:
(a) the initial reign of President Paz Estenssoro from 1952 to 1956; (b)
the more moderate regime of President Hernán Silco Zuazo from 1956 to
1960; and (c) the second reign of President Paz Estenssoro from 1960 to
1964. During these periods there was a gradual decline in revolutionary
rhetoric and revolutionary zeal as well as increased U.S. identification
with the revolution's goals and objectives. At the same time there was a
steady acceleration in social change, particularly at the bottom of the
society, coupled with a tendency away from destruction towards reconstruction and economic development.

THE 1952-1956 PERIOD

The revolution's first stage, 1952-1956, was marked by a passionate
reaction against the existing feudal system and its gross abuses, as well
as by much personal vengeance and hatred, all aimed at the destruction
or reformation of the old society. Yet sight should not be lost of the fact
that most of the MNR leaders responsible for the 1952 revolution were
substantially from the urban middle class rather than radical revolutionaries. At least originally, these leaders had few ties with the peasants.

This apparent paradox can be explained by examining the society
the leaders were out to destroy. Bolivia before the revolution represented a dual society made up of a modern foreign-owned mining sector,
which largely dominated the country's political system, and an agricultural sector marked by medieval feudalism and de facto slavery insofar
as the peasants were concerned. While a few large landlords controlled
most of the good land, the majority of the peasants had no choice but to
cultivate their own small marginal plots in return for the privilege of working without wages on the large *haciendas*. With the landlord having virtual control over life and death in his area and the Indians living in abject
misery, the system was repulsive to anybody interested in even a modicum
of social justice.

Similar abuses could be found in the tin mines where life often ended
at age thirty-five due to incredible working conditions and the incidence
of silicosis and other occupational diseases. Likewise, the fact that for
years Bolivia's political destiny had been largely under the control of the
Big Three tin mining companies, Patiño, Hochschild and Aramayo, was
enough to enrage any patriotic Bolivian. Here again the MNR found
eager support on the part of middle class Americans aiding in the country's development program.

This feudalism was exactly what most of the MNR leaders wanted to
change. Rather than being radical revolutionaries in the Castro or Arbenz
style with the intent of introducing twentieth-century-style communism
in Cuba or Guatemala, most of the leaders of the 1952 Bolivian revolution
were content with bringing about a measure of nineteenth century social
justice. Almost instinctively they seemed to realize that the change from
fifteenth century feudalism to a modern industrial society could not be
achieved in one broad sweep. This does not mean that the MNR did not
harbor elements intent on pushing Paz Estenssoro and others of his kind
farther to the left with the ultimate goal of brushing them aside in a complete leftist take-over. However, these people were in the minority, as
was clearly borne out by the subsequent political developments.

The original five goals of the revolution clearly reflected this philosophy: (a) universal voting rights aimed at turning the Indian into a citizen; (b) nationalization of the Big Three tin mining companies intended to make the Bolivians masters of their own political destiny; (c) labor participation in the management of the nationalized mines; (d) land reform aimed at giving the land back to those who worked it; and (e) dissolution of an all too often repressive army.

The existence of a *just cause* was also a motive for the close U.S.-Bolivian cooperation during the period in question. During the first four years, U.S. officials had a fairly clear understanding, often somewhat disapproving, of President Paz Estenssoro's need to give priority to social rather than economic development as a means of keeping himself and his group in power. Given the pre-1952 conditions, the new government needed little persuasion that the MNR's first impact had to be the destruction of the foundations of the old society. Yet in the process both parties had to make compromises based on political realities.

While the Bolivians often felt frustrated about U.S. aid and a level of financial support which merely kept them gasping for breath, the Americans were perturbed about the fact that so much of the foreign aid had to go for consumption. Moreover, there was much U.S. concern with the galloping inflation which increased the money in circulation from 11.3 billion bolivianos to 382.3 billion bolivianos over a period of five years.[3] By and large this inflation was due to a conflict between the small coterie which held the MNR's formal power as represented by Paz Estenssoro, Siles Zuazo and a few others, and the real power of the armed miners as represented by the Bolivian Workers' Central (COB) and the labor left, whose power could only be eroded over a period of time. To most Bolivians, at least initially, the inflation was not as tragic as the above numbers would indicate since it helped to destroy the wealth and power of the ruling class and the intelligentsia—long accustomed to having a free ride on the rest of the society. Likewise the lack of labor discipline in the mines merely represented a political reality for the Bolivians, while it became a constant obsession with the U.S. officials in La Paz who visualized the tin mines as a continuing source of income. Because of the fact that for several decades no substantial new mineral deposits had been discovered in Bolivia, the MNR leaders had already written off the mines as a dynamic factor in the national economy.

At the individual level relations between the Bolivians and U.S. foreign aid technicians working within the *Servicio* framework[4] were generally good, being much helped by the seeming justness of the Bolivian cause, of which the MNR seemed the true prophet. Major and minor differences showed up at the higher levels of the bureaucracy, many of which could be brushed away during the first phase due to a good sense of reality on the part of all participants, a Bolivian tendency towards frankness bordering on the blunt, and finally President Paz Estenssoro's sense of humor, which often contributed to the breaking up a deadlock.

Since in the Bolivian context both the U.S. and the MNR needed each other— after all Paz Estenssoro was about ten years ahead of the Alliance for Progress which in the early 1960s, warmly espoused the MNR position on the need for social change in Latin America—the first fact of life was that the MNR had to stay in power at all costs and that in order to do so it had to give priority to social rather than economic development. The cost was high indeed. Widespread smuggling activities undermined the foundation of the society. Corruption ranged all the way from the manipulation of differential tariffs, the so-called *revertibles* at the top and intermediate levels of the government, to a group of weeping Indians carrying a coffin across the border, their crocodile tears trying to disguise the fact that the coffin was filled with contraband coffee![5]

As time passed, however, and American patience was tried, some of the differences between the countries tended to become more serious. This is reflected in the concern over a number of major issues such as the above mentioned inflation and lack of labor discipline, the direct and daily interference in the management of the tin mines on the part of the MNR bureaucracy, the giving of priority to state petroleum development over that of mining, the use of American counterpart funds, the requirement of tied U.S. loans, the monopoly of the Bolivian State Mining Bank in the purchasing of minerals from the small mines, the implications of the U.S. tin stockpile, the role of Bolivia's public sector and budgetary reform, the issue of private foreign investment and Bolivia's policy towards Cuba. Finally there was the human rights issue, which became a sore point with a number of Americans as the Paz Estenssoro regime, in an effort to sustain itself, filled the jails as well as its detention camps at Corocoro, Uncia and Curahuara de Carangas with its opponents, including both men and women.

The MNR started out with the benefit of some 356 million dollars in the treasury in 1952.[6] As the options became more limited, the government had to become more repressive, resulting in a polarization between the MNR and important sectors of the society such as the church, the university and the MNR's main adversary the Bolivian Socialist Falange (FSB). This in turn drove the MNR more to the left, much to the dismay of those Americans who favored controlled social change in Latin America. Subsequently, when large numbers of intellectuals and technicians started to leave Bolivia, the MNR deprived itself of a valuable asset for the economic development process, or as President Siles Zuazo once told the writer: "If we really want to have economic development we cannot have too many capable Bolivians in jail!"

To this the standard MNR reply was, please bear with us; in order to destroy Bolivia's old oligarchy, the *Rosca,* and to obtain a massive political base, we must first share the poverty before we can start to stimulate production to create wealth. Such an assertation was not unwarranted since by distributing what little wealth there was to the various pressure groups, the MNR was able to stay in power. Without the MNR, what little desirable economic and social change had taken place would again be in jeopardy.

Not all was negative during the 1952-1956 period, however, even if the emphasis was on the need to reform or destroy the existing society. The fact that Paz Estenssoro's initial gamble on petroleum did pay off proved that the U.S. could be wrong. More credit should be given to the Bolivians for realizing that their initial and highly successful public sector efforts to find petroleum and export it to several neighboring countries could not substitute for private foreign investment in the industry. Thus, shortly after the promulgation of a petroleum code in 1955, some 100 million dollars in foreign petroleum investment started to come into Bolivia, thus laying the basis for an important diversification in the structure of the Bolivian economy.

The question has often been raised, particularly by Bolivians opposed to the MNR regime, as to whether the Americans were taken in by Paz Estenssoro's charm. It is true that during the early 1950s relations between Bolivia's top echelon and the American establishment in La Paz were quite cordial. Questions regarding the direction and magnitude of the U.S. aid effort were at times discussed by American officials in full sessions with all the key ministers present while an occasional Sunday morning horseback ride with the *Compañero Jefe* afforded easier access to the President. Little cabinet-level jokes about the "litmus paper test" whether Paz Estenssoro was pink enough to rate more foreign aid, or offsetting falangist with communist influence, are illustrative of social relations prevailing at the time.[7]

In answer to the above question, however, it might be said that relations were generally too close for the Americans not to see the true realities. This closeness had both its good and bad effects. On the positive side it provided the U.S. with a means to make suggestions on important issues. Several examples are: (a) the need to curb inflation through monetary stabilization, (b) the attraction of foreign investment through the promulgation of an attractive petroleum code, (c) the evaluation of the future of the Bolivian mining industry with the help of an American consulting firm resulting in the well-known Ford, Bacon and Davis Report, and (d) the introduction of a highly successful road maintenance program to reduce transportation costs.

In some cases, such as that of the monetary stabilization program, these suggestions may well have been redundant, since after a while Bolivian officials realized quite clearly that inflation, lack of labor discipline, low productivity and widespread contraband activities would ultimately destroy the revolution. For example when a number of market women smugglers formally organized themselves into a Union of Travelers from Arica to La Paz it was clear that inflation was harmful!

The closeness and the give-and-take between the Bolivian and U.S. groups also had its negative effects. It helped to lay the basis for the subsequent and greatly enhanced visibility of both United States embassy and technical assistance personnel, a problem which was to haunt President Paz Estenssoro during his second term. At any rate, in retrospect it would seem that a number of important decisions reached in the early 1950s, which more or less decided the course of events during the following period of 1956-1960, resulted from this close collaboration.

THE 1956-1960 PERIOD

The Bolivian constitution prohibits that the president immediately succeed himself in office. Thus during this period the immensely popular Hernán Siles Zuazo succeeded to the office of President while Víctor Paz Estenssoro left the Bolivian scene to become Ambassador to the Court of St. James. Since the MNR had openly admitted that its goal during the first stage of the revolution was largely the destruction of the old order to lay the foundation for a new society, Siles Zuazo needed to stress the constructive aspect. However this was difficult to do with an empty treasury. By 1957 corruption and inflation had reached an all time high. Resale of subsidized commissary articles provided the powerful miners with a cushion against inflation while the peasants could live off their newly acquired lands. The rest of the population had to stand in line endlessly to obtain its bare necessities at controlled low prices. Or, if they had the money to do so, they could obtain everything they wanted on the black market.

Whereas in the beginning inflation had helped the MNR to destroy its opponents, it had now become counterproductive and was in fact threatening the party's future existence. As a result a monetary stabilization program was introduced with the help of the United States government and the International Monetary Fund (IMF). Briefly, this program provided for the following:

(1) Government expenditures were to be reduced 40 per cent; taxes and tariffs were to be raised. The budget was to be balanced with the assistance of counterpart funds generated from the sale of U.S. surplus agricultural commodities to the public. This money had

formerly been directed toward financing development projects in the country.

(2) The deficits of the public enterprises were to be eliminated and the subsidization of their commissaries abolished.

(3) The exchange rate was unified at the rate of 7,700 bolivianos to the dollar, and all exchange, import, price controls, and subsidies were abolished.

(4) Cost-of-living increases for wage and salary earners were to be granted for the anticipated increase in prices resulting from the proposed tax increases and abolition of price controls and consumer subsidies. After one year there was to be a freeze on all wage increases.

(5) Legal reserve requirements on commercial bank deposits were raised, and deposits were to be limited by the capital and reserves of the private and state banks. [8]

To aid Bolivia over the initial impact of this drastic program, the country was to receive a total of 25 million dollars. This amount was composed of a loan of 7.5 million dollars from the IMF plus a 7.5 million dollar loan and a 10 million dollar grant from the United States for development projects.

As a result of this program, which was headed by the American George Jackson Eder, all subsidies and artificially low prices were eliminated so that shortages and long queues disappeared overnight and prices became so high that few people could afford to buy anything. As a solution to this problem, cost of living increases were to be granted for a limited period; thereafter all wages would be frozen. The impact of this program can best be compared to the medical profession undertaking major surgery prior to the availability of anesthesia. Yet Mr. Eder was able to convince President Siles Zuazo of the need for the program and the President went on a hunger strike to sell it to—or rather to impose it upon—the Bolivian populace. In the long run the program proved to be a boon as well as a turning point for Bolivia. Perhaps less desirable was Mr. Eder's high visibility and his drafting of official but unpopular memoranda for the President. This accentuated American involvement in the program and provided the opponents of the MNR with some welcome ammunition.

As the split in the MNR became more apparent, Siles Zuazo had to look for other forms of support. He did this by bringing back some conservative leaders among whom was the very capable Walter Guevara Arce, who had served as Foreign Minister in the original cabinet of President Paz Estenssoro. Forced by his own program to turn against the miners, Siles Zuazo started to build up the army again, hoping that this would enable him to *reason* better with the popular militias. He also relaxed some of the more vindictive measures of the MNR against the opposition and allowed the return of a number of exiles. Likewise he sought the support of the peasants in an effort to counter the power of the miners and industrial unions. The only way to do this, however, was to make peace with the peasant leaders who by now had become as powerful as Chinese war lords. This meant that any political support from this quarter would be rather fickle. Peasant leader José Rojas Guevara was brought to La Paz to become Minister of Peasant Affairs, the first Indian to hold such a post. Apparently Siles Zuazo believed that while the revolution was largely made with the miners, it could be continued with and brought to a moderate end with the peasants. While correctly anticipating some gratitude on the part of the peasants who had gained much from the revolution, the president failed to recognize that peasant support would be mobilized through deals with local *caudillos* rather than through public appeals from La Paz.

Siles Zuazo's effort to undermine the labor left and to neutralize Juan Lechín Oquendo, the powerful leader of the miners, tends to confirm our basic thesis that from its beginning the MNR was predominantly guided by moderates. To be facetious, if the MNR leaders ever visualized an industrial revolution, it was one where high wages would certainly not deprive them of their servants. At best it would do away with the locks which some people had on their refrigerators to prevent the servants from having access to the goodies!

At any rate, under Siles Zuazo the stage was set for a gradual transition to state capitalism and a possible subsequent return to a laissez faire economy which was to provide Bolivia with one of the highest economic growth rates in Latin America during the early 1960s. It is debatable that this compromised the revolution since the goals of the original MNR revolutionaries were never as all-encompassing as some would maintain.

THE 1960-1964 PERIOD

The third stage of the initial impact of the revolution, the period from 1960 to 1964, can be briefly treated. After waiting out the required term while serving as Ambassador to England, Víctor Paz Estenssoro returned to the Presidency in 1960. At that time the decay and disorder within the MNR Party had reached such proportions that even he himself seemed disgusted with the local political scene. Apart from that, the sputtering Bolivian economy seemed to put a damper on the much touted economic effects of the revolution.

Fortunately, as in the early 1960s, the change of administration in the United States brought new hopes and perspectives to the Bolivian leader. Almost overnight President John F. Kennedy's Alliance for Progress discovered the Bolivian revolution. This discovery provided the testimony that the moderate leaders of the revolution had been right all along. Bolivia was an example of a country which had introduced needed social change without resorting to communism or similar radical solutions. Consequently it provided a model which had possibilities for export to other countries. In 1966, when the Bolivian peasants proved to be immune to the leftist teachings of a Che Guevara and Regis Debray, some Alliance enthusiasts even went so far as to compare the MNR revolution with "a vaccine against communism."[9]

Under the Alliance the level of United States aid to Bolivia was suddenly doubled, allowing President Paz Estenssoro to swap aid for a disastrous loss in popularity within his own divided party. Always a cautious man, he looked for additional insurance by trying to make a deal with the peasants and the military in order to neutralize the power of the militant labor groups. Both approaches misfired. The peasants obviously had reason to be grateful to the man who had brought about land reform, but as most Bolivians well know, in any revolution the Indian merely changes masters. Thus by 1960 peasant support depended no longer on the president's image of distributing the land to the peasants, as was the case in the early 1950s, but rather on getting support from the powerful rural caciques who now controlled the peasants.

By strengthening the military's hand, Paz Estenssoro violated his own advice on the advisability of maintaining a strict balance among the army, the police and the powerful local militias. Further complication resulted from the army's embarking, by 1960, on a civic action program which included colonizing land, building rural schools, constructing access roads, bridges and similar projects eminently suited to enhancing its image at the grass root level. By trusting some of the military officers he had handpicked for promotion in earlier years, Paz Estenssoro unwittingly laid the groundwork for Bolivia's return to the old *cuartelazo* or barracks mentality which would ultimately destroy what little gain the revolution had brought to Bolivia in terms of political—as distinguished from socioeconomic— progress. Even in the economic sphere the MNR policies proved to be inconsistent because of the revolution's limited goals. Whereas the mining and electric power sectors were largely nationalized, the development of the agricultural and industrial sectors was patterned after a more capitalistic model in the expectation that they would be taxed to finance economic diversification. This scheme failed to work since the government failed to provide the proper incentives to these sectors for their development.

Yet the gamble of substituting military and peasant support for the power of the always troublesome miners was a dilemma which could no longer be avoided during Paz Estenssoro's second presidential term. In order to bring about a badly needed rehabilitation program for the nationalized mines, he had to insist on labor discipline and the introduction of more rational managerial policies. These resulted in the laying off of thousands of unneeded miners. By doing otherwise he would have risked losing the 37.5 million dollar package of loans for the rehabilitation of the Bolivian State Mining Company (COMIBOL) offered by the United States, West Germany and the Inter-American Development Bank.

And there was more. During the early part of Paz Estenssoro's second term there were ever increasing indications that the MNR's restructuring of Bolivian society, including the development of the *Oriente,* was finally beginning to pay off. Moreover, mineral prices were rising. In other words, as an astute economist the president could feel reasonably sure that Bolivia's fundamental economic position was going to improve.

Since prior emphasis had been placed on social development, Paz Estenssoro was faced with the challenge of leading Bolivia out of its economic morass into the promised land of state capitalism and eventually, perhaps, real democracy. Consequently, the president increasingly turned his attention to economic issues such as the development of the Beni Province and the Chapare region as well as the already booming Santa Cruz area. Since the president was from Tarija, it is not surprising that he obviously believed that much of Bolivia's future was to be found in the nation's vast lowland areas. He also tried to improve technical education in order to develop a cadre of Mexican-style technocrats in support of the various development projects. Unfortunately this effort alienated him from the influential groups in the universities which were afraid that their prerogatives would be diminished by competing educational institutions.

Paz Estenssoro—having been proclaimed a hero by President Kennedy and heavily courted by two United States ambassadors who were constantly at his coattails—was eager to serve a third term. He wished to do so even if this required an amendment to the constitutional precept that presidents should not immediately succeed themselves and even if he had to renege on an informal promise, made in 1956, that after his second term Juan Lechín Oquendo would assume the presidency in 1964. Since the powerful boss of the miners was obviously not a favorite of the United States Embassy, all this maneuvering made Paz Estenssoro appear as a tool of American imperialism. This alienated the Left, which was horrified by the blatant display of American meddling in local politics. Likewise, it did not get the president any kudos from the Right and the middle classes. These latter groups hoped for an ultimate return to a laissez faire economy, and didn't see Paz Estenssoro as the leader to provide a gradual revival of their comfortable pre-revolutionary existence after twelve years of the MNR nightmare. Whereas the middle class approved the demise of the Big Three mining companies and payed lip service to liberation of the Indian, they felt little gratitude towards the man who had started it all.

In conclusion, it became increasingly clear that the MNR revolutionary movement, after the twelve years of being in power, had never been able to unite Bolivia's highly fragmented society into a Mexico-style one party system supported by a major portion of the population. Perhaps the historical fragmentation of Bolivian society was even further accentuated by the revolution since it had deliberately added a new geopolitical dimension in the form of an economic diversification away from tin, La Paz and the *Altiplano* and towards petroleum, commercial agriculture and industrial development in the *Oriente*.

By 1963 it was also clear that the miners and peasants, who had made the revolution possible, were again the losers. Highly respectable annual increases in Bolivia's gross domestic product obscured the fact that at the same time income distribution was becoming more and more skewed. For the first time in Bolivia's history many young people turned away from politics to become interested in the possibilities of making money in the private sector.

THE REVOLUTION IN RETROSPECT

In 1964, when Juan Lechín Oquendo was eliminated as a presidential candidate in favor of Víctor Paz Estenssoro, the road was blocked to radical or populist solutions in favor of more state capitalism and military rule with an ever expanding public sector.

Paz Estenssoro's move to run for another term as president—which had been cleverly legalized in 1961 by the establishment of a new constitution which permitted the incumbent president to succeed himself—contributed to a clearcut miscalculation of the political elements. With his popularity greatly eroded among important sectors of the population such as the urban middle class, the universities, the MNR members who had lost their jobs, and the entire labor left, the removal of Lechín—in spite of Paz Estenssoro's earlier promises to support Lechín for the presidency—proved to be the straw that broke the camel's back.

During the convention of 1964 the party fell apart. Lechín broke away to form his own leftist party and Siles Zuazo openly declared his opposition to Paz Estenssoro while the rest of the party struggled over the vice presidency. As a further indication of the president's eroded support, he was forced to drop his own candidate for the vice presidency in favor of the popular air force chief, General René Barrientos Ortuño, a move which would turn out to be fatal to the incumbent president. The end came on November 4, 1964, when General Alfredo Ovando Candía, the Commander-in-Chief of the armed forces, intervened, telling the president that he would take him "either to the cemetery or to the airport." Paz Estenssoro then opted for the latter and flew off to Lima and exile. For a brief period the two generals acted as co-presidents until General Barrientos took over as head of state, promising to hold elections in May, 1965. Elections were not held, however, until July 1966 when he easily won, carrying a good part of the urban middle class and the peasantry. As a next move Barrientos tried the old strategy, initiated under Siles Zuazo, of using a coalition of peasant and military power to break the political power of the Left. As his position became gradually more precarious, the end came unexpectedly with the death of the former air force general in a helicopter accident on a trip into the interior to cultivate peasant support. After Vice President Luis Adolfo Siles Salinas took over, he was in turn replaced by a coup led by General Alfredo Ovando Candía, who then issued a 14-point leftist-nationalist program and immediately proceeded to nationalize all Bolivian Gulf Oil properties. This action opened up a controversy that would last for years.

While it is beyond the purview of this paper to discuss the period from 1964 to the present in any detail, what happened during these years merely confirms, in spite of all the economic progress since the revolution, that the problem of political stability had not been solved in Bolivia.

Even the brief nationalistic leftist and basically anti-American interregnum of General Juan José Torres in 1970 and 1971 would show that at the time Bolivia's fractured society was not yet ready to be molded into a more unified and more egalitarian political system. As Mitchell points out, in cases where populist parties have lost interest in reform and represent chiefly the short-run interest of their leaders, they may be displaced by a more genuinely progressive military elite. [10]

Even in the economic sphere the revolution could not bring about a change from an outward-looking and open economy, highly dependent on sales of raw materials to the world, to a more inward-looking development strategy based on economic nationalism and active participation in the Andean Group. Whereas there obviously have been significant gains in economic diversification as well as in a greater diversification in mineral exports, the performance of the agricultural sector is most disappointing. After a successful attempt at land reform, the MNR government failed to follow up with sufficient inputs such as credit and technical assistance to help the peasant become more productive, while the large commercial farmers, other than those growing cotton, concentrated on high-cost crops such as rice and sugar, which had little future beyond supplying Bolivia's domestic needs.

Yet, looking at what is realistically and humanly possible within the span of one generation, Bolivia's uncompleted revolution should not receive too harsh a judgement. [11] If the revolution is accepted for what it was intended to be, i.e., a moderate movement towards social change—in practice the long overdue abolition of slavery—the initial impact was quite constructive. Moreover, successful colonization schemes brought many Indians from the high plains to the lowlands where they started a new existence, thus lessening the distinction between Kollas and Cambas. [12] A substantial diversification in the Bolivian economy resulted in new sources of income such as petroleum and natural gas, new export crops such as cotton and coffee, and an impressive level of import substitution.

Of course, it can be argued that the cost of this economic development was high measured in terms of per capita U.S. aid. That country provided some 380 million dollars in economic and military aid between 1952 and 1964. Furthermore, such aid in itself, particularly if combined with a blatant U.S. presence, tends to have a degrading psychological effect, as some of Bolivia's leftist leaders have not failed to note. [13]

The United States' role in the revolution went from quiet support in the early 1950s to openly being in bed with the revolution in the 1960s. Given this position it is obvious that a radical revolution could not have succeeded in 1952 because of U.S. opposition, while a modest form of social change such as actually took place could only come about with U.S.

support. The assumption that the MNR leaders as well as most Bolivians never wanted a radical reform anyway seems to be confirmed by the fact that the 1970 leftist coup by General Torres ended in abject failure with the successful military coup in 1971 headed by the relatively conservative, Colonel Hugo Banzer Suárez.

There are those who regret that after 1964 the military again took over as the arbiters of Bolivian progress and who continue to point out that oppression still lingers in Bolivia some twenty-five years after the 1952 revolution. [14] They can take consolation, however, from the fact that as a result of this revolution these military leaders at least have a better and economically more viable Bolivia with which to work.

ENDNOTES FOR CHAPTER III

1. Milton Eisenhower, *The Wine is Bitter, The United States and Latin America* (Garden City, N.Y.: Doubleday, 1963), pp. 67-68.

2. Víctor Andrade, *My Missions for Revolutionary Bolivia 1944-62* (Pittsburgh: University of Pittsburgh Press, 1976), p. 162.

3. Cornelius H. Zondag, *The Bolivian Economy 1952-64, The Revolution and its Aftermath* (New York: Fred A. Praeger, 1965), p. 55.

4. The *Servicio* constituted a unit composed of Americans and their Bolivian counterparts working within the framework of each of several ministries such as Public Health, Education and Agriculture. It was funded jointly by the two governments.

5. *Revertibles* constituted a variable tariff on imports designed to bring the local cost of imports more in line with the value of the bolivianos in the free market. The revenues obtained through this device were employed to subsidize the prices of basic consumer goods, finance investment and cover the general expenses of the government. While somewhat better conceptually than the previous system of multiple exchange rates, the system obviously contributed much to corruption since it required that an individual rate be established for every product.

6. Alberto Ostria Gutiérrez, *The Tragedy of Bolivia* (New York: The Devin Adair Company, 1958), p. 185.

7. The fact that a number of Bolivian intellectuals less than friendly to the regime--often FSB party members--were able to find employment in the American offices sometimes led to minor frictions as is reflected in the jocular remark attributed to Paz Estenssoro: "If you Americans will get rid of your falangists, I will get rid of my communists."

8. See Robert J. Alexander, *The Bolivian National Revolution* (New) Brunswick: Rutgers University Press, 1958), pp. 208-209, and George Jackson Eder, *Inflation and Development in Latin America* (Ann Arbor: Program of International Business, School of Business Administration, University of Michigan, 1969), pp. 275-307.

9. Regis Debray, *Che's Guerrilla War*, trans. Rosemary Sheed (Marmodsworth, Middlesex, England: Penguin Books, Ltd., 1975), passim.

10. Christopher Mitchell, *The Legacy of Populism in Bolivia from MNR to Military Rule* (New York: Praeger, 1977), p. 173.

11. James M. Malloy, *Bolivia: The Uncompleted Revolution* (Pittsburgh: University of Pittsburgh Press, 1970), passim.

12. The terms *Kollas* and *Cambas* are used to distinguish between the residents of the departments of La Paz and Santa Cruz, respectively.

13. Sergio Almaraz, *Requiem para una república* (La Paz: Universidad Mayor de San Andrés, 1969), p. 27.

14. Moisés Sandóval, "Bolivia Oppression Lingers" *Maryknoll Magazine*, Vol. 72, No. 1 (1978), 3-9.

Part Two

Political Development

The Praetorianization of the
Revolution: 1964-1967

James M. Malloy and Sylvia Borzutsky

INTRODUCTION

Since the overthrow of the National Revolutionary Movement Party (MNR) government in November of 1964, Bolivia's public life has been dominated by the nation's armed forces. The military came to power primarily because the MNR was incapable of defining and imposing a new coherent model of political economy to reshape Bolivian society in the wake of the revolution the movement initiated in 1952. The MNR failed for many reasons some of which have been intrinsic to populist political coalitions in the general Latin American context. More fundamental, however, was the fact that the MNR was deeply split between two alternative models to organize the nation's efforts to develop economically: a "radical populist" model espoused by the movement's labor-based left wing and a "state-capitalist" model favored by its middle class-based center right wing. The two models had sharply differing implications for Bolivia's external relations with the world's rival power blocs and clearly different internal implications particularly with regard to the distribution of the costs and benefits of the revolution and any new process of development.

By 1960 the center right of the MNR led by Víctor Paz Estenssoro had achieved a position of formal dominance, but this faction had neither the power capacity nor the legitimacy to impose its state capitalist solution on an aggressive and armed working class—especially mine workers—which was scheduled to bear the brunt of the costs of the strategy. It was in this context that the military, reorganized and modernized through substantial United States military assistance, stepped into the breach to provide a concentrated source of force at the national level to impose a political and economic solution on the highly fragmented Bolivian society.

With the exception of the brief radical populist interludes of Generals Alfredo Ovando Candia and Juan José Torres, military regimes in Bolivia, first under General René Barrientos and more recently under General Hugo Banzer Suárez, have sought assiduously to impose the state-capitalist model of political economy. Both regimes pursued this goal with Draconian tenacity, especially in their dealings with organized labor. In the economic field both regimes, but especially that of Banzer, were relatively successful as measured by the rise in gross national product. In both, however, the aggregate economic performance was purchased at a very high social and political price, the costs of which have fallen disproportionately on the working class, urban popular sectors and the mass of traditional peasants.

Economic success, however, has not been matched by any long-term political success. As recent events have indicated the *pax* Banzer has been much more apparent than real. Like Barrientos before him, Banzer has mounted a highly personalized authoritarian regime based on the clientelistic manipulation of civil and military elite factions and the suppression of organized opposition.

At its base Bolivia remains a deeply fragmented society divided along class, regional and racial lines. While many of the forces mobilized by the revolution of 1952 have been contained and suppressed, there exists no institutional infrastructure to link state and society and provide a fundamental structural stability. Indeed the rising political and economic power of the department of Santa Cruz has added another destabilizing factor to the already complex equation which brought the MNR to grief.

In the end it has been the guns of the soldiers that have guaranteed the Banzer regime and its state capitalist development model. In this sense the Bolivian revolution has been praetorianized. But this reality goes much deeper. The Bolivian armed forces hardly constitute a coherent institutional force capable of defining and sponsoring a reconstruction of a viable political infrastructure. The fragmentation of the larger society has invaded the military, undermining its already precarious institutional unity. Likewise the old political parties are in total disarray and there is no new viable civil coalition or party formation on the horizon.

From the point of view of this paper, there is no immediate facile solution to Bolivia's political dilemma. The best that can be done now is to analyze the structural factors that contribute to this situation.

STRUCTURAL FACTORS

Dependent Capitalist Development

Bolivia is an extreme case of the general Latin American phenomenon of delayed dependent capitalist development. Thus Bolivia shares many of the essential characteristics of the region's twentieth century patterns of political and economic development but in more exaggerated form.

Like the region as a whole, Bolivia developed first within the contours of an export-based, outward-oriented capitalist growth model. This region-wide model experienced a deep political crisis in the 1930s with the exhaustion of the growth potential of the primary product export structure. The characteristic political response to this crisis was the emergence of broad-based multi-class populist movements: in Bolivia the MNR. These movements sought to promote a new "nationalist" process of state guided capitalist growth by mobilizing support from the urban middle classes, the working class and rhetorically at least the peasantry. In effect they promised to achieve economic growth and distributive social justice simultaneously.

Even where such movements did not come to direct power, they had a profound impact by increasing general levels of political mobilization, restructuring the terms of national political debates and forcing established elites to meet at least some of the demands of the middle classes and the better organized sectors of the working class. The larger more diversified countries like Argentina, Brazil and Chile were able to ride out the crisis without a mass-based revolutionary upheaval by promoting a new process of import-substitution growth which allowed political elites to co-opt critical sectors of the middle and working classes. This was only a temporary solution however. By the early 1960s the exhaustion of the import-substitution model provoked a new political crisis which in turn led to the emergence of a number of new military-based development-oriented authoritarian regimes.

These new "bureaucratic-authoritarian" regimes differ from the post-1964 Bolivian military governments in a number of important ways. Nonetheless there are also some important similarities. All of these regimes emerged in situations characterized by extreme political immobilism in which civil elites were incapable of coping with a growing volume of demands from popular sectors that were increasingly mobilized, organized and militant in pressing their demands. Fearing revolutionary upheavals, military organizations seized power to impose order and discipline on their respective societies.

Once in power all of these regimes have sought to create a structure for what might be called a new pattern of anti-populist state-capitalist development. They have been anti-populist in the sense that they have imposed the costs of development on the popular sectors and sought by force if necessary to reverse the process of mobilization of these sectors.

Thus all of these regimes in a sense can be seen as reacting to the cumulative political effects of populist attempts to grapple with the structural realities of underdevelopment in Latin America. Despite the experience of the MNR, it is clear that populism in Latin America was never really revolutionary in intent. Rather populism was and is a reformist attempt to retain the essential framework of the region's political economy by promoting a kind of neo-mercantilism. The recent history of the region indicates the essential fallacy of the populist approach. Populism appeared as a political response to the periodic crises of the underlying structural reality of delayed-dependent capitalist growth. Yet the same structure in the end subverted populism's reformist attempts to pursue economic development, distributive justice and mobilization at the same time. Again Bolivia is best understood as an extreme case of this general pattern.

Radical Populism

A central feature of twentieth century political economy in Bolivia was the fact that the country did not have the structural capacity to ride out the crisis of the 1930s through a process of import-substitution growth. Hence, established elites were incapable of buying time by co-opting segments of the middle and working classes. As a result the situation deteriorated rapidly. Two important features of the Bolivian context were the transformation of the MNR from a small cadre party of middle class reformers into a tenuous multi-group alliance, and the internal disintegration of the Bolivian armed forces.

In many respects the revolution of 1952 came as a surprise to many including the leadership of the MNR. In any event it is clear that many of the structural transformations, e.g., the land reform, that came in the wake of the revolt of 1952 went far beyond the intentions or expectations of a substantial part of the MNR's original middle class core of support.

Aside from the structural transformations, the most significant result of the revolution of 1952 was the tremendous wave of political mobilization it set in motion. Bolivia became a hyper-mobilized society; a reality that was complicated considerably by the virtual collapse of the official armed forces, the broad dispersal of weaponry into civilian hands and the quick formation of autonomous worker and peasant militia units.

The MNR had never been an integrated, disciplined and ideologically coherent political organization. After the revolt it was even less so. As Christopher Mitchell has pointed out, the MNR was an uneasy alliance of disparate and contradictory ".social sectors" who sought to use the formal structure of the party to further their own sectoral interests and particular visions of the revolution. [1] In a sense the MNR recapitulated within itself the extremely fragmented nature of that hyper-mobilized society. On paper the elaborate formal party organization became the spinal column of a new "corporatist" political structure modeled at least in part on that of Mexico. In reality the party elite lacked even the most rudimentary capacity to discipline its own support groups and as a result could do little more than cling to the formal trappings of power and react on an ad hoc basis to the increasing clamor of contradictory demands rising from its ostensible supporters.

The Bolivian revolution quickly demonstrated some inescapable facts of the reality of the situation of economic backwardness and structural dependency, namely that (a) a relatively backward country cannot follow a simultaneous policy of economic development and popular consumption and (b) any process of restructuring for development demands that some social groups pay the "costs" of the new course. Finally the revolution, in characteristically extreme fashion, made clear that the populist premise of a community of interests among the middle classes, workers and peasants is illusory.

The MNR like other regimes came up against the fact that it would have to choose which of its support groups would gain and which lose in the short run at least; more importantly it would have to fashion a coalition powerful enough to impose such a solution on the rest of the society.

In confronting these questions the MNR's options were limited by a number of internal and external constraints. While anti-imperialist in rhetoric, the core MNR leadership never seriously considered breaking with the Western Capitalist world; and in the context of the early 1950s it is highly doubtful that the Soviet Union had either the will or the capacity to become the protector and patron of an anti-U.S. revolution in Bolivia. Owing to its early policies, the regime became extremely dependent on external aid to keep afloat, which in that context meant mainly the United States and U.S. dominated international institutions such as the International Monetary Fund (IMF). Instead of breaking or lessening the structural reality of dependency, the revolution actually increased it. Thus the United States acquired significant leverage over the regime which it used to push the revolution in an essentially state capitalist direction. This reality was made clear in the monetary stabilization of 1956, the Triangular Plan and the terms of aid under the Alliance for Progress. [2]

State Capitalist Model

The shift of the revolution away from the radical populism of the first four years toward a state capitalist model was the product of the basic orientation of the core MNR elite and the realities of Bolivia's international situation. The central internal problem hampering the shift was the essential weakness of the central government in the face of the determined resistance of the MNR's left wing backed by the autonomous armed power of sectors of the working class, especially the miners. To overcome this reality, the MNR core first under Hernán Siles Zuazo and then under Víctor Paz Estenssoro and backed by substantial U.S. assistance, began to rebuild and modernize the Bolivian armed forces.

The first prerequisite of imposing the new model was the ability of the regime backed by the U.S. to definitively break the political-cum-

military power of the labor left. In this struggle the state capitalist coalition came to rely more and more on the power of the revitalized military.
In addition the Siles Zuazo and Paz Estenssoro governments skillfully used
a blend of symbolic rhetoric, particularistic privileges and clientelistic
patronage to mobilize important sectors of the peasantry (especially Cochabamba) against the labor left. The bulk of the rest of the peasantry
was effectively marginalized from the main political and economic dynamics
of the process.

The increasingly violent sectoral clashes over the issue of the costs
of the new course constituted the most obvious factor that brought the
MNR down in 1964. However, at least two other structural factors ultimately led to the MNR's fall: the structural reality of the Bolivian urban
middle class and the party organization itself.

The Middle Class

The Bolivian urban middle class is again an extreme manifestation of
a general Latin American reality produced in part by the situation of delayed dependent capitalist development. The Bolivian middle class is essentially a bureaucratized stratum which has traditionally relied directly
or indirectly on the public sector to support its status and position in the
overall system of stratification. This fact has been manifested at least
since the 1920s when it became clear that whatever else they were, Bolivia's political parties were at base loosely knit personalistic elite factions
struggling among themselves over the circulation of the jobs, contacts and
largesse of the public sector. At one level Bolivian politics was and is an
elite and sub-elite battle among "ins and outs." As one local saying aptly
puts it: "The major industry of this country is politics." If anything,
this underlying reality has become even more pervasive since the revolution of 1952.

The root problem has been, however, that the Bolivian economy has
never been able to support a public sector sufficiently large to support
all the elite and sub-elite claimants on its resources. Thus Bolivian political life has been plagued by a swollen and expensive public sector and
built in fragmentation at the elite and sub-elite level.

Over the years the MNR as a party came increasingly to mirror this
basic fact. Lacking even rudimentary membership controls, the party
became bloated with job and contact hungry supporters. Like the political parties before it, the MNR behind its formal facade was a top heavy
coalition of personalistic factions seeking to control portions of the public
sector. Thus aside from its deep sectoral divisions, the MNR was also
irrevocably fragmented at the elite and sub-elite level. To maintain even
the semblance of rule, national political leaders had to become adept at
manipulating an extremely complex pattern of patron client networks.
The ability of leaders to play the clientelistic game turned on the amount
of surplus the state could extract from the society which in turn fluctuated mainly with the fortunes of Bolivia's export sector. Even at the
best of times there was not enough to go around and each division of
patronage generated substantial opposition within the MNR itself.

The reality of elite and sub-elite fragmentation stood out during the
second presidential term of Paz Estenssoro. By his end the president was
obviously ruling through a rump faction of the party, made up of many
new faces, and there were many attacks from within the MNR itself against
this coterie of Paz Estenssoro. Indeed there is little doubt that a substantial number of MNR factions played either a direct or indirect role in
the coup of 1964 which in many ways was, in their eyes at least, not an
overthrow of the MNR as such but of a highly personalistic faction of the

MNR. One might in fact argue that by that point there was no real MNR.
    Yet the problem of the middle class goes even deeper. The state capitalist development model demands more than simply a capacity to impose costs. Specifically, as Jaguaribe has pointed out and as the Brazilian case demonstrates, it demands a middle class developed and modern enough to generate a substantial cadre of technocrats capable of rationally manipulating the public sector as well as a national stratum of entrepreneurs ready and willing to respond to incentives emanating from the state on a long-term basis.[3] Thus far the Bolivian middle class has not been able to generate either.
    The national entrepreneurial stratum remains small, favors traditional state dependent activities such as construction and tends to seek short-term windfall profits as the agri-industry cycles of the eastern region amply demonstrate. The middle class not only has not produced the requisite technocratic elite but in fact has resisted government attempts to transform the educational system in that direction. Witness, for example, the fate of the Paz Estenssoro government's attempt to create the Bolivian Technology Institute (ITB). This fact combined with the reality of middle classed-based job and contact factionalism has contributed to the conversion of the universities into a chronic source of political instability.

The Armed Forces

    These structural considerations have contributed to another factor that has weakened the ability of subsequent regimes to build up a political infrastructure to underpin the state capitalist model. Namely the Bolivian armed forces do not constitute an unified national institution with either a strong corporate identity or a coherent vision of the nation's future and the role of the armed forces in bringing that about. Drawn largely from the middle classes the officer corps reflects the patrimonial orientation and intra-elite factionalism of the broader bureaucratic middle class. Compared to military organizations in countries like Brazil and Peru the Bolivian armed forces are less professionally developed as an organization. Since 1964 the government has not been dominated so much by the military as an institution but by shifting coalitions of factions within the military. Presidents like Barrientos and Banzer have clung to power by the clientelistic manipulation of personalistic factions in the military much the same as that used to stay on top of the civil elite. The Bolivian armed forces still reflect a quasi-*caudillesque* dynamic demonstrated by the fact that in moments of political crisis the chain of command within the military breaks down. If the military was once a coherent institution, it is not clear that it too has been invaded and subverted by the fragmentation of the society at large. All indications are that this process of the institutional disaggregation of the military is apt to continue as long as the armed forces are constrained to assume formal governmental responsibility. Given the disarray of the civil political elite there seems little doubt that the military will be induced to play a more or less open role in the governance of Bolivia.
    Since at least the early 1960s, Bolivia has been an almost paradigm case of what Huntington has defined as a praetorian society:

> In a praetorian system social forces confront each other nakedly; no political institutions, no corps of professional political leaders are recognized or accepted as the legitimate intermediaries to moderate group conflict. Equally important no agreement exists among groups as to the legitimate authoritative methods for resolving conflicts.[4]

Since overthrowing the MNR military regimes have merely ratified this fact and while they have been able to suppress the more open manifestations of the situation they have not been able to change it.

1964-1969: BARRIENTOS AND STATE CAPITALISM

In examining the dynamics of the political economy of state capitalism in Bolivia since 1964, it is necessary to take into consideration the continuing reality of external dependence. Bolivia, like other Latin American countries, has been forced to attempt to adapt its internal structures to succeeding phases in the development of the global Western Capitalist system. The recent history of Latin America shows that this has meant that the dependent nation seeks to adapt up to the latest level of the advanced nations rather than through some linear internal progression from lower to higher stages; thus the marked structural dualism of the region characterized by highly developed modern sectors and backward traditional sectors--the former not developing separately from the latter but at its expense.

We can see some of the aspects of this reality in Bolivia during the Barrientos period from 1964 to 1969. Structurally development during the period had two chief aspects: (a) a resurgence of the private sector; and (b) an attempt to modernize the economy by favoring almost exclusively modern corporate enterprises in both the public and private sector. The resurgence of the private sector was most notable in the economically critical areas of mining and petroleum. In both of these activities, which previously were the symbols of Bolivian nationalism, private sector national and international interests by 1968 had become the major sources of production; in the case of oil the preponderant one. The government's main direct efforts went into revitalizing and reorganizing the major public sector corporations and to financing infrastructure to serve the modern sector and most particularly to stimulate the development of a new modern agri-industrial sector in the eastern provinces or *Oriente*. In effect there was an attempt to force an alliance between the public sector and modern-oriented national and international enterprises in the private sector. At that juncture the emphasis was on pushing private modern activities while rolling back and stabilizing public activities. If we see state capitalism as an attempt to strike a dynamic balance between the public and private sectors, under Barrientos the scale was tipped toward the private sector.

The Barrientos approach clearly discriminated against the traditional economic sectors, particularly agriculture. During this period Bolivia posted a respectable rate of growth in gross national product led by growth in petroleum production and construction. In fact the only sector not to post substantial gains was the agricultural sector. And of the agricultural growth that did take place (ranging from a high of 6 percent in 1966 to a low of -1 percent in 1967) by far the bulk was in commercial products such as rice, sugar and meat. The vast bulk of traditional peasant small holders were simply left behind.

This distorted growth pattern came about at a very high cost in human and political terms. The major beneficiaries of the thrust were the small national entrepreneurial class and foreign multi-national investors such as Gulf Oil. In addition the urban middle class as an aggregate benefited from increased employment and a stable currency. More specific indicators of the benefits accruing to the middle class were the boom in urban construction and a doubling of government expenditures in wages and salaries. As might be expected the military benefited directly from a very substantial rise in military expenditures.

The bulk of the costs of the process fell none too gently on the great mass of Bolivians in the popular classes in whose name the revolution of 1952 was launched. The most obvious and direct costs were imposed on the working class, particularly the miners. In the mines there were mass layoffs and salaries were cut by half. Aside from small privileged groups, the rest of the working class were forced to accept wage freezes in an economy that was averaging better than 6 percent inflation per year.

Despite Barrientos's carefully cultivated image as the patron of the *campesino*, it is evident that the bulk of the rural peasants were also losers. Aside from highly publicized personal acts of largesse by the *Caudillo*, little of substance went into the countryside. Investment in agriculture was almost nil and what little there was went to agri-industry. Finally, overall government spending for goods, services and transfers declined sharply.

To impose these costs the Barrientos government escalated considerably the level of repression of independent popular organizations. Again, worker organizations were the main targets of the repression. The Bolivian Worker's Central (COB) was disbanded and most unions quashed or taken over by docile government leaders. But the repression followed the historical pattern of being particularly vicious toward the miners. The mines were invaded on at least two occasions and for most of the period were under military occupation.

Under the so-called military-*campesino* pact, the regime appeared to have massive peasant support. This was an illusion. Barrientos did generate some visible support through his frequent highly publicized trips to the rural areas on which occasions he personally doled out some highly symbolic rewards. But key to his ostensible peasant support was the cooptation of some key leaders such as Jorge Soliz from the Cochabamba Valley. Other less cooperative peasant leaders felt the harsh hand of the government. The point is that the bulk of rural syndicates no longer functioned as autonomous organizations and the peasant leadership was estranged more and more from its own base. The bulk of the peasantry was not only marginalized from the economic process, but from the political as well. The logic of the state capitalist model aims for a largely excluded and docile peasantry which occasionally can be manipulated for political purposes.

From the political point of view, the Barrientos regime sought assiduously to destroy the remnants of the political infrastructure that emerged between 1952 and 1964: namely the MNR and the worker and peasant unions. The regime did succeed in quashing this structure but it did not eliminate it. More importantly the government was completely incapable of building an alternative structure. It was painfully evident that the new Barrientos party was nothing more than an old fashioned personalistic clique of office seekers with absolutely no organizational links to any segment of Bolivian society.

Aside from the suppression of any organized opposition, the ability of the regime to garner any positive support so as to govern was based on two factors. The first was the classic ability to co-opt significant sectors of the middle class elite by manipulating clientelistic access to positions in the public sector. This ability in turn depended on the capacity of the state to extract a surplus from either internal or external sources. Given Bolivia's economic dependence this ability has always fluctuated with the vagaries of the international market. By the late 1960s this picture was dimming. The balance of trade, always precarious in Bolivia, began to shift against the regime; in part because of the importation of consumer goods destined for the urban middle class. In addition foreign private investment declined as did direct economic aid from the U.S. Thus the regime was forced to borrow heavily and to incur a growing debt. Barrientos was in a situation similar to that of Paz Estenssoro. There was never enough to go around and each division of the largesse generated its own dissidents from within the urban middle class which in turn kept the opposition parties alive and plotting.

In the final analysis popular support for the Barrientos government was a chimera and the General's hold on power was based on the support of the military. However, the regime's support in the military was also based on the manipulation of factional politics within the military and the fact that there was no readily available alternative. Support for the regime did not spring from the institution itself nor was the Barrientos regime an expression of a coherent military image of its role in governing and developing the nation. In short it was more transient support by default than a positive expression of the military's approach to governance.

Barrientos's military support was always precarious to say the least. His relationship with the commander of the armed forces, General Alfredo Ovando Candia, as well as other senior officers was fraught with tension born of conflicting personal ambitions. The fragility of his relationships with the army in particular was made clear in the handling of the Ché Guevara episode and especially in the disposition of Ché's diary. In addition there was at least one serious coup attempt by General Vásquez Sempértegui and rumors of plots and counter-plots were the order of the day throughout his presidency. Above the suppressed popular sectors of society, national politics was characterized by an intense and unstable process of intra-elite factional politics.[5] In a tragic end Barrientos was killed in a helicopter crash in April 1969. The civilian vice-president Luis Siles Salinas assumed the presidency. However, his regime was short lived for in September of the same year he was overthrown in a coup led by General Ovando.

1969-1971: A RETURN TO POPULISM

If anything, the short-lived radical populist governments of General Ovando and the General Juan José Torres confirmed the complete institutional disintegration of Bolivian national political life. Ovando openly attempted to model his government along the lines of the then fashionable "revolution of the armed forces" in neighboring Peru. His nationalization of Gulf Oil was a page straight out of the Peruvian book.

Structurally he followed the Peruvian approach of forming a government based on an alliance between the military and a civilian technocratic elite, which then reached out to the popular sectors with structural reforms designed to mobilize a legitimating base of popular support. However the political situation in the two countries was quite different.

Prior to the revolution of 1968 in Peru, there had not been anything near the level of political mobilization Bolivia had experienced nor had there been any significant structural reforms. The Peruvian military was in effect attempting to forge its own populist coalition to impose from above much the same agenda of structural reforms that had already been carried out in Bolivia during the early days of the MNR revolution. Moreover from the beginning the Peruvian military was determined to avoid the uncontrolled mobilization Bolivia had experienced. In short it was an attempt—only partially successful—to impose a controlled populist revolution from above.

Most important, the Peruvian military, while not monolithic, had achieved a degree of corporate identity and a sense of its mission as an institution far beyond that of the Bolivian armed forces. The Coup of

1968 was a consensual institutional act informed by a well-defined doctrine of national security and development. In addition, the Peruvian middle class, while similar to that of Bolivia in many respects, was able to provide some truly technocratic cadres ready and willing to cooperate with the military in its venture. Finally, while the Peruvian regime sought to crush its old institutional enemy, the Popular Alliance of American Revolutionaries (APRA), it also was able to garner the active support of the Peruvian Communist Party and its labor federation. Although the relationship was tense the Communist party did support the generals, and even more important, consciously determined a strategy of not pushing the military too hard nor of publicly taking political positions in advance of the military.

Ovando, in contrast, tried to put together a government organized around some factions of the military and a small group of quasi-technocratic civilian independents. From the first the civil wing pushed in a more radical direction than the military, and the government split into hostile camps. Yet the independent civilian ministers simply could not produce any coherent popular support by lifting the blanket of suppression of the previous period. Given some maneuvering room the old autonomous popular structures sprang back into place, but not as a structural base of support for the populist wing of the regime. Rather, and most understandably, the old labor left immediately pushed far ahead of the regime in an attempt to recoup its economic and political losses and reverse the state capitalist thrust. In a sense it was an abrupt return to the political situation of the early 1960s but in an even less structured context.

The situation deteriorated rapidly and culminated in the tragic comic coups and counter coups of October 1970 from which emerged the figure of Juan José Torres. The Torres interlude was a fascinating historical moment that deserves an analysis beyond the scope of this paper. Under Torres the process of mobilization speeded up and threatened to become general again. The old labor left dropped any semblance of supporting the formal government and in a revival of the old doctrine of dual power sought to form an alternative governmental structure in the Popular Assembly aimed at pushing a complete socialist revolutionary transformation.

But while the old labor left organizations proved their durability and survival capacity in the face of years of brutal repression, the fact remains that they did not possess anything resembling the power they had achieved in the early days of the MNR revolution. Moreover the left elite was as factionalized and strife-riven as every other political stratum. Harass and harry a government that was all but epiphenomenal to the situation the left could do—but the constitution of a structure of governance and revolutionary change was simply beyond their capacity. As Hobbes put it long ago in that type of political situation "clubs are trump" and the clubs were neither in the hands of Torres's official government nor in those of the Popular Assembly. They were still in the hands of the soldiers.

Some leaders of the Assembly grasped this fact and made the logical but crucial mistakes of seeking to overturn the structure of authority within the military and mobilize the troops to back their cause. Faced with this threat to its very institutional existence the officer corps was able to momentarily overcome its own fragmentation and move against the perceived common enemy. The result was a brief but bloody civil war in 1971 which brought to an end this radical populist interlude.

1971-1978: THE *ORIENTE* COMES TO POWER: THE BANZER PERIOD

Ideological factors obviously played an important role in the over-throw of Torres. But ideological and class questions have never been the sole substance of Bolivian politics. Although the military has never been able to develop a positive sense of a governmental mission, it did have enough coherence to act out of sheer self-preservation. This aspect of military behavior will remain a constant in Bolivian politics for some time. What specific content this capacity to act out of institutional self-preservation will take in the future, however, is unpredictable.

Equally, if not more significant for the future of Bolivia, was the role played by the *Oriente* and particularly the Department of Santa Cruz in the overthrow of Torres. At one level the action was a civil war that pitted Santa Cruz and the east against the *Altiplano*. It is no coincidence that in 1971 the coup began in Santa Cruz and was led by two officers, Colonel Hugo Banzer Suárez and Colonel Andrés Selich, both native to the region.

Regional conflicts tinged with racial and cultural animosity are by no means new to Bolivia. Historically, Bolivian political life has been structured in part by global geo political shifts occasioned by shifts in the nation's economic structure. Such a shift took place in 1898 with the rise to dominance of La Paz and tin over the previously dominant Sucre and silver. Until the revolution of 1952, La Paz, tin and the *Altiplano* constituted the political and economic core of Bolivia much to the chagrin and anger of other regions, particularly the isolated *Oriente*. [6]

Since the 1930s populist ideology has been predicated on a perceived need to buttress the economy and integrate the nation through a general program of economic diversification and a specific plan of marching to the east. Particularly since the 1960s the state capitalist model in Bolivia has been based on a plan of stabilizing and rationalizing the old *Altiplano* base of the economy so it would at least not be a drain to the economy. This, in a sense negative, orientation has been accompanied by a more positive belief that the country's real future growth potential lay toward the *Oriente* and all state capitalist oriented regimes have followed policies reflecting this belief in the eastern *El Dorado*.

Fueled by the growth in the importance of oil and natural gas and the rise of agri-industry, Santa Cruz was transformed into an economic boom zone. Moreover, thanks to the department's control over a sub-stantial portion of oil and gas revenues, it was able to funnel the funds into its own local development. These regional developments have been converted into a growing level of political power which the department and its local entrepreneurial elite have deployed with increasing aggressiveness at the national level.

Both the Ovando and Torres administrations were perceived to be populist and pro-*Altiplano* regimes and as such direct threats to the continued capitalist growth of Santa Cruz. The coup was in a sense a successful blow by Santa Cruz and the *Oriente* against the *Altiplano*. In short Bolivia is experiencing a new geo-political shift characterized by the relative decline of the *Altiplano* and tin and the rise of the *Oriente* with its oil, gas and agri-industry. This shift is fraught with significant regional, racial and cultural tensions that will be a constant factor in the Bolivian political equation for some time to come.

Since 1971 the Banzer regime has put Bolivia firmly back on the state capitalist path. This time around, however, there has been a marked shift in the balance between the public and private sectors toward the former. In fact, one of the striking characteristics of this period has been the preponderant economic role assumed by the state.

Some sources indicate that the public sector now accounts for some 65 to 70 percent of the investment. [7] Between 1971 and 1975 governmental expenditures grew at an annual real average rate of 16.5 percent, or more than twice the real rate of growth of GNP. This growth in the role of the public sector has been the result of a dramatic increase in direct government expenditures and a significantly higher rate of expenditure by public corporations.

This shift to a preponderant public sector probably reflects in part the structural weakness of the local private entrepreneurial stratum and its inability and or unwillingness to assume a leading role in pushing the state capitalist model. Yet, probably much more basic has been the political reality of the faction-ridden, job-hungry Bolivian middle class.

Harking back to the previous analysis, it is interesting to note that during the 1963-1975 period the total labor force grew at a yearly average of 2.73 percent while that of the central government grew at an annual average rate of 5.7 percent. As a result, government employment as a percentage of total employment went from 2.54 to 3.37. This general trend in state employment was accelerated in the 1971-1975 period when government employment grew at an annual rate of 9.9 percent or three times more than growth in the total labor force. [8] At least one study notes that this has not reflected an increase in technical personnel, but rather the fact that hiring in the public sector has been done on "distributive grounds rather than on grounds of efficiency." [9] The situation is so out of kilter that the Ministry of Education--a traditional source of middle and lower middle class employment--spends 99.2 percent of its total direct expenditures on wages and salaries while the Ministry of Health spends some 77.6 percent. [10] In our view this hyper-growth of the public sector is reflective of Banzer's continuing need to buy short-term political support through the clientelistic manipulation of Bolivia's fractious traditional middle class.

Since 1971 the state capitalist strategy in Bolivia has again favored the modern corporate enterprises to the detriment of what are perceived as small traditional and inefficient activities. The regional biases of the earlier versions of the approach have not only continued but have been considerably increased. These dimensions of the strategy were articulated as national policy in the Five-Year Development Plan published in June of 1976.

The Plan aims at export-led growth accompanied by selective import substitution. It gives the preponderant leading role to the public sector projecting some 7.1 billion pesos in public sector investment projects compared to some .7 billion in private sector projects, and over the entire 1976-1980 period a total investment goal of 50 billion pesos with 71 percent coming from the public sector. Following the earlier logic, it aims at stabilizing the mineral sector (4.3 billion pesos investment) and pivoting the economy toward hydrocarbons (6.7 billion investment). [11]

The bias against agriculture, and particularly the traditional peasantry, continues. Of total planned investment only 4 percent or 2 billion pesos is earmarked for agriculture and again the bulk of this will go to nurture the agro-industrial sector in the *Oriente*. [12]

Within this traditional-modern, dichotomized scheme, a clear pattern of regional differentiation and discrimination is also articulated. The nation has been divided into three investment zones: a primary zone of La Paz-Cochabamba-Santa Cruz; a secondary zone of Oruro-Potosi-Chuquisaca; and a tertiary zone of Pando-Beni with investment shares of 63, 32 and 5 percent, respectively. As we see it, the scheme represents a political reality of attempting to link the more traditional pole of political economy in La Paz to the emergent giant, Santa Cruz, with Cochabamba serving as the connector.

The pattern of government-enforced "cost" allocation among social sectors of the state capitalist model has remained essentially the same. The heralded prosperity of the *Pax* Banzer has benefited only a small part of the population—specifically, entrepreneurial elites in the public and private modern sectors and a portion of the traditional middle class absorbed in the burgeoning governmental bureaucracy. This stands out sharply in the fact that despite its "populist" revolution of 1952, Bolivia today has one of the most unequal patterns of income distribution, both internationally and within Latin America. In terms of labor income, the highest 5 percent earns 21.4 times more than the lowest 5 percent; a picture that becomes even more unequal if property income is added. [13] These and other measures show that Bolivia's popular classes have gained little from the revolution made in their name.

The largest group of losers has been the traditional peasantry who have been all but completely marginalized from the main stream of economic life. Again, the most direct and forceful imposition of costs has been against the organized working class groups who were the backbone of the revolution of 1952 and the radical populist model. There is no need to detail here the systematic suppression which these groups have experienced since 1971. In Bolivia as elsewhere in Latin America, the state capitalist model has been predicated on a militarized breaking of the political back of the bulk of organized labor.

Like Barrientos before him, Banzer has been completely incapable of building a political structure to support his regime let alone institutionalize Bolivia's political life. While many factors account for this, in our view the key structural problem remains the intense fragmentation at the elite and sub-elite level of society, which in turn is rooted in Bolivia's bureaucratized middle classes. These groups do not act as a class but as a shifting melange of personalistic factions capable of being wielded only into short-term and unstable factional alliances. Once in power each such alliance of "ins" generates from within the same class formation its own counter alliance of "outs." This general class pattern carries over into the military, undercutting its ability to provide an institutional base of support.

Thus, at the elite and sub-elite level the name of the game continues to be the clientelistic manipulation of civil and military factional alliances. Banzer's ability to play this game has been rooted in the surplus created by the generally favorable terms of trade that have held for much of his term thus far. But as bureaucratic absorption reaches its outward limits within the efficiency needs of the development model and the terms of trade show signs of weakening, the president's room for maneuver has been narrowing accordingly.

In his first three years, Banzer attempted to play this game and simultaneously achieve a facade of institutional support and legitimacy by wielding the military, the MNR and its old rival the Bolivian Socialist Falange (FSB) into a tripartite regime. He soon learned, however, that this play merely formalized the claims on the public sector of the job-hungry cadres of these parties, while providing very little stable support. Moreover, this arrangement put the control of patronage into the hands of party faction leaders who used it to advance themselves and their allies. When he eliminated political parties in 1974, Banzer was able to assert some personal control, but hardly resolve the structural dilemma itself. Moreover, that brief period showed that the old parties either alone or in alliance cannot themselves provide any institutional base for a regime.

Bolivia therefore remains a praetorian society characterized by a fragmented elite struggling to form alliances to preside over a severely repressed society. [14] It is hard for us, at least, to see any electoral solution to this reality in the offing. Indeed elections will probably only serve to bring these and other factors into the open. Even should elections be brought off, which is highly doubtful, the possibility of a legitimate regime capable of governing in anything resembling a stable democratic manner is dubious in the extreme.

As recent events have demonstrated, repression has kept the organized expression of sectoral opposition under control, but the organizational infrastructure itself is far from being dead. Given the chance, the labor left will at the least seek to reconstitute its political power and reverse some of its economic losses; hence, it will be quickly back on collision course with the forces that support and benefit from the state capitalist mode. But it is extremely doubtful that the populist left could reverse the basic thrust of Bolivia or provide a base to support an alternative model of political economy. The cycle of stand off and repression, evident since the 1960s, is apt to continue.

The newest and most difficult factor to assess in the Bolivian political equation is the emergence of Santa Cruz as a regionally self-conscious political force. While it is doubtful that Santa Cruz could dominate the rest of the nation, it does seem to have achieved the power to veto either governments or policies deemed hostile to its interests. Thus, any government that tried to adopt a pro-*Altiplano* image against the perceived interests of Santa Cruz could at the least expect harassment and coup attempts. Should a government emerge that projected a radical populist as well as pro-*Altiplano* image, the possibilities of secession and civil war become a grim possibility.

PROJECTIONS FOR THE FUTURE

In sum, seven years of superficially stable government have done little to transform the underlying political instability in Bolivia. If anything, it is more complex. The most likely scenario in the short run is for a continuance of the state capitalist course within an unstable political framework of shifting alliances of elite "ins" and "outs" presided over by *caudillos* drawn from factions within the military. The longevity of specific regimes will vary with the constraints imposed by the international context on the extractive capabilities of the state and the ability of individual leaders like Barrientos and Banzer to manipulate the complex web of clientelistic factions within the Bolivian elite and sub-elite. The extremely unequal distribution of income enforced by recurrent cycles of repression is also apt to remain. In spite of any contrary intentions, the military will remain at the pivot of political life, deciding the fate of governments and imposing costs. The outlook for Bolivia's popular classes is, to say the least, not very bright.

ENDNOTES FOR CHAPTER IV

1. See Christopher Mitchell, *The Legacy of Populism in Bolivia: From the MNR to Military Rule* (New York: Praeger Publishers, 1977).

2. For a study of the relations between the U.S. and the revolutionary regimes in Bolivia, see Cole Blasier, *The Hovering Giant: U.S. Responses to Revolutionary Change in Latin America* (Pittsburgh: University of Pittsburgh Press, 1976).

3. See Helio Jaguaribe, *Political Development: A General Theory and a Latin American Case Study* (New York: Harper and Row, 1973).

4. P. Samuel Huntington, *Political Order in Changing Societies* (New Haven: Yale University Press, 1968), p. 196.

5. For a detailed analysis of the Barrientos's period, see Melvin Burke and James M. Malloy, "From National Populism to National Corporatism: The Case of Bolivia (1952-1970)," *Studies in Comparative International Development,* Vol. IX, ed. I. L. Horowitz (New Brunswick: Rutgers University Press, 1974), pp. 49-73.

6. This problem has been analyzed by James M. Malloy in *Bolivia: The Uncompleted Revolution* (Pittsburgh: University of Pittsburgh Press, 1970).

7. Sebastián Piñera, "Public Expenditure Structure and Employment," in *Fiscal Reform in Bolivia, Staff Papers,* Vol. I (Cambridge, Mass.: Musgrave Mission, 1977), p. 2 (Mimeographed.)

8. Ibid., p. 2.

9. Ibid., pp. 4 5.

10. Ibid., p. 29.

11. Armando Pinell-Siles, "Alternative Strategies for the Economic Development of Bolivia," *Fiscal Reform in Bolivia, Staff Papers,* Vol. I, No. 3 (Cambridge, Mass.: Musgrave Mission, 1977), p. 48. (Mimeographed.) All data are calculated in constant 1973 prices.

12. Ibid., p. 48.

13. Sebastián Piñera, "The Structure of Income Distribution in Bolivia," *Fiscal Reform in Bolivia, Staff Papers,* Vol. I (Cambridge, Mass.: Musgrave Mission, 1977), p. 21, (Mimeographed.)

14. The problems of the weakness of the Bolivian State and the fragmentation of her society have been analyzed by James M. Malloy in "The Case of Bolivia," *Authoritarianism and Corporatism in Latin America,* James M. Malloy, ed. (Pittsburgh: University of Pittsburgh Press, 1977).

Chapter V

The Labor Movement During and Since the 1952 Revolution

Robert J. Alexander

THE EARLY ROLE OF LABOR IN THE REVOLUTION

Organized labor played a key role in launching the Bolivian national revolution in April 1952. Groups of miners seized control of principal cities near the mining areas, while the workers of La Paz were armed by the National Revolutionary Movement Party (MNR) and the *Carabineros*, constituting a major factor in the victory of the revolution in the national capital.

After the MNR regime came into power, the trade union movement was a principal factor in the maintenance of the regime, particularly during the first administration of President Víctor Paz Estenssoro from 1952 to 1956. Throughout that period and for some time thereafter, the country's government was officially a co-government by the MNR and the Bolivian Workers' Central (COB), established within a few days of the triumph of the uprising. The COB had the right to name three of its principal figures to key posts in the cabinet, and did so.

Furthermore, the security of the regime rested largely on the organized labor movement for the year or so following the revolt. Armed militiamen of the various labor groups, particularly the miners, were the principal force behind the regime, since one of the MNR government's first acts was officially to dissolve the Bolivian armed forces.

The organized labor movement's role was particularly important in the mining regions where *control obrero* was established. This was a system whereby officials named by the Bolivian Federation of Miners' Unions (FSTMB) had a veto power on any decisions of the management of the tin mines, which were nationalized late in 1952. Furthermore, the local miners unions and the FSTMB had the decisive voice in saying who would remain on the managerial staff of the nationalized mining enterprise.

Decline of Labor Influence in Revolutionary Regime

However, the influence of the organized workers declined as the MNR regime progressed. Perhaps the decisive showdown between the MNR government and the organized labor movement came in the early months of 1957. Shortly before, the new government of President Hernán Siles

Zuazo had enacted an economic stabilization program which had the effect of ending many of the privileges which the miners, and particularly their leaders, had enjoyed in the preceding years. After first accepting the stabilization program, the FSTMB leaders, headed by Executive Secretary Juan Lechín Oquendo, later sought to thwart it. They declared a general strike, but after impassioned appeals by President Siles Zuazo and other leaders of the government, the miners generally refused to follow their leaders, and the strike was broken. The stabilization program became a reality.

Thereafter, several other factors served to mitigate the influence of the organized labor movement, and particularly the miners, in the government and the general political situation. One was the growing importance of the peasants as an element in the MNR regime. In 1953 the revolutionary government had decreed a land reform, which served to put most of the land in the *Altiplano* and Mountain Valley areas of the republic in the hands of the Indian peasants. Even before the land reform decree, the government had largely organized the peasants into unions, and armed militia groups. Much of the armament of the military forces dissolved after the 1952 revolution was placed in the hands of the peasants.

As a result, the peasants became strong supporters of the MNR government. Their armed militia came to be a vital force in the security of the revolutionary regime. Much more numerous than the workers militia, and particularly the miners, the peasant militia were for awhile the most important armed force supporting the government of the MNR.

The Siles Zuazo government, however, undertook to reinforce another element which could challenge the workers and their militia. This was the regular military. The first Paz Estenssoro government had, after a year or so, reestablished the national army, air force and navy, but had been careful to keep them relatively small, lightly armed, and largely dispersed on civic action projects in the provinces, so that they would constitute no menace to the stability of the regime.

However, the Siles Zuazo government with considerable encouragement from the United States, which at that point was extending very considerable economic aid to the Bolivian revolutionary regime, undertook a considerable strengthening of the official armed forces. This policy was continued and intensified under the second Paz Estenssoro government which came into power in 1960. Although the reconstituted military apparently was under the influence of the MNR, the armed forces again acquired a level of armament and an esprit de corps which ultimately allowed them to challenge the MNR regime itself.

Thus by the early 1960s the organized labor movement and the workers militia, which had been decisive in the first year or so of the regime, had been reduced to a secondary role. Both the peasant movement and its militia and the official armed forces had surpassed it in strength and effectiveness.

The result of this development was shown by the policies which were followed by President Paz Estenssoro during his second term in office. One of his major programs was the reorganization of the tin mining industry in accordance with the Triangular Plan. This was a program for rehabilitation and recapitalization of the country's government-owned mining sector, in collaboration with the Inter-American Development Bank and West German mining firms. There is little doubt that the Bolivian mining industry, and particularly the government firm, the Bolivian State Mining Company (COMIBOL), needed reorganization. Tin remained the country's principal export. But production and productivity of the government mines had declined steadily since the revolution in 1952. If this trend with its negative impact on the general economic position of Bolivia was to be halted (and hopefully, reversed), drastic action was certainly required.

The Triangular Plan called for increasing the efficiency of the operation of the COMIBOL mines with extensive mechanization and the reduction of production costs. As part of this program, President Paz Estenssoro ended the *control obrero*, formally reestablishing full control of management in COMIBOL. This move engendered strong opposition among the miners' unions.

Shifting Political Influence in Organized Labor

As a result of the MNR's leadership of the 1952 revolt it had strong control over the labor movement during the first years of the revolution. Under the leadership of Juan Lechín Oquendo, the COB was established immediately after the triumph of the revolution. However, during the first few months the MNR labor leaders, including Lechín, were too busy leading the government and the revolution to spend much time on the problems of the COB. As a result they allowed their supposed allies of the Trotskyite Revolutionary Workers' Party (POR) to run the machinery of the COB. However, shortly before the government nationalized the Big Three mining companies, the COB, under Trotskyist leadership, condemned the terms of nationalization. This spurred the MNR unionists, led by Lechín, to organize their majority in the COB and to take full control of the organization.

From late 1952 until the last months of 1963, the COB and most of the union groups affiliated with it were firmly under MNR control. The MNR forces, however, split among themselves. At the time of the monetary stabilization crisis early in 1957, Lechín sought to mobilize the labor movement against the Siles Zuazo government's program to curb the inflation but failed. At the same time efforts by supporters of Siles Zuazo to organize a rival COB to that led by Lechín Oquendo also failed.

The division in MNR labor forces was clear after 1957. On the one hand were Lechín Oquendo, his FSTMB and various other groups, and on the other there were anti-Lechín forces, particularly the railroad and the industrial workers. Until late 1963 they all remained under MNR control, but the MNR labor leadership was divided. A final break came in 1963 as a result of a struggle over the MNR candidacy for president in the 1964 election. Lechín Oquendo, who was Vice President during the second Paz Estenssoro administration, had much right to believe that he should be his party's candidate. There is considerable evidence that in 1960 he had been promised the nomination in 1964. Instead of Lechín's being picked, however, the MNR chose Paz Estenssoro for a third term, an alternative made possible in 1962 by an amendment to the National Constitution which made it possible for an incumbent president to be reelected.

When Lechín Oquendo was denied the nomination of the MNR, he withdrew with his followers from the party and formed a rival one, the National Revolutionary Party of the Left (PRIN). It promptly named him as Paz Estenssoro's opponent, but Lechín withdrew from the contest before the final election.

In the meantime, unrest in the mines continued to surge. One of the penultimate events before the fall of the Paz Estenssoro regime was a miners strike, which occasioned the mobilization of the peasant militia by the government. Reportedly the relatively weak peasant forces, which the regime was able to mobilize to deal with both the striking miners and dissident students in La Paz, served to incite those military men who were contemplating a move against the MNR regime.

Structure of the Bolivian Labor Movement

By the end of the MNR government, the structure of the labor movement, which to a greater or lesser degree has persisted ever since, had been established. It was capped by the COB which from its inception had been headed by Lechín Oquendo, the leader of the FSTMB.

Below the COB were organized a series of confederations and federations. The most powerful of these was the FSTMB, which included the country's tin miners, particularly those in COMIBOL. Other such organizations were those of factory workers—railroaders, airline and allied employees—bank clerks, chauffeurs, commercial workers, petroleum workers and artisans.

There was also another level of union organization, this one on a departmental level. In each of these the COB had a local Department Workers Central, to which all of the local units of unions of the COB belonged.

Labor in the Overthrow of the MNR Government

It is clear that when the military, headed by General René Barrientos Ortuño and General Alfredo Ovando Candia, moved to overthrow the Paz Estenssoro government, important labor elements were aligned with the coup d'état, and the government was unable to mobilize strong labor forces in its defense. The miners supported the coup against Paz Estenssoro, and Lechín Oquendo was among those who had plotted his overthrow. Some of the industrial workers of the city of La Paz took up arms to defend the government, and fighting went on for many hours after Paz Estenssoro had left the country for exile. However, these efforts were to no avail. The new regime, for its part, promised to be more friendly toward the needs of the organized labor movement, and particularly the miners, than the government of Paz Estenssoro had been.

Changes in Government Since 1964—An Overview

After the overthrow of the Paz Estenssoro government in November 1964, Bolivia was ruled by a succession of governments, all but one of which were presided over by military men. Although these regimes have not done away with many of the basic achievements of the Bolivian revolution—the land reform, nationalization of the Big Three tin mining companies, etc.—few of them have been favorably disposed towards the organized labor movement.

Immediately after the ouster of the Paz Estenssoro government a diumvirate of Generals Barrientos and Ovando took over. However, in preparation for the election of 1966 Co-president Ovando took full charge to allow General Barrientos to run for constitutional president. Barrientos was elected, serving until April 1969 when he was killed in a helicopter accident. He was succeeded by the only civilian chief executive of the period, Vice President Luís Adolfo Siles Salinas, half brother of former President Hernán Siles Zuazo.

President Siles Salinas was overthrown by Army Commander General Ovando in September 1969. The Ovando government nationalized the Gulf Oil Company's concessions and professed a more or less friendly attitude towards the labor movement. However, in October 1970 Ovando was overthrown by a further military coup, and after several days of confusion General Juan José Torres emerged as the new president. General Ovando went off to be Ambassador to Spain.

The administration of General Torres, which lasted only 10 months, was marked by a "pre-revolutionary" atmosphere. During this period, the leaders of the labor movement played a particularly active and important role in public affairs, particularly in the Popular Assembly. It proved impossible, however, for organized labor to adopt a consistent policy and to give strong leadership to the process of change which seemed to be under way at the time. During this period, elements of the MNR left and Lechín Oquendo's PRIN seemed to be gaining more influence than they had experienced until that time, not only in the labor movement but also in general national politics.

In August 1971 the Torres government was overthrown by a military insurrection led by Colonel Hugo Banzer Suárez, and supported by the country's two major political parties, the MNR and the Bolivian Socialist Falange (FSB). The Banzer government dismantled the Popular Assembly. The labor movement was by no means completely suppressed during this period, but within it there took place a struggle for power between elements of the MNR and those groups which had played a major leadership role in the Torres period. In late 1973 President Banzer broke with the MNR. As a result, virtually all of the labor movement was thrown into opposition to the government which led to various strikes and other protests by the organized workers against the Banzer regime.

These movements of opposition to the Banzer government culminated in November 1974. The Banzer regime decided virtually to decapitate the labor movement by removing all of its elected officials and placing its own nominees in charge of virtually all of the country's labor organizations. This government control of the organized labor movement continued until the last months of 1977. At that time, as a result of internal and international pressure, President Banzer decided to undertake the "reconstitutionalization" of the regime. A general amnesty was declared, exiled trade union and political leaders were allowed to return, and a new chapter in the history of organized labor began.

Organized Labor in the Barrientos Period

The years immediately following the overthrow of the MNR government were marked by Generals Ovando and Barrientos playing a game of musical chairs with the presidency. However, in July 1966 General Barrientos was finally elected constitutional president. In any case, the dominant figure in the Bolivian regime between the overthrow of Paz Estenssoro and his own death was Barrientos.

The organized labor movement did not fare well during the Barrientos period. The general, who had been Paz Estenssoro's last vice president, and until the coup against the MNR regime head of the "military cell" of that party, based his control on two elements, the armed forces and the organized peasantry. He came from Cochabamba, spoke Quechua, and took particular interest in trying to keep support of the peasants and giving them modest help to make their small landholdings more productive.

Therefore Barrientos made little serious effort to maintain support of the organized workers of the cities and the mines. In the case of the latter, Barrientos's determination to go about with the Triangular Plan for rehabilitation and nationalization of COMIBOL was a serious barrier to any lasting rapprochement between the general and the miners.

Lechín Oquendo, the miners and some other elements of the labor movement supported the overthrow of Paz Estenssoro. Immediately thereafter, as Dwight Heath has written, "Lechín emerged from hiding and led the miners to demand rewards for their part in the revolution." Heath adds that "Leftists took advantage of the confusion and stepped into a power vacuum left in the mining unions."[1]

The honeymoon between Barrientos and organized labor was short-lived, however. In May 1965 Barrientos issued a number of decrees providing for massive layoffs in the mines, the reduction of wages by some 50 percent, and limitation of the right of miners to buy goods at subsidized prices in the COMIBOL stores.[2] At the same time that these decrees were issued, Lechín Oquendo was arrested and exiled, on charges of "fraud and dual citizenship."[3] The government thus threw down the guantlet to the labor movement.

Melvin Burke and James Malloy have described what followed next:

> When the miners reacted . . . the military invaded the mines, smashed the strike, and disarmed the militias. After the remainder of organized labor protested, the military moved against the entire movement killing or exiling leaders and submitted what was left of the once powerful unions to strict governmental control.[4]

The crisis of May 1965 was not the end of the story. Twice again, in September 1965 and June 1967, the troops occupied the mining camps. Burke and Malloy have commented on the effect of this temporary destruction of the labor movement on the living conditions of the workers:

> With the possible exception of the oil workers, the Bolivian laborers experienced a relative decline in living standards during the Barrientos period, primarily because they were forced to live on fixed or reduced wages in an economy that was running an inflation of approximately 6 percent per year. Although some new jobs were created, especially in construction, they were more than offset by an influx of country people to the cities which held down wages, reduced employment security and increased dramatically the urban marginal population of the unemployed and underemployed.[5]

So long as Barrientos remained president, the labor movement was unable to organize effective resistance against the government and its labor policies. Although Lechín Oquendo returned clandestinely to Bolivia in May 1966 even before Barrientos's election, he was not able to mobilize the workers in an effective movement against the Barrientos government.[6]

Organized Labor Under Ovando Candia

On April 27, 1969, after President Barrientos met his tragic death, the civilian Vice President Luís Siles Salinas assumed the presidency. However, on September 28, 1969, he was overthrown by General Ovando Candia. The seizure of power by General Ovando seemed to promise a restoration of trade union freedom. One of the first decrees of his regime provided for restoration of the liberty of the labor movement to function without government interference.[7]

In his maiden speech as president, from the balcony of the presidential palace, General Ovando declared that "This revolution is leftist, it is nationalist and revolutionary." The first ministers he chose seemed to reflect this statement, many of them being young or youngish men from the left wing of the MNR or from groups which had split from that party. His decision to nationalize the Gulf Oil Company's holdings also seemed to conform to the President's description of his regime. There were antecedents, however, in his career which probably aroused doubts concerning his revolutionary bona fides. His first political affiliation had been with the FSB. He had been the principal executor of the anti-labor policies of the Barrientos period. Marcel Niedergang of the Paris daily *Le Monde* noted, "In 1965, in 1966, then in 1967, General Ovando directed a ferocious military repression in the mining camps of the *Altiplano*, where the workers unions, which had profited from the Paz Estenssoro government to become strong, were not willing to accept the tutelage of an openly pro-American president. Catavi, Siglo Veinte, Oruro were occupied and hundreds of miners were massacred."[8]

In fact very little time passed before President Ovando began to move against the leadership of the labor movement. On October 17, 1969, Lechín Oquendo was arrested and deported to the Chilean port of Arica. The government insisted that in deporting Lechín it was "attacking the politician, not the labor leader." At the same time the government promised wage increases to the mine workers and said that it would withdraw the soldiers who had been stationed in the mining areas for about four years.[9] However, the Ovando government continued to have some influence in the organized labor movement. Thus in December 1969, when the employees of the Miners' Bank declared a strike, President Ovando was able to get them to go back to work by a personal appeal.[10]

In May 1970 Ovando reorganized his cabinet, removing most of its more leftist members. As Marcel Niedergang commented subsequently, by this reorganization "Ovando chose, at the last moment, the unity, albeit fictitious, of the armed forces rather than having recourse to the popular and trade union forces."[11]

The Torres Interregnum

President Ovando was overthrown in October 1970. The events of October 4th and 5th proved to be a veritable comedy, although it might well have degenerated into a tragic civil war. First, the Army commander-in-chief, General Rogelio Miranda, declared Ovando deposed early on October 4th, but in spite of this Ovando returned from Santa Cruz to La Paz and took over the presidential palace without resistance. However, to avoid fighting between the Ovando and Miranda forces it was decided to poll all the top military officers, who decided by a vote of 317 to 40 that both men should step down in favor of a military junta of three other generals. This government, which Bolivian journalist Samuel Mendoza, writing in the Brazilian newspaper *O Estado de Sao Paulo*, called "the briefest government in the history of Bolivia," lasted only a few hours.[12] It was overturned by forces led by General Juan José Torres, which seized control of the *El Alto* airbase, above La Paz, and sent planes to strafe the capital. At the same time civilian elements led by the COB and the University Students Confederation declared a general strike and began erecting barricades, in support of General Torres.

Once in power Torres invited the COB and the student organizations to join the government. However, after consultations they refused, although expressing support for the new regime. From then until it was overthrown, the Torres government received the critical support of the COB, the students and various left-wing parties.[13] Although the organized labor movement did not take any part in the Torres government, it revived its own forces with new vigor after the years of persecution following the overthrow of the MNR government and played a major political role during the few months of the Torres regime.

A number of the labor organizations held congresses during this period, among them the FSTMB. At the miners convention, elements of the MNR joined forces with those of Lechín Oquendo's PRIN to block attempts by elements farther to the Left to oust Lechín from the post of Executive Secretary which he had held for nearly thirty years.

The longer the Torres government stayed in power, the more radical the government and the general political situation became. Although at first proclaiming his government to be "revolutionary nationalist," President Torres, in a speech to the glass workers in January 1971, argued that it would lead to socialism "within a few years, when conditions permit," while urging caution on those who wished to change everything "from night to day."[15] Nonetheless, it is clear that the president did not have much actual control of the progress of events. As the months of his administration drew on the situation became increasingly chaotic. Growing numbers of large and small businesses were seized by armed groups and kidnappings for ransom became commonplace. In some cases, to paraphrase Dr. Johnson, revolutionary rhetoric became the last refuge of scoundrels. The middle class--Bolivia virtually had no upper class-- became thoroughly frightened, and the military as a group became increasingly concerned about the future of their institution and their own personal security.

Throughout the ten months in which the Torres government was in power the leaders of organized labor played a major role in the political situation. At the same time, the labor movement itself was torn by conflicting political currents, including Lechín Oquendo's PRIN, the MNR, the pro-Moscow and pro-Peking Communists and one or more of the Trotskyist groups. The most striking event of the period was the installation and functioning of the so-called Popular Assembly. Obviously patterned after the Soviets of 1917 Russia, it groped towards the complete reorganization of Bolivian society, and workers' representatives played a major role in its organization and its deliberations.

The first formal meeting of the Assembly took place on May 1, 1971, in the Congress Building in La Paz. It was presided over by Lechín Oquendo and consisted of 221 delegates.[16] Of these, the organizers of the group provided that 60 percent would be from trade unions, 30 percent from peasant and middle class organizations, and 10 percent would represent various political parties.[17] In terms of political representation, the largest single bloc was reported to consist of members of the MNR, the second largest group of people belonging to the pro-Moscow Communist Party. Other political groups represented included the PRIN, the pro-Chinese Communists, the Socialist Party, the MIR, the Revolutionary Christian Democrats, and the faction of the Trotskyist POR led by Guillermo Lora.[18]

After the formal organizational meeting on May 1, the Assembly did not meet again until June 23. In that session it proclaimed an "emergency of the whole people," and declared that that emergency would not end until "the defeat of imperialism." This session also declared that "the historical representative of the construction of socialism in the country" had aroused the ire of the Right, which continued to plot a coup against the Torres regime.[19] At a further session a week later, the delegates of the FSTMB presented a motion calling for co-participation by the workers on all levels of management of COMIBOL. The motion was adopted, and the Assembly went on record condemning the bureaucratization of the government mining enterprise.[20]

Meanwhile, the COB had issued a directive calling on all of its affiliates to organize militia groups. Their purpose was to be to guard the workplaces in which their members were employed and to fight against any possible coup attempt by right-wing military men.[21]

There were several attempted coups before the Torres government, was finally overthrown in August 1971. The most serious of these took place in La Paz in January, led by Colonel Banzer Suárez. The COB contributed to its defeat by mobilizing its members in support of the government. [22] After the collapse of this movement, the COB organized a meeting in front of the presidential palace which was said to have been attended by as many as 50,000 people. One of the chants heard at the meeting was "Torres, socialism, socialism." [23] A local uprising in April took place in the Department of Santa Cruz. Peasant elements seized the departmental capital with the apparent support of the local garrison commander, ousted the local governor and demanded the ouster of five of President Torres's ministers. The local COB proclaimed a strike, and the movement was finally suppressed. [24]

Organized Labor and the Banzer Coup

Finally, a military uprising led by Colonel Hugo Banzer Suárez did succeed in August 1971, and President Torres was overthrown. Unlike the earlier coup attempts, this one had the backing and collaboration of the country's two major parties, the MNR and the FSB. The new uprising began on August 20th, in the eastern city and department of Santa Cruz, long resistant to too tight control from far-off La Paz. It quickly spread to Cochabamba, Tarija and subsequently to Oruro. Sucre, Potosi and La Paz itself were the only centers which held out for some time against rebel troops.

The principal resistance to the uprising came from within the trade unions and the student movement. Upon the outbreak of the revolt, the Popular Assembly met and passed a resolution ordering "the mobilization of pickets and security squadrons of the COB to everyone of the unions on a national scale." [25]

On the afternoon of August 20th, the Assembly mobilized a march and demonstration "against imperialism" and in support of the government, through the center of La Paz. President Torres addressed the demonstrators from the balcony of the presidential palace. [26] Meanwhile, in Potosí, the local COB declared its support for the government and organized a demonstration against the military insurrection. Local labor leaders conferred with the regional military commander. [27]

In Oruro, the major mining center, the COB ordered that the workers take control of the city, which they proceeded to do. [28] However, the massed miners and other workers were no match for the Ranger troops who moved in to occupy the city, and one U.S. observer who was there at the time noted that by the time the two groups clashed, most of the local union leaders had fled. [29]

Within forty-eight hours of the outbreak of the rebellion, it had triumphed. With the victory of the insurgents, Colonel Banzer began his long period, for Bolivia, as president.

Organized Labor in the Banzer Suárez Years

The new regime was officially a tripartite coalition among the MNR, the FSB and the Bolivian Armed Forces or, as it was called, the Popular Nationalist Front. This phase of the Banzer government lasted for a bit more than two years. It came to a close, for all practical purposes, when ex-President Paz Estenssoro was once more deported on January 8, 1974.

Paz Estenssoro's explanation for the failure of the Popular Front is of some interest. He has written:

The scheme of the Popular Nationalist Front . . . had implicitly within it certain elements of contradiction. There were the emotional remains of the long struggle with the Falange . . . . There was also a latent counter-position of a group of apparent personal friends of President Banzer, who were in reality representatives of economic interests. These were some of the "medium-sized" mining entrepreneurs . . . .

With the unexpected increase in their economic power, they came to desire to exercise political power directly, without intermediaries. Thus, they sought posts for themselves, their managers or lawyers in the highest levels of the state apparatus, to carry out measures favorable to their interests. Necessarily this produced divergence with the MNR, made up of peasants, workers and members of the middle class. [30]

From the breakup of the Popular Front until the early months of 1978, the government was one of the armed forces, relying for its principal civilian support on the new class of private mine owners. The whole period of the Banzer government divides, insofar as the labor movement is concerned, into four phases: that of the Popular Front; that of frank confrontation between organized labor and the military regime in 1974; that of the period of the so-called Law of Compulsory Civil Service; and that of late 1977 and early 1978, when the regime seemed seriously to move towards "constitutionalization" and full trade union freedom was restored.

Labor Under the Popular Nationalist Front

Throughout the existence of the Popular Front the government continued to talk in terms of a more or less rapid return to constitutional government. At the same time, it claimed to be seeking the "normalization" of the trade union movement.

The immediate impact of the uprising of August 1971 on the labor movement was severe. Logically enough, the Popular Assembly was dissolved. At the same time, the structure of the organized labor movement was dramatically disrupted. Many hundreds of labor leaders were jailed, deported, or went into hiding and a few were killed in the August conflict and its aftermath. At the same time, the COB was declared temporarily dissolved and elections were called throughout all of the other labor organizations.

The elections in the FSTMB largely returned to power those political elements which had dominated that organization prior to August 1971. Thus in the Catavi mines a ticket backed by PRIN and a number of far Left parties won over three pro-government lists by 1,688 votes to 600. In the Potosí region, a coalition headed by elements of the pro-Soviet Communists came in first, one led by pro-Chinese Communists second, the MNR a not very good third. [31] However, the MNR did regain influence in a number of other unions. Slates organized by them won in the Industrial Workers Confederation and the Railroad, Airline and Allied Workers Confederation. [32]

By a year after the overthrow of Torres some of the country's national labor groups were functioning more or less normally. These included the Railroad, Airline and Allied Workers Confederation, the Industrial Workers Confederation, the Commercial Workers Confederation, and several others. Some of the regional organizations of the COB had also been reorganized under new leadership. However, neither the FSTMB nor the COB had yet been allowed to hold congresses. [33]

It was not until late October 1972 that the armed forces issued a declaration that they supported the full reestablishment of trade union activities "on the condition that the unions remain outside politics." [34] Finally, in November 1972 the Banzer government took this position. It was reported that "Banzer said that, 'henceforth the government will recognize the free association of workers,' and as proof of this he gave guarantees for the resumption of the combative FSTMB." [35]

A few weeks after this announcement, the FSTMB held a national conference at which the exiled Lechín Oquendo was once more confirmed as Executive Secretary of the Federation. A year later, in November 1973, he was once more renamed to the post by the Fifteenth National Mine Workers Congress meeting in Potosí, although at the time he was still living abroad at the government's insistence. The other two top incumbent leaders, Simón Reyes and Víctor López Arias, were also reelected Organizational Secretary and General Secretary, respectively. [36]

Shortly after Lechín Oquendo's nomination once more by the Potosí conference, the conservative Cochabamba newspaper *Los Tiempos* speculated on his perseverance as the mine workers' top leader. It noted that, "It has been remembered that in periods of normal development of public life, when Lechín is in the government or quasi-opposition, his trade union authority is put in question, and it appears that his political and trade union career is approaching its end, but repressive measures of one or another government bring it about that the miners and other workers, as a natural reaction, revive the popularity of Lechín, reconfirming him in the leadership posts which he has held for so many years." [37]

The one organization which the Banzer government did not allow to be legally reestablished was the COB, although various affiliates continued to demand its reestablishment. Thus on May Day, 1973, the FSTMB issued a special demand that the COB be reopened, and its demand was endorsed by the manufacturing, printing, and railroad workers' confederations, among others. [38]

Meanwhile, in November 1972, on the initiative of the Industrial Workers Confederation, the Bolivian Workers' Defense Committee was established to coordinate the activities of the various labor groups. The statement issued at the time of the establishment of this committee noted the need to coordinate resistance to the government's economic policies and said that the committee was being set up because of the failure of the government to legalize the COB. [39] Finally, on August 1, 1973, a meeting of delegates of most of the country's important trade union groups signed an agreement which brought the COB back into existence, albeit without government approval. The unions continued--unsuccessfully-- to try to get the government to change its attitude. [40]

Strikes were not unusual during the Popular Front period. After the labor movement had recovered from the first shocks following the fall of Torres, the number of walkouts began to increase. These included strikes by textile workers, bank clerks and several local miners' unions.

The Banzer government's decision--which was taken against the advice of Paz Estenssoro and some other MNR members associated with the government--to devalue the Bolivian peso on October 27, 1972, aroused a great deal of labor resistance. There were street clashes between workers and police in La Paz, and the Industrial Workers Confederation called an eight-hour protest strike throughout the country on October 30. [41] Throughout 1973 there were frequent protests by unions against the government's economic policies and there were a number of strikes.

Growing Labor Unrest in 1974

After the Popular Front had practically disappeared, labor discontent grew considerably during 1974, and strikes became increasingly frequent. On January 23rd all of the country's mine workers struck for twenty-four hours to protest the government's economic policies. [42] During the next few days bank clerks and commercial workers throughout the country, as well as construction workers and bakers in La Paz also struck against government decisions to raise prices for a number of key commodities. [43] The factory workers carried out a protest strike and demanded three times the 20 percent wage increase which the government had proposed that they receive. The workers employed in railroad workshops also declared a twenty-four hour protest strike. [44] Early in February five thousand miners of Siglo Veinte and Catavi struck for forty-eight hours in protest against a lack of sufficient food in the COMIBOL commissaries. [45] These and other walkouts were sufficiently important to evoke a protesting editorial from *Los Tiempos*, entitled "Pernicious Labor Stoppages." [46] Late in March the air crews of the national airline went on strike, charging that the government airline was not fulfilling the conditions of the collective agreement then in force. [47] At about the same time a strike in the Gamboa shoe company in Cochabamba brought about the deportation of the local union's principal leader. [48] In August there was a general strike of school teachers [49] at the same time that the employees of the National Social Security System went out. [50]

This continuing wave of strikes, of which we have only mentioned a sample, brought another editorial protest from *Los Tiempos* entitled, "Trade Union Agitation Upsets the Tranquility of the Country." This editorial argued that much of the unrest in the country's unions was due to "outside agitators," who were not members of the various unions. It complained of "the damage which the republic suffers from the distortion of the true purposes of trade unions, which should be only concerned with the social and economic problems of workers." [51] Without any doubt, editorials such as this stimulated the drastic approach to the labor problem which the Banzer government soon adopted.

Establishment of the System of Coordinators

In November 1974 the Banzer regime sought to reorganize completely the country's trade union movement and to subordinate it totally to state control by utilizing the Compulsory Civil Service Law. This statute gave the government power to draft people for a wide variety of civilian jobs in and out of government "for socio-economic development of the Republic, with the objective of fully and integrally developing the Bolivian man, and developing the potentialities of the country, for its internal and external security." [52]

This law was particularly applied to the organized labor movement. All leaders of every union were formally removed from office, and in their place the government named so-called Trade Union Coordinators. These individuals—usually three in a union—were designated to take over the affairs of the union until further notice. Those who refused to accept these posts were subject under the Law of Compulsory Civil Service to both fines and imprisonment.

To apply the Compulsory Civil Service Law to the organized labor movement, President Banzer issued Supreme Resolution No. 174780 which set forth the functions of the Coordinators, banned all strikes and lockouts, and suspended all trade union dues, assessments and other charges on union members. The same Supreme Resolution named the Coordinators of the various labor confederations. [53]

The people who were named as coordinators in most unions did not refuse to serve. Usually they were chosen from the ranks of incumbent trade union officials. For instance, the three men named as national co-ordinators in the Petroleum Workers' Federation included one who was an elected national official of the Federation and two others who were elected officers of locals belonging to it. [54] In the case of the Bank Workers' Confederation, the national coordinators were chosen from among the elected officials of the various departmental federations which made up the organization. [55] In the Health Workers' Local Union in Santa Cruz, the secretary general and two other elected officials of the organization were chosen to be the coordinators. [56]

It is probably true that in most cases those who were chosen by the Ministry of Labor to be coordinators knew that by accepting the position they were discrediting themselves in the eyes of their fellow workers. However, since most people are not heroes, they accepted rather than going to jail.

The one instance in which the people named as coordinators refused to accept the posts was in the FSTMB, particularly in the unions of workers in the COMIBOL mines. There, both local union and federation officials were sent to jail, staying there for five to six months. This provoked a number of strikes in the mines, and the government finally agreed to a face-saving maneuver in which, although proclaiming that it was naming new leaders of the mining unions, it in fact left the old leaders in their jobs. The old officials of the COMIBOL unions and of the FSTMB continued to use their old titles rather than calling themselves coordinators. However, in the private mines the government was successful in naming coordinators who accepted the positions. [57]

One of the reasons why the government gave up the attempt to punish the union leaders who refused to become coordinators was probably the resistance of members of the judiciary to trying cases involving such "criminals." At least three judges refused to hear cases involving mine union leaders who refused such nominations. [58]

The ability of the coordinators to be effective as labor leaders apparently varied a great deal. During a visit to Bolivia in July, 1975, I talked to a number of these people and they reported a variety of different kinds of situations in their respective organizations. Generally, they said that the employers had assumed more hardline positions since November 1974 than they had previously taken. With more or less difficulty, however, the coordinators had been able to process grievances of their members. Some of them reported that they had successfully resorted to the strike weapon to force employers to make concessions.

Colonel Mario Vargas, the Labor Minister, sought to explain and justify the measures which the government had taken against the labor movement. He complained that before November 1974 the labor movement had been "too political," and that most of the labor leaders had been very corrupt and unprincipled. He argued that the best proof of the correctness of the government's action was that eight months after it had been taken, the country was in a state of social peace and stability. He professed to believe that there was great enthusiasm among the workers for the coordinators system. However, Colonel Vargas ended his conversation with me by saying that he feared that if union elections were held again too soon, the old leaders would all return to office, adding that what was needed was four or five years of the coordinators system to allow time for a new generation of leaders to arise in the labor movement. [59]

The new system by no means ended the militancy of the organized labor movement. In fact, the first labor crisis with which the Banzer government was faced after November 1974 was one with the miners. On January 13, 1975, the workers of Quluvi and Siglo Veinte went on strike against the government's closing of several radio stations in the Oruro area. [60] Subsequently, the government professed to see a "plot" in the miners' move. [61] On January 18 the government blockaded the mines, forbidding anyone to enter or leave the mining areas. [62] This lockout went on for several weeks. During the rest of 1975 there were various other strikes of different groups of workers. The government had obviously not been able completely to curb the militancy of the Bolivian labor movement.

The Role of the American Institute for Free Labor Development

The American Institute for Free Labor Development (AIFLD), an organization largely manned by members of the United States labor movement, and largely financed by the Agency for International Development, played an important role in Bolivia during this period. It had been operating in the country for nearly a decade, conducting a labor education program and helping both urban workers unions and peasant groups establish a variety of "social projects," including cooperatives, small housing projects, special educational facilities and the like.

After the government intervention of November 1974, the AIFLD sought to intensify its activities. The expanded series of courses which it ran, in La Paz and other parts of the country, served to provide occasions and places where leaders of the various union groups could get together without being accused of "conspiring." Under these circumstances the leaders could not only exchange information on what was happening in various parts of the labor movement, but also upon occasion could work out common strategy. The importance of the AIFLD activities to the unionists was demonstrated by the extensive participation of the leaders of the FSTMB and its constituent unions, as well as coordinators and militants from other unions. In fact, the head of the AIFLD in La Paz, Charles Wheeler, went out of his way to indicate his moral and material support for union leaders who were being persecuted by the government. Thus, when various leaders of the miners were sent to jail for refusing to allow the government to name them as coordinators, Wheeler dispatched food, blankets and other things to them in prison. When they came out, they are reported to have commented that the AIFLD seemed to have been the only group outside of the mining communities which was interested in their fate. [63]

One aspect of the AIFLD labor education activities during this period which may have a lasting impact on the Bolivian labor movement is the emphasis put on the negotiation of collective contracts. Only a relatively small minority of the Bolivian labor organizations have traditionally had formal collective agreements with the employers. But there seemed to be considerable receptivity among the unionists, with whom I talked, to the idea of trying to negotiate such agreements once trade union freedom had been restored.

The Strikes of 1976

In spite of all of the Banzer government's efforts to curb the labor movement, the regime was by no means completely successful in doing so. For one thing, the miners continued to maintain a substantial degree of independence, and to constitute a major source of opposition to the regime itself. A number of other unions also successfully defied the government's efforts completely to curtail their autonomy.

During 1976 the Banzer regime faced several important strike situations. The first of these occurred in January. The workers of the Manaco shoe factory in Cochabamba, owned by the Bata firm, went out on strike to protest a management plan to dismiss two hundred of them. Although the government ordered the Manaco strikers to return to work, they refused to do so, and instead there were solidarity strikes by a number of other worker groups including thousands of tin miners.

Minister of Labor Mario Vargas was finally dispatched to Cochabamba to try to put an end to the situation which had developed into a challenge to the government itself. After long negotiations among the Labor Minister, the Manaco management and the workers, the company finally agreed to take back all of those workers whom it had dismissed. [64]

Early in May the FSTMB held a clandestine congress. This meeting elected a new slate of leaders and drew up a series of demands to be submitted to COMIBOL. The key demand was for a wage increase of 200 percent. On June 8th, shortly before the newly elected leaders of the FSTLB were to begin negotiations with COMIBOL, twenty-four of them were suddenly arrested by the government. They were deported to Chile, where the government relegated them to an area in the far South.

The result of this action by the government was a general strike of the tin miners. After the outbreak of the walkout, the government offered a 35 percent wage increase which was turned down by the miners, who continued to demand a 200 percent wage boost and added demands for the withdrawal of troops from the mining areas and the return of the arrested mine union leaders to Bolivia and to their positions in the FSTMB.

The walkout lasted for over a month. The government's position was strengthened by the fact that there were on hand large stocks of minerals which had not yet been shipped abroad, so that tin exports were not interfered with. By mid-July, although the workers of Catavi and Siglo Veinte were still out on strike, those in the other half-dozen mines involved were reported to be slowly returning to work. [65]

The 1977-78 Revival of the Labor Movement

By the last months of 1977 it was clear that the political position of the Banzer regime, both internally and internationally, had been seriously weakened. This fact set in motion a rapidly accelerating process which led early in 1978 to a revival of the legitimate labor movement.

Several factors had undermined President Banzer's position. For one, his attempts to gain an "access to the Sea" from Chile were clearly a failure, and he was no longer able to wave that nationalist banner to gain popular backing. In the second place, his regime was under considerable diplomatic pressure from the Carter administration in the United States to clean up its record on human rights. Finally, in neighboring Peru the military regime had announced elections for 1978 to start the process of return to constitutionalism and an elected government. Under these circumstances, President Banzer, who had hitherto been talking somewhat vaguely about a return to constitutional government by 1980, announced early in November 1977 that general elections would be held on July 9, 1978. At the same time, he lifted a ban on the country's major political parties--the MNR and Falange--which had been in effect since November 1974. [66]

For the time being this shift in policy did not directly affect organized labor. Early in December the government submitted proposals for a constitutional rewriting of the country's labor laws, to both management and labor groups. However, they were generally rejected even by the union coordinators. The reasons for this rejection were indicated by the British periodical *Latin America Political Report,* which noted that, "They restrict the right to strike, banning strikes completely in 'strategic industries' (such as, undoubtedly, the tin mines). They also allow for the existence of more than one national labor organization." The periodical added that "The clandestine *Central Obrera Boliviana* (COB) has already said that the labor movement will refuse to take part in any discussions unless its elected leaders are present." At the same time, the exiled leaders of the FSTMB called for a general strike on December 21 to demand a complete amnesty for persecuted trade union and political leaders. [67] The miners' protest walkout was carried out as the FSTMB leaders had ordered it should be, and it was supported by various political parties and by the university students. [68]

Meanwhile, things had in fact begun to change in the labor movement. It was reported in mid-December that Lechín Oquendo "is back in La Paz...in well publicized clandestinity, and hoping to be included in an amnesty." [69]

In January 1978 it was clear that President Banzer was losing control of the situation, and the process of change notably accelerated. The catalyst for this change was a hunger strike, in which groups of participants gathered in churches and other buildings and announced that they would not move and would not take nourishment until the government declared a general amnesty and removed the soldiers from the mining areas. Various political parties, including even the Falange, declared their support for the hunger strikers and their objectives. [70]

Finally, on January 18th President Banzer surrendered to the hunger strikers. In a gesture which was certainly humiliating to the regime, the government gave in to the insistence of the hunger strikers that they would not call off their demonstration until the Minister of Interior signed a formal agreement with them. It provided for an unlimited amnesty to political opponents of the regime, establishment of committees to study the reinstatement of all workers who had been dismissed for trade union activities, and agreement that there would be no reprisals against those who had participated in the hunger strike. [71] By the middle of February the FSTMB announced that 80 percent of its members who had been ousted from their jobs for trade union activities had been returned to work. [72]

The hunger strike and its success were new phenomena in Bolivian history. As one Bolivian correspondent wrote me, "This was the first time non-violent tactics were used for a political objective with such effectiveness in Bolivia." He noted that those involved "were not necessarily identified as political groups but rather as civic groups," and added that "I think the hunger strike movement became significant because by and large the people involved in it came from the middle and upper-middle classes which are supposed to provide Banzer's power base." [73]

On the same day that the agreement with the hunger strikers was signed, Minister of Labor Vargas announced that all restrictions on trade union activities would be lifted. Meanwhile, a mass movement had begun within the various unions to get rid of the coordinators and to elect regular union officials. Nine of the elected leaders of the FSTMB took over the building of the Federation, located on the main street of La Paz. [74]

When it ended its control over the unions, the Ministry of Labor decreed that elections should be held in all local unions within thirty days, within federations in sixty days, and within confederations within ninety days. [75] However, in some cases, groups associated with the underground COB leadership proclaimed themselves to be the new officials of particular unions without benefit of formal election. The Ministry of Labor refused to recognize these groups, insisting that elections be held according to its schedule. [76] The elections brought an end, at least for the time being, to the trade union careers of most of those who had served as government coordinators in the unions. The only known group of coordinators to be elected consisted of those in a few locals of the Bank Workers Confederation. [77]

By mid-February the effort to reestablish the COB openly was well under way. "A national meeting of leaders and delegates" convened to "define its future policies." It was also announced that a national congress of the COB would be held on May 1, 1978. As in the past the work of restoring the COB was being conducted largely from the offices of the FSTMB, and under the supervision of Juan Lechín Oquendo. [78]

One possible stumbling block to the emergence of the COB once again as the dominant force in the labor movement was the fact that the government had amended the Labor Law to provide for the possibility of there being more than one legally recognized central labor organization. It seemed unlikely, however, that so long as the labor movement continued to be able to choose its own leaders and establish its own organizations that it would be possible to establish any substantial rival to the COB.

The new influence of organized labor became almost immediately apparent as soon as the hold of the Banzer regime on the unions began to loosen. Late in January the government announced a 10 percent increase in electricity rates, but protests by union leaders forced President Banzer to cancel the decision. [79]

The events of the early months of 1978 seemed to set the stage for another period in Bolivian history in which the organized labor movement will play a major role in national politics. It is too early at this point to be able to define just what the relative strength of the political elements active in the labor movement will be. Much will depend upon the general development of the political situation, and upon such factors as the success—or lack of it—of efforts to reunite the four dispersed elements of the MNR, that is, the followers of Paz Estenssoro, Hernán Siles Zuazo, Juan Lechín Oquendo and Walter Guevara Arce. The first three of these certainly have substantial followings among the organized workers, and a successful effort to reunite their groups would certainly present the far Left (including the Moscow and Peking Communists, the much splintered Trotskyites, and other groups which gained strength since the fall of the MNR government) with a major stumbling block. The only thing which is clear at the moment is that the organized workers are free once again to choose their own leaders and to make their own decisions concerning which political groups, if any, to follow.

ENDNOTES FOR CHAPTER V

1. Dwight Heath, "Revolution and Stability in Bolivia," *Current History*, December 1965, pp. 332-333.

2. Melvin Burke and James Malloy, "From National Populism to National Corporatism, The Case of Bolivia 1952-70," (Manuscript), p. 35.

3. Heath, op. cit., p. 333.

4. Burke and Malloy, op. cit., p. 36.

5. Ibid., p. 36.

6. Ernesto Santiago, "Bolivia: En el Filo de la Navaja", *Ercilla*, September 21, 1966, p. 19.

7. *El Mercurio* [Santiago, Chile], International Edition, September 22-28, 1969.

8. *Le Monde* [Paris], October 8, 1970.

9. *Le Monde* [Paris], October 18, 1969.

10. *El Mercurio* [Santiago, Chile], International Edition, December 8-14, 1969.

11. *Le Monde* [Paris], October 8, 1970.

12. Samuel Mendoza, "Torres conquista a poder", *O Estado de São Paulo* [São Paulo] June 13, 1971.

13. Ibid.

14. Statement by Víctor Paz Estenssoro, personal interview, Lima, Peru, July 10, 1971.

15. *O Jornal* [Rio de Janeiro], January 9, 1971.

16. "'People's Assembly Installed on May Day," *Intercontinental Press* [New York], May 24, 1971, p. 483.

17. Gerry Foley, "Torres Regime Buffeted by Polarizing Forces," *Intercontinental Press* [New York], April 12, 1971, p. 329.

18. Statement by Víctor Paz Estenssoro, personal interview, Lima, Peru, July 10, 1971.

19. "Bolivia: Constituida la Primera Asamblea Popular," *El Siglo* [Santiago, Chile], June 24, 1971.

20. "Cogestion Obrera en Empresa Minera Estatal en Bolivia", *La Prensa* [Santiago, Chile], July 1, 1971.

21. Gerry Foley, "Workers Seek to Strengthen 'People's Assembly,'" *Intercontinental Press* [New York], July 19, 1971, p. 676.

22. "Semana Latinoamericana", in *Informacion Latinoamericana* [Buenos Aires], January 18, 1971, p. 12.

23. Gerry Foley, "Torres Regime Buffeted by Polarizing Forces," op. cit., p. 329.

24. Ibid., pp. 330-331.

25. *Presencia* [La Paz], August 20, 1971, p. 3.

26. *Presencia* [La Paz], August 21, 1971, p. 5.

27. *Presencia* [La Paz], August 21, 1971, p. 1.

28. *Presencia* [La Paz], August 20, 1971, p. 7.

29. Talk by June Nash, anthropologist, at Rutgers University, New Brunswick, New Jersey, March 9, 1972.

30. Letter from Víctor Paz Estenssoro, from Buenos Aires, February 27, 1974.

31. Gerry Foley, "Workers Call Nationwide Strike," *Intercontinental Press* [New York], November 13, 1972, p. 1234.

32. Statement by Juan José Rivera Salinas, *Secretary General, Movimiento Nacionalista Revolucionario,* personal interview, La Paz, July 13, 1972.

33. Statement by Humberto Aguilar, ex-railroad union leader, personal interview, La Paz, July 14, 1972.

34. Foreign Broadcast Information Service, October 26, 1972.

35. *Times of the Americas* [Miami], November 22, 1972.

36. *Presencia* [La Paz], November 20, 1973.

37. "Vigencia politica y sindical de Lechín", *Los Tiempos* [Cochabamba], November 27, 1973.

38. Foreign Broadcast Information Service, May 2, 1973.

39. *Presencia* [La Paz], November 7, 1972.

40. *Presencia* [La Paz], September 16, 1973.

41. Gerry Foley, "Workers Call Nationwide Strike," op. cit., p. 1234.

42. *Presencia* [La Paz], January 22, 1974.

43. *Los Tiempos* [Cochabamba], January 24, 1974.

44. *Los Tiempos* [Cochabamba], January 23, 1974.

45. *Presencia* [La Paz], February 2, 1974.

46. *Los Tiempos* [Cochabamba], February 3, 1974.

47. *Los Tiempos* [Cochabamba], March 24, 1974.

48. *Los Tiempos* [Cochabamba], March 29 and April 2, 1974.

49. *Los Tiempos* [Cochabamba], August 13, 1974.

50. *Los Tiempos* [Cochabamba], August 17, 1974.

51. *Los Tiempos* [Cochabamba], October 6, 1974.

52. *Presencia* [La Paz], January 25, 1978.

53. *Presencia* [La Paz], November 13, 1974.

54. Statement by Hugo Tapia Sandoval, *Coordinador Nacional, Federación Sindical de Trabajadores Petroleros,* personal interview, La Paz, July 21, 1975.

55. Statement by Eduardo Tapia, *Coordinador Nacional, Confederación Sindical de Trabajadores Bancarios,* personal interview, La Paz, July 21, 1975.

56. Statement by Silvio Gutierrez, *Coordinador, Sindicato de Sanidad de Santa Cruz,* personal interview, La Paz, July 21, 1975.

57. Statement by Arturo Crespo, *Secretario de Hacienda, Federación Sindical de Trabajadores Mineros de Bolivia,* personal interview, La Paz, July 21, 1975.

58. *Los Tiempos* [Cochabamba], November 27, 1974.

59. Statement by Colonel Mario Vargas Salinas, Minister of Labor, personal interview, La Paz, July 22, 1975.

60. *Los Tiempos* [Cochabamba], January 14, 1975.

61. *Los Tiempos* [Cochabamba], January 17, 1975.

62. *Los Tiempos* [Cochabamba], January 19, 1975.

63. Statement by Charles Wheeler, Country Program Director for Bolivia, American Institute for Free Labor Development, personal interview, La Paz, July 21, 1975.

64. *Latin America* [London], February 20, 1976, p. 63.

65. *Latin America* [London], July 16, 1976, p. 223.

66. *Latin America Political Report* [London], November 18, 1977, pp. 357-358.

67. *Latin America Political Report* [London], December 9, 1977, p. 378.

68. *Latin America Political Report* [London], December 23, 1977, p. 393.

69. *Latin America Political Report* [London], December 16, 1977, p. 386.

70. *Latin America Political Report* [London], January 20, 1978, p. 22.

71. *Latin America Political Report* [London], January 27, 1978, p. 29.

72. *Latin America Political Report* [London], February 24, 1978, p. 60.

73. Letter from Bolivian ex-labor leader who wishes to remain anonymous, March 2, 1978.

74. *Latin America Political Report* [London], January 27, 1978, p. 29.

75. *Presencia* [La Paz], January 25, 1978.

76. *Presencia* [La Paz], January 26, 1978.

77. Letter from Bolivian ex-labor leader, op. cit.

78. *Latin America Political Report* [London], February 17, 1978, p. 52.

79. *Latin America Political Report* [London], February 10, 1978, p. 46.

Part Three

Foreign Influence and Foreign Relations

Chapter VI

U.S. Foreign Policy and Economic Assistance in Bolivia: 1948-1976 *
James W. Wilkie

INTRODUCTION

Given the fact of Bolivia's small population, the United States has undertaken a relatively large-scale program to financially assist Bolivian regimes. What have been the United States' goals in providing this aid? How important have U.S. funds been to Bolivia? What have been Bolivia's goals in accepting United States grants and loans? At what point is it feasible to phase out U.S. aid? These questions help to analyze quantitatively United States policy in relation to Bolivian achievements. This paper is limited to an examination of economic policy, and particularly aid, the convolutions of diplomatic and CIA policy deserving separate treatment when and if top-secret archives are opened. It is the author's contention, however, that the expenditure policy discussed here has more political significance than a study of politics itself. Analysis of historical statistics to 1976, the latest year for which data are available, reveals the long-term impact of U.S. funds in relation to Bolivian central government expenditure, thus permitting development of new interpretation here.

AN OVERVIEW

Since 1948 United States aid, defined to encompass the funds and the personnel to administer them, has been expended with different emphases in three distinct periods of Bolivian history: 1948-1951, 1952-1964 and 1965-1976. Although this paper emphasizes the post-1948 periods it should be noted that U.S. economic assistance to Bolivia began during the Second World War. In 1942 the United States, in exchange for access to important Bolivian tin, entered into wartime cooperation with Bolivia to develop roads, agricultural extension and research programs, and health centers. There was also assistance for mobile campaigns to eradicate malaria, yaws and smallpox, as well as to reform the public administration and customs collections. About 1.4 million dollars were obligated and probably spent in this United States assistance through fiscal years from 1942 to 1947.[1] Also in 1942, the U.S. Export-Import Bank (Ex-Im Bank) agreed to a 25 million dollar loan for Bolivia, including a large amount for the newly established Bolivian Development Corporation. [2] Data for Ex-Im Bank expenditures through 1945 are not available but the Bank spent 1.2 and 7.4 million dollars in 1946 and 1947 respectively, for low-interest, long-term loans that otherwise might not have been available to the La Paz government. [3] The low figure for 1946 no doubt involved the U.S. Department of State's fearfulness that the National Revolutionary Movement Party (MNR), the party then in power, was "pro-Nazi." The much higher 1947 figure came after the MNR leadership left the country for exile in 1946. [4]

The 1948-1951 Period

In the first period considered in this study, 1948-1951, United States aid to Bolivia declined in both current and real terms for the initial three years. As is shown in Table VI-1, with the involvement of the United States in the Korean War in 1950, U.S. aid to Bolivia rebounded from the low of 1.5 million dollars in 1950 to reach 7.9 million in 1951. Total U.S. outlay for the four-year period came to over 19 million dollars.

The 1952-1964 Period

At the beginning of the second period considered, 1952-1964, United States aid declined. Not only was there the 1952 revolution of the MNR, but also the end of the Korean War in 1953. In the latter year the U.S. outlay declined to 4.7 million dollars. After Milton Eisenhower's 1953 visit to Bolivia, however, the United States government became convinced that it could work with the MNR government. Because of post-revolution peasant invasions of estates and resultant food shortages in the urban areas, Bolivia was in desperate need of foodstuffs. In fiscal year 1954-1955, the first 6.2 million dollars of food under U.S. Public Law 480 reached Bolivia. [5] Under this program much of the food was sold for local currency that would then be used for development projects. Thus, the total U.S. outlay came to almost 310 million dollars for the 13 years, between 1952 and 1964, during which the MNR governed.

The 1965-1976 Period and Military Aid

Early in the third period, 1965-1976, aid was needed to prop up the unstable Bolivian military governments as they began to establish their own political infrastructure throughout the country. The threat of "Che" Guevara in 1966 and 1967 caused expanded U.S. military funds and arms transfers to Bolivia. This was in addition to the military assistance begun during the late 1950s as part of the economic stabilization program to help the MNR government build a national army that could stand up against unruly civilian militias. In the third period total U.S. outlay for both military and economic assistance rose to 341 million dollars, meaning that Bolivia continued to receive one of the highest amounts of per capita aid of any country in Latin America. [6] Column F in Table VI-1 portrays the rise of Bolivia's military during the period of the MNR as measured by the relative importance of U.S. military aid. The military share of U.S. assistance (defined as technical cooperation and developmental grants; cash and other grants, including budgetary support; food transfers under U.S. Public Law 480, including expenditure of local currency generated by food sales; and loans) and total outlay (defined as aid including assistance, military transfers, Ex-Im Bank, and Peace Corps)

TABLE VI-1

U.S. GOVERNMENT ACTUAL OUTLAY TO BOLIVIA,[a] 1948-1976

| Fiscal Year | Millions of Current Dollars | | | | | Percent | |
| | A. Total Outlay[b] | B. Assistance[c] | C. Export-Import Bank | D. Military Funds and Arms Transfer Costs | E. Peace Corps | F. Military Share | |
						Of Assistance D/B	Of Total D/A
1948	6.4	.4	6.0				
1949	3.6	.4	3.2				
1950	1.5	.5	1.0				
1951	7.9	.5	7.4				
1952	5.9	.6	5.3				
1953	4.7	1.3	3.4				
1954	14.8	13.1	1.7				
1955	12.4	11.3	1.1				
1956	27.6	23.7	3.9				
1957	28.2	27.2	1.0				
1958	25.9	25.8	0	.1[d]		.4[d]	.4[d]
1959	23.2	22.9	0	.3		1.3	1.3
1960	17.9	17.8	0	.1		.6	.6
1961	17.3	16.9	0	.4		2.4	2.3
1962	30.3	28.0	0	2.2	.1[d]	7.9	7.3
1963	39.6	36.2	0	2.7	.7	7.5	6.8
1964	62.1	57.6	.1	3.6	.8	6.3	5.8
1965	23.4	19.2	0	2.0	2.2	10.4	8.5
1966	21.7	17.8	0	2.5	1.4	14.0	11.5
1967	26.7	22.3	0	3.0	1.4	13.5	11.2
1968	35.4	30.6	0	3.7	1.1	12.1	10.5
1969	20.5	17.3	0	1.7	1.5	9.8	8.3

(continued)

TABLE VI-1 (continued)

| Fiscal Year | Millions of Current Dollars | | | | | Percent | |
	A. Total Outlay [b]	B. Assistance [c]	C. Export-Import Bank	D. Military Funds and Arms Transfer Costs	E. Peace Corps	F. Military Share Of Assistance D/B	Of Total D/A
1970	40.2	29.7	8.0	1.2	1.3	4.0	3.0
1971	22.8	19.5	.2	2.0	1.1	10.3	9.0
1972	45.9	42.6	0	2.6[f]	.7[e]	6.1	5.7
1973	24.4	20.0	0	4.4		22.0	18.0
1974	23.9	16.0	0	7.9		49.4	33.8
1975	18.6	11.3	0	7.3		64.6	39.3
1976	37.5	20.8	4.3	12.4		59.6	33.1

[a]For obligations, in contrast to actual outlay, see AID/Washington, *U.S. Overseas Loans and Grants* (Washington, D.C., 1968), reprinted for years 1946 to 1968 in James M. Malloy and Richard S. Thorn, eds., *Beyond the Revolution: Bolivia Since 1952* (Pittsburgh: University of Pittsburgh Press, 1974), pp. 390–391; for more complete data on obligations, see Phillip Boucher, "U.S. Foreign Aid to Latin America: Hypotheses and Patterns in Historical Statistics, 1934–1974" (unpublished Ph.D. dissertation in history, University of California, Los Angeles, 1979).

[b]This table excludes amounts from the Social Progress Trust Fund, administered by the Inter-American Development Bank.

[c]Includes: (1) technical cooperation and developmental grants; (2) cash grants and other grants; (3) foodstuffs under U.S. Public Law 480—see Appendix E—–, and local currency programs since 1958; (4) development loans.

[d]Inception of program in Bolivia.

[e]Program phased out in Bolivia.

[f]After 1973 data may include up to 1 million dollars in private commercial military sales.

TABLE VI-1 (continued)

Sources:
A. Calculated.

B. 1948–1957, James W. Wilkie, *Statistics and National Policy* (Los Angeles: UCLA Latin American Center Publications, 1974), p. 369; 1958–1972, AID/Bolivia, *Estadísticas económicas*, Vols. 7, 9, 13, 14 (La Paz, 1965, 1968, 1972, 1973, respectively); and 1973–1976, AID/Bolivia, Comptroller's Office.

C–E. Wilkie, *Statistics and National Policy*, op. cit., p. 369; and James W. Wilkie and Peter Reich, eds.: *Statistical Abstract of Latin America*, Vol. 19 (Los Angeles: UCLA Latin American Center Publications, 1978), tables 1101, 1102, and 3105.

F. Calculated.

did not exceed 8 percent until the MNR was overthrown by the military. During the late 1960s the share of military aid reached as high as 11.5 percent of total U.S. aid. The impact of these figures on military spending can be deceiving, however, because an increase in aid for economic purposes could allow the Bolivians to take their own funds from development objectives and shift them to military purposes.

Military funds did not maintain their proportional share of U.S. aid as the populist government of General Alfredo Ovando Candia came to the fore in October 1969, when it nationalized U.S. Gulf Oil. Although military aid had increased in absolute terms there was movement afoot to reduce the influence of the armed forces. In 1970 the Popular Legislative Assembly was convoked by leftists to assign power to the people at the expense of the military. [7] Consequently, the military share of U.S. aid fell to 3 percent of total U.S. outlay in 1970. With restricted funds, scission between rightist and leftist militarymen was heightened, the right arguing that if U.S. aid were cut off as leftists demanded, development of the nation, and of the military, would come to a stop.

The terms "leftist" and "rightist" military are somewhat misleading in the Bolivian context because when the rightists overthrew the leftists in August 1971—extreme leftist General Juan José Torres had taken the presidency away from moderate leftist Ovando in October 1970—they did not undo the nationalizations of land, mines, or petroleum that had come under the leftist MNR or leftist militarymen. Indeed, the plan after 1971 was intended to unite the country against economic and political disorganization engendered by the Popular Assembly; disorganization that angered middle and upper social classes and caused old archenemies in the MNR and Bolivian Socialist Falange (FSB) to join forces with the military. Whereas the FSB had opposed the MNR as being communist in its governing of Bolivia between 1952 and 1964, the MNR's programs seemed moderate in contrast to the talk of the Popular Assembly heard by the FSB. The assembly, for example, had discussed urban reform including the nationalization of private houses in La Paz and other cities. Moreover, whereas the MNR had opposed the FSB as being fascist, at least the Falange's programs stood for traditional political organization and not for a national congress wherein only "workers" would rule the country with the aid of communist-bloc countries.

THE RELATIVE IMPORTANCE OF U.S. AID TO BOLIVIAN GOVERNMENT EXPENDITURE

Originally, United States aid was intended to help Bolivia mobilize for the U.S. effort to win World War II by supplying raw materials at low prices. In return for low prices, the United States offered to buy all the minerals that Bolivia could produce. In a sense, Bolivia gave up precious nonrenewable resources to help the United States in time of need. In this light, perhaps the United States might have paid "fair" prices for Bolivian tin, antimony, tungsten, rubber, etc., instead of having tried to compensate for the artificially low prices with aid. However, the advantages for the United States in the latter arrangement outweighed "fair" prices. The United States bureaucracy could always attach strings to aid, thereby assuring the bureaucrats an excuse for managing Bolivian affairs. At the same time, U.S. exports to Bolivia could be stimulated through Ex-Im Bank loans for construction equipment. The problem for Bolivia was how to absorb the massive inflow of new funds. According to Richard S. Thorn:

In order to utilize the U.S. funds, the government was required to contribute substantial
sums of dollars to the projects. For example,
in the initial agreement concluded with the Export-Import Bank in December 1942 for $15.5
million in credits to be made available to the
newly established Bolivian Development Corporation, $3.5 million was to be contributed by the
government. This sum was equal to 14 percent
of the total government expenditures in 1943.
The government deficit rose from the equivalent
of $326,000 in 1943 to $2.5 million in 1944. The
Bolivian budget simply could not absorb such a
substantial increase in expenditure as required
by the Export-Import agreement and other similar agreements concluded with the United States.
On the other hand, the government could not
ignore the opportunity of receiving such a large
credit under such favorable terms. The result
was a continued resort to the printing press and
renewed inflation. [8]

By 1948, total U.S. aid amounted to over one-third of Bolivian central government expenditures, as can be seen in column H of Table VI-2.
Although in 1950 the share of U.S. financial input to Bolivia declined to
only 8 percent of the amount spent by the central government, in 1951 it
increased to about 45 percent of that amount. This shift, as the economy
continued to contract because of the 1952 revolution and its aftermath,
caused Paz Estenssoro's MNR government to find itself in a very difficult
position. Political victory was not possible without consolidating the impact of the social and economic victories as reflected in the new labor
laws, the right of illiterates to vote, the land reform, and the nationalization of the big tin mining industry. Although U.S. aid fell to only 4.7
million dollars in 1953, the sharp decline of Bolivian expenditures in that
year meant that U.S. outlay was equal to over half of the central government expenditures.

A shifting of funds to the new autonomous agencies from the government budget accounted for some of the decline in central government expenditures. This was of little consolation to Paz Estenssoro, however,
who could not control the income and expenditures of such autonomous
agencies as he could have done if the agencies depended entirely upon
a direct allocation from treasury funds instead of directly charging the
populace for their services. In addition to controlling their own revenues, the decentralized agencies received subsidies from the central
government to offset losses during the period of disorganization resulting
from the political upheaval. Theoretically, the agencies were decentralized to keep them out of politics and to use their profits for national
development. However, it would take several decades before profits
were earned with any consistency, especially because the newly nationalized mines had been allowed to deteriorate by their former owners in
anticipation of the end of their property rights, and because an imperative of the revolution required the rehiring of workers who had been
fired unjustly for having demanded fair wages and working conditions.
Decentralized agencies could not be allowed to go bankrupt and their
losses were fully subsidized without question in the confusing years of
national reorganization under the MNR. [9]

In 1954 and 1955 U.S. outlay in Bolivia was almost double actual central government expenditures, and in 1956 it spent almost three times what

TABLE VI-2

BOLIVIA'S GROSS DOMESTIC PRODUCT (GDP), ACTUAL CENTRAL GOVERNMENT EXPENDITURE, AND SHARE OF U.S. TOTAL ACTUAL OUTLAY, 1948-1976[a]

| | Millions of Pesos | | | Millions of Dollars | | | Percent | |
| | A. | B. | C. | D. | E. | F. | G. | H. |
Year	GDP	Central Govt. Actual Exp.	Dollar Exchange Rate[b]	GDP	Central Govt. Actual Exp.	U.S. Total Actual Outlay	U.S. Share of GDP (F/D)	U.S. Share of Central Govt. (F/E)
1948	N.A.	1.7	.09	N.A.	18.9	6.4	N.A.	33.9
1949	N.A.	1.8	.12	N.A.	15.0	3.6	N.A.	24.0
1950	46	2.4	.13	353.8	18.5	1.5	.4	8.1
1951	80	3.7	.21	381.0	17.6	7.9	2.1	44.9
1952	107	4.2	.28	382.1	15.0	5.9	1.5	39.3
1953	327	8.4	.95	344.2	8.8	4.7	1.4	53.4
1954	632	14.7	1.82	347.3	8.1	14.8	4.3	182.7
1955	1,501	25.8	4.05	370.6	6.4	12.4	3.3	193.8
1956	2,757	77.1	7.76	355.3	9.9	27.6	7.8	278.8
1957	2,960	265.8	8.33	355.3	31.9	28.2	7.9	88.4
1958	3,361	326.2	9.70	346.5	33.6	25.9	7.5	77.1
1959	3,862	357.2	11.88	325.1	30.1	23.2	7.1	77.1
1960	4,497	355.0	11.88	378.5	29.9	17.9	4.7	59.9
1961	4,872	414.5	11.88	410.1	34.9	17.3	4.2	49.6
1962	5,327	454.8	11.88	448.4	38.3	30.3	6.8	79.1
1963	5,736	505.1	11.88	482.8	42.5	39.6	8.2	93.2
1964	6,463	575.2	11.88	544.0	48.4	62.1	11.4	128.3
1965	7,180	763.5	11.88	604.4	64.3	23.4	3.9	36.4
1966	7,950	809.2	11.88	669.2	68.1	21.7	3.2	31.9
1967	8,979	945.3	11.88	755.8	79.6	26.7	3.5	33.5
1968	10,192	1,019.6	11.88	857.9	85.8	35.4	4.1	41.3

(continued)

TABLE VI-2 (continued)

Year	Millions of Pesos		C. Dollar Exchange Rate[b]	Millions of Dollars			Percent	
	A. GDP	B. Central Govt. Actual Exp.		D. GDP	E. Central Govt. Actual Exp.	F. U.S. Total Actual Outlay	G. U.S. Share of GDP (F/D)	H. U.S. Share of Central Govt. (F/E)
1969	11,044	962.9	11.88	929.6	81.1	20.5	2.2	25.3
1970	12,080	1,248.9	11.88	1,016.8	105.1	40.2	4.0	38.2
1971	13,677[c]	1,388.6	11.88	1,151.3	116.9	22.8	2.0	19.5
1972	17,413	2,068.3	13.23	1,316.2	156.3	45.9	3.5	29.4
1973	26,466	2,882.0	20.00	1,323.3	144.1	24.4	1.8	16.9
197-	44,339	5,524.7	20.00	2,217.0	276.2	23.3	1.1	8.7
'97	50,156	6,359.4	20.00	2,507.8	318.0	18.6	.7	5.8
1974	58,949	8,239.8	20.00	2,947.5	411.9	37.5	1.3	9.1

N.A. - No data available

a J.S. data on fiscal-year basis; Bolivian data on calendar-year basis.

b Through 1955 data are for black market rate at year's end; 1956 data are for average market rate.

c Revised series begins, 1971 equals +4.0 percent after revision.

Sources: A. James W. Wilkie, *Statistics and National Policy* (Los Angeles; UCLA Latin American Center Publications, 1974) p. 402; and International Monetary Fund, *International Financial Statistics*, Oct. 1978.

B. James W. Wilkie, *The Bolivian Revolution and U.S. Aid Since 1952* (Los Angeles; UCLA Latin American Center Publications, 1969), p. 26; Wilkie, *Statistics and National Policy*, op. cit., p. 162; Bolivia, Banco Central, *Boletín Estadístico*, marzo 1977, p. 46.

C. Wilkie, *Statistics and National Policy*, op. cit., p. 241; and International Monetary Fund, *International Financial Statistics*, May 1977. Cf. Bridget Reynolds, "Exchange Rate History, 1937–1974," in James W. Wilkie and Paul Turovsky, eds., *Statistical Abstract of Latin America*, Vol. 17 (Los Angeles: UCLA Latin American Center Publications, 1976), p. 262.

D-E. Calculated.

F. Table I, above.

G-H. Calculated.

the central government did. Beginning in 1957, under the more stable regime of President Hernán Siles Zuazo expenditures of the Bolivian central government increased more than threefold over the levels of 1956; and, whereas U.S. aid also increased substantially, the proportional share of U.S. outlays to total government expenditures sharply declined.

Bolivian central government expenditures reached the 30 million dollar mark in the late 1950s after having fallen to less than 10 million from 1953 to 1956. After 1961 the total climbed steadily, except for 1969. With increased central government expenditures, in 1961 U.S. aid out lays fell to less than half of those of the Bolivian government. However, during the second Paz Estenssoro presidency, 1960-1964, United States officials were concerned that he would be succeeded by extreme leftists within the MNR, therefore U.S. outlays approached those of the Bolivian central government in 1962 and 1963, and exceeded them by 28 percent in 1964. Such a pattern was certainly in line with Paz Estenssoro's close relationship with Washington. This does not mean, however, that he "sold out" to the United States. Paz Estenssoro was an able bargainer and was able to bring Bolivia through difficult years when the real trade balance showed negative results (see Appendix A, column C) as Bolivia attempted to diversify its economy and escape from its reliance on a few trading partners. [10]

Under the military governments that have held power since 1965, the percentage of U.S. aid to Bolivian central government expenditures reached the lowest figures since 1950. Column H of Table VI-2 shows that by the mid-1970s U.S. aid was less than 10 percent of central government outlay in Bolivia. The same pattern appears in the U.S. aid outlay in relation to Bolivia's gross domestic product (GDP). U.S. totals rose to 11 percent of Bolivian GDP by 1964. Subsequently they fell to about 1 percent of GDP by the mid-1970s.

In attempting to unite Bolivia against a "workers' takeover" of government, from 1971-1978 the military, under President Hugo Banzer Suárez, sought to end the chronic instability of the post-MNR period. According to Alfredo Arce Carpio, ideologue for Banzer, the post-1971 military government institutionalized the following economic system: all nationalized spheres were reserved for government control and all other areas were open for free enterprise, both spheres being closely regulated by the government. [11] At the same time, new generations educated after the 1952 revolution came to maturity and began to staff technical posts within the government.

BOLIVIA'S TRADE DIVERSIFICATION

With the success of the MNR in achieving import substitution of sugar, rice, and petroleum products, the new *técnicos* could turn their high-level expertise to export diversification. Bolivia's historic goal of constructing a tin smelter had to be postponed during the MNR period not only because Bolivia had to provide remuneration for the nationalization of the tin mines by sending the ore to some of its former owners who smelted it in England, [12] but also because the U.S. Congress in effect forbade aid of most kinds that could develop industry which would raise U.S. import prices. Therefore, the United States Agency for International Development (AID) in Bolivia was hampered in meeting Bolivia's demands for building certain new industries such as the smelters.

After the capture and killing of "Che" Guevara in 1967 had redounded to make him a hero and had set off waves of guerrilla movement in the country (the CIA was accused of having conspired with the Bolivian

military to murder Guevara),[13] the U.S. State Department finally realized
that it could not expect to keep Bolivian development within a too nar-
rowly conceived limit or the United States would "lose" Bolivia. The
days when the United States Ambassador could intervene openly in politics had passed. The U.S. government did not cut off aid when Bolivia
established diplomatic relations with Moscow in 1969 nor when it accepted
Eastern European assistance to build an antimony smelter in the mid-
1970s--the long awaited tin smelter already having gone into operation
by 1970 with West German financing.[14] The military government made
much propaganda in the 1970s about these new conquests on Bolivia's
road to economic independence.

In other spheres, by the 1970s Bolivia had also begun to achieve
goals originally set by Paz Estenssoro and the MNR. As Table VI-3
shows, the average real trade balance that Bolivia had enjoyed in the
pre-revolutionary era, but lost between 1952 and 1964, was regained
after 1965 even as the country increased its capital goods imports at an
average of 10 percentage points per period. The value of tin exports
declined from almost 70 percent of total exports in pre-revolutionary days
to less than half of the total export value by the period of military rule.[15]
Thus, metallic tin exports that had been impossible before the 1970s
garnered an average of an additional 10 percent share of the value of
exports in each period. The petroleum and natural gas exports foreseen
by the MNR also came to reality under the military. True, exports were
still mineral based, but they were based less heavily than in the past upon only one mineral, the first step toward greater diversification.

Bolivian revolutionary goals for diversification of trading partners
also made important gains, as can be seen in Table VI-4. Imports from
the United States fell from an average high of 43 percent of all imports
under the MNR—when U.S. aid was most influential because of relatively
low GDP and central government outlay—to 33 percent, which was also
lower than the pre-revolutionary average. Two other import partners,
Japan and Brazil, gained at the expense of Argentina as well as the
United States.

If the United States hoped to increase its hold on the purchase of
Bolivian exports, it was also frustrated in this sphere. The U.S. share
in purchases of Bolivian exports fell 9 percentage points from the average level of 52 percent in the pre-1951 period to 43 percent in the MNR
period, and declined another 9 percentage points to 34 percent in the
post-1965 era. Great Britain's importance in the purchase of exports
fell between 10 and 14 percentage points to the 30 percent level in 1965-
1976, to the gain of Argentina. Although Bolivian governments have argued that national exports would be less subject to declines in volume
and value if Bolivia could trade with more countries, it now seems that
such a hope is limited by the fact that increasing international interde-
pendence means that when one country is affected by adverse economic
conditions all may be. Nevertheless, Bolivia has made strong progress
in diversification of its foreign trade position, progress that took several
decades to begin to show new patterns.

BOLIVIA'S INTERNAL GOALS

Bolivia's internal goals since 1950 have emphasized economic growth.
In spite of problems in measuring Bolivian GDP, it appears that Bolivia
sustained a minor miracle in terms of economic growth between 1963 and
1970.[16]

TABLE VI-3

BOLIVIA'S REAL TRADE BALANCE AND PERCENTAGE VALUES OF MAJOR IMPORTS AND EXPORTS, BY PERIOD SINCE 1939

| Period[b] | No. of Years in Average | A. Real Trade Balance[a] | | Average Percentage Value | | | | |
		Total	Average	B. Capital Goods[c] Imports	C. Tin Concentrate and Metallic Tin Exports	D. Metallic Tin Exports[d]	E. Petroleum and Natural Gas Exports	F. Natural Gas Exports[g]
1939–1951	13	602.6	46.4	22	69	0	.2[f]	0
1952–1964	13	147.3	11.3	33	62	0	2.3	0
1965–1976	12	393.8	32.8	44	48	10.2[e]	15.4	6.3[h]

[a] Millions of dollars of 1951, CIF, except imports FOB through Sept. 1954.

[b] For prior years, see Wilkie, *Statistics and National Policy* (Los Angeles: UCLA Latin American Center Publications, 1974), p. 80.

[c] Minor change in methodology—percentage for first two periods may be slightly understated. (Consumer goods series excluded here as not comparable between first two and third periods owning to major change in methodology for this aspect of import analysis.)

[d] Included in column C.

[e] Since 1971.

[f] Only 1950–1951.

[g] Included in column E.

[h] Since 1972.

(continued)

TABLE VI-3 (continued)

Source: A. Calculated from Appendix A; and Wilkie, *Statistics and National Policy* op. cit., p. 80.

B. Through 1964, Wilkie, ibid., p. 79, revised with AID/Bolivia, *Estadísticas económicas*, Vol. 14, p. 20; since 1965, Bolivia, Banco Central, *Boletín estadístico*, septiembre 1976 and marzo 1977.

C-D. Wilkie, *Statistics and National Policy*, op. cit., p. 69; Bolivia, Ministerio de Minería y Metalurgia, *Bolivia minera en números* (La Paz, 1975), p. 192; and Bolivia, Banco Central, *Boletín estadístico*, marzo 1977.

E-F. Wilkie, *Statistics and National Policy*, op. cit., p. 72; AID/Bolivia, *Estadísticas económicas*, p. 14; and Bolivia, Banco Central, op. cit., marzo 1977.

TABLE VI-4

BOLIVIAN TRADE WITH MAJOR COUNTRIES, BY PERIOD SINCE 1939
(Average Percent)

	No. of Years in Average	Imports				Exports			
		United States	Japan	Argentina	Brazil	United States	Great Britain	Argentina	Brazil
1939-1951	5[a]	37	1	19	3	52	40	2	1
1952-1964	13	43	4	9	1	43	44	3	2
1965-1976	12	33	13	12	6	34	30	10	2

[a]Sample years, 1939, 1942, 1946, 1950, 1951.

Source: James W. Wilkie, *Statistics and National Policy* (Los Angeles: UCLA Latin American Center Publications, 1974), pp. 83-84; AID/Bolivia, *Estadísticas económicas*, Vol. 14; American Security Bank, "Republic of Bolivia," (New York, 1976), p. 40; and Bolivia, Banco Central, *Boletín estadístico*, marzo 1977.

The highest annual growth rates after 1960 were in 1966 and 1968 but all years except 1961 and 1971 were affluent ones for national development. Part of the problem in 1961 no doubt came once Paz Estenssoro began to push land titling to legitimize holdings occupied by peasants after the 1952 land reform; as long as only a few titles had been granted, former owners felt that all hope of recovering their lands was not lost. On the one hand, Paz Estenssoro wanted to resolve ownership problems in the countryside, yet at the same time he wanted to attract national and foreign capital into Bolivia to open new industry; these mixed signals hampered economic confidence in 1961.[17] In 1971 the problem of growth coincided with activities of the Popular Assembly, scaring new investors or reinvestors. By the mid-1960s, however, it was clear that Bolivia had escaped from the year-to-year economic crises that had marked the 1950s.

Petroleum

Economic health of Bolivia rested to a large degree on the emergence of a healthy petroleum industry as well as relative prosperity of the tin mines. Although the latter earned much larger export revenues, it still had a much larger number of employees with whom to contend. The petroleum industry, in contrast, did not have an inflated labor force demanding its "traditional rights" and its "historic vindication." By the late 1970s some observers have been concerned about the rather dramatic contraction of Bolivian oil exports, a decline shown in Appendix D. Whether exports were down because of a collapse in output or expanding domestic demands is not clear. It could be argued that Bolivian officials have placed emphasis on natural gas production and export, income from which has expanded dramatically in only a few short years, especially because of ready sales to Argentina. Appendix D reveals that petroleum prices have increased favorably to yield over 55 million dollars in 1976 and over 67 million dollars in 1977, thus compensating for the concurrent decline in crude petroleum exports.

Energy and Communications

In another important aspect of national development Bolivia has been remarkably successful in bringing to fruition an extensive network of energy and communications systems. The success of this time-consuming task did not become apparent until the early 1970s, twenty years after the revolution got underway. With the achievement of expanding economic activity of the Santa Cruz area, Bolivian life began to give full credit for the first time to the *Oriente*. New hydroelectric systems formed part of this dynamic activity and spontaneous colonization tended to prosper where colonization directed by the government had not. In all, it can be said that by the 1970s, when the expanded road and air systems tied the country together, it became possible for the first time in Bolivia's history to speak of a Bolivian nation. Until the 1970s transportation boom, Bolivia lacked the possibility for national identity, a situation that had caused many an observer to suggest that Bolivia should be divided among its neighbors because it was not a viable state—such observations were all the more easy given the apparently chaotic political life.

AN EVALUATION OF GROWTH POTENTIAL

In short, Bolivia can now be seen in a new light: it has had two periods of relatively long political stability, 1952-1964 and 1971-1978. Some Bolivians would even say that since 1952 Bolivia has had steady presidential power and the problems in 1964 (when Paz Estenssoro was overthrown) and 1969-1971 (when the extreme left juggled leaders in the presidency) were aberrations in an institutionalized process wherein regardless of political leadership, economic programs begun by the MNR have been carried forth and even expanded.

In the author's view Bolivia's growth potential is not similar to that of Uruguay. Whereas Uruguay has a small geographic area with few natural resources and a small population to support a modern economy balanced between growth in agriculture, mining, energy, and industry, Bolivia has a large territory of varied climate and rich resources with room for the population to expand productively. If Uruguay was once a leading country in economic and social terms, it may have reached the limit of its possibilities; witness its long-term economic, social, and political decline since the 1950s. On the other hand, Bolivia has only begun to tap its wealth. As it does so, social advances are bound to come. This is not to say that Bolivia does not face grave problems; but it has the opportunity to realize a potential that many small countries such as Uruguay, El Salvador, Nicaragua, Honduras, etc., do not have.

Bolivia already has a comparative advantage in Latin America with regard to the rate of food production. Table VI-5 reveals that after its low output in 1953, a year of massive land invasions under the revolution when Bolivia's level of food production ranked among one of the lowest in Latin America, Bolivia registered one of the region's highest increases in output through 1961-1965. If by 1971 Bolivia ranked eighth in gains in food production compared to the 1961-1965 base period, by 1976 it registered the third highest gain of Latin America's twenty countries, being exceeded only by Costa Rica and Brazil. It appears from Table VI-5, then, that following the expected declines in food production after land reform, Bolivia made rapid recovery, the country's per capita index of output increasing 88 percent between 1953 and 1976. This progress stands in strong contrast to that of three other countries that have undergone major reorganization ·of land tenure: Cuba has continued to be plagued by food production problems; Mexico has made only modest gains; and Peru has seen stagnation in food output since the 1950s. Of the land reform countries, only Venezuela has made gains equal to those of Bolivia, but with a vastly greater amount of available money.

At what cost has this "success" been achieved? Did political dictatorship under the MNR—with illiterates trucked to the polls to vote for whom they were told, as some critics alleged—and military dictatorship—with workers suppressed in political rights as well as fair wages—negatively outweigh the benefits of economic growth? Did Bolivia sell out to the United States and abort its social revolution in return for U.S. favors?

Political scientists have tended to answer these questions in a way that determines Bolivia's revolution to have failed. Christopher Mitchell has painted the Bolivian scene since 1952 as follows:

> Although the MNR promised social and economic
> reform, the abolition of political privilege, and
> a nationalistic foreign policy, the party was un-
> able to sustain these efforts beyond an initial
> period of achievement. Instead, within five

TABLE VI-5

INDEX OF PER CAPITA FOOD PRODUCTION IN LATIN AMERICA,
1953-1976[a]

(1961-1965 = 100)

Country	1953[b]	1961-1965	1971	1976
Argentina	98	100	98	116
Bolivia	66	100	110	124
Brazil	88	100	112	128
Chile	102	100	105	92
Colombia	105	100	102	106
Costa Rica	123	100	134	140
Cuba	114	100	100	93
Dominican Republic	108	100	104	98
Ecuador	65	100	100	98
El Salvador	N.A.	100	105	110
Guatemala	97	100	112	123
Haiti	N.A.	100	103	105
Honduras	102	100	117	107
Mexico	78	100	110	104
Nicaragua	N.A.	100	115	109
Panama	90	100	123	113
Paraguay	106	100	104	99
Peru	100	100	102	102
Uruguay	124	100	88	106
Venezuela	82	100	120	124

N.A.--No data available.

[a]Includes cereals, vegetables, starchy roots, sugar, pulses, edible oil
crops, nuts, fruits, livestock and livestock products, cocoa, and wine.

[b]Includes also coffee, tea, and linseed not counted as food products
after 1961.

Source: UN, Food and Agricultural Organization, *FAO Production Yearbook*, Vols. 24 and 30 (Rome, 1970 and 1977), pp. 31 and 77,
respectively. Index base standardized for 1961-1965 = 100 .
For data on individual Bolivian crops, see E. Boyd Wennergren
and Morris D. Whitaker, *The Status of Bolivian Agriculture*
(New York: Praeger, 1975).

years after vaulting to power in 1952, the "multi-class" party's policies had become socially divi-sive, leaving Bolivia internationally vulnerable. In my view, this turnabout resulted from the MNR's underlying identification with Bolivia's middle class—a class which turned conservative once its most basic objectives were achieved in 1952-53.

By the same token, [we can see] new em-phasis on the political continuity between the MNR's civilian populism and the military regimes which have ruled Bolivia since 1964. As for in-terrupting basic trends in the Andean nation's political life, the 1964 coup can now be seen clearly as the transition to an even more vigor-ous and rigid middle-class domination than existed before. In addition, it seems that Bo-livia's inheritance from the MNR period—bitter-ness among politically-mobilized groups, and a difficulty in forming broad-based political coali-tions—will be among the major obstacles to polit-ical progress away from military authoritarian-ism. [18]

James Malloy has written of the "Uncompleted Revolution," but has not defined explicitly what the completed revolution would entail. Pre-sumably urban and rural workers would be the immediate beneficiaries who would run national affairs or at least receive redistributed income at the expense of the "bourgeois state capitalism" that emerged under the MNR. According to Malloy:

Under Paz [Estenssoro] the attempt was made, with heavy United States assistance, to achieve a solution to the revolution and begin a drive toward development in the image of an updated version of the older democratic bourgeois model. This drive included a power strategy directed at the regional, intersectoral, and intra-elite levels. First there was an attempt to replace anti-Paz caudillos with pro-Paz caudillos. Si-multaneously, there was an attempt to "national-ize" the pro-Paz caudillos and the regions under their control, and to establish a national insti-tutional presence through the military. At the intersectoral level, there was an attempt to make the peasants the mass base of the revolution by meeting both their objective and subjective (identity) demands. The peasants were then to be used in conjunction with the army to deny labor's demands for control and to push off onto that sector, at least temporarily, the major social costs of development. At the elite level, the attempt was to push aside the entrenched fac-tionalized party elite and to bring into existence a new party elite. At the same time, the ground-work was laid to create a general middle-class elite trained for, committed to, and capable of presiding over a state capitalist developmental system. [19]

And Malloy continues:

> One observer has aptly referred to the Bo-
> livian experience as the "revolution at starvation
> level." Before the revolution of 1952, Bolivia
> was, with the exception of Haiti, the least-
> developed Latin American country. Aside from
> a few families, even the legendary Rosca was
> only moderately wealthy when compared to the
> ruling elites of Bolivia's sister republics. Old
> Bolivia, therefore, had very little to contribute
> to the new. After it was stripped, there just
> wasn't enough to meet the demands of social jus-
> tice and economic development. As the saying
> current among the Bolivian middle class has it,
> "All this revolution did was to socialize poverty."
> Moreover, as the Cuban experience demon-
> strates, dependence on a single export product
> cannot be banished by revolutionary fiat. But
> whereas the Cubans could eventually (although
> with difficulty) fall back on a reorganized sugar
> industry, the Bolivians had little beyond empty
> mountains, antiquated mining equipment, and
> an inflated work force.
>
> Poverty and backwardness may create con-
> ditions which motivate men to rise up in violence.
> Such violent uprisings may successfully destroy
> the fabric of a pre-existent social order. But
> the question of "making the revolution" in the
> modern developmental context is a different kind
> of problem than the process of destroying the
> old. The modern revolution is a process of
> stripping previously dominant social groups (in
> some cases, not so dominant groups as well) and
> reorganizing them and their resources within a
> new political and economic framework with the
> avowed aim of national development. The ability
> to complete the process successfully depends, at
> least in part, on the previous level of develop-
> ment. The relative success of the Mexican and
> Cuban revolutions in institutionalizing new polit-
> ical economic models is undoubtedly related to
> the fact that both societies were among the more
> developed of Latin America when the revolu-
> tions occurred. The Bolivian case appears to
> demonstrate, on the other hand, that the pros-
> pects of completing a development-oriented
> revolution in countries below a certain level of
> development are, at best, extremely difficult. [20]

In response to such bleak statements, it is necessary to ask whether
or not political scientists do not tend to see political solutions as the first
step in national development rather than viewing political growth as growing out of, or coterminously coming with, basic economic reorganization
and often taking years to carry out. Also, social classes and traditions
cannot be fully reorganized in even several decades. With regard to Bolivia, without education and communications for the dissemination of
ideas, isolated populations can hardly participate in society with any

understanding of issues or events. "Power to the people" is a fine concept if the people have a certain degree of education and some sophisti-
cation about the complexity of matters affecting them. Bolivia did not
inherit such a population in 1952; rather, it has had to begin almost from
the beginning to develop new generations who could staff the government
and master complex technical processes necessary for Bolivia to compete
in the modern world, be it in mining, smelting, petroleum development,
agricultural extension, transportation, and so on. Twenty-five years is
a short time to have made the gains that Bolivia has made, let alone to
begin to break down social isolation by attempting to make all citizens
fluent in the Spanish language--the basic language necessary to understand and protect legal rights as well as to generate effective cooperation between the country's regions. [21]

Malloy admits that Bolivia started far behind Cuba and Mexico, Bolivia ranking as Latin America's poorest nation only a quarter of a century
ago. How then can Bolivia be judged to have failed when, facing the
same political problems of Cuba and Mexico, i.e., one-party dominance
and repression of dissidents, [22] it has laid the basis for the diversified
economy needed to compete in the twentieth-century world marketplace.
Cuba has not escaped dependency on sugar as the primary export, and
like Uruguay it faces immense problems in its lack of size and scarcity
of resources. Moreover, the case of Cuba no longer stands as a model
for many countries seeking independent national development--it has become as dependent, if not more so, on the Soviet Union than it ever was
on the United States.

Mexico is more comparable to Bolivia, both in size and resources
and also in ethnic makeup, but the former faces a population-growth
problem that is grave indeed. Bolivia has accomplished much of what
Mexico did, yet in a much shorter time. It took Mexico some seven years
after its political revolution began in 1910 to get its plan of social revolution into written form in 1917. It did not get real land reform until 1934,
24 years later. Oil was not expropriated until 1938. Agriculture did not
recover for over 30 years after the 1910 revolution. And government
sponsorship of new industry became full-fledged only in the 1940s and
1950s. Mexico today still has very unequal income distribution. Why
demand full success from Bolivia in 25 years, then, that which Mexico
could not accomplish in two or three times as long? [23]

THE IMPORTANCE OF U.S. AID

Kenneth F. Johnson has argued that in spite of all the money spent
by the U.S. Alliance for Progress, Latin America is presumably much
worse off than if it had not accepted funds. [24] Such commentary implicitly raises a question as to whether or not U.S. aid has been responsible
for the relative success of Bolivian growth portrayed in the present
paper. In this vein, it could be argued that the United States provided
aid costly to Bolivia after 1960 by shifting from grants to loans, loans
that have helped place Bolivia in a heavy position of foreign indebtedness. [25] An additional point for argument is to what extent the thrust of
U.S. aid always caused the Bolivian government to evade the issues of
development.

In 1969 the author suggested that only about half of U.S. aid had
ever been expended on economic functions, thus not having taken up
the developmental slack left by the fact that Bolivia had been locked into
social as well as administrative, including military, expenditure since
1945 when Paz Estenssoro served as Minister of Treasury for President

TABLE VI-6

BOLIVIA'S ACTUAL MILITARY EXPENDITURE, AND CENTRAL GOVERNMENT BUDGETARY SUPPORT
AS SHARES OF U.S. OUTLAY, BY PERIOD SINCE 1957

| Period | No. of Years in Period | Bolivia's Military Expenditures | | Central Govt. Budgetary Support by the United States | |
		Million Dollars[a]	As Percent of Total U.S. Outlay[b]	Million Dollars[c]	Percent of Total U.S. Outlay[b]
1957-1964	8	33.4	13.7	55.8	22.8
1965-1976	12	304.5	89.3	42.4	12.4

[a] Calculated from Appendix A, column D.

[b] Calculated with data in Table VI-1, column A: total U.S. dollar outlay 1957-1964, 244.5 million; 1965-1976, 341.0 million.

[c] Data are from James W. Wilkie, *The Bolivian Revolution and U.S. Aid Since 1952* (Los Angeles: UCLA Latin American Center Publications, 1969), p. 12; and AID/Bolivia, Comptroller's Office.

Gualberto Villarroel. Because U.S. and Bolivian expenditures had thereto never been published, both governments lived with the myth that the United States had put most of its aid into economic functions; in fact, both governments' expenditures tended to be frozen in non-economic activities. [26]

Military Assistance

In two important ways the United States has supplied noneconomic funds to help support the Bolivian military. First, as noted when discussing Table VI-1, U.S. outlay for non-military purposes freed Bolivian funds for use by the military. Table VI-6 presents another view of that phenomenon, U.S. outlay amounting to 13.7 percent of Bolivia's military expenditure between 1957 and 1964, thereafter jumping to 89.3 percent. Second, U.S. funds were needed to cover Bolivian central government deficit spending; thus the United States provided direct budgetary support amounting to 22.8 percent of Bolivian central government expenditures in the years 1957-1964, thereafter it declined to 12.4 percent. Indirectly, if not directly, U.S. funds, therefore, released Bolivian funds so that the military's percentage of central government funds could rise from Bolivia's historical low of 6.7 percent in 1957 and about 14 percent by 1964 when the MNR fell from power, as can be seen in Appendix A. In 1965, after the military coup, the military share of central government expenditure jumped to over 18 percent in that one year alone. Although this percentage declined to 13.4 percent in 1971 (giving substance to the fears of many generals that the country's workers would gain at the expense of the military) once leftist military officers were eliminated from command, the military share of the budget gained once more. That share reached 18.4 percent in 1975, the highest figure since the 1952 revolution.

In the past, most U.S. liberals would have assumed that if military expenditure went up after the MNR fell from power, the share of central government expenditure devoted to education would go down. [27] However, the military governments since 1965 have devoted a much greater share of central government expenditure to education than the MNR ever did. Under the MNR the annual percentage devoted to education ranged from 10 to 24 percent, the average being 16 percent. Under the military governments up to 1976 the percentages ranged from 21 to over 32 percent, the average being 27 percent. (See Appendix A, column E.)

Given these apparently contradictory patterns, what is to be made of U.S. aid that has at once helped both the militarymen and the student—traditional enemies. And although it appears that U.S. outlay to Bolivia increased after the MNR fell (the MNR received an average of 23.8 million dollars per year compared to the military's receipt of 28.4 million per year, as Table VI-7 shows), once inflation is accounted for, the average U.S. outlay declined from 22.7 to 20.1 million dollars between the MNR period and the military period. In short, what one may easily assume to be "bad" about U.S. aid to Bolivia since 1965 is here seen to be complex. It is possible that the "good" aspects outweigh "bad" aspects as traditionally measured. [28]

U.S. Aid Advisors and Program Formulation

Another important dimension of the role of U.S. aid to Bolivia is the management activity of AID officials, many of whom have generally tried to foist their views on the host country. Whereas it may have been true

TABLE VI-7

REAL U.S. ACTUAL OUTLAY TO BOLIVIA, BY PERIOD SINCE 1948

Period	No. Years in Period	Million Current Dollars Total	Million Current Dollars Average	Million Real Dollars[a] Total	Million Real Dollars[a] Average
1948–1951	4	19.4	4.9	20.2	5.1
1952–1964	13	309.9	23.8	294.8	22.7
1965–1976	12	341.0	28.4	241.4	20.1
Totals	29	670.3	23.1	556.4	19.2

[a] Dollars of 1951.

Source: Calculated from Table VI-1 and Appendix A.

in the 1950s that Bolivia lacked the trained manpower to administer the huge influx of U.S. funds during a time of national reorganization, by the 1960s the situation had begun to change. This change was not recognized by U.S. Ambassador Douglas Henderson, who felt that he himself had to partially govern the country during his term from 1963 to 1968. [29] This attitude was finally reversed by U.S. Ambassador William P. Stedman, who served from 1973 to 1977. Stedman brought an end to U.S. advisory services to Bolivia on development of planning, tax reform, public administration, reorganization, etc. [30]

"Advisory activities" by U.S. officials had long abused Bolivia's hospitality by compromising the country's national integrity. By claiming to carry out U.S. congressional mandates with regard to administration of U.S. assistance, AID officials too often implemented programs in ways that were counterproductive for both Bolivia and the United States. Some officials meddled at will in Bolivian affairs to impress their own biases on projects. They threatened to hold up U.S. funds for the projects unless their own petty demands were met. Only in this way could some AID officials prove to themselves that they were "managing" U.S. assistance to Bolivia. Their behavior showed an insecurity caused, in part, by frequent and sudden transfers from job to job or country to country.

A case in point is the U.S. technical assistance in the development of Bolivian sheep and wheat production, as reported by members of the Utah State University technical mission to Bolivia, who found their efforts impeded by AID. According to E. Boyd Wennergren and Morris D. Whitaker, the programming of U.S. investment in technical assistance resulted in this case in a serious misallocation of resources. Between 1967 and 1969 sheepshearing and wool-marketing programs had been introduced by Utah State with relative success and by 1975 new livestock management practices had been proven, and the estimated rate of return to investment was 44.1 percent. But AID officials were more interested in wheat production, despite warnings by Utah State that scarce resources could not be used with much success. In the words of Wennergren and Whitaker.

Early in 1966, contract consultants thoroughly studied the economic and agronomic potential for a wheat program. They concluded
such a program would encounter serious difficulties because production of wheat was clearly
uneconomic compared with other crops . . . .

Despite the possimistic 1966 report of the
consultants, the wheat project was added to the
technical assistance program late in the same
year. Then, in 1969, the AID mission director
and rural development officer were changed;
shortly thereafter, the wheat project was significantly expanded without adequate testing of
campesino acceptance of improved varieties or
the probability of their widespread diffusion.
We have argued elsewhere that rotation of AID
personnel tends to promote changes in program
emphasis . . . Bolivia is a case in point. The
contract focus on wheat was precipitately increased relative to sheep, and $1.8 million was
spent on the wheat project between 1970- 1973
compared with $.4 million in the previous four
years . . . .

[Thus], Bolivian society suffered real
losses due to the initial decision to invest in the
wheat project, especially because of greatly increased emphasis on this program in preference
to the much more successful sheep project. In
essence, the return to total U.S. investment was
reduced by investment in the wheat project. [31]

The rate of return to investment on the wheat project is estimated to
have been a negative 47.5 percent.

A case with which the author is personally familiar took place in 1977
long after Ambassador Stedman's attempt to stem the power of petty officials: a lower-eschelon AID officer, newly arrived in Bolivia, immediately
embarrassed himself and AID in Washington by attempting to force his
will upon a proposed independent assessment of activity by earlier AID-
sponsored mobile land brigades. The assessment was to be undertaken
by an outside non-AID authority and had the support of U.S. officials in
Washington and Bolivian officials in La Paz. The newly arrived AID official had been so busy unpacking his belongings that he did not have time
to acquaint himself with negotiations for the proposal by the time he met
with Bolivia's director of land reform. He noted, however, that he would
approve of funding the project only if it were completed in seven months
rather than in twice that time. His reason was ingenuous to say the
least: any project taking over seven months is academically oriented
rather than practically oriented. Although he recognized that the assessment was for evaluative purposes and not for immediate implementation,
he held to his position on the grounds that, because most of past AID
programs essentially had failed, there was no reason to study them.
Thus, at once he not only had insulted implicitly the Bolivian official involved but AID as well. The AID official was transferred out of Bolivia
within weeks, demands elsewhere needing his "expertise."

The "Imperative of AID to Fail"

This case of the instant AID expert who sees most aid as having failed is instructive because it reveals an unwritten rule that guides many AID officers. Such experiences are all too common and lead to the rule, "The Imperative of AID to Fail." In practice, this rule promotes only the new programs of each succeeding AID bureaucrat. To some degree this rule stems from, and is reinforced by, a bureaucratic phenomenon wherein officials rise in rank by coming up with new programs. Once a new program gets underway it becomes almost immediately an old one; and with transfer of officials the new ones have more interest in developing new projects than in implementing somebody else's old ideas. If past and present AID programs are doomed from the start, then, why bother to evaluate them. Hence, AID is famous for being an "agency without a memory."

The odd thing about the 1977 case discussed above, however, is that AID in Washington had intended to overcome some of its memory problems by evaluating AID-sponsored land reform throughout the world, Bolivia being one major case, but its plan was circumvented by a lower-eschelon figure who was only temporarily in Bolivia. Too, the AID mission director was cool to assessment on the grounds that any Washington generated evaluation would have to be managed by AID in Bolivia, even if Washington did not want it to be managed. Lost in all of this was the fact that Bolivian land reform had not failed at all; rather its mixed results and the work of AID's mobile titling brigades awaited (and still await) evaluation.

As in AID-sponsored land reform, most AID programs cannot be said to have failed. Still, if mixed results have been the hallmark of AID's programs, can we say that Bolivia has benefited from U.S. assistance? In the author's view, the answer is affirmative. U.S. assistance with all of its problems has helped Bolivia over several major developmental hurdles and helped to buy the time necessary for Bolivia's economy to grow into a diversified, self-sustaining force. But no single factor—be it the United States, the Bolivian government, or the Bolivian private sector—has been responsible for the country's expanding national economic base. All have been necessary to place Bolivia in a new position from which to tackle unresolved political and social problems.

CONCLUSION

Various U.S. leaders have said in the past that U.S. aid cannot continue forever, yet it has never been curtailed. At what point does U.S. aid become irrelevant?

On the basis of evidence presented here, it is concluded that U.S. aid is certainly not as important as it once was. Its importance in the Bolivian economy has declined to a pre-revolutionary low, less than 10 percent of central government expenditure and only about 1 percent of Bolivian GDP, as observed in Table VI-2. If there was ever a time to end U.S. assistance to Bolivia, that time would appear to be near. The relative lack of importance of such aid was highlighted July 21, 1978, when President Banzer was overthrown by his hand-picked successor, General Juan Pereda Asbún, whose election "victory" of July 9 had been annulled by the country's electoral court. Although President Carter had made continued U.S. aid contingent upon free and honest elections, such assistance was no longer committed to Bolivia, let alone to ousted military leaders. True, U.S. cancellation of 14 million dollars in 1979 for the Bolivian military may have been a blow to the Bolivian general staff as a whole, [33] thus encouraging self-serving officers to move the military out of politics, but the United States must realize that past military funding already has distorted seriously the U.S. role in Bolivia. As revealed in Table VI-1, the Bolivian military received U.S. funds equal to over half of U.S. assistance and over one-third of total U.S. outlay. Such massive funding can serve only two purposes: to create a Bolivian army capable of crushing "democracy" or to encourage Bolivian militance for regaining its outlet to the sea lost to Chile in the War of the Pacific, 1879–1883.

To look at United States-Bolivian financial relations in a somewhat different light, Bolivia has gained the ability to become independent from the need for U.S. funds. The historical series given in Tables VI-1 and VI-2 portray declining direct U.S. financial impact on the country. Such a situation is healthy for Bolivia in the sense that U.S. influence becomes less awesome, influence that always has attempted to promote the United States' own best interests. How can those interests be justified as involving military funding on a scale that hampers civilian control of the country?

A convincing case can be made for ending U.S. aid to Bolivia by the 1980s. To avoid still possible "withdrawal pains" and a return to the political chaos of 1971, it could be argued that U.S. outlay aid should be phased out in three steps. First, end permanently all direct military funding—if Bolivia chooses to use funds released by U.S. non-military assistance for the military, that is a matter of Bolivian priorities. Second, recall all AID officials except those involved in audit and statistical gathering functions—Bolivia now has enough *técnicos* to work out its problems without meddlesome U.S. AID middlemen who continue to stand between U.S. and Bolivian developmental policy goals. [34] Third, in the near future gradually reduce U.S. expenditures to Bolivia, however, a total end to aid need not be the final aim.

In conclusion, it is the contention of this paper that U.S. policy and actual expenditures in Bolivia between 1948 and 1976 helped that country—by accident or by design—to modernize its social and economic infrastructure. Now that the impact of U.S. outlay has declined in the face of Bolivia's growing economic power and Bolivian technical manpower has reached relatively strong levels, it is time to phase out the majority of U.S. officials, if not funding. In the meantime, it must be recognized that Bolivia's formerly pessimistic situation has taken on optimistic overtones. In the 1970s Bolivia has achieved for the first time in its history the economic possibility of supporting new social and political change.

ENDNOTES FOR CHAPTER VI

*Original data series offered here on United States foreign aid and Bolivian government actual expenditures have been constructed from sources in La Paz and Washington, D.C. Thanks are due to the following persons for assistance: AID Comptroller's Office in La Paz (especially Guillermo Peñaranda, Berta de Lanza, Mario Salvatierra, and Melvin L. Van Doren); U.S. Embassy officials in La Paz (especially Hernán Solares Risco and James S. Landberg of the Economic Section); AID Statistics and Reports Division in Washington (especially Jack Cohen and Albert H. Huntington, Jr.). Dr. Carlos Serrate Reich, Bolivian Ambassador to the Soviet Union, facilitated my research in La Paz immediately prior to his departure for Moscow.

1. Projected data without yearly breakdown arc given in U.S. Operations Mission to Bolivia, *Point Four in Bolivia, 1942-1960* (La Paz, 1960), pp. 10 and 94. From the total of 3.2 million dollars given as obligated for 1942-1951, 1.8 million actually spent between 1948 and 1951 have bccn deducted (see Table VI-1, column B) to arrive at 1.4 million dollars. No total data on actual expenditures are given but some detail shows that between 1942 and 1951 the United States contributed 2,035 thousand dollars to the Health Service, 466 thousand to the Education Service, and 33 thousand to the Agriculture Service (see ibid., p. 91).

2. Richard S. Thorn, "The Economic Transformation," in James Malloy and Richard Thorn, eds., *Beyond the Revolution: Bolivia Since 1952* (Pittsburgh: University of Pittsburgh Press, 1971), p. 165.

3. Although AID/Washington no longer classifies Ex-Im Bank as "aid," such loans do indeed constitute aid; for further discussion of the matter, see James W. Wilkie, *Statistics and National Policy* (Los Angeles: UCLA Latin American Center Publications, 1974), p. 148.

4. On the MNR problem with the U.S. Department of State, see Cole Blaiser, "The United States, Germany, and the Bolivian Revolutionaries (1941-1946)," *Hispanic American Historical Review* 52:1 (1972), pp. 26-54. In real terms, as measured in 1951 prices, Bolivia received 8 million dollars in 1947. This figure is calculated from actual U.S. expenditure given in Wilkie, *Statistics and National Policy,* op. cit., p. 369 and deflated with the U.S. export price index given here in Appendix A, column A, carried back in ibid., p. 80 (base converted). Although the U.S. export price index cannot precisely eliminate inflation to calculate real Bolivian purchasing power, it does give a good indication of change in world-market place prices upon which Bolivia has been dependent. It is the best measure to use in this study which seeks to gauge the impact of U.S. aid to Bolivia (aid that must also be deflated by the same index), especially because so much U.S. aid has been tied to purchase of U.S. exports.

5. For yearly breakdown of actual P.L. 480 funds, see Appendix E.

6. See Phillip Boughon, "U.S. Foreign Aid in Latin America: Hypotheses and Patterns in Historical Statistics, 1946-1974" (unpublished Ph.D. dissertation in history, University of California, Los Angeles, 1979).

7. For general discussion of the Popular Assembly, see Jerry W. Knudson, *Bolivia's Popular Assembly of 1971 and the Overthrow of General Juan José Torres* (Buffalo: Council on International Studies, State University of New York, 1974) and Samuel Mendoza, *Anarquía y Caos* (La Paz: Universo, 1973).

8. Thorn, "The Economic Transformation," op. cit., p. 182.

9. See James W. Wilkie, "Public Expenditure Since 1952," in Malloy and Thorn, eds., *Beyond the Revolution,* op. cit., pp. 217-231; reprinted in Wilkie, *Statistics and National Policy,* op. cit., pp. 67-97, with further discussion on pp. 470-472. See also James W. Wilkie, "Recentralization: The Budgetary Dilemma in the Economic Development of Mexico, Bolivia, and Costa Rica," in David T. Geithman, ed., *Fiscal Policy for Industrialization and Development in Latin America* (Gainesville: University of Florida Press, 1974), pp. 200-247; reprinted in Wilkie, *Statistics and National Policy,* op. cit., pp. 101-131.

10. See James W. Wilkie, *Bolivian Foreign Trade: Historical Problems and MNR Revolutionary Policy, 1952-1964* (Buffalo: Council on International Studies, State University of New York, 1971). Reprinted in Wilkie, *Statistics and National Policy,* op. cit., pp. 67-86.

11. Interview with Alfredo Arce Carpio, La Paz, Bolivia, June 18, 1976.

12. According to George Jackson Eder: "Because of the low metal content and complex composition of the Bolivian ores, there were few smelters in the world equipped to handle the concentrates economically. For years, Bolivian tin had been refined chiefly by Williams, Harvey & Co., Ltd., of Liverpool, who managed to reduce smelting costs by combining it with the high-content concentrates from the Straits Settlements. The lowest-quality Bolivian concentrates were smelted by Capper Pass & Sons, Ltd., in Yorkshire, and by the U.S. government-financed Longhorn Tin Smelter in Texas City, Texas. The contract with the Texas smelter expired in 1945, but, as a disguised subsidy to Bolivia, the plant was kept operating at a loss until January 31, 1957. Patiño owned a substantial interest in Consolidated Tin Smelters, Ltd., which in turn owned Williams, Harvey & Co., Ltd. It was not difficult, therefore, for Patiño to have that company withhold from the COMIBOL [Bolivian State Mining Company] shipments a proportion of all tin refined, as a deposit against whatever settlement might ultimately be reached with the Bolivian government. On June 10, 1953, this arrangement was embodied in a formal agreement with Bolivia, whereby an agreed percentage of revenues, on a sliding scale, was withheld from all shipments from the former Patiño, Aramayo, and Hochschild properties." Quoted from Eder, *Inflation and Development in Latin America: A Case History of Inflation and Stabilization in Bolivia* (Ann Arbor: Graduate School of Business Administration, University of Michigan, 1968), p. 51.

13. See, for example, Gregorio Selser, *La CIA en Bolivia* (Buenos Aires: Hernández, 1970). Guevara's influence on Bolivia after his death is clearly seen in President Ovando's interview with the left-wing magazine *Marcha* wherein he stated that while he was still opposed to communist guerrilla activities, Guevara had "renewed certain moral and intellectual values in the country"—quoted in *Facts on File,* 1969, p. 748.

14. The Soviet Union is currently engaged in a pilot program near Potosí to develop a cost efficient way of recovering tin ore from Bolivia's millions of tons of tin mine tailings. Such a program could give a spectacular fillip to Bolivia's tin exports.

15. The volume and price of tin-exports increased in the 1970s compared to the 1960s even as its value in all Bolivian exports declined. See Appendix C.

16. Data changes in GDP are subject to redefinition and revision, as is suggested in Appendix B. Both the Economic Commission for Latin America (ECLA) and the International Monetary Fund (IMF) series are in agreement for the period from 1953 to 1960, but only the ECLA series extends back to 1946. After 1961 the ECLA series shows significantly higher growth rates than does the IMF series for 1961, 1962, 1964, 1974 and 1975. The IMF series shows more growth only in 1972.

17. See James W. Wilkie, *Measuring Land Reform* (Los Angeles: UCLA Latin American Center Publications, 1974), p. 57.

18. Christopher Mitchell, *The Legacy of Populism in Bolivia: From the MNR to Military Rule* (New York: Praeger, 1977), p. vii.

19. James M. Malloy, *Bolivia: The Uncompleted Revolution* (Pittsburgh: University of Pittsburgh Press, 1970), pp. 309-310.

20. Ibid., pp. 340-341.

21. Such a statement does not necessarily deny the desirability of government sponsorship of plural cultures. Problems of regional culture will have to be worked out as Bolivia attempts to provide basic literacy training for its scattered, rural Indian-speaking population which exists often completely or very much outside of modern technological society. Curiously, in the first quotation of Malloy above, Malloy seems not concerned with this issue, but with implicitly, if not explicitly, condemning Paz Estenssoro's attempt to establish central government authority at the expense of regional caudillos. In order to have prevented the imposition of a "democratic bourgeois model," would Malloy have had Paz Estenssoro *not* bring the regions under "national" control?

22. Bolivia is not as politically free as Mexico, which has regular elections to validate the continued resolution of Mexico's permanent crises by the Revolutionary Institutional Party (PRI), but it is more free politically than Cuba, which continues to hold thousands of political prisoners. On the case of Mexico, see James W. Wilkie, "Mexico: Permanent 'Revolution,' Permanent 'Crisis,'" *Los Angeles Times,* December 5, 1976, p. VIII-17. On the case of Cuba, see Norman Luxenburg, "Facts on [Cuban] Political Prisoners Ignored," *Times of the Americas,* June 7, 1978. According to James S. Landberg, political-economic officer of the U.S. Embassy in La Paz, in 1977 Bolivia had between 75 and 150 political prisoners--interview La Paz, July 13, 1977.

23. Too, in light of democratic failure in such "politically advanced" countries as Chile and Uruguay one may ask without condoning political dictatorship the following question: How can Bolivia be expected to have achieved more political development in a country

of less education and economic amenities than its "advanced" neighbors where democracy failed in the 1970s?

24. Kenneth F. Johnson, "Research Perspectives on the Revised Fitzgibbon-Johnson Index of the Image of Political Democracy in Latin America, 1945-1975," in James W. Wilkie and Kenneth Ruddle, eds., *Quantitative Latin American Studies: Methods and Findings* (Los Angeles: UCLA Latin American Center Publications, 1977), p. 90.

25. This problem is not as serious as the author envisaged that it might become in earlier writings. Appendix F shows that by 1976 the ratio of Bolivia's external debt service to value of exports was only 16.7 percent, up from 11 percent in 1970, but down from 27.6 percent in 1960. In 1976 the record compared favorably to five countries with higher percentages, three of which had ratios of 30 percent or more.

26. See James W. Wilkie, *The Bolivian Revolution and U.S. Aid Since 1952* (Los Angeles: UCLA Latin American Center Publications, 1969) and Wilkie, "Public Expenditure Since 1952," op. cit., with regard to expenditure of aid by function, the former work examines in Table 3 the role of AID per se, whereas the latter defines it in the same terms as Table VI-1, column A, here.

27. For an important test of U.S. liberal views in another case, see Enrique A. Baloyra, "Democratic *versus* Dictatorial Budgeting: The Case of Cuba with Reference to Venezuela and Mexico," in James W. Wilkie, ed., *Money and Politics in Latin America* (Los Angeles: UCLA Latin American Center Publications, 1977), chapter 1.

28. Cf. Marcel Quiroga Santa Cruz, *El Saqueo de Bolivia* (Buenos Aires: Ediciones de CRISIS, 1973).

29. Interview by Edna Monzón de Wilkie and the author with Douglas Henderson, Los Angeles, June 24-25, 1970. Henderson said that by 1964 Paz Estenssoro had completely politicized the Bolivian scene to the detriment of the country; thus in his view Paz's fall in the 1964 military coup by General René Barrientos was justified, especially because Barrientos was "personally stable, aware of economic complexities, and politically open to resolve the country's problems." According to Henderson, Paz Estenssoro, who rose to power after years of conspiring to overthrow the old regime, always continued to live with a mood of suspicion, being distrustful of others and always balancing potential competitors against each other.

30. Interview with James S. Landberg, La Paz, July 13, 1977.

31. E. Boyd Wennergren and Morris D. Whitaker, "Social Return to U.S. Technical Assistance in Bolivian Agriculture: The Case of Sheep and Wheat," *American Journal of Agricultural Economics* 59 (1977), p. 568. These authors also note (p. 568) the 1968 view of consultant Delworth B. Gardner that "a significant reduction in Bolivia's relatively large imports of wheat is possible within a ten-year period if improved varieties, which have produced relatively high yields under experimental conditions in Bolivia, could be generally extended to farmers. His analysis indicates that, for wheat to become competitive with other crops, yields at the farm level have to double.

Also, land area in wheat would have to double, and more than 80 percent of all land in wheat would have to be planted to improve varieties in order for imports to be reduced by 50 percent in ten years."

For some examples of AID success, however, see Cornelius Zondag, *The Bolivian Economy, 1952-1965* (New York: Praeger, 1966), Chapter 16.

32. Shirley Christian, "Bolivia Awaits Reaction to Coup;" *Idaho Statesman* (Boise), July 24, 1978. According to Christian, the United States had approved an 85 million dollar aid package when Banzer was wavering on elections, then stopped the signing of the agreement until the new government could be elected and installed. The U.S. Department of State/Washington Bolivia Desk officer, however, was unaware of such an agreement (telephone conversation, Nov. 13, 1978).

33. The figure is from the *Los Angeles Times*, August 9, 1978. According to the U.S. Department of State/Washington Bolivia Desk (telephone conversation November 13, 1978), although 1978 military assistance was suspended, it may be renewed for 1979.

34. It can be argued that in agriculture Bolivia is short of technobureaucrats and administrative efficiency and that the country has failed to build a fertilizer plant, but U.S. government technicians have not helped this situation much either, as we saw in Utah State University problems with AID. Bolivia would be better off contracting directly with foreign experts rather than using AID officials as brokers to do so. In any case, some countries such as Mexico, Cuba, and the Soviet Union seem to have an imbalance of *técnicos* in urban compared to rural affairs, the problem does not seem to be uniquely a Bolivian one.

APPENDIX A

FACTORS FOR ANALYZING BOLIVIAN DEVELOPMENT, 1948-1976

| | A. | B. | C. | D. | | E. | |
| | | | | Bolivia's Actual Military Expenditure | | Bolivian Central Govt. Actual Expenditure | |
Year	U.S. Export Price Index (1951=100)	Real U.S. Total Outlay To Bolivia Million Dollars	Real Bolivian Trade Balance[a] Million Dollars of 1951	Million Pesos	Million Dollars[b]	Military	Education Percent
1948	97	6.6	45.5	.4	4.4	22.9	22.5
1949	91	4.0	27.1	.5	4.2	26.2	20.2
1950	87	1.7	44.1	.6	4.6	25.8	22.0
1951	100	7.9	64.8	.9	4.3	24.7	20.6
1952	99	6.0	49.2	1.0	3.6	23.0	23.7
1953	99	4.7	45.1	1.2	1.3	13.7	18.8
1954	98	15.1	34.7	1.7	.9	11.4	16.9
1955	99	12.5	20.2	3.3	.8	12.8	16.0
1956	102	27.1	22.9	6.7	.9	8.7	22.0
1957	105	26.9	7.0	18	2.2	6.7	9.7
1958	105	24.7	-14.1	28	2.9	8.6	12.3
1959	105	22.1	12.0	38	3.2	10.6	13.6
1960	106	16.9	- 3.4	39	3.3	10.9	15.7
1961	108	16.0	- 1.4	51	4.3	12.3	14.4
1962	107	28.3	-19.4	61	5.1	13.5	15.8
1963	107	37.0	-15.8	68	5.7	13.5	17.1
1964	108	57.5	10.3	80	6.7	13.9	15.8
1965	112	20.9	- 1.8	140	11.8	18.3	21.0
1966	113	19.2	10.6	141	11.9	18.0	24.4
1967	117	22.8	13.1	143	12.0	15.5	31.4
1968	119	29.7	14.9	144	12.1	14.1	31.0
1969	123	16.7	27.0	153	12.9	14.7	32.4
1970	130	30.9	51.1	197	16.6	15.8	30.0
1971	134	17.0	34.6	187	15.7	13.4	30.2

(continued)

APPENDIX A (continued)

	A.	B.	C.	D.		E.	
		Real U.S.	Real Bolivian	Bolivia's Actual Military		Bolivian Central Govt.	
	U.S. Export	Total Outlay	Trade	Expenditure		Actual Expenditure	
	Price Index	To Bolivia	Balance^a			Military	Education
Year	(1951=100)	Million Dollars of 1951		Million Pesos	Million Dollars^b	Percent	
1972	138	33.3	39.9	272	20.6	14.8	26.4
1973	160	15.3	68.1	492	24.6	17.4	24.7
1974	204	11.7	127.7	839	42.0	16.1	25.1
1975	229	8.1	-15.9	1,157	58.0	18.4	23.4
1976	238	15.8	24.5	1,325	66.3	16.6	23.1

a Exports and imports on CIF basis, except imports FOB through Sept. 1954.

b Converted with exchange rate given in Table VI-2, above.

Source:

A. James W. Wilkie and Peter Reich (eds.), *Statistical Abstract of Latin America*, Vol. 19 (Los Angeles: UCLA Latin American Center Publications, 1978), table 2506, base converted here. See also James W. Wilkie, *Statistics and National Policy* (Los Angeles: UCLA Latin American Center Publications, 1974), p. 80.

B. Data in column A in Table VI-1, above, divided by data in column A, here.

C. Data in the following sources divided by data in column A here: Wilkie, *Statistics and National Policy*, op. cit., p. 80; Bolivia, Banco Central, *Boletín estadístico*, septiembre, 1976, p. 54; and International Monetary Fund, *International Financial Statistics*; February, 1978.

D-E. James W. Wilkie, *Bolivian Revolution and U.S. Aid Since 1952* (Los Angeles: UCLA Latin American Center Publications, 1969), Appendix N; AID/Bolivia, *Estadísticas económicas*, Vol. 14, p. 33; Bolivia, Banco Central, *Memoria*, p. 24-B; and Bolivia, Banco Central, *Boletín estadístico*, marzo, 1977.

APPENDIX B

ALTERNATIVE ESTIMATES OF CHANGE IN
BOLIVIAN GROSS DOMESTIC PRODUCT
1946–1976

(In Constant Prices of 1970)

| | Percentage Change | |
| | A. | B. |
Year	Estimate by ECLA	Estimate by IMF
1946	1.8	N.A.
1947	1.7	N.A.
1948	2.1	N.A.
1949	2.1	N.A.
1950	2.1	N.A.
1951	7.1	N.A.
1952	3.0	N.A.
1953	-9.5	-9.5
1954	2.1	2.1
1955	5.3	5.3
1956	-5.9	-5.9
1957	-3.3	-3.3
1958	2.4	2.4
1959	- .3	- .3
1960	4.3	4.3
1961	2.1	1.3
1962	5.6	2.4
1963	6.4	6.8
1964	4.8	4.0
1965	4.9	4.6
1966	7.2	7.2
1967	6.2	6.3
1968	8.5	8.4
1969	4.5	4.6
1970	5.2	5.3
1971	3.8	3.8
1972	5.1	5.9[a]
1973	6.9	6.9
1974	6.7	6.1
1975	6.8	5.5
1976	6.9	6.5

N.A. - Not available

[a]Revised series begins, and converted to 1975 prices.

Source: A. UN, Comisión Económica para América Latina (ECLA), *Series históricas de crecimiento de América Latina* (Santiago: Cuadernos estadísticos de la CEPAL, 1978), pp. 15–19. Estimated on dollar basis.

B. James W. Wilkie and Peter Reich, eds., *Statistical Abstract of Latin America*, Vol. 19 (Los Angeles: UCLA Latin American Center Publications, 1978), table 2203, updated with revisions since 1972 calculated from International Monetary Fund, *International Financial Statistics*, Oct., 1978. Estimated on peso basis.

APPENDIX C
VALUE AND VOLUME OF BOLIVIAN TIN EXPORTS,
1948-1977

Year	Millions of Dollars	Index: 1975 = 100 Unit Value[a]	Index: 1975 = 100 Volume
1948	80.2	32	154
1949	72.8	32	140
1950	63.4	30	129
1951	93.4	40[b]	135[b]
1952	84.7	38	129
1953	72.6	30	142
1954	60.1	30	118
1955	57.3	29	114
1956	59.2	32	110
1957	57.4	30	113
1958	36.4	29	72
1959	52.9	32	98
1960	42.9	32	79
1961	50.6	35	84
1962	54.0	36	88
1963	57.3	36	93
1964	80.9	48	98
1965	93.0	56	97
1966	93.3	52	105
1967	90.9	48	110
1968	92.5	46	118
1969	102.5	50	120
1970	108.1	56	112
1971	105.9	51	122
1972	113.5	54	122
1973	131.0	66	114
1974	230.1	116	116
1975	171.4	100	100
1976	216.1	110	115
1977	326.9	152	124

[a] Unit value equals reported value data divided by reported volume data.

[b] Change in methodology.

Source: International Monetary Fund, *International Financial Statistics*, Supplement 1972, May 1976, May 1977, May 1978, and Oct. 1978. Index base standardized for 1975 here.

APPENDIX D

VOLUME AND VALUE OF BOLIVIAN CRUDE PETROLEUM AND NATURAL GAS EXPORTS, 1955–1977

	Crude Petroleum			Natural Gas		
	Millions of	Index: 1975=100		Millions of	Index: 1975=100	
Year	Dollars	Unit Value[a]	Volume	Dollars	Unit Value[a]	Volume
1955	1.7[b]	27	6			
1956	1.9	26	6			
1957	3.6	26	12			
1958	4.3	28	14			
1959	3.1	25	11			
1960	3.4	25	12			
1961	1.9	22	8			
1962	1.3	19	6			
1963	1.6	23	6			
1964	.6	19	3			
1965	.7	19	3			
1966	6.5	17	35			
1967	22.9	17	121			
1968	24.3	17	125			
1969	23.0	18	117			
1970	13.2	22	55			
1971	23.9	22	99			
1972	31.7	22	128	9.9[c]	36	65
1973	48.9	32	139	18.1	42	101
1974	163.9	117	126	29.2	69	99
1975	111.4	100	100	42.5	100	100
1976	112.6	107	94	54.9	128	101
1977	67.4	115	53	66.8	149	105

[a] Unit value equals reported value data divided by reported volume data.

[b] Crude petroleum exports did not round to 1 million dollars prior to 1955.

[c] Natural gas exports did not round to 1 million dollars prior to 1972.

Source: International Monetary Fund, *International Financial Statistics*, May 1971, May 1978, Oct. 1978. Index base standardized for 1975 here.

APPENDIX E

U.S. PUBLIC LAW 480 FOOD ASSISTANCE TO BOLIVIA,[a]
1955–1977
(Actual Expenditure)

Fiscal Year	Millions of Dollars
1955	6.2
1956	6.5
1957	2.1
1958	0
1959	.2
1960	.2
1961	.3
1962	6.0
1963	10.5
1964	11.1
1965	6.4
1966	6.8
1967	7.0
1968	4.3
1969	4.1
1970	6.2
1971	2.1
1972	6.2
1973	3.0
1974	15.1
1975	4.8
1976	4.9
1977	6.3

[a]Data included in Table VI-1, column B, above.

Source: James W. Wilkie, *Statistics and National Policy*, (Los Angeles: UCLA Latin American Center Publications, 1974), p. 369; and U.S. Department of Agriculture, Economic Research Service, *Foreign Agricultural Trade of the United States*, April 1976, March 1977, and January 1978.

APPENDIX F

RATIO OF LATIN AMERICA'S EXTERNAL DEBT SERVICE TO VALUE OF EXPORTS OF MERCHANDISE AND SERVICES, 1960-1976
(Percent)

Country	1960	1970	1976
Argentina	20.5	21.7	18.3
Bolivia	27.6	11.0	16.7
Brazil	38.7	14.3	15.2
Chile	14.2	18.7	33.0
Colombia	13.9	11.8	9.5
Costa Rica	4.8	10.0	9.4
Cuba	N.A.	N.A.	N.A.
Dominican Republic	N.A.	5.1	6.1
Ecuador	7.1	8.9	5.8
El Salvador	2.6	3.5	4.2
Guatemala	1.5	7.4	1.9
Haiti	3.6	7.5	8.6
Honduras	2.8	3.0	6.3
Mexico	15.5	24.1	33.2
Nicaragua	3.8	10.6	12.3
Panama	1.6	7.6	12.2
Paraguay	6.8	11.2	9.0
Peru	10.5	13.7	21.6
Uruguay	5.8	21.7	29.5
Venezuela	4.4	2.9	4.1

N.A. - Not available.

Source: Inter-American Development Bank, *Economic and Social Progress in Latin America* (Washington, D.C., 1977), p. 440.

APPENDIX G
U.S. AMBASSADORS TO BOLIVIA SINCE 1946[a]

Assumption of Office	Name
April 27, 1946	Joseph Flack
November 19, 1949	Irving Florman
December 14, 1951	Edward J. Sparks
October 11, 1954	Gerald A. Drew
March 28, 1957	Philip W. Bonsal
April 8, 1959	Carl W. Strom
June 24, 1961	Ben S. Stephansky
December 3, 1963	Douglas Henderson
September 3, 1968	Raul Hector Castro
November 19, 1969	Ernest V. Siracusa
October 3, 1973	William P. Stedman
October 14, 1977	Paul H. Boeker

[a]For prior years from 1928, see James W. Wilkie, *The Bolivian Revolution and U.S. Aid Since 1952* (Los Angeles: UCLA Latin American Publications, 1969), p. 77.

Source: U.S. Embassy/La Paz and U.S. Department of State/ Washington Bolivia Desk.

Chapter VII

Bolivian Relations with Chile and Peru: Hopes and Realities
E. James Holland

INTRODUCTION

Bolivian relations with Chile and Peru since the fall of Paz Estenssoro's government in 1964 have carried forward many of the themes which have characterized these contacts for decades. The consequences of the War of the Pacific (1879-1883) remain contentious issues in this triad of bilateral relationships and continue to prejudice the processes for resolving the problems between these bordering states. In this respect, the 1964-1977 period does not differ markedly from previous ones.

At the same time, noteworthy developments in these relations have taken place in recent years, and it is upon such areas of movement and change in Bolivian relations with its Pacific neighbors that this study focuses. Emphasis will be given to the political dimension of these relations, especially in regard to recent negotiations concerning Bolivia's maritime aspirations. Secondarily, the study indicates how the Bolivian concern with its landlocked status influences diplomatic activities relating to other important issues of security, trade, and development.

The general nature of Bolivian relations with Chile since 1964 is suggested by the fact that for most of the period under consideration formal diplomatic relations were broken between the two countries.[1] The decision to restore full diplomatic relations at the ambassadorial level for the first time since April 1962 was announced in an official communiqué emanating from a meeting between Chilean President Augusto Pinochet Ugarte and Bolivian President Hugo Banzer Suárez held at Charaña, Bolivia, on February 8, 1975. Contact between the governments had been maintained in the interim by various means, including the maintenance of consular staffs in La Paz and Santiago, occasional meetings of joint commissions established to treat common problems, and the participation by representatives of both countries in regional and international organizations. It should be noted, also, that in spite of the continuing controversy with Santiago with respect to obtaining a sovereign outlet on the Pacific, Bolivia's trade and transportation ties with Chile constitute the basis for a perpetual and natural relationship between the two countries.[2]

Within this context of ruptured diplomatic relations, their political differences did not prevent the two countries from joining in efforts to promote regional economic integration in the Andean integration movement and, by the late 1960s, from assuming compatible positions in favor of a Latin American front in relations with the United States.[3] Presidents Alfredo Ovando Candia and Juan José Torres responded favorably to Chilean support of the nationalization of Bolivian Gulf Oil Company in 1969 and to Chileanization of United States-owned copper industries.

Serious differences in domestic and foreign policy directions arose, however, in Bolivian relations with the Allende government after the leftist nationalist Torres regime in La Paz was replaced by a military government led by Colonel Hugo Banzer Suárez. The strong anti-Marxist posture of the Banzer government led to divergent Bolivian and Chilean positions on relations with Washington and Cuba. Frequent charges, also, were made in La Paz that leftist Bolivian exiles in Chile were organizing to overthrow the Banzer government.[4] Relations improved after the fall of Allende in September 1973, leading to the restoration of diplomatic relations in 1975.

Bolivian relations with Peru throughout the period generally were more amicable than with Chile. Normal diplomatic relations were maintained, and the two governments worked cooperatively through joint commissions on a number of development projects. Bolivian government leaders in 1969 expressed great admiration for the vigorous nationalist leadership of the military government of Peru under General Juan Velasco Alvarado, especially in such actions as the nationalization of the International Petroleum Company in 1968.[5] However, the improvement in Bolivian-Chilean relations in 1975 and subsequent bilateral discussions between La Paz and Santiago on ways of resolving Bolivia's maritime problem placed some stress on relations with Peru.

INTERNATIONAL CONTEXT

Bolivian relations with Chile and Peru exist within the complex context of the international relationships maintained by these three countries. Selected features of this context deserve brief consideration due to their special relevance for ties between La Paz, Santiago, and Lima.

Bolivia

It is important to note initially that Bolivia, Chile, and Peru together contend with a relatively large number of neighboring countries. Bolivia and Peru have frontiers with five states; Chile counts three adjacent states. In fact, all but two of South America's principal countries (Uruguay, Venezuela) have a common boundary with Bolivia, Chile, or Peru. This situation suggests numerous possibilities for conflict and cooperation for each of these countries in their relationships with adjoining states. At the same time, the attention given by foreign policy-makers in La Paz, Santiago, and Lima to their mutual relationships seldom is undivided, usually contending simultaneously with issues in relations with other neighbors.

The long-standing conflicts with Chile have inclined La Paz more and more to its powerful neighbors to the east, Argentina and Brazil. Since the Chaco War, numerous trade and assistance agreements have been signed with the Argentine government that have assisted in the development of important highway, railway, and pipeline links between the two countries. Among Bolivia's neighbors, Argentina is the most significant trading partner, purchasing to date all of its natural gas exports. Under the Banzer government, Bolivian-Brazilian relations expanded significantly, taking the form of agreements in which this richer and larger neighbor agreed to lend substantial financial and technical assistance for Bolivian pipeline, railway, and industrial projects in return for natural gas, other natural resources, and access to the production from newly developed Bolivian industries. [6]

These close relations with Argentina and Brazil are important in La Paz for a variety of reasons, not the least of which is the desire to have support in Brasilia and Buenos Aires for Bolivia's policy of obtaining sovereign access on the Pacific. Although significant domestic opposition to closer ties with Brazil exists in Bolivia, these relations are important, also, in offsetting somewhat the traditional Brazilian-Chilean friendship based upon a common interest in containing Argentine influence.

In a wider context, Bolivia has vigorously sought support for its policy of maritime reintegration from other Latin American countries in bilateral and multilateral relations. One of the characteristic tactics of Bolivian diplomacy is to utilize the international forums provided by regional and global international organizations to present its case for territorial realignment on the Pacific. Bolivian relations with the United States since 1964 generally have been friendly, although ties with Washington were strained in the 1969-1971 period when properties owned by U.S. companies were nationalized and the "revolutionary nationalism" of the Torres regime assumed strident anti-U.S. overtones.

Chile

Robert N. Burr's study of Chilean foreign relations during the nineteenth and early twentieth centuries demonstrates the importance of Chilean relations with Argentina and Brazil in its quest to maintain a favorable power position on the Pacific Coast. [7] Chilean relations with Brazil's military government have improved since 1973 under the Pinochet government. However, in recent years, a boundary dispute with Argentina involving islands in the Beagle Channel has troubled relations with Buenos Aires and has escalated into a serious problem in their bilateral relations.

The tension level in Chilean relations with Peru has increased precipitously on several occasions during the past decade as Peruvian purchases of tanks, aircraft, and other military equipment from the Soviet Union, France, and elsewhere have installed Peru as the leading military power on the Pacific Coast of South America. [8] This disturbing development was taking place as periodic rumors circulated of Peruvian plans to regain the territories lost to Chile in the War of the Pacific by the one-hundredth anniversary of the outbreak of the conflict in 1979.

Chile also has faced strong criticism from democratic and socialist segments of the international community for the harsh repressive measures taken against Allende supporters and sympathizers by the military junta that assumed power in September 1973. In recent years, international human rights organizations and human rights commissions of the United Nations and the Organization of American States frequently have called upon the junta to desist from violating the fundamental human and civil rights of persons detained by the new government. Measures taken by the United States and British governments in 1974, in disapproval of human rights violations, made it difficult for Chile to obtain military equipment from these sources to keep pace with Peru. The repressive domestic policy and the independent economic strategies employed by the new military government since 1973 have created difficult relations with many of the countries of Latin America, with the notable exceptions of Brazil and Uruguay.

Peru

Following its humiliating defeat by Chile in the War of the Pacific, Peru devoted its attention during much of the first half of the twentieth century to serious territorial disputes with Colombia and Ecuador, disputes which still trouble relations with the latter state. As Peru has developed the oil resources of its rich northeastern jungle region, government leaders have followed closely Brazilian westward development efforts approaching the Peruvian border. In 1974, after completing arms purchases from the Soviet Union, Lima expressed concern about Brazilian efforts to form an anti-communist axis across the continent with Uruguay, Bolivia, and Chile.[9] Nevertheless, relations with Brazil are proper, and Peru has agreed to join with Brazil, Bolivia, Colombia, and Ecuador in a pact for the economic integration of the Amazon basin. Peru in the late 1970s enjoys friendly relations with both the United States and the Soviet Union, and has gained some prominence in international circles through its efforts to exert leadership among Third World countries.[10]

It is within this wider international context that Bolivian relations with Chile and Peru must be studied. The fundamental problem in these relations is Bolivia's insistence upon obtaining a sovereign seaport on the Pacific.

THE PRINCIPAL PROBLEM

The principal problem in Bolivian relations with Chile and Peru is the apparently unrelenting aspiration in the *Altiplano* to establish again a sovereign territorial presence on the Pacific Ocean. The developments in this fundamental issue since 1964 hold some promise for being of lasting significance. As such, they merit attention. A review of some of the high points in the evolution of the problem sets the stage for this latest round.

Background

A number of studies have carefully traced the history of Bolivian relations with Chile and Peru, especially in regard to the problem of Bolivia's landlocked status.[11] Therefore, the purpose of this brief section is simply to make reference to several of the major agreements and diplomatic exchanges which have been significant in the long development of the portuary issue.

Following the military victories by Chilean forces in the years from 1879 until 1883 and the Chilean occupation of the Bolivian littoral and the Peruvian provinces of Tarapaca, Arica, and Tacna, an uneasy peace was reestablished on the Pacific through agreements reached by Santiago with Peru and Bolivia. The Treaty of Ancon with Peru, signed on October 20, 1883, ceded to Chile "in perpetuity and unconditionally" the conquered province of Tarapacá, but postponed a definitive decision on the provinces of Arica and Tacna by providing for a future plebiscite to determine if the territories were to be Chilean or Peruvian.[12]

Bolivia signed a formal pact of truce with Chile almost six months later which left the victorious nation in complete possession of Bolivia's Atacama Desert coastal region, but did not acknowledge its final cession to Santiago. For many of the next twenty years, Chile and Bolivia sought ways to resolve the territorial problems derived from the war, not the least of which was Bolivia's insistence upon an outlet to the Pacific. Although much discussion took place during this period with respect to the possibility of granting the disputed Peruvian provinces of Arica and Tacna to Bolivia, no definitive agreements of this type could be implemented in the face of strong opposition from Peruvian leaders. Confronted by a powerful adversary in Santiago, which itself appeared to have limited options for granting Bolivia a Pacific outlet, the La Paz government signed a formal peace treaty with Chile on October 20, 1904. The essential terms of the treaty included Bolivia's cession of its coastal territory to Chile in return for the construction by Chile of a railroad linking Arica to La Paz. Chile, also, granted Bolivia free transit in perpetuity for its commerce across Chilean territory and the right to build customs houses in designated Chilean ports, including Arica and Antofagasta.[13]

Successive Bolivian governments after 1904 continued pressing for some arrangement with Peru and Chile which would provide the landlocked Andean nation a sovereign seaport on the Pacific, but without effect. While the Tacna-Arica question remained unsettled, both Bolivia and Peru presented separate requests to the League of Nations in 1920 to revise their respective peace treaties with Chile on the grounds that they were incompatible with the newly adopted international principle of non-recognition of the rights of territorial conquest, only to find that the League was not prepared to involve itself in matters of treaty revision.[14] Bolivian hopes were raised in 1926 when United States Secretary of State Frank B. Kellogg proposed on November 30 that the Tacna-Arica impasse between Chile and Peru be resolved by ceding both provinces to Bolivia, a suggestion which, when rejected in Santiago and Lima, soon led to the end of United States "good offices" in the dispute.[15]

In June 1929, Chile and Peru reached an agreement on the Tacna-Arica question providing for the cession of Arica to Chile and the return of Tacna to Peru. An additional agreement entered into by the two parties by means of a secret Supplementary Protocol provided that neither Chile nor Peru, "without previous agreement between them," would cede to any third party all or part of the territories allocated by the principal treaty.[16] By virtue of the secret protocol, the tripartite nature of any subsequent discussions of a sovereign Bolivian seaport on the Pacific in the provinces of Tacna or Arica was assured. However, in 1937, the Bolivian government narrowed its options for obtaining access to the Pacific by signing a treaty with Peru in which it relinquished any future claims to Peruvian territory. Since that time Bolivia has sought to satisfy its maritime aspirations primarily through discussions with Chile. The territorial settlements made in the treaties of 1883, 1904 and 1929 are shown in Fig. VII-1.[17]

Consistently, but with varying degrees of intensity, Bolivian governments since the Chaco War have stated the nation's position in favor of obtaining a sovereign port on the Pacific as a means of promoting economic development, assuring national independence, and establishing international justice. Chilean responses to these Bolivian overtures have ranged from a hard line position asserting that no territorial questions were pending between the two countries to a more flexible position involving, at least, the expression of a willingness to discuss the problem with La Paz.

An example of the more flexible line was contained in a diplomatic note from Chilean Foreign Minister Horacio Walker Larraín, dated June 20, 1950. In his reply to a note from the Bolivian ambassador in Santiago, Alberto Ostria Gutiérrez, requesting direct bilateral negotiations on the portuary problem, Walker Larraín stated that "my government , , , animated by a spirit of fraternal friendship toward Bolivia, is ready to enter formally into direct negotiations designed to find a formula that can make it possible to give Bolivia its own sovereign outlet to the Pacific Ocean and for Chile to obtain compensation of a non-territorial character and consis-

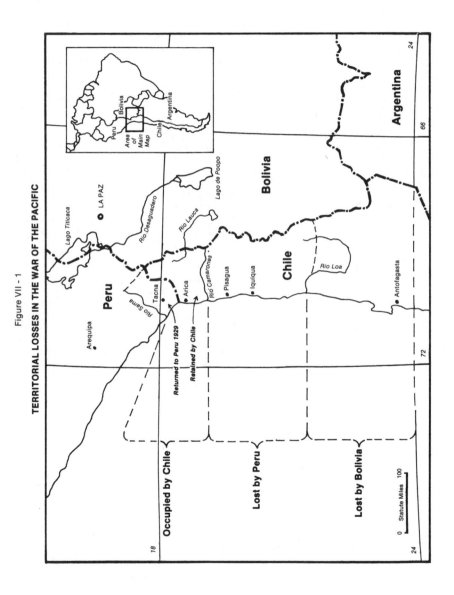

Figure VII - 1

TERRITORIAL LOSSES IN THE WAR OF THE PACIFIC

tent with its real interests."[18]   The ensuing discussions ended when Peruvian objections were raised vigorously to a plan under consideration which would have granted Bolivia a corridor to the Pacific north of Arica in exchange for giving Chile access to the waters of Lake Titicaca on the Bolivian-Peruvian border.[19]

A similar willingness on the part of the Chilean government to discuss Bolivia's maritime problem apparently was displayed in July 1961, when the Chilean ambassador in La Paz, Manuel Trucco, delivered an *aide memoire* to the Bolivian Foreign Ministry reiterating Chilean readiness to discuss the question of Bolivia's sovereign access on the Pacific and making reference to the Walker Larraín note of June 1950.[20]   Apparently, the Chilean Foreign Office had grown concerned about reports that Bolivia was planning to raise the maritime issue at the eleventh Inter-American Conference scheduled that year in Quito and to insert the principle of maritime reintegration into a new constitution.   However, Santiago rejected ensuing Bolivian efforts to link discussions involving a current dispute over Chilean use of the waters of the Lauca River with the issue of a port for Bolivia.   When La Paz, early in 1962, attempted to follow up on the Chilean offer to discuss the maritime question contained in the Trucco communication, it received a chilly reception in Santiago.   The Chilean Foreign Minister, Carlos Martínez Sotomayor, indicated that talks regarding the Lauca waters should be pursued with the understanding that the dispute was entirely separate from the port question.[21]

Faced with failure in seeking to use the Lauca issue in efforts to achieve a settlement with Chile on the port question, Bolivia carried its case in the Lauca dispute to the Council of the Organization of American States (OAS) early in April 1962, a decision that eventually led to a rupture in diplomatic relations with Santiago on April 16.[22]   In September, Bolivia withdrew from participation in the political and administrative activities of the OAS in protest over the council's refusal to take more decisive action in resolving the Lauca River dispute.

Irked by the Bolivian escalation of the Lauca dispute, the Chilean Foreign Office adopted a firm stand against discussions on the port question.   In March 1963, Chilean Foreign Minister Martínez Sotomayor accused Bolivia of having used the Lauca dispute simply to "raise its portuary problem."   In an address on March 27, he assailed the domestic public agitation in Bolivia directed against Chile, claimed that relations had been worsened by the diplomatic strategy employed by La Paz, and stated that "the good disposition" of Chile in favor of bilateral discussions on the outlet issue no longer existed.[23]

Thus, one aspect of the legacy of Bolivian diplomacy from the revolutionary period was the relatively poor state of relations with Chile.   The military junta that assumed power in La Paz in November 1964, confronted a situation in which diplomatic relations with Santiago were not only broken, but the Chileans, also, had assumed a posture whereby they were unwilling to talk with Bolivia about the latter's portuary objectives.

Until 1974 the two governments remained firm in their postures assumed on the portuary question in 1962 and 1963.   Successive Bolivian governments wanted Chile to agree to enter into bilateral discussions regarding the sovereign outlet issue as a condition for restoring full diplomatic relations and pursuing final settlement of the Lauca River dispute. Santiago continued to maintain that no territorial issues were pending in its relations with Bolivia, but that it was prepared, at any time, to enter into discussions with La Paz on ways to improve transportation facilities and procedures for Bolivian shipments across its territory and through its ports.[24]

During the years of Barrientos's leadership, the maritime issue maintained its visibility through the annual "Week of the Sea" celebration in

March and by consistent Bolivian efforts to place the item on the agenda of various inter-American meetings of foreign ministers.[25] Barrientos dramatized the problem in 1967 when he refused to attend the April meeting of American chiefs of state at Punta del Este, Uruguay, as a symbolic protest of the refusal by western hemisphere leaders to consider Bolivia's landlocked status. However, the disputes with Chile did not prevent the Bolivian government from entering into negotiations in 1967 with Chile, Colombia, Ecuador, Peru, and Venezuela on the formation of the Andean sub-regional group or from adhering to the Declaration of Bogota the same year. Enthusiastic Chilean support for the Andean integration movement, coupled with statements by Chilean Foreign Minister Gabriel Valdés that regional cooperation would minimize the differences between the two countries, did prompt concern among some Bolivian leaders that Santiago would attempt to propose regional integration as the more practical solution to Bolivia's maritime problem, thus making a sovereign port unnecessary.[26]

Although relations with Chile grew somewhat more cordial during the relatively brief presidencies of Alfredo Ovando Candia (1969-1970) and Juan José Torres (1970-1971), little progress was made in either restoring full diplomatic relations or in sustaining talks on the principal problem between the countries. Soon after the military government led by Colonel Hugo Banzer Suárez was established in August 1971, Bolivia's Foreign Minister Mario Gutiérrez Gutiérrez made it clear that his country's basic foreign policy objective of obtaining a sovereign port on the Pacific by means of direct discussions with Chile remained the same.[27]

Resumption of Diplomatic Relations

The overthrow of the Allende regime in September 1973 and the establishment of Chile's first military government in forty-one years created a situation somewhat more conducive to improving Bolivian-Chilean relations. Strongly anti-Marxist, military regimes had assumed the responsibilities of governance in Santiago and La Paz and were confronted with serious economic problems, domestic unrest, and international criticism of its treatment of political opponents. The Chilean junta contended with a serious image problem in the international community, a growing military inferiority vis-à-vis Peru, boundary differences with Argentina, and broken diplomatic relations with Bolivia.

In March 1974 Bolivian President Banzer and Chilean President Pinochet met for talks while in Brasilia attending the inauguration of Brazilian President General Ernesto Geisel. Denying that the port issue had been discussed, both presidents stated that they had reviewed basic problems in the relations between their two countries with the objective of opening the way to closer ties between them.[28] However, reports of a proposal by Brazilian President Geisel for a solution to Bolivia's landlocked situation by way of a narrow corridor across Chile prompted increased speculation that a new round of discussions on the matter was in the offing.

Within Bolivia, President Banzer moved to unify domestic support for his government around the port issue. In April 1974 he convened a national meeting of consultation in Cochabamba bringing together political leaders of various persuasions to urge national unity behind efforts to solve the portuary problem as the first step toward national development. The national consultative meeting adopted a declaration identifying the return to the sea as the nation's most important objective and agreeing not to place pressure on the government while it was organizing to confront the challenge of maritime reintegration.[29]

Bolivian relations with Chile improved somewhat during the year. Discussions were held through a Joint Commission on Transportation that culminated in an agreement in early November on ways to improve the transit of Bolivian goods through Chilean ports. [30] Although the Chilean government apparently hoped to avoid facing the maritime question with Bolivia, closer ties with La Paz were important for the Pinochet government at this time. Reports of Peruvian purchases of Soviet tanks and the presence in Peru of Soviet military technicians worried the Chilean military government. The possibility of a Peruvian attack was raised frequently in the Chilean press, in spite of denials of any such plans from Lima. [31] Obviously a friendly and neutral Bolivia would be important should military conflict occur.

The regional arms races were a major topic of discussion among the chief executives and other representatives of eight Latin American countries, including President Banzer and Peruvian President Juan Velasco Alvarado, who gathered at Ayacucho, Peru, on December 9, 1974, to commemorate the one-hundred-fiftieth anniversary of the Battle of Ayacucho. The Declaration of Ayacucho signed on that date pledged the signatory nations to limit their armaments and to refrain from acquiring offensive weapons. In the multi-faceted declaration, President Banzer also managed to obtain a promise from the participants to show the greatest understanding of the landlocked situation affecting Bolivia, a problem described as demanding the most considerate attention and constructive understanding. The acceptance of this pledge by President Velasco and the representative of Chile was an encouraging signal to Bolivian leaders, who interpreted the action as a commitment from the two countries to view favorably Bolivian portuary needs. [32]

The decision to restore full diplomatic relations between the two countries was made at a presidential meeting held in the Bolivian frontier town of Charaña on February 8, 1975. In the official communiqué emanating from the meeting it was reported that the two presidents had agreed to "continue the dialogue at different levels" in seeking solutions "to the vital matters facing both countries such as the landlocked situation affecting Bolivia within a framework of reciprocal convenience and attending to the desires of the Chilean and Bolivian peoples." [33] The statement concluded by saying that in order to obtain these objectives, the presidents had decided to normalize diplomatic relations at the ambassadorial level.

While the decision to restore diplomatic relations between Bolivia and Chile was acclaimed in Santiago and drew praise from Washington, it received mixed reviews in Bolivia. Banzer faced a public skeptical of Chilean intentions, critical, at least in some sectors, of the resumption of relations without benefits other than a vague agreement to engage in dialogue about mutual problems, and anxious about the prospects for making any real progress in the maritime issue.

Although Banzer cautioned his countrymen against expectations of an early solution to the problems with Chile, as the months passed without signs of progress, no way could be found to avoid a growing public unease that the president had been outsmarted in the decision to renew relations with Chile. By August, at least some sectors of the Bolivian press were calling for a new break in relations in the face of signals coming from Santiago which were perceived as negative signs of Chilean intransigence in the maritime issue.

A partial explanation of the slow pace of discussions at this stage was that it was not until August 26, 1975, that Ambassador Guillermo Gutiérrez Vea Murguía delivered a Bolivian proposal to Chilean officials which sought a sovereign port on the Pacific linked by a corridor to Bolivian territory, and one or more territorial enclaves on the coast south of Arica. [34] While the proposal was being studied in Santiago, domestic

Figure VII - 2

PROPOSED BOLIVIAN CORRIDOR TO THE SEA (Approximate Alignment)

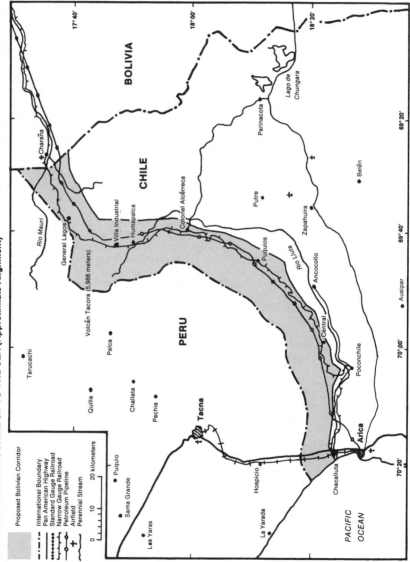

pressure continued to build on the Bolivian government, and in late September President Banzer threatened to resign if the negotiations were
unsuccessful, a decision that might lead to another leftist government in
La Paz.[35] Whether or not the threatened resignation by Banzer was indeed a factor, the Chilean government responded to the Bolivian proposal
with a significant offer in December.

The Chilean Proposal

The proposal presented on December 19, 1975, represented perhaps
the most specific Chilean plan for resolving Bolivia's landlocked situation
since 1895.[36] Santiago offered Bolivia a narrow land corridor extending
from the Bolivian border to the Pacific coast north of Arica. The corridor would parallel the present Chilean-Peruvian boundary and apparently
would encompass the Chilean sector of the Arica-La Paz railroad and the
Chacalluta airport. The approximate alignment of the proposed corridor
is shown in Figure VII-2.[37]

In return for the cession of the corridor, Chile asked a high price.
In effect, Santiago was proposing an exchange of territories in which Bolivia would grant to Chile a land area equal in size to the corridor territory and the surface area of the territorial sea extending two hundred
miles from the narrow coastal outlet. Bolivia would pay Chile for the
Chilean section of the Arica-La Paz railroad and withdraw its objections
to Chilean use of the Lauca River. Furthermore, Chile proposed that the
exchanged territories be demilitarized and that the inviolability of the
territories be guaranteed by the UN or the OAS.[38]

In reporting to the nation on December 21, President Banzer acknowledged difficulties with the proposal, including the necessity of gaining
Peruvian consent for the arrangement in accordance with the 1929 Supplementary Protocol and the Chilean requirement for territorial compensation.
He announced, nevertheless, that the proposal answered the basic point
of the Bolivian request and, therefore, merited "the agreement of the
national government."[39]

Though Bolivian public reactions to the Chilean proposal were mixed,
most were critical. Banzer's success in eliciting a concrete proposal from
Chile did not readily convert to political capital domestically in terms of
unified support for the government in its negotiations with Santiago.
Criticism from the press and opposition political leaders focused primarily
on two issues: the Chilean demand for territorial compensation and the
feasibility of constructing a port on the narrow Pacific outlet. Several
former presidents suggested also that any final agreement with Chile on
the proposal be submitted to a public referendum. The idea gained wide
support and soon was expanded into a growing demand to restore constitutional political guarantees and to grant unrestricted amnesty for political
prisoners so that the widest national debate would be possible.

Such criticisms and questions certainly encouraged the Bolivian
President to establish by formal decree on January 6, 1976, the National
Maritime Council (CONAMAR) and a lower level Maritime Advisory Committee to give the Chilean proposal the most careful and complete consideration.[40] President Banzer also indicated on several occasions that no
final decision would be reached on the issue without consultation with the
Bolivian people, but the nature of such consultation remained vague.

Even though Bolivian President Banzer was able to obtain qualified
support from the armed forces and several labor and civilian groups for
negotiations with Chile on the basis of Santiago's proposal, opposition from
other labor and political groups made it necessary for the Foreign Ministry
to announce on March 10 that it would not accept the terms in the Chilean

offer: demilitarization of the exchanged territories, an unpopular concept among the Bolivian military; territorial exchange as defined by Chile; and full Chilean utilization of the waters of the Lauca. [41] Negotiations in Santiago continued during the year in an effort to narrow the differences between the two countries on the Chilean proposal, but the critical question that loomed larger and larger as 1976 passed was that of Peru's response to the Chilean proposition for resolving Bolivia's port problem.

The Peruvian Counter-Proposal

The resumption of diplomatic relations between Bolivia and Chile and their discussions of the port issue were matters of concern in Lima. Although Peruvian leaders had given considerable rhetorical support to efforts designed to find a solution to Bolivia's port aspirations, it may be doubted that they believed that Chile would actually propose a territorial solution. [42] However, Peruvian spokesmen, including President Velasco, consistently had coupled their sympathetic rhetoric with reminders that it was the port of Antofagasta which had been lost by the Bolivians to Chile in the War of the Pacific and that Peru maintained an interest in its former territories now belonging to Chile. [43]

When the Chilean government informed Lima of its proposal to Bolivia shortly before it was announced publicly, the Peruvian government of General Francisco Morales Bermúdez was placed in a difficult position, a situation which helps to explain the eleven-month delay in submitting a Peruvian reply. A simple veto of the Chilean proposal would have placed added stress on relations with Santiago and would doubtless have had the effect of moving La Paz closer to Chile, while irritating those Latin American countries sympathetic to Bolivia's cause. At the same time, strong nationalist sentiment domestically would not easily accept the transfer of former Peruvian territory, a notion which would be completely abhorrent to any harboring revanchist sentiments. To handle the challenge, Morales Bermúdez established a consultative commission headed by former Peruvian President José Luis Bustamante y Rivero and consisting of military and civilian political leaders. Negotiating sessions between Peru and Chile were held in April and July, 1976.

On November 18, Peru presented its counter-proposal to Chile. The plan accepted the notion of a narrow land corridor eight and one-half miles wide under Bolivian sovereignty, extending from the Bolivian frontier to the Pan American Highway linking Arica and Tacna. But Peru proposed that the coastal zone between the highway and the Pacific be placed under the tripartite sovereignty of Peru, Chile, and Bolivia. Figure VII-3 sketches the proposed coastal arrangement. [44] Within the zone of joint control, Bolivia would be allowed to construct a port under its sovereign jurisdiction and the adjacent two-hundred mile territorial sea would also be Bolivia's. Peru proposed that the coastal zone under joint control become an industrial development region with the assistance of international financial organizations and that a trinational port authority be established in Arica. [45]

The political climate within the region in late 1976, due in part at least to continuing arms purchases by Peru and Chile, was not propitious for a settlement of the dispute. [46] Shortly after receiving the written Peruvian proposal on November 19, the Chilean Foreign Office, on November 26, rejected the plan on the grounds that it called for a modification of Chile's sovereign jurisdiction over the port of Arica, which had been established in the 1929 treaty. Santiago also took exception to the proposed shared sovereignty arrangement for the coastal zone as an unacceptable revision of the 1929 Treaty and an unwelcome alteration of its

Figure VII - 3

THE PERUVIAN PROPOSAL

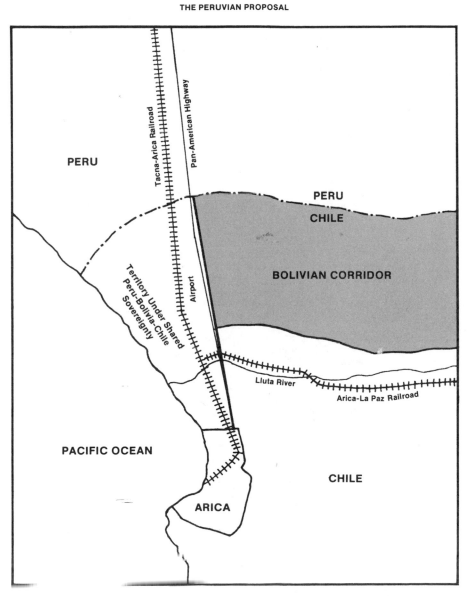

proposal to Bolivia. In addition, Chile objected to the memorandum for-
mat of the Peruvian communication of November 19, and this twin rejection
of form and content amounted to a refusal by the Chilean Foreign Office
to consider the Peruvian proposal as an official response to its note of
December 19, 1975.[47] Lima immediately responded by stating that its
November 19 memorandum should be considered the Peruvian reply to the
Chilean note of December 19, 1975.

Press and political opinion within Bolivia was divided with respect to
the Peruvian proposal, which had been made public on November 20.
Several features of the plan, including the concepts of shared sovereignty
and joint administration and the fact that Peru was asking for no territorial compensation for the corridor to be granted to Bolivia, were received
favorably by various sectors of public opinion. However, government
officials in La Paz responded critically, labeling the proposal "obscure,
uncertain, vague and dangerous."[48] During 1976, while the Peruvian
plan was unacceptable officially, opposition to the Chilean proposal had
continued to mount within Bolivia amidst criticism of the manner in which
the Banzer government had conducted negotiations on the portuary issue.
The Peruvian counter-proposal and its rejection by Chile afforded La Paz
an opportunity to seize the initiative again.

An Impasse

In his 1976 Christmas address to the nation, President Banzer stated
that since Chile and Peru had offered their proposals for resolving the
problem of Bolivia's landlocked situation, it was now time for the Bolivian
government to "define its position." After reiterating Bolivia's objective
of acquiring "a free and fully sovereign outlet from the national territory
to the Pacific Ocean," he then proposed that Chile delete its demand for
territorial exchange and that Peru "change its proposal in relation to the
establishment of a territorial area of shared sovereignty." In return,
Banzer pledged that Bolivia would offer "whatever contributions might be
necessary, in equitable terms," for establishing a tripartite development
region in its newly acquired coastal area which would be beneficial to all
parties.[49]

Nineteen seventy-seven was a year of growing frustration within
Bolivia with respect to portuary negotiations as responses to Banzer's
proposals were awaited. Early in the year, assurances were received in
La Paz from Santiago and Lima that these governments wished to continue
their efforts to find a solution to Bolivia's problem. In May the Bolivian
government convened a meeting of consultation in La Paz for its western
hemisphere ambassadors, apparently to seek their assistance in formu-
lating a plan for future moves on the sea outlet question.[50] In June a
series of bilateral discussions between foreign ministers were conducted
in Santiago and Lima, resulting in reports that new formulas for resolving
Bolivia's landlocked situation were under discussion in Santiago and La
Paz and would be submitted to Lima if agreement could be reached.[51]

In September, on the occasion of the signing of the Panama Canal
treaties in Washington, D.C., President Banzer arranged a meeting with
Chilean President Pinochet and Peruvian President Morales Bermúdez to
deal with the port problem. Historically significant as a rare meeting of
the chief executives of the three countries whose relations have been
seriously troubled throughout their history, the gathering managed to
produce only a weak agreement whereby the foreign offices of the countries were to be instructed to continue efforts designed to reach a solution of the portuary problem.[52] More significant than the agreement
reached, however, were the statements reportedly made by the Chilean

and Peruvian presidents to President Banzer during the meeting. The Chilean President reasserted his country's position that any future arrangement would have to be based on territorial exchange. Peruvian President Morales Bermúdez stated that he favored the attainment of a satisfactory settlement, as long as the agreement respected Peru's historical rights. [53] Essentially, the statements represented replies to Banzer's 1976 Christmas proposals, although the exact implications of President Morales Bermúdez's statement were unclear. Later in September, Chilean Foreign Minister Carvajal reiterated his country's insistence upon territorial compensation in any final solution to the problem. [54]

Although the foreign ministers of Bolivia, Chile, and Peru met in New York City at the United Nations in October and agreed to designate special envoys to continue talks on the problem, it was soon clear that all momentum in the diplomatic process had been lost. During October, the Bolivian ambassadors in Santiago and Lima, together with other diplomatic personnel in the hemisphere, were recalled to La Paz for consultation. Responding to Chile's firm position on territorial exchange, President Banzer announced that the question of accepting or rejecting Chile's demand for territorial compensations must be referred to the elected representatives of the Bolivian people in a future congress. On November 9, 1977, the Bolivian President announced that the armed forces planned to restore constitutional government through elections for president, vice-president, and congress in July 1978. Elections for a constituent assembly also had been called for in June 1978 by Peruvian President Morales Bermúdez.

Thus, a diplomatic stalemate with respect to the several outlet proposals and growing domestic pressures in behalf of restoring elective governments in Peru and Bolivia signaled that the nearly three-year process of attempting to solve the problem of Bolivia's landlocked situation had ended without success. This failure was verified on March 17, 1978, when the Bolivian government announced that it was breaking diplomatic relations with Chile as the result of Santiago's intransigent position in the maritime issue negotiations. [55] Future initiatives on the problem undoubtedly would await the outcome of the 1978 elections.

Negotiations on the Principal Problem: Analysis and Future Prospects

The diplomacy of the three central actors in recent years with respect to Bolivia's maritime objectives can best be understood in terms of the variety of challenges confronting each of them domestically and internationally. After the overthrow of the Allende government, Chile under General Pinochet was confronted by strong international criticism of its repressive measures against political opponents, critical economic problems, tension in its relations with a militarily superior Peru, and persistent border problems with Argentina. Given such a situation, Santiago felt that it needed improved relations with Bolivia, whose anti-Marxist military government appeared ideologically compatible with the Pinochet government. The restoration of relations with Bolivia would signal a modest but positive step for Chile in restoring its international image and would enhance its prospects for keeping Bolivia from allying itself with Peru should war actually break out with that country. Chile's December 1975 proposal for resolving Bolivia's maritime needs apparently was designed to further the *rapprochement* with La Paz, while gaining approval from other hemispheric states which had given Bolivia moral support in the matter, such as Colombia, Venezuela, and Panama.

Bolivia, as the political plaintiff in the maritime reintegration problem, was willing to take advantage of Chile's need for friendlier relations.

As we have seen, Bolivian officials were prepared to resume full diplomatic relations in February 1975, on the basis of Chile's pledge to enter into bilateral discussions on methods of resolving the portuary problem. Later, in December 1975, they were ready to accept the terms of the Chilean proposal as the basis of negotiations. During the three-year period the Bolivian government continued to emphasize that it was necessary for the nation to have a sovereign outlet on the Pacific in order to pursue successfully its plans for economic development and to regain national independence in terms of access to the great maritime routes of world trade. However, the Banzer government also sought to gain wider and more unified domestic political support through its vigorous pursuit of a Pacific port.

The Bolivian government also supported a dampening of Chilean-Peruvian tensions by participating in periodic military consultations involving high-ranking officers from each country and by favoring regional declarations on arms limitations in 1974 and 1975. Bolivian officials consistently stated the government's intention of maintaining a posture of neutrality in any Chilean-Peruvian military confrontation. Obviously, La Paz viewed the Chilean-Peruvian arms race and the periodical war scares as a threat to the talks on its maritime problem. The stated intention of remaining neutral, of course, enabled the Banzer government to maintain its access to the governments in both Santiago and Lima.

As noted earlier the Peruvian government was placed on the defensive, at least temporarily, when Chile submitted to Lima its December 1975 proposal in accordance with the Supplementary Protocol of 1929. Revanchist and nationalist sentiment had grown in Peru under the revolutionary military regime, and strong domestic pressure existed in opposition to accepting the cession to Bolivia of territory which once belonged to Peru. Nor was Lima prepared to grant Chile success in a major diplomatic coup in which Santiago could claim credit for resolving Bolivia's perennial maritime problem. On the other hand, however, since Peru was interested in retaining friendly relations with Bolivia, the Peruvian government could not afford to disregard completely its earlier expressions of support for finding a formula to solve Bolivia's maritime problem. A total rejection, moreover, would have cast Lima in a poor light within the hemisphere among Bolivian sympathizers.

The Peruvian counter-proposal therefore offered alternative means for meeting Bolivia's portuary needs involving revisions in the territorial arrangements contained in the 1929 Treaty. These revisions, however, were virtually certain to provoke serious Chilean objections. As the triangular discussions floundered, Peru continued its rhetorical posture in favor of a permanent solution, while awaiting some new proposal based upon Bolivian-Chilean agreement.

Although no settlement of Bolivia's maritime problem was achieved during the so-called Charaña negotiations, several possible short-term and long-range gains from the process can be identified. First, diplomatic relations were restored between Bolivia and Chile, a situation that at least provided improved opportunities for communication between the two governments during the 1975-78 period. Such channels of communication did facilitate efforts to deal cooperatively with common problems in the region such as the acquisitions of armaments by regional governments, trade, transportation facilities, and development projects. Chile's withdrawal from the Andean Group in 1976 made direct communication channels even more important.

In terms of perceivable gains with respect to Bolivia's principal problem itself, it appears as if the exchange of proposals in 1975 and 1976 erected a new conceptual floor beneath future discussions. The idea of a sovereign Bolivian corridor along the Chilean-Peruvian border has been endorsed by Chile and, up to a point, by Peru. Regardless of what the future holds, Bolivia will undoubtedly make it difficult for either Santiago or Lima to forget such offers. [56] Both the Chilean and the Peruvian proposals also accepted the principle of a sovereign Bolivian port on the Pacific, although it would have to be a new facility constructed north of Arica. The twin ideas of shared sovereignty in the coastal zone north of Arica and of the joint administration of the port of Arica were introduced in the Peruvian proposal and gained substantial support in Bolivian press and political circles. Possibly some key ingredients of a future formula for resolving the problem have emerged from these recent talks.

A third category of achievements relates to the experience gained since 1974 by Bolivian leaders with respect to the maritime problem. One lesson which may be learned is that while a large majority of Bolivians undoubtedly support the goal of acquiring a sovereign outlet on the Pacific, unified public support for any specific formula cannot be relied upon, especially if compensation is demanded. President Banzer managed some increased support for his government early in 1974 on the strength of the maritime issue. However, when the provisions of the December 1975 Chilean proposal became known, the president discovered that public opinion was not only seriously divided over the proposal, but also was critical of the way his government had conducted negotiations. If indeed the championing of the maritime issue has been regarded by various Bolivian government leaders through the years as a means of rallying political support for a faltering regime, as many observers have suggested, the experience of recent years suggests that as these discussions move toward specific means for solving the problem, the supportive consensus of the Bolivian public is likely to dissipate into divisive pro and con factions. Future Bolivian leaders may view the maritime issue as a potentially destabilizing domestic political theme. In somewhat of a reversal of traditional tactics, civilian opponents of the government seized upon the Chilean and Peruvian proposals as matters of such national significance that they demanded the restoration of the constitutional political process to assure full public consultation.

Another significant aspect of recent developments may well be the recognition by important sectors of the Bolivian leadership of the practical difficulties associated with gaining a useful sovereign outlet on the Pacific. Although President Banzer gave assurances in December 1975 that it was feasible to build a port on the coastal terminus of the territorial corridor offered by Chile, at least some expert opinion felt that it would be exceptionally difficult and expensive to construct such facilities. [57] In addition, the limited volume of traffic through nearby Arica hardly seems to justify the construction of a new port in the region, at least, in economic terms. Comments by several prominent critics of the Chilean proposal suggested that these practical considerations were being given serious attention.

If some gains from the recent round of negotiations can be identified, the serious obstacles to reaching a satisfactory solution to the Bolivian maritime problem must be acknowledged also. Assuming that the 1975 Chilean proposal or a modified version of it will be at least the starting point for any future discussions of the issue in the next several years, the main problems appear to be obtaining Peruvian agreement for transferring to Bolivia a corridor through its former territory, the resolution of the question of territorial compensation, and the practical aspect of Bolivia's desire for a port on the Pacific.

In order to gain a final settlement to Bolivia's maritime problem it appears as if some compelling benefits for each of the three nations must be included in any successful negotiating formula. Without obtaining some clear rewards for the national good, it will be difficult for governments in Lima and Santiago to accept any final agreement on the matter.

Since Chile has assumed such a firm position with respect to territorial compensation, in all likelihood any settlement in the foreseeable future would require Bolivian acceptance of such terms. Since opposition to this basic approach has been so vigorous in Bolivian public opinion, a settlement will be most difficult. Should Chile, however, find ways of granting Bolivia increased privileges in Arica, perhaps territorial exchange would become somewhat more palatable.

Identifying appropriate rewards for Peru in a successful formula would perhaps be the most difficult problem. Minor territorial revisions could be considered along the proposed Bolivian corridor boundary with Peru, allowing that country to reintegrate under its full sovereignty a system of irrigation channels now located partially in Chile. [58] Other possible benefits of a settlement for Peru could be sought in terms of the regional economic development envisaged by Bolivian spokesmen in this zone of trinational confluence.

CONCLUSION

The lasting significance of recent developments in Bolivian relations with Chile and Peru, if any, remains to be determined. The temporary restoration of diplomatic relations with Santiago and the subsequent Chilean proposal for resolving Bolivia's landlocked situation were positive steps which may be built upon in the future. At the same time, however, the conditions that prompted Chile to seek improved relations with Bolivia have changed to some degree in the period since 1975. The threat of war with Peru has diminished, economic gains have been made, and Chile's "human rights" image has improved to some extent. Santiago, moreover, has turned its foreign relations focus to the current boundary dispute with Argentina. Thus the urgency for bettering relations with La Paz has passed.

Although the maritime negotiations created some tension in Bolivian-Peruvian ties, the ensuing stalemate in discussions apparently has restored the normally amicable relations between the two countries. In all likelihood, Bolivian public opinion will be inclined to place most of the responsibility for the failure of the negotiations upon Chile.

As Peru and Bolivia confront the uncertain process of restoring constitutional governments in 1978, the twin problems of political stability and legitimacy should be considered in relation to the solution of the portuary issue. While political stability in the two countries would appear to be more conducive to a settlement, the prospects for instability grow as civilian political parties resume their activities. However, the Bolivian experience of recent years raises the question of whether a nonelective military government can give the necessary legitimacy to an agreement for resolving the sensitive maritime issue without substantial civilian political involvement.

Certainly an early resolution of Bolivia's principal foreign policy problem with Chile and Peru does not appear likely. The recent exchange of proposals highlighted the problematic realities of the situation. Neither is there a compelling reason to accept the opposite view that the problem is insoluble. President Banzer on numerous occasions during the diplomatic discussions acknowledged the difficulties of the negotiations in calling upon his countrymen to be patient in the government's pursuit of this national objective. It appears that in such patience and perseverance, Bolivia's hope for eventual satisfaction of its portuary aspirations must finally rest.

ENDNOTES FOR CHAPTER VII

1. Relations were broken on April 16, 1962, over a dispute arising from Chilean use of the waters of the Lauca River which flows from Chile into Bolivia. See Robert D. Tomasek, "The Chilean-Bolivian Rio Lauca Dispute and the OAS," *Journal of Inter-American Studies*, IX, No. 3 (July 1967), 351-366.

2. Bolivia historically has transported a substantial portion of its mineral exports by railroad to the Chilean ports of Antofagasta and Arica. An oil pipeline links Bolivian oilfields with Arica. Although the value of Bolivian trade with Chile is considerably less than that with Argentina and Brazil, the value of exports to and imports from Chile since 1970 has increased significantly. See James W. Wilkie and Paul Turovsky, eds., *Statistical Abstract of Latin America*, XVII (1976), UCLA Latin American Center Publication (Los Angeles: University of California, 1976).

3. Richard W. Patch, "The Manifest Ethics of North and South: Nixon Speaks, Bolivia Replies," *American Universities Field Staff Reports*, West Coast South America Series, XVII No. 1 (November 1, 1970), 4.

4. *New York Times*, February 9, 1972, p. 7.

5. *New York Times*, September 30, 1969, p. 9. Shortly after dismissing the civilian government of Luis Adolfo Siles Salinas on September 27, 1969, General Alfredo Ovando Candia was quoted as saying, "Fundamentally our revolution is the same as Peru's."

6. *New York Times*, April 5, 1972, p. 3; April 9, 1972, p. IV, 4.

7. For a summary of his thesis, see Robert N. Burr, *By Reason or Force, Chile and the Balancing of Power in South America, 1830-1905* (Berkeley: University of California Press, 1965), pp. 260-263.

8. *The Times of the Americas* (Washington, D.C.), XXI, No. 14, July 6, 1977, p. 2. Also, see "The Military Balance 1977/1978," (Latin America section) compiled by the International Institute for Strategic Studies, London, *Air Force Magazine*, LX, No. 12 (December 1977), 106-109.

9. *The Times of the Americas* (Washington, D.C.), XVIII, No. 9, May 1, 1974, p. 2.

10. Thomas J. Dodd, "Peru," *Latin American Foreign Policies: An Analysis*, eds. Harold Eugene Davis and Larman C. Wilson (Baltimore: The Johns Hopkins University Press, 1975), pp. 376-378.

11. A good recent summary of Bolivian efforts to obtain a Pacific port is found in Ronald Bruce St. John, "Hacia el Mar: Bolivia's Quest for a Pacific Port," *Inter-American Economic Affairs*, XXXI, No. 3 (Winter 1977), 41-73. A highly regarded Bolivian study is Jorge Escobari Cusicanqui, *El derecho al mar* (La Paz: Librería "Juventud," 1964). Also, Burr, op. cit,

11. Burr, op. cit., pp. 160-162.

13.   Ibid., pp. 257-259.

14.   St. John, op. cit., p. 66.

15.   Ibid.; an excellent summary of United States involvement in the Tacna-Arica affair is contained in William L. Krieg, "Legacy of the War of the Pacific," (A unpublished study prepared for the Department of State under its External Research Program, Washington, D.C., October 1974), pp. 48-61.

16.   Text of the Supplementary Protocol (No. 2157), League of Nations, *Treaty Series,* Vol. XCIV, Nos. 1,2,3,4, 1929, pp. 410-411.

17.   U.S. Department of State.   The map is contained in Krieg, op. cit. following p. iv.

18.   The text of the Walker Larraín note is printed in Ministerio de Relaciones Exteriores y Culto, *Rumbo al mar,* (La Paz: Documentes Trascendentales, 1963), pp. 11-12.

19.   Krieg, "Legacy of the War of the Pacific," op. cit., pp. 81-84.   Bolivian spokesmen also objected strenuously 'on the basis of the "Thesis of 1921" that water should not be diverted from its natural geographical basin to a different geographical area. This thesis was recalled and reaffirmed in Jorge Escobari Cusicanqui, *El desvió del río Mauri, integración y reintegración marítima* (La Paz: Universidad Mayor De San Andrés, 1969), pp. 15-16.

20.   The text of the Trucco Memorandum is contained in *Rumbo al mar,* op. cit., p. 13.

21.   Krieg, "Legacy of the War of the Pacific," op. cit., pp. 84-91.

22.   Bolivia's decision to break relations with Chile was precipitated by the action ordered by Chilean President Jorge Rodríguez Alessandri to proceed with the diversion of the Lauca River.   Apparently Bolivia's decision to take the dispute before the OAS Council had prompted this Chilean action (*New York Times,* April 17, 1962, p. 9).

23.   The text of the Chilean Foreign Minister's address of March 27, 1963, is printed in *Rumbo al mar,* op. cit., pp. 26-41.

24.   In December 1964, serious discussions aimed at normalizing Bolivian-Chilean relations collapsed when Bolivian spokesmen apparently insisted that Chile be prepared to discuss the portuary matter (*New York Times,* December 13, 1964, p. 76; December 26, 1964, p. 2). Reports of Chilean offers to discuss Bolivia's transportation needs and joint economic projects are contained in the *New York Times,* October 24, 1966, p. 2.

25.   Jorge Escobari Cusicanqui, op. cit., pp. 76-77.

26.   Ibid., p. 75.

27.   William L. Krieg, "Bolivia: En Route To The Sea?"   (A study prepared for the Department of State under its External Research Program, Washington, D.C., October 1977), p. 12.

28. *New York Times*, March 17, 1974, p. 3.

29. Krieg, "Bolivia: En Route To The Sea?" op. cit., pp. 20–21.

30. Ibid., p. 22.

31. *Facts on File*, XXXIV, No. 1743 (April 7, 1974), 277.

32. Krieg, "Bolivia: En Route To The Sea?" op. cit., p. 26.

33. The text of La Declaración de Charaña is contained in Mariano Bap-
    tista Gumucio, *En lugar del desastre: Bolivia y el conflicto Peruano-
    Chileno* (La Paz: Editorial Los Amigos Del Libro, 1975), pp. 97–98.

34. The exact details of the Bolivian proposal are somewhat unclear.
    See Krieg, "Bolivia: En Route To The Sea?" op. cit., p. 36.

35. Banzer's threat to resign appeared in an interview in the September
    24, 1975, issue of the Santiago, Chile magazine *Ercilla* and was re-
    ported in the *New York Times*, October 19, 1975, p. 5.

36. In 1895 Bolivia and Chile signed several agreements in which Santiago
    committed itself to providing Bolivia with a sovereign outlet on the
    Pacific. The agreements, of course, were never implemented. See
    Burr, op. cit., pp. 208–209, 215.

37. Map 2 was prepared by the Office of the Geographer, U.S. Depart-
    ment of State, in 1977. It is included in Krieg, "Bolivia: En Route
    To The Sea?" op. cit., following p. ii.

38. Contents of the Chilean proposal are reported in various sources.
    See Buenos Aires LATIN News Agency report in U.S. Department of
    Commerce, Foreign Broadcast Information Service (FBIS), *Daily
    Report*, Latin American ed., Vol. VI, No. 248 (December 24, 1975),
    p. E 1; Mexico, Banco Nacional de Comercio Exterior, S.A., *Comer-
    cio exterior de México*, Vol. XXXIII, No. 3 (March 1977), 92–94;
    Krieg, "Bolivia: En Route To The Sea?" op. cit., pp. 37–38.

39. La Paz Domestic Services reported in FBIS, *Daily Report*, Latin
    American ed., VI, No. 246 (December 22, 1975), C1–C2.

40. CONAMAR membership included several cabinet ministers, the joint
    command of the armed forces, the secretary-general of the presi-
    dency, and other advisors named by the president. Krieg, "Bolivia:
    En Route To The Sea?" op. cit., p. 42.

41. *The Times of the Americas*, XX, No. 7 (March 31, 1976), 14.

42. A statement by Peruvian Foreign Minister General Miguel Angel de
    la Flor Valle on October 29, 1975, illustrates the rhetorical position
    assumed by Peruvian officials before Chile's December 1975 proposal
    was submitted. He stated, "We realize that Bolivia faces great prob-
    lems because it is landlocked, and we would like to see this issue
    settled." Buenos Aires LATIN news agency in FBIS, *Daily Report*,
    Latin American ed., VI No. 211 (October 31, 1975), #1.

43. *The Times of the Americas*, XVIII, No. 8 (April 17, 1974), 11.

44. *Comercio exterior de México*, op. cit., p. 93.

45. Contents of the Peruvian proposal are contained in *La prensa* (Lima), November 20, 1976. Reports on the proposal were printed in *New York Times*, November 21, 1976, p. 14, and December 9, 1976, p. 13. Major provisions are identified in Krieg, "Bolivia: En Route To The Sea?" op. cit., pp. 50-51.

46. See reports in the *New York Times*, December 9, 1976, p. 13, and in *Time*, January 10, 1977, pp. 24-25.

47. Krieg, "Bolivia: En Route To The Sea?" op. cit., p. 53.

48. This comment was attributed to Mario Ojara, adviser to President Banzer. *Facts on File*, XXXVI, No. 1886 (December 31, 1976), 975.

49. *Presencia* (La Paz), December 25, 1976, reported in FBIS, *Daily Report*, Latin American ed., VI, No. 252 (December 30, 1976), C1-C5.

50. U.S. Department of State, Incoming Telegram from American Embassy, La Paz, No. 3364, May 6, 1977.

51. *The Times of the Americas*, XXI, No. 18 (August 31, 1977), p. 3, and U.S. Department of State, Incoming Telegram from American Embassy, Lima, No. 4950, June 14, 1977.

52. Text of declaration was released to the author by the Chilean Embassy, Washington, D.C. on November 11, 1977.

53. UPI dispatch, La Paz, September 15, 1977. Also texts of broadcasts by *Radio Cruz del Sur* Network, La Paz, FBIS, *Daily Report,* Latin American ed., VI (September 15, 1977), C1.

54. *The Andean Report* (Lima), Vol III, No. 11, November 1977, p. 215.

55. Organization of American States, Permanent Council, OEA/Ser. G, CP/INF. 1257/78, March 20, 1978. The text of the Bolivian diplomatic note to the Interim Chargé d' Affaires of Chile in La Paz is enclosed with Note Number 301, submitted by the Permanent Delegation of Chile to the Organization of American States, March 18, 1978, Washington, D.C.

56. In his "Day of the Sea" address on March 23, 1977, President Banzer suggested that the Chilean and Peruvian proposals represented at least have official recognition by those countries of Bolivia's right to have a sovereign coastline linking the nation to the sea. U.S. Department of State, airgram from the U.S. Mission to the United Nations with text of address, A-416, April 22, 1977.

57. *The Times of the Americas*, XX, No. 5 (March 3, 1976), 9. This was the position of the Bolivian maritime geographical specialist Jaime Taborga Torrico.

58. Portions of the Mauri and Uchusuma canals pass through Chilean territory, although Peru enjoys "a perpetual and absolute easement" over these sections under Article 2 of the Treaty of 1929. Text of the Treaty Between Chile and Peru For The Settlement of The Dispute Regarding Tacna and Arica (No. 2157), League of Nations, *Treaty Series*, Vol. XCIV, Nos. 1,2,3,4, 1929, pp. 406-410.

Part Four

Economic Development

Chapter VIII

The Economic Structure of Bolivia After 1964
Juan L. Cariaga

INTRODUCTION

Since the well-known events of 1952, a great many changes have occurred in the Bolivian economy. These changes reflect to a great extent the transformation of the government and social structure during the same period—a transformation which has created an economic situation very different from that which prevailed at the beginning of the National Revolutionary Movement Party (MNR) government.

In order to understand this new economic situation, one must first be aware that today's Bolivia is radically different from the Bolivia of 1952 and even from the Bolivia of the early 1960s. Although still active, the leaders of that revolution are aging, divided among themselves, and to a considerable extent absorbed into the new governing establishment. The prolonged rule of military governments and the long abandonment of forums for open debate by freely elected representatives of the public has prevented the emergence of a new leadership. In the absence of one, an admittedly highly qualified group of technocrats has attempted to establish itself as part of the political system—but without a real appreciation and understanding of the unique reality that is Bolivia. This sensitivity to the Bolivian situation, which today's highly trained technocrats frequently lack, may, in fact, have been one of the greatest strengths of the old revolutionaries—many of whom, ironically, are the fathers of the present generation of technocrats.

In this and in many other particulars Bolivia today differs from the Bolivia of twenty-five years ago precisely because a generation has come and gone in the interim. Today's rulers are the young officers whose recently initiated military careers were interrupted during the first years of the revolutionary government. Some are also the university students who received their political baptism in the anti-Movement groups which were formed in the universities of San Andrés and San Simón. Above all, the new ruling establishment were the adolescents who experienced--and remember with considerable resentment--the political jailings, the sometimes unruly militia of revolutionary miners and peasants, and above all, the long lines to buy flour, bread, and coffee under the economic administration of the 1952 revolution.

Finally, to understand today's Bolivia, one must be aware of the great changes which have overtaken the social and productive structure of the nation. For example, the preliminary findings of the 1976 census indicate that Bolivia has become a young nation with more than 50 percent of her population under twenty years of age and 37 percent under ten years of age. These same findings show considerable improvement in the quality of these human resources. For example, illiteracy among persons over ten years of age has fallen to 33 percent of the general population.

The means of production have also undergone considerable alteration in today's Bolivia. The small landholder has begun to use commercial fertilizers, which have helped him to overcome the difficulties of the *minifundia* and of the dry Andean climate. The farmer has also begun to recognize the advantages of irrigation, crop rotation, and scientific cattle-raising. In the valleys which cut through the Andean highlands, the production of dairy products is becoming industrialized; and poultry raising, thanks to the introduction of prepared feeds, has become so advanced that its large-scale production now meets the entire national demand for poultry products. In the tropical lowlands, sugar, rice, cotton and soybean production has increased sufficiently to make Bolivia a net exporter, albeit on a relatively small scale, of these commodities.

Bolivia now has its own facilities for smelting tin, making the nation an exporter of minerals rather than mineral concentrates, and generating additional employment for increasing the aggregate value of Bolivian exports and, supposedly, also increasing savings by reducing transportation costs for the Bolivian State Mining Company (COMIBOL).

Not every aspect of the current economic situation is favorable, nor are they all the result of the 1952 revolution, which did achieve a great deal of benefit for the national well-being. Bolivia still faces great problems and will continue to face them for many years.

Bolivian agriculture, notwithstanding the advances mentioned above, has for the most part undergone very little fundamental change since the 1950s. Investment in this sector has been limited and slow to develop, and recent governments have taken few steps to remedy the situation. COMIBOL still suffers from the same problems that plagued it twenty years ago: large numbers of marginal employees, too little exploration for new mineral resources, and an unwieldy and inefficient administration incapable of attacking even the problem of its own organization.

In addition, the public enterprises of Bolivia, with the exception of two or three, have become independent fiefdoms which, despite the fact that they control a significant portion of the public sector income, are not responsive to the national government for their investments, their dividend policy or even their tax payments.

The following sections of this paper will attempt to identify some of the most important economic transformations that have taken place in Bolivia since the fall of the well-documented MNR government. We will begin with a brief analysis of the characteristics of the Bolivian economy, an analysis which will set the stage for an examination of the effects on given economic sectors of the economic measures instituted in 1952.

CHARACTERISTICS OF THE BOLIVIAN ECONOMY

The Degree of Openness of the Bolivian Economy

Despite great efforts by various Bolivian governments to achieve even small-scale industrialization in order to limit Bolivia's dependence on foreign trade, the Bolivian economy is still one of the most open on the American continent. Between 1970 and 1975 exports and imports averaged 21 and 25 percent, respectively, of the gross domestic product (GDP). In countries such as Colombia, Peru, Chile and Paraguay, these percentages never exceeded 15 percent during the same period.

This is not to say that the openness of the Bolivian economy is an evil in and of itself. Japan, for example, depends to a very great degree on foreign trade. On the South American continent, Venezuela is similarly dependent on its exports and imports. The negative aspect of Bolivia's economic openness is that the national economy, in addition to being very open, depends on a highly limited number of exports--basically minerals and petroleum products. More important still, Bolivia has no leverage whatsoever in the markets where its products are sold.

Dependence on Foreign Trade for Government Revenues

In addition to the openness of its economy, Bolivia also depends heavily on foreign trade to provide revenue for the national government. In effect, as Table VIII-1 indicates, in 1975 taxes which were not related to foreign trade accounted for only 37 percent of overall government revenues. The remaining 63 percent depended in one form or another on Bolivian participation in the international market.

The same table shows that from 1968 to 1975 direct taxes rose from 44 to 52 percent, taxes on non-renewable resources rose from 8 to 33 percent, and taxes on the state-run public enterprises (generally for the export of non-renewable resources) from 8 to 34 percent. All this points to a single conclusion—the great dependence of Bolivia's tax structure on foreign trade.

These figures also reflect the dependence of government tax revenues on export taxes, principally on the taxation of non-renewable resources—minerals and petroleum products—and on the taxation of state-owned companies, which themselves derive most of their income from raw material exports.

Most important, this dependence brings with it a great vulnerability to international price fluctuations. If, as has been the case in Bolivia during the last few years, government expenditures show little downward flexibility, a fall in export prices can have serious repercussions. First, it can affect planned public investment, since investment outlays are usually the first to be sacrificed in the face of fiscal constraints. Second, a fall in export prices can unleash a round of inflation since the government usually has recourse to the "printing of new money," a solution it finds preferable to implementing other methods for controlling deficit spending. Finally, a fall in export prices can contribute to Bolivia's foreign debt, a well-known and readily accessible substitute for a raise in taxes.

To avoid these repercussions, the national government could instead go for an overall increase in taxes—provided, of course, it is willing to pay the political price of such an action. Even this, however, will require a prior comprehensive reform of the antiquated tax structure now in existence in Bolivia.

Rigidity of Supply in Strategic Sectors of the Economy

Another characteristic of the Bolivian economy is the relative inelasticity of supply in certain strategic sectors of the economy. In these sectors, supply does not respond readily, even in the medium term, to changes in demand or changes reflected in prices. The rise in international and domestic prices during the 1973-1975 period is a prime

TABLE VIII-1

COMPOSITION OF TAX REVENUES OF THE CENTRAL GOVERNMENT
(Percent)

	1968	1972	1973	1974	1975
Direct vs. Indirect Taxes					
Direct	43.7	51.6	58.6	65.0	52.3
Indirect	56.3	48.4	41.4	35.0	47.7
TOTAL	100.0	100.0	100.0	100.0	100.0
Taxes on Foreign Trade vs. Internal Taxes					
To foreign trade					
To imports	34.2	28.5	21.3	20.4	29.6
To exports	8.5	20.5	35.7	47.9	33.4
TOTAL	42.7	49.0	57.0	68.3	63.0
Internal					
Direct[a]	35.2	31.1	22.9	17.1	18.8
Indirect[b]	22.1	19.9	20.1	14.6	18.2
TOTAL	57.3	51.0	43.0	31.7	37.0
TOTAL	100.0	100.0	100.0	100.0	100.0
To the Non-Renewable Resources vs. Others					
Non Renewable	8.4	19.8	35.2	47.5	33.4
Other	91.6	80.2	64.8	52.5	66.6
TOTAL	100.0	100.0	100.0	100.0	100.0
To Public Enterprises vs. Other					
Public Enterprises	7.6	26.9	31.5	44.4	34.2
Other	92.4	73.1	68.5	55.6	65.8
TOTAL	100.0	100.0	100.0	100.0	100.0
TOTAL TAXES	100.0	100.0	100.0	100.0	100.0

[a]Excludes export taxes.

[b]Excludes import duties and taxes on foreign exchange.

Source: Musgrave Mission, *Fiscal Reform in Bolivia, Vol. III. Tax Structure and Tariff System* (Cambridge, Mass.: Musgrave Mission, September 12, 1978), p. D-4. (Mimeographed.)

example, since it had almost no effect on the national level of production. This inflexibility of supply occurs primarily in the most important export industries, particularly in mining and agriculture. The same phenomenon also occurred in the traditional portion of the agricultural sector when domestic prices rose in 1973.

Given this situation, it is apparent that it is very difficult to stimulate production by means of price increases. For this reason, an expansion of the money supply may accomplish little beyond stimulating a rise in domestic prices.

THE HERITAGE OF THE REVOLUTION

In his analysis of the Bolivian economic structure, Richard Thorn acknowledges that land reform, the nationalization of mines, and the implementation of the 1939 Labor Law were the most important economic measures of the 1952 revolutionary government. The MNR, of course, also instigated other social and economic measures, among which two are sufficiently important to merit separate mention. These are educational reform, which accounts for the astounding relatively low levels of illiteracy reported in the 1975 census, and the Petroleum Code, which has awakened interest in exploring and developing Bolivia's energy wealth. These measures are addressed in the following five sections.

AGRICULTURE SINCE THE LAND REFORM

As the following quote from Thorn points out, the MNR government had no master plan for reorganizing economic activity so as to stimulate Bolivia's development:

> The MNR, unfortunately, was so thoroughly occupied with the problems of seizing and maintaining political power that it was never able to formulate a well-defined program of how planning was to be organized under the new society that it was to create. [1]

Land reform is a prime example of the situation Thorn was referring to. After distributing available land among the landless, a step dictated by strong political pressures in the early years of the revolution, the MNR government considered the problem of agricultural development solved. Thus it left the agricultural sector—or at least the traditional portion thereof—practically without resources, plans for the future, or real opportunities for development. As a result, agricultural production declined drastically during the early years of the revolution and has not recovered completely to date.

Unfortunately, little has been done since the fall of the MNR government to remedy this situation despite many political contacts and "pacts" established since that time between the nation's rulers and the rural population. [2] In actuality, all that most of the *campesinos* have received are vague promises and a piece of paper giving them title to land. Even now, however, twenty-four years after the land reform, there is land that has yet to be distributed to more of Bolivia's rural population. This sweeping statement, which may appear somewhat inflammatory, is, in fact, perfectly justifiable. The following evidence substantiates the lack of true government interest in traditional agriculture.

First, although from 1967 to 1973 the agricultural sector produced 50 percent more GDP than mining and employed two-thirds of the labor force, it received a scant 6 to 8 percent of total public expenditures (Table VIII-2). If the contributions of the Bolivian Agricultural Bank (BAB) and the Bolivian Development Corporation (CBF) are excluded, the fraction of government expenditures received by the agricultural sector shrinks to a mere 1 to 2 percent. This minimal level of public investment is obviously not in accord with the strategic importance of the agricultural sector.

Second, although it is necessary to protect domestic products from import competition, the present tariff system appears to encourage the importation of food products rather than import substitution in the agri-

TABLE VIII-2

PUBLIC EXPENDITURE IN AGRICULTURE
(In millions of pesos)

Expenditures	1967	1968	1969	1970	1971	1972	1973
(1) Agricultural Sector	14.7	27.6	24.7	37.3	35.8	56.8	56.0
(2) Public Expenditure	293.7	367.0	414.0	496.4	467.2	540.2	688.2
(3) (1)/(2) (Percent)	5.0	7.5	6.2	7.5	7.7	10.4	7.8
(4) Public Expenditure BAB & CBF	5.6	10.7	11.5	10.9	8.8	11.9	7.6
(5) (4)/(2) (Percent)	1.9	2.9	2.8	2.2	1.9	2.2	1.1

Source: Albert Berry, "The Potential of Increased Public Investment in Agriculture: The Current Situation and the Potential of Public Policy," *Fiscal Reform in Bolivia, Staff Papers*, Vol. I, No. 11 (Cambridge, Mass.: Musgrave Mission, 1977), p. 41. (Mimeographed.)

cultural sector. The effective tariff protection of certain agricultural products is, in fact, (and despite all logic to the contrary) negative.[3] As a result, Bolivia has had a negative commercial balance of trade in food products since 1951. Admittedly, the gap between food exports and imports has decreased considerably despite the present tariff policy, but Bolivia still imported 39 million dollars worth of foodstuffs in 1975, a figure which represented almost 6 percent of total imports for that year.

Third, although it is necessary to provide incentives to the agricultural sector, government stabilization policies have adversely affected its development and expansion. On the one hand, the policy of a fixed exchange rate, which has been in effect since 1956, has served to raise the price of domestic agricultural products relative to imports, and this has encouraged the smuggling of imported products from the surrounding countries. On the other hand, the control of agricultural prices in order to limit overall inflation only contributes to discouraging the production of agricultural goods, in spite of changes in demand.

Fourth, although all effective agricultural endeavors require adequate financing, the BAB, until recently the only institution providing much credit for agriculture, has unfortunately dedicated almost all of its assets to financing the modern portion of the agricultural sector. There is scant hope that this situation will change in the near future. Nor is it unfair to characterize BAB as unduly cumbersome, tolerating as it does a percentage of delinquent loans that would horrify the most generous of commercial bankers.[4]

Finally, the lack of an adequate plan for marketing agricultural products in the traditional sector and the lack of an adequate system to ensure farmers ready access to necessary agricultural inputs both demonstrate how little interest there has been in achieving a good understanding of the problems of Bolivian agriculture.

Obviously, even this brief review of the agricultural situation in Bolivia serves to indicate why it is that in a nation of more than one million square kilometers, less than two percent of that huge land area--a mere

28,794 square kilometers—is under cultivation in spite of the fact that Bolivia has a total of 918,535 square kilometers of arable land.

The information presented in Table VIII-3 dramatically expresses the potential of Bolivian agriculture, a potential which contrasts sharply with the many problems mentioned above.

TABLE VIII-3

UTILIZATION OF BOLIVIAN LAND SPACE

	Area in sq. km.	Percentage
Range and/or shrublands	338,307	30.81
Forests	564,684	51.40
Cultivated land	28,794	2.62
Wet lands	24,201	2.20
Bodies of water	14,107	1.29
Barren lands	126,101	11.47
Permanent snow- and ice-covered	2,148	0.20
Other	149	0.01
TOTAL	1,098,491	100.00

Source: Servicio Geológico de Bolivia, Programa del Satélite Tecno-lógico de Recursos Naturales "ERTS-Bolivia", *Memoria explicativa* (La Paz: Geobol, agosto, 1978), p. 41.

The foregoing discussion has concentrated on the lamentable stagnation in the traditional sector of Bolivian agriculture. This is in sharp contrast, however, to the substantial progress made in the commercial agricultural sector. As Table VIII-4 indicates, sugar cane and rice production both quadrupled between 1961 and 1975. Cotton production, a mere 1,000 metric tons in 1961, increased to 37,600 metric tons in 1973, albeit declining to 22,020 in 1975.

Nevertheless, despite the noteworthy development of modern and commercial agriculture in Bolivia, it is unlikely that this sector will absorb the excess of labor created by inefficiencies in the traditional sector. In the 1960s and 1970s it is estimated that about 10,000 and 17,000 persons annually migrated from the rural areas to urban centers. These figures account for about 0.33 and 0.44 percent of the annual rural population in the two decades respectively. [5]

The obvious conclusion to be drawn from these figures is the need to emphasize investment in the traditional sector of Bolivian agriculture. Additional investment in this sector would help achieve not only the economic goal of providing employment, but also the social goal of distributing the benefits of investments more widely.

TABLE VIII-4

PRODUCTION IN THE COMMERCIAL AGRICULTURAL SECTOR
(Metric tons)

Year	Sugar Cane	Cotton	Rice
1961	600	1.000	24.000
1967	1.065	2.800	39.650
1971	1.101	9.800	59.730
1972	1.515	15.500	59.670
1973	2.082	37.600	54.465
1974	2.049	26.700	29.665
1975	2.366	22.020	88.590

Source: Ministerio de Asuntos Campesinos y Agropecuarios, División de Estadísticas, *Estadísticas agropecuarias*, Boletín No. 2. (La Paz, diciembre, 1976), pp. 54, 56 and 58.

MINING SINCE NATIONALIZATION

Despite its stagnation in recent years, mining remains one of the most important sectors of the Bolivian economy, representing between 11 and 12 percent of GDP, employing 3 percent of the Bolivian labor force, and providing 75 percent of all foreign exchange and 25 percent of government revenues.

Its importance notwithstanding, mining, like agriculture, is a strategic economic sector in which supply is relatively inelastic and does not respond readily to changes in demand or in prices. In part, this situation is due to the difficulties which have beset the mining sector since 1952, the obsolescence of the mining laws, and the poorly coordinated tax structure which applies to this industry.

Of course, mining in Bolivia is also closely related to the topography of the country. Most of the mines are located at high altitudes. Many, if not most of them, follow thin veins, and their high operating costs relate directly to the depth of the faces and the complexity of the mineral concentrates they yield. The limited physical infrastructure of Bolivia—roads, railroad lines, etc.—also adds to the very high operating costs of what can only be described as an extremely capital-intensive industry.

Another factor which has limited the development of mining in Bolivia is the lack of exploration and development of new mineral deposits during the last twenty-five years. Less than 10 percent of the national land area has been systematically explored since 1952. This is due in part to the mining laws, which stipulated that large land areas thought to contain mineral wealth be declared government reserves. Such areas were reserved exclusively for the state enterprise COMIBOL. Paradoxically, COMIBOL, which has prevented private mining firms from undertaking such exploration, has nevertheless refused to make more than a token effort in this direction on its own behalf. Fortunately, the national government is now taking steps to rectify this situation.

Yet another factor which limits mining development in Bolivia has been the somewhat irrational system of taxation applied to this industry. Tax assessments are based on the gross value of exports, and do not take production costs into consideration. Thus they have an adverse effect on investment for exploration and mine development, since such investments cannot be deducted from production costs.

COMIBOL: The Heritage of Nationalization

The World Bank, in an unpublished economic analysis of Bolivia in 1977, notes that COMIBOL, since its creation in 1952, has experienced a multitude of problems due to its excessive centralization, the slow erosion of its capital assets, its inefficient use of labor, and excessive welfare benefits for its employees. The World Bank analysis of the national mining company certainly comes as no surprise, since it does little more than repeat the contents of many other reports concerning COMIBOL.

> Since its creation in 1952 COMIBOL has experienced problems of overcentralization, decapitalization, inefficient use of labor and excessive welfare expenditures. The organization's structure seems to be centralized to an extent inconsistent with running such a large, diversified firm in an efficient manner. Most of COMIBOL's mines are decapitalized and operate with very low levels of ore reserves. Operational costs are rising as mines become progressively deeper and the ore grades mined deteriorate. COMIBOL's equipment was already depreciated and technically obsolete at the time of nationalization in 1952 and no significant new investment has been carried out until very recently. Investment has been channeled mainly into ore processing (including volatization) which has succeeded in increasing recovery ratios despite falling mineral content of ores. Employment in COMIBOL is well in excess of requirements due to the commitment of the Government to social reform and the concentration of political power in the miner's unions. Moreover, there is a serious lack of middle management at the mine and plant levels. The Government recognizes that improvements in COMIBOL are essential to the future of the sector and has recently appointed a new management team. [6]

Although these reports are correct in pointing out that COMIBOL has wrestled unsuccessfully with the same problems for more than twenty years, they usually err in not realizing that the most important of COMIBOL's problems are political rather than managerial. Indeed, the solution of the managerial problems that do exist cannot possibly take place unless the political problems are dealt with first. For example, the ineffective utilization of COMIBOL personnel and the payment of excessive social welfare benefits are in fact complex *political* problems which have their roots in the compromises made on October 31, 1952, when Bolivia decreed the nationalization of mines. These compromises, sanctioned by custom in succeeding years, cannot now be ignored by the national government without risking a serious breach with organized labor. Such a breach would have the gravest political consequences for the nation as a whole.

In addition to its role as a political instrument, COMIBOL also serves, in effect, as a continuing law and of the ills and reverses suffered by the

Bolivian economy. The best example of this phenomenon is, perhaps, the question of exchange rates. For many years, Bolivia has had a policy of fixed rates of exchange. Obviously, when domestic prices rise, the price of foreign exchange falls in relation to that of domestic goods. COMIBOL is then obliged to accept payment for its mineral products in undervalued foreign currencies, and this situation is reflected in its earnings. Clearly, COMIBOL would benefit greatly if it did not have to pay the price for a poorly conceived fixed exchange policy, especially while attempting to deal with the resource allocation and labor utilization problems mentioned previously.

The fact that COMIBOL serves at times as a scapegoat for ills it has not caused cannot, however, be taken as an excuse for its true failures. On the contrary, this example, like the others mentioned above, shows the essentially political nature of COMIBOL as an institution and high-lights the political rather than managerial causes of its well-known deficiencies. While these political problems remain unresolved, even the best managers can do little to improve the functioning of this state-owned industry.

Medium and Small-Scale Mining

In sharp contrast to the experience of COMIBOL since 1952, medium-scale mining enterprises during the same time period have demonstrated a notable efficiency, a strong tendency towards modernization, and an intensive utilization of capital. In the first years after the nationalization of large holdings, fear of still more extensive nationalization inhibited the development of the privately owned medium-scale mining enterprises. But at present the only serious problem facing this sector is the lack of qualified personnel to operate its installations and bring its products to market.

Small-scale mining has generally not partaken of this same dynamism, and, like COMIBOL, has changed little since 1952. This sector embraces a relatively large number of small private companies and mining cooperatives, which employ antiquated methods and seldom live up to the minimum standards for protecting the health and safety of their workers. They also have severe marketing problems due to their dependence on the State Mining Bank, the *Banco Minero,* an institution which buys and markets their products, and which has for twenty-five years provided a minimal level of service in exchange for charges reflecting its high operating cost. [7]

Fiscal Reform for Mining

Under the auspices of the World Bank, a group of economists and engineers headed by Malcom Gillis of the Harvard Institute for International Development has proposed steps to solve the tax problems of the mining sector. These steps involve replacement of the present inefficient tax system by two economic packages which include the following measures:

(1) A tax on presumptive income, which takes into account actual development costs, combined with a low-rate levy to stabilize fiscal revenue.

(2) Once this system is well established, a change-over to a tax on profits is to be applied, at least to companies such as COMIBOL and the twenty-five to thirty largest non-state-held companies which can render an adequate accounting of their financial operations. These firms to-

gether account for approximately 80 percent of all mineral production in Bolivia. Producers unable to prepare adequate accounts will continue to be taxed on the presumptive income basis.

Recommendations of the report also include:

(1) The drawing up of a list of depreciable items (a partial tax credit for exploration and development instead of a depletion is recommended).

(2) The elimination of preferential treatment for the mining of low-grade deposits (at the present time a highly uneconomical pattern of exploitation and processing is encouraged, which results in utilizing the richest ores which are then exported as very low concentrates).

(3) The establishment of a system of effective taxes designed to increase with income.

(4) An additional tax on windfall profits.

(5) Economic rationalization of patents and other small fees.

The report of this mission represents a comprehensive analysis of the mining situation in Bolivia and proposes viable solutions to urgent problems. Nevertheless, three years have gone by without any government action on its recommendations. The medium-scale mining enterprises, which strongly supported the implementation of these recommendations when mineral prices were low and their production costs equaled or surpassed the export value of their products, have apparently lost much of their great interest now that prices have risen.[8] However, as a result of the failure to implement this reform, the Bolivian government must get along without the considerable additional income which a reform of the present mining taxes would undoubtedly provide.[9]

SMELTERS

When President René Barrientos announced the intention of the Junta to build the first Bolivian tin smelters, his speech from the balcony of the County Government Building in Oruro on February 10, 1965 began with the cry "We are free!" This cry, although it may seem somewhat melodramatic to foreign ears, was nevertheless a sincere expression of the sentiments of many Bolivians. Bolivia, by and large, presumed that the establishment of smelters in-country would liberate the national economy from "foreign exploiters," increase revenues by saving transport costs and by moving "downstream" in the production process, and reduce unemployment by generating new jobs.

Unfortunately, only the last of these expectations has been realized even in part. On the one hand, the mere fact that Bolivia can now produce metal rather than mineral concentrate does not automatically guarantee the marketing of her products. On the other hand, the operation of the smelters has not proven sufficiently profitable to guarantee large additional revenues.

The Bolivian authorities later became aware of the problem of marketing and Decree Number 07695, issued July 15, 1966, placed this activity in the hands of the National Smelting Company (ENAF). To date, however, ENAF has limited its participation in this field to the formation of a very small marketing department, capable only of serving as a sort of liaison with the true marketing agents, Phillip Brothers of New York.

The expectation of increased revenues has proven equally unfounded. Supposedly, such revenues would be based on the profitability of the enterprise itself, and on the savings occasioned by reducing transportation costs. It appears, however, that from the beginning the question of profitability received very little attention. Reportedly, two attempts that proved that the project was not feasible were rejected before the German firm Klockner agreed to provide the necessary equipment. These prior rejections were based on doubts concerning the profitability of smelting in Bolivia. Indeed, ENAF has justified these doubts by losing money every year between 1971 and 1975.[10]

With respect to the projected saving of transportation costs, an unpublished World Bank study on the Bolivian mineral-extraction and metallurgic industries estimates that, at 1971 prices, transportation savings on concentrates of less than 40 percent (grade) cannot in themselves justify the building of smelters.[11] Of course, given the present tin prices and transportation costs, it is possible that this situation may have changed. There are even some reports, such as the one prepared by *Metals Week*, which would go so far as to affirm that a price of five dollars per pound on the London market would justify transporting tin by air![12]

In general, however, the foregoing considerations suggest that present plans to set up new smelters should be carefully reviewed. During the 1977-1980 period, ENAF plans to invest 250 million dollars in tin trebling and the smelting of zinc, silver, lead, and even copper. The extremely low price of copper on the international market and the expectation that the United States will soon impose severe protective restrictions on zinc imports are both subjects of grave concern in relation to these perhaps over-ambitious plans.

PETROLEUM PRODUCTS SINCE THE PETROLEUM CODE

As noted previously, the implementation of the Petroleum Code was one of the most significant actions of the MNR government, serving as it did to awaken interest in the discovery and development of Bolivia's energy wealth. Interest in Bolivian petroleum resources actually dates from many years earlier. However, the MNR government played a key role in encouraging this interest. Despite its ultra-nationalist political stance, the MNR recognized the importance of acquiring foreign exchange, even at the price of sacrificing one of its basic principles--freedom from dependence on foreign companies.

President René Barrientos, who succeeded the MNR government in 1964, stoutly defended the petroleum policy of his predecessors, which had sought to create a favorable climate for foreign investment. However, President Ovando, who took office in 1969, opted shortly thereafter to nationalize the holdings of the Gulf Oil Corporation. As a result petroleum exploration in Bolivia came to a halt until the 1972 enactment of a new set of petroleum laws entitled The General Hydrocarbons Law.

This new legislation authorized The Bolivian State Petroleum Company (YPFB) to sign thirty-year contracts with private firms entitling the latter to undertake petroleum exploration and production. The laws establish the minimum investment required, the number of wells to be drilled in the first four years of operation, and the rules under which petroleum products can be exported by the international oil companies. More than fifteen such contracts have been signed to date, guaranteeing that for each contract YPFB will receive 50 percent of the resulting gross income.

These contracts have raised the hopes of Bolivians in general, but unfortunately little petroleum has been discovered to date. The results of the Montecristo explorations remain unconfirmed, occasioning rumors that the location is rich in natural gas rather than oil. The recent discoveries by Occidental Petroleum will increase national petroleum production by only 3,000 to 5,000 barrels per day. No other company has yet indicated the discovery of important deposits.

Nevertheless, petroleum experts apparently remain convinced that large deposits do exist in Bolivian territory, and it is to be hoped that their expectations will not prove false. If, however, the present lack of results continues, existing reserves will diminish rapidly under the pressure of accelerating internal consumption, and it may even become necessary to import petroleum products. If the current unfavorable commercial balance continues into the future, such importation will be difficult. It is estimated that supporting present consumption with imported petroleum products would add 148 million dollars per year to the unfavorable balance of trade. Even half that amount of petroleum imports would raise Bolivia's total imports by about 12 percent. [13]

The failure to find oil would also have grave consequences for investment in the five-year period 1976-1980. The Bolivian government plans to invest approximately 3,500 million dollars during that period, 69 percent of which must come from savings in the domestic economy--most of it from the savings of the Public Enterprises. [14] If mineral production does not double and petroleum production does not quadruple during that period--as the plan postulates--this will have a sharp impact on the level of investment in the national economy, with additional impacts on the level of production.

This situation would also affect Bolivia's image in international circles. The Bolivian economy has benefited greatly from the mere possibility that Bolivia might become a more important exporter of petroleum. The benefits which have accrued to the national economy include substantial amounts of credit from international organizations and the international capital market. The utilization of these new lines of credit have contributed significantly to the outstanding foreign debt.

Although not directly related to the question of production levels, the subsidizing of high levels of internal consumption should also be mentioned in any discussion of Bolivia's petroleum resources. This subsidy has proven undesirable in terms of resource allocation. In a study, "Taxation of the Domestic Consumption of Petroleum," Charles McLure estimates that the cost of importing, transporting, refining and retailing petroleum is more than 85 percent higher than its cost on the domestic market, and that the government subsidy of this product amounted in 1975 to 1.385 billion pesos each year. [15]

TABLE VIII-5

EXTERNAL DEBT IN BOLIVIA
(In millions of U.S. dollars)

Year	Contracted Debt	Debt Service
1972	94.800	53.6
1973	1.018	53.4
1974	1.191	78.0
1975	1.524	91.5
1976	1.979	111.3
1977	2.510	161.1

Source: Ministerio de Finanzas, Instituto Nacional de Financiamiento, *Memorandum sobre el financiamiento externo de Bolivia* (La Paz, enero, 1978).

NATURAL GAS PRODUCTION

The possibilities for natural gas production in Bolivia are considerably brighter than those for the near-term production of oil. It is estimated that Bolivia's gas reserves total some 3.8 trillion cubic feet, a figure which does not take into account recent discoveries by the foreign oil enterprises. Presently, Bolivia sells 57 million cubic feet per day to Argentina, and employs about 3.5 million cubic feet for domestic uses.

The principal obstacle to the sale of this abundant resource is the lack of customers. Unless an additional pipeline is built through Brazil or another neighboring country, Bolivian gas exports will continue to be limited by the conditions of the poorly negotiated sales contract with Argentina. The conditions of this contract have been somewhat improved, especially as regards price, but even the modified terms favor Argentina far more than Bolivia. Bolivia could probably use its leverage to raise gas prices still further, at least until they reach the level of the Argentine opportunity cost, i.e., the cost to Argentina of importing fuel oil from other sources. This price would be quite high, since Bolivia is Argentina's best natural gas supplier—especially for the northern section of the country—and the employment of other energy sources to replace Bolivian gas would be extremely complicated.

Currently there is a project under consideration to sell 240 million cubic feet of gas to Brazil, but this would require the construction of a 400-mile pipeline. Brazil has offered to finance the construction costs, but the Bolivian government has decided that the entire project should form part of a joint package that would include development of the Mutun iron deposits. At present, both governments are considering negotiations based on this package.

EMPHASIS ON EDUCATION

A comparison of the 1950 census with the preliminary results of the 1976 census leaves no doubt whatsoever that the educational efforts of the MNR government during the 1950s were fruitful. These efforts, which included increased expenditures for education and better incentives for rural teachers, have been far more effective than expected. The approximately 67.8 percent illiteracy rate reported in 1950[16] has fallen to 37.3 percent, and to a surprising 15 percent for Bolivians between the ages of fifteen and twenty. It is no exaggeration to say that Bolivia's educational investment has been recovered many times over.

This does not necessarily signify that Bolivia's education problem has been solved. Much remains to be done, and the present system is in need of considerable reform. The existing misallocation of expenditures in the educational sector places too much emphasis on current outlays, primarily for salaries, and too little emphasis on long-term investment in schools, educational equipment and other facilities. Provisions of existing educational legislation which intended to provide incentives for necessary basic education in prior years should also be reconsidered in the light of the current conditions, since many of them have outlived their usefulness.[17]

CONCLUSION

In reviewing Bolivia's economic situation since 1952, it must be kept in mind that the efforts which began in that year to transform the national economy, and which have continued since, have not succeeded in altering three features of the economy which represent potential bottle-

necks to future progress: (1) dependency on foreign trade, with resulting vulnerability to international price fluctuations; (2) related government dependence on foreign trade taxes which, together with inflexible
minimum levels of government expenditure, can occasion serious problems
of resource allocation, price levels, and levels of public debt; (3) inflexible supply in some of the most strategic economic sectors, especially agriculture and mining.

Although land reform and the nationalization of the mines might have
served to ameliorate the effects of these bottlenecks, they have not done
so, in part because the reforms of the 1950s took place in the absence of
an economic and social infrastructure which would have greatly enhanced
their effectiveness. Thus agriculture, particularly traditional agriculture, has tended to stagnate; and mining, particularly COMIBOL, continues to suffer from the same problems that beset it twenty years ago.

In order to rescue agriculture from its present stagnation, it will be
necessary to: increase agricultural investment; modify the price controls,
which discourage production; rationalize tariffs to discourage import competition; set up adequate systems for distributing agricultural inputs and
marketing foodstuffs; and extend more agricultural credit to small-scale
producers in the traditional sector. The last of these points is by no
means the least important.

With respect to mining, it is now high time to end the seemingly in-
terminable reports on the problems of COMIBOL and to recognize that
these problems are basically political rather than administrative, or at
least that the administrative problems which do exist have their roots in
the political system. As long as Bolivia continues to receive undervalued
foreign currencies in return for its mineral products and COMIBOL raises
its production costs in response to political pressures, the state-owned
enterprise's profits and its managerial structure will continue to suffer.
This being the case, COMIBOL will continue to serve principally as a
scapegoat for Bolivia's economic problems—an easy target due to its many
deficiencies—but in many respects an unjust target for criticism which
would be better directed against political decisions which the Bolivian
government feels obligated to make.

Bolivia's smelters—another program inspired by the 1952 revolution—
should be recognized as an industry of traditionally low profits. This
characteristic should be given careful consideration before proceeding
with the plans for additional zinc, silver, lead and copper smelters. Perhaps the most important point to keep in mind is that the relatively small
benefits to be obtained from the investment in the smelters could make it
much more attractive to employ those same resources in other projects—
projects capable of generating more income, more employment, and a
better distribution of investment benefits than the new smelters.

Finally, two of the many socioeconomic measures initiated by the MNR
are particularly pertinent to the present situation in Bolivia: the encouragement of education—which has resulted in considerable improvement of
Bolivia's human resources—and the Petroleum Code—which takes into
account the need to encourage exploration and development.

After undertaking this brief analysis of the effects of the revolution
of 1952 on modern-day Bolivia the question needs to be asked what can
be expected for Bolivia in the near future? The answer to this question
will depend on the political decisions that will come from the forthcoming
elections this July, the results of Bolivia's development plan, and above
all the resolution of the three important problems confronting Bolivia that
must be solved in the short run, namely: increase in wages, the devaluation of the Bolivian peso, and the determination of petroleum prices.

ENDNOTES FOR CHAPTER VIII

1. Richard S. Thorn, "The Economic Transformation," *Beyond the Revolution: Bolivia Since 1952*, eds. James M. Malloy and Richard S. Thorn (Pittsburgh: University of Pittsburgh Press, 1971), p. 159.

2. Obviously, it is not fair to say that "nothing" was done for agriculture during the MNR years, since the truth is that the MNR has attempted to stimulate production in the traditional agricultural sector, both by encouraging the formation of agricultural communities and by creating incentives for internal migration to the eastern region of the nation. In 1953, a commission was established for the latter purpose headed by the then-Vice President Siles Zuazo. The Mexican agricultural economist Edmundo Flores served as principal advisor to the commission. Nevertheless, the implementation of this program obviously required a master plan backed up by adequate financing, neither of which the MNR possessed or was willing to acquire as it was preoccupied with maintaining and consolidating its own political power.

3. Juan Antonio Morales, "Tariff, Internal Indirect Taxes and Allocative Efficiency," *Fiscal Reform in Bolivia, Staff Papers*, Vol. II, No. 21 (Cambridge, Mass.: Musgrave Mission, 1977), pp. 39-41 (Mimeographed.)

4. In recent years, United States Agency for International Development (AID) FRA II credits have attempted to serve as a vehicle for extending credit to small producers in the traditional agricultural sector. However, limitations on the amount of these loans and difficulties in finding a means to guarantee their repayment have served to limit the impact of this program. The AID-financed T-053 small farmer credit program has had better results.

5. Albert Berry, "The Potential of Increased Public Investment in Agriculture," *Fiscal Reform in Bolivia, Staff Papers*, Vol. I, No. 11 (Cambridge, Mass.: Musgrave Mission, 1977), p. 30.

6. International Bank for Reconstruction and Development, "Economic Memorandum on Bolivia," Unpublished report (Washington, D.C.: March, 1977), p. 16.

7. Ibid., pp. 17-18.

8. Asociación Nacional de Mineros Medianos, *Informe anual: julio 1976-junio 1977* (La Paz: 26 de septiembre, 1977), p. 11 and *Informe anual: julio 1977-junio 1978* (La Paz, 28 de agosto, 1978), p. 14. In this last report, fiscal reform is hardly mentioned.

8. The combination of export taxes and royalties in the present system makes the present tax structure more proportional than progressive when the prices are high. The opposite occurs when the prices are low.

10. Malcom Gillis and Charles McLure, Jr., "Tax Policy and Public Enterprises," *Fiscal Reform in Bolivia, Staff Papers*, Vol. I, No. 8 (Cambridge, Mass.: Musgrave Mission, 1977), p. 59 (Mimeographed.)

11. International Bank for Reconstruction and Development, International Development Association, Industrial Projects Department, "The Mining and Metallurgical Sector, Bolivia," Vol. III. Annex 2- Metallurgical (Smelting and Refining) Survey, Confidential Report No. PI-14 (Washington, D.C.: The International Bank for Reconstruction and Development, November 15, 1977), p. 3.

12. *Metals Week* (New York), October 17, 1977, p. 2, col. 2.

13. Based on the 1976 consumption and an opportunity cost of 18.50 dollars per barrel (consumption defined as oil internally refined).

14. Presidencia de la República, Ministerio de Planeamiento y Coordinación, *Plan de desarrollo económico y social (Resumen)*, (La Paz: Minplaneamiento, agosto 1976), p. 84.

15. Charles McLure, Jr., "Taxation of Domestic Consumption of Petroleum," *Fiscal Reform in Bolivia, Staff Papers*, Vol. I, No. 9 (Cambridge, Mass.: Musgrave Mission, 1977), pp. 20-21 (Mimeographed.)

16. Population over fifteen years of age.

17. For example, certified teachers receive a government salary whether or not they actually work as teachers. Originally intended to encourage Bolivians to become teachers, this legislation now leads to an obvious distortion of its original intention.

Chapter IX

Structural Change and Development Policy in Bolivia[1]
L. Enrique García-Rodríguez

INTRODUCTION

The purpose of this paper is to analyze the main structural changes that have occurred in Bolivia after the 1952 revolution, and to determine the role of development policy in the process—particularly after 1960. The presentation is divided into four parts.

The first section examines the main structural changes. The second and third sections discuss the institutional setting and development policies of the various governments that have been in power since 1960 along with some suggestions for the future development of Bolivia. Special attention is placed on planning, which can be considered as the main tool for a definition of priorities and the implementation of sound strategies in a developing country. The fourth section presents a summary with conclusions.

STRUCTURAL CHANGES SINCE 1952

General Framework

Bolivia—a large country with low population density, rich in natural resources and located strategically in the heart of South America—has always had the potential to become a prosperous nation. In the twentieth century there have been, however, a number of obstacles to rapid growth and social betterment. Some of the major ones are: dormant industrialization, underdeveloped economic and social infrastructure, lack of access to the ocean, small population, insufficiently trained human resources, inadequate institutional framework and considerable political instability.

The Bolivian economy from the early years of Spanish colonization until 1952 had a dual character. One part of the economy, orientated to the world market, was concerned with natural resources, mainly minerals, which were not only exported but also were largely processed beyond its borders. At first, silver was the main product and principal source of export earnings of the country. This continued until near the beginning of the twentieth century when world prices fell drastically; since then tin replaced silver as the main export of Bolivia. The almost exclusive dependence upon minerals as a source of foreign exchange created a situation, whereby the Big Three tin companies that controlled the mines also had absolute control over the political life of the country.

The remaining part of the economy, mainly agricultural, was organized in small subsistence farms or large *latifundia*, whose products flowed to local markets that were little affected by world prices. The agricultural economy was practically based upon slave labor and Spanish manorial customs. The religious beliefs of the rural population were a contributing factor as they served to immobilize the peasants in a traditional style of life.

Since the concentration of the modern sector of the economy was in mining, most of the infrastructure—roads, railroads and electricity—was built to support that industry. Consequently, very little was done to connect the vast areas of the nation outside of the mining centers. The eastern lowlands, where a great potential for development existed, was noticeably neglected. The lack of a sound development strategy and of sufficient government revenues were also serious obstacles to channeling resources to health, education, housing and other social services. Bolivia presented, indeed, one of the worst social situations in Latin America, with no hope for change due to the vested interests of the small but powerful ruling classes.

The 1952 revolution is the turning point in Bolivia's modern history. The resultant major structural changes have had deep repercussions: of particular importance were the nationalization of the Big Three tin mines, the land reform, the opening of the Santa Cruz region, the initial efforts to diversify the productive base of the country and the social conscience developed by the majority of the population. The impacts of these changes were felt during the 1950s when most political and social changes took place, but were most important after 1960 when economic development accelerated.

The present analysis concentrates on the important changes occurring since 1952 in the following areas: (a) the rates of growth and inflation; (b) the structure of production, exports and imports; (c) the level per capita of income; (d) the magnitude of the investment effort; (e) the capacity for internal savings; (f) the improvement in social indicators; and (g) the role of the public sector in the development process. It is useful when analyzing these changes to make comparisons of the early fifties with the sixties and the seventies. The observed trends permit some speculation concerning the future. It is in this context that each of the seven areas is discussed in the following sections.

Growth and Inflation

It was not until the early 1960s, when financial equilibrium was restored after several years of hyperinflation and negative growth, that Bolivia actually started to grow within a framework of financial stability.

In fact, as shown in Table IX-1, in the 1950s the gross domestic product (GDP) and per capita GDP cumulative annual rates of growth were less than -1 and -3 percent, respectively. In the 1960s recovery began such that the rates were almost 5 and 3 percent, respectively, and in the 1970s they increased to about 6 and 4 percent. At the same time, the average annual rate of inflation, which was as high as 122 percent for the 1952-1955 period, decreased to 32 percent in the 1956-1959 period and then remained below 6 percent until 1972. Between that year and 1975 inflation rates averaged 25 percent. An important causal factor was the 66 percent devaluation of the Bolivian peso in 1972. Excluding the effect of the exchange rate adjustment, inflation has been kept below 15 percent a year since 1975.

TABLE IX-1

GROWTH AND INFLATION IN BOLIVIA 1952-1977
(Percent)

	1952-55	1956-59	1960-63	1964-69	1970-71	1972-77[a]
GDP cumulative annual rate of growth in real terms	-0.90	-1.85	4.60	6.20	5.10	6.10
GDP per-capita cumulative annual rate of growth in real terms	-2.58	-3.44	2.90	4.40	3.45	4.25
Average annual rate of inflation	122.4	32.40	5.60	5.10	5.10	25.00

[a]The data for the period are influenced by the price adjustments of 1972 and 1973 following the 1972 devaluation of the Bolivian peso. In the 1972-1974 period the annual inflationary rate was 40 percent. In the 1975-1977 period it declined to 11.9 percent.

Source: Ministerio de Planificación y Coordinación, *Cuentas nacionales 1950-1969* (La Paz, 1970); Banco Central de Bolivia, *Cuentas nacionales 1970-1975* (La Paz, 1977); Ministerio de Planeamiento y Coordinación, *Planes anuales operativo 1977; 1978*, (La Paz, 1977; 1978).

The Structure of Production

Table IX-2 shows that in the 1950s the productive sectors contributed more than 60 percent of total GDP, but that their share has continuously declined since then. During the 1960s the productive sectors contributed about 58 percent of GDP and during the seventies they have been responsible for only about 46 percent of the total. Since the proportion of GDP attributed to economic infrastructure has remained between 9 and 10 percent during the last twenty-five years, it is clear that the counterpart to the reduction in the productive sectors' contribution was a considerable increase in social infrastructure and services.

It is also shown in Table IX-2 that there were major changes in the sectoral composition of GDP over the time period under consideration. Of particular importance were the changes in the shares of the productive sectors--agriculture, mining, hydrocarbons, manufacturing and construction. Agriculture, which represented about 29 percent of GDP in the early fifties, decreased to less than 20 percent in the seventies. Moreover mining's share fell from almost 16 percent in the early fifties to less than 9 percent in the seventies. While manufacturing, energy, and transportation and communications maintained approximately their same shares during the whole period under consideration, hydrocarbons, construction, commerce and finance, general government, housing and other services increased their participation.

TABLE IX-2

SECTORAL COMPOSITION OF GDP 1952-1977
(Percent)

	1952-55	1956-59	1960-63	1964-69	1970-71	1972-77
Productive Sectors	63.5	60.6	58.6	58.1	46.5	46.4
Agriculture	28.5	30.3	30.6	26.4	18.0	17.1
Mining	15.8	11.3	8.6	8.7	8.9	8.3
Hydrocarbons	0.8	2.0	1.7	2.9	1.4	2.1
Manufacturing	15.8	13.9	13.8	15.3	14.2	15.8
Construction	2.7	3.1	3.9	4.8	4.0	3.9
Economic Infrastructure	9.0	10.0	9.9	9.8	8.9	9.8
Energy	1.5	1.6	1.5	1.9	1.4	1.4
Transportation & communications	7.5	8.4	8.4	7.9	7.5	8.4
Social Infrastructure and Services	27.4	29.4	31.5	32.1	44.6	43.8
Commerce & finance	12.9	13.1	12.8	13.1	18.8	18.5
General government[a]	6.2	6.8	8.6	9.6	8.1	8.8
Housing	3.2	3.5	3.6	3.4	8.6	7.9
Other services	5.1	6.0	6.5	6.0	9.1	8.6
TOTAL	100.0	100.0	100.0	100.0	100.0	100.0

[a]Includes health, education and other social services.

Source: Ministerio de Planificación y Coordinación, *Cuentas nacionales 1950-1969* (La Paz, 1970); Banco Central de Bolivia, *Cuentas nacionales 1970-1975* (La Paz, 1977); Ministerio de Planeamiento y Coordinación, *Planes anuales operativos 1977; 1978* (La Paz, 1977; 1978).

There are several conclusions that can be drawn with respect to the changes in the structure of production during the last twenty-five years. First, the fact that the productive sectors only represented about 46 percent of GDP in the seventies as compared to more than 64 percent in the early fifties, is unfavorable in terms of the objectives of self-sustained growth.

Second, it is quite a plus that within the productive sectors considerable economic diversification has taken place; for example, hydrocarbons increased considerably their relative importance. This diversification, however, has not favored development by directly creating numerous new jobs or by providing for a substantial shift of the labor force out of agriculture. The agricultural sector still employs more than 60 percent of the labor force.

Third, the increased contribution of the social sectors—health and housing—has favored not only economic but also social development. These sectors increased their share of GDP from less than 15 percent in the early fifties to around 18 percent in the sixties and to 25 percent in the seventies.

Fourth, the increased share of the financial sector in GDP is favorable since the growth of financial intermediation is suggestive of a more dynamic economy. In contrast the increased share of commerce is unfavor-

able   since this activity has not been related fundamentally to the productive sectors, but rather has been closely linked to consumption, oftentimes
that of unnecessary imports.

The Structure of Exports and Imports

The significant changes in the composition of exports are shown in
Table IX-3. Minerals accounted for 97 percent of Bolivia's total exports in
1952. During the fifties and sixties they maintained around a 90 percent
share. However, by the 1972-1977 period they had fallen to only around
63 percent of the total.

The principal export, tin, has fluctuated in its importance. It accounted for 61 percent of total exports in 1952, 79 percent in 1964, and
less than 46 percent of total Bolivian exports in 1977. It is noteworthy that
40 percent of tin was exported in a semi-processed smelted form. Estimates indicate by 1983 total production of tin and most of other minerals
will be exported in this form.

TABLE IX-3

STRUCTURE OF EXPORTS 1952-1977
(Percent)

	1952-55	1956-59	1960-63	1964-69	1970-71	1972-77
Minerals	97	90	91	86	87	63
Hydrocarbons	1	4	3	8	8	24
Other	2	6	6	6	5	13
TOTAL	100	100	100	100	100	100

Source: Banco Central de Bolivia, *Memorias anuales 1952-1977* (La Paz,
1952-1977).

Petroleum and gas exports have increased substantially. Less than
1 percent of Bolivia's total exports in the early fifties were from this source.
In the sixties and the early seventies they accounted for 6 and 8 percent
of the total, respectively. In 1977 approximately 25 percent of total exports came from this sector.

In recent years there has been a considerable increase in the export
of other products, particularly those of agricultural and manufacturing
origin. In the early fifties they accounted for less than 3 percent of total
exports. The sixties showed an increase to more than 5 percent, but in the
last four years their importance has risen sharply to where they accounted
for close to 13 percent of total exports.

The structure of imports also changed. As shown in Table IX-4, there
was a decline in the relative importance of consumer good imports and an
increase in the importance of intermediate goods. In the fifties about 30
percent of total imports corresponded to consumer goods and 13 percent to
intermediate goods, whereas in the seventies only 20 percent of imports
were consumer goods, but 38 percent corresponded to intermediate goods.
These changes reflect the advances in the industrialization. Capital goods

TABLE IX-4

STRUCTURE OF IMPORTS 1952-1977
(Percent)

	1952-55	1956-59	1960-63	1964-69	1970-71	1972-77
Consumer goods	33	25	25	23	20	21
Intermediate goods	13	7	26	34	34	38
Capital goods	53	67	48	42	46	40
Other	1	1	1	1	--	1
TOTAL	100	100	100	100	100	100

Source: Banco Central de Bolivia, *Memorias anuales 1952-1977* (La Paz, 1952-1977).

have always accounted for the largest portion of imports. The percentage of capital goods imports, however, declined after the early 1960s and since then has remained at about 40 percent of total imports.

GDP and Per Capita Income

After the revolution of 1952 the real value of GDP declined (Table IX-5). It wasn't until 1962 that it again reached the level of 1953 and in the remainder of the decade there were continual increases. Real per capita GDP followed a similar pattern. Measured in 1977 pesos it was approximately equivalent to 464 dollars in 1952. It fell to 373 dollars in 1960, but increased to 431 dollars in 1964 and up to 560 dollars in 1970. At the end of 1977 it was close to 750 dollars.

In other words, this means that per capita GDP doubled in real terms between 1960 and 1977. Taking into account the favorable terms of trade experienced by Bolivia for most years between 1960 and 1977 (Table IX-6), per capita purchasing power can be estimated to have increased, in real terms, by more than 120 percent during the period.

Investment, Savings and Other Macroeconomic Indicators

The increase in per capita income provided for the simultaneous improvement in the investment and savings capacity of Bolivia. As shown in Table IX-7 the considerable increases in the investment and savings ratios demonstrate that the country was able to capitalize on this potential. The investment ratio was around 16 percent of GDP from 1952 until the early seventies. It increased, however, to 21 percent in the 1972-1977 period in response to Bolivia's recent development efforts. The current ratio is one of the highest in the developing world.

The internal savings ratio, which was as low as 7 percent in the early sixties, has improved since 1964 to reach 20 percent in the period 1972-1977. If the years of 1973 and 1974 are excluded, when extraordinarily high export prices favored the savings performance of the country, the savings ratio for the 1972-1977 period is close to 18 percent.

TABLE IX-5

REAL GDP AND GDP PER CAPITA 1952-1977[a]

Years	GDP (Millions of 1977 pesos)	Population	GDP per capita (1977 pesos)	GDP per capita (1977 US dollars)
1952	28,948.8	3,120,709	9,276	464
1953	26,205.7	3,172,824	8,259	413
1954	26,750.6	3,225,811	8,293	415
1955	28,170.0	3,279,682	8,589	429
1956	26,499.7	3,334,452	7,947	397
1957	25,619.4	3,390,138	7,557	378
1958	26,231.4	3,446,753	7,610	381
1959	26,145.5	3,504,314	7,461	373
1960	27,269.2	3,562,836	7,654	383
1961	27,839.0	3,622,335	7,685	384
1962	29,392.1	3,682,828	7,981	399
1963	31,280.8	3,744,331	8,354	418
1964	32,787.1	3,806,862	8,613	431
1965	35,050.5	3,870,436	9,056	453
1966	37,509.0	3,935,073	9,024	451
1967	39,881.7	4,000,788	9,968	498
1968	42,745.9	4,067,601	10,509	525
1969	44,782.9	4,135,530	10,829	541
1970	47,125.4	4,204,594	11,208	560
1971	49,465.7	4,275,231	11,570	579
1972	52,367.6	4,347,055	12,047	602
1973	55,996.6	4,420,086	12,669	633
1974	59,429.7	4,494,343	13,223	661
1975	62,749.8	4,569,848	13,731	687
1976	66,801.0	4,647,836	14,372	719
1977	70,170.0	4,724,685	14,852	743

[a]A price index utilizing 1977 as the base year and calculated by the Ministry of Planning and Coordination was employed.

Source: Ministerio de Planificación y Coordinación, *Cuentas nacionales 1950-1969* (La Paz, 1970); Banco Central de Bolivia, *Cuentas nacionales 1970-1975* (La Paz, 1977); Ministerio de Planeamiento y Coordinación, *Planes anuales operativos 1977; 1978* (La Paz, 1977; 1978).

TABLE IX-6

TERMS OF TRADE INDEXES 1952-1977[a]

	1952-55	1956-59	1960-63	1964-69	1970-71	1972-77
Export price index	100	1.640	2.110	3.109	3.243	10.900
Import price index	100	1.764	2.090	2.222	2.208	7.053
Terms of trade index	100	93	101	140	147	155

[a]The base period is 1952-1955.

Source: Ministerio de Planificación y Coordinación, *Cuentas nacionales 1950-1969* (La Paz, 1970); Banco Central de Bolivia, *Cuentas nacionales 1970-1975* (La Paz, 1977); Ministerio de Planeamiento y Coordinación, *Planes anuales operativos 1977; 1978* (La Paz, 1977; 1978).

Quasi money—savings deposits, time deposits, etc.—has become more important in this latter period. Holdings of these items rarely existed in the fifties, but represented more than 4 percent of GDP in the 1972-1977 period. Since an investment-savings gap prevailed during the whole period under consideration, internal savings had to be supplemented by external resources. It is noteworthy that, notwithstanding the significant flows of United States foreign assistance during the early years of the revolution, the external debt ratio in the period was below 10 percent of GDP. This is explained by the fact that all of these funds came to Bolivia on a grant basis. Thus, the creditworthiness of the country was not affected whereas its political autonomy was affected. It is also noteworthy that in relative terms Bolivia's external debt was higher from 1955 up to the early seventies than during the 1972-1977 period. The debt-service ratio deteriorated, however, from a negligible level in the early fifties to 4 percent of exports in the late sixties, to near 20 percent in the 1972-1977 period and to about 25 percent in 1977.

Investment Priorities

Table IX-8 presents the sectoral composition of investment between 1952 and 1977. Changes in this composition serve as indicators of changing investment priorities. During the fifties, about 60 percent of total investment was concentrated in hydrocarbons. Transportation and mining were the next most important. Each of these sectors accounted for about 16 percent of the total. The other sectors had little relevance. In the 1960-1963 period, although hydrocarbons had again the largest share of investment with 42 percent of the total, transportation and communications as well as manufacturing increased their shares considerably. Agriculture and social services also increased their shares. In the 1964-1969 period there were changes which reflected new investment priorities. Transportation and communications had the largest share with 31 percent of the total. Hydrocarbons fell to 23 percent and services increased to 18 percent. The other sectors maintained approximately their same investment shares.

TABLE IX-7

MACROECONOMIC RATIOS 1952-1977
(Percent)

	1952-55	1956-59	1960-63	1964-69	1970-71	1972-77
Consumption/GDP	84	91	93	88	85	80
Investment/GDP	17	16	15	16	17	21
Internal Savings/GDP	16	9	7	12	15	20
External Savings/GDP	1	7	8	4	2	1
Exports/GDP[a]	18	18	17	21	18	22
Imports/GDP[a]	25	25	25	25	20	23
Current Account Deficit/GDP	-1	-6	-7	-5	-3	-2
External Debt/GDP	10	41	46	45	51	40
Debt Service/Exports	b	b	b	4	15	19
Money Supply/GDP	4	9	10	13	12	10
Quasi-Money/GDP	0	0	1	1	3	4
Bills and Coins/GDP	70	78	83	79	76	65

[a]The export and import ratios for the 1952-1956 period were adjusted to reflect exchange rate policies which incorporated multiple exchange rates.

[b]Data are not available to calculate ratios for these years.

Source: Ministerio de Planificación y Coordinación, *Cuentas nacionales 1950-1969* (La Paz, 1970); Banco Central de Bolivia, *Cuentas nacionales 1970-1975* (La Paz, 1977); Banco Central de Bolivia, *Memorias anuales 1972-1977* (La Paz, 1972-1977).

    In the 1970-1977 period, the share for agriculture increased to 6 percent, which was in sharp contrast to the 1960-1963 period when it was 2 percent. Over the same time period the share for manufacturing rose from 5 to 16 percent and that for the services and social sectors from 18 to 26 percent. Over the same period there were declines in the shares of transportation and communications from 31 to 17 percent, in energy from 8 to 4 percent, and in mining from 14 to 11 percent. The share of hydrocarbons fell the most, from 42 to 20 percent.

    The composition of investment described in the preceding paragraphs has directly influenced the structure of GDP and exports analyzed earlier. On the one hand, the low investment in agriculture was an important determinant in the relatively slow growth of this sector's GDP. On the other hand, the high investment in hydrocarbons was important in improving this sector's share of GDP and exports. Finally, the high investment in services after 1964 was important in causing the improvements in social indicators which are examined in the following section.

TABLE IX-8

SECTORAL COMPOSITION OF INVESTMENT, 1952-1977
(Percent)

	Actual						Planned	Implemented		Planned
	1952-55	1956-59	1960-63	1964-69	1970-71	1972-77	1976-80	1976	1977	1978
Agriculture	---	---	2	4	4	6	10	4	4	13
Mining	21	11	14	11	13	11	8	11	7	6
Hydrocarbons	57	61	42	23	29	20	16	17	15	9
Manufacturing	2	2	5	5	6	16	20	19	14	13
Energy	1	1	2	8	5	4	3	4	6	7
Transportation & Communications	14	18	26	31	21	17	16	12	23	22
Services & Other[a]	5	7	9	18	22	26	27	33	28	30
TOTAL	100	100	100	100	100	100	100	100	100	100

[a]Includes construction.

Source: Estimates of the Ministry of Planning and Coordination for the 1952-1958 period; Ministerio de Planificación y Coordinación, *Cuentas nacionales 1959-1969* (La Paz, 1970); Banco Central de Bolivia, *Cuentas nacionales 1970-1975* (La Paz, 1977); Ministerio de Planeamiento y Coordinación, *Plan nacional de desarrollo económico y social 1976-1980* (La Paz, 1976); Ministerio de Planeamiento y Coordinación, *Planes anuales operativos 1977; 1978* (La Paz, 1977; 1978).

Social Indicators

There are at least six social indicators that can also be cited as illustrative of the changes Bolivia has experienced.[2] First, it is estimated that in the sixties open unemployment represented less than 5 percent of the labor force. This estimate increased to more than 10 percent in the early seventies, but by 1977 had fallen again to less than 3 percent. Disguised unemployment, however, is a serious problem, especially in the rural areas where it is estimated to be more than 25 percent. Second, life expectancy has improved. Estimates in the early fifties placed it at less than 40 years. In the sixties it rose to 44 years and 1977 it was estimated to be 48 years. The birth and mortality rates per thousand inhabitants, which were 47 and 23 respectively in the early fifties, improved to 44 and 19 in the sixties and to 42 and 17 in 1977. Third, a rural-urban shift in the population has taken place since the revolution. In the early fifties 74 percent of the population was rural, whereas, only 56 percent lived in the countryside in 1977.

Fourth, there has been a dramatic increase in literacy. In the fifties almost 85 percent of the population over 15 years of age was illiterate; by 1976 only 37 percent were so classified. Fifth, there has also been improvement in nutrition. In the fifties the average daily intake of calories was below 1,400. By 1960 it improved to 1,600 and in 1976 it was 1,900. This figure is still below the United Nations' minimum acceptable level of 2,300 calories a day. Protein intake, which according to the United Nations should be at least 62 grams a day, was close to 52 grams in 1976 as compared to 40 grams in the sixties and 45 in the early seventies.

Sixth, there have been significant improvements in the availability of potable water. Less than 40 percent of the urban population had access to potable water in the fifties, whereas in 1975 more than 60 percent of the urban population had access. Improvements in rural areas have not been so strong. Practically no potable water was available to the rural population in the early fifties and in 1975 only 10 percent of that population had access to it.

Income Distribution

Lack of adequate information makes it impossible to accurately evaluate what changes have occurred since 1952 in the patterns of income distribution. The general pattern of income distribution is believed not to be improving, and it remains highly unequal. According to the Musgrave Study, the combined distribution for all work income (including employees and self-employed) is such that the lowest 40 percent receive only 13 percent of total income, the next 40 percent receive 26 percent, and the top 20 percent obtain 61 percent of the total. It is noteworthy that the average per capita income of the self-employed, which includes farmers, is only one-fifth of the average level of employees. These persons fall almost entirely within the lowest 40 percent.

The Bolivian distribution is not dissimilar to that of the rest of Latin America. The Musgrave Study concludes that the shares received by the lowest 40 percent and by the top 20 percent in Bolivia appear to be slightly above the average, while the share received by the middle 40 percent is somewhat below it.

Public and Private Participation

The public sector plays a very important role in Bolivia, not only insofar as government policy is concerned, but also through its direct participation in production. In 1976 all governmental units including decentralized agencies and mixed enterprises provided for 33 percent of GDP, 13 percent of employment, 59 percent of exports, 70 percent of investment, and 23 percent of national savings.

The increasing importance assigned to the public sector since 1960 is evidenced by the rise in this sector's level of total investment from 40 percent in 1959 to 75 percent in the 1970-1975 period. Even between 1964 and 1969 during the Barrientos regime, which was clearly favorable to private investment, the public sector's share was 52 percent. The role of the public sector was accentuated between 1971 and 1977. Today the public sector is composed of two hundred institutions, of which twenty-one correspond to the central administration, eighty-nine to the decentralized agencies, sixty to the public or mixed enterprises, nine to the regional corporations and nine to the municipalities.

From the standpoint of total expenditures, only 19 percent of the national budget corresponds to the central administration while 72 percent is for the decentralized agencies and enterprises. In terms of public external debt, 64 percent corresponds to decentralized agencies and enterprises.

Public enterprises play an important role in the Bolivian economy. They account for 13 percent of GDP, 3 percent of total employment, 40 percent of external public debt, and for 37 percent of central government revenues. They also account for 60 percent of public investment, which means almost 50 percent of total national investment.

In addition, the fifteen major enterprises have received substantial government budgetary support from equity investment in recent years. According to a survey performed by the Ministry of Planning and Coordination, between 1970 and 1975 total equity contributions from the central government amounted to more than 100 million dollars. Adding the contributions of the last two years the sum would be close to 200 million dollars.

Activities of the public enterprises are widespread. Important elements are: mining, producing and refining petroleum, generating electric power, manufacturing cement, milling sugar, processing milk, owning and operating virtually all modes of transportation, intermediating financial markets and distributing of rice.

Given that most of the public enterprises are not efficient in their operations and that they do not generate enough surplus to undertake new investments, it is either through government equity contributions or internal or external financing that the investment-savings gap is closed. This means, however, that a permanent deterioration of the public finances takes place and that the level of both the public sector deficit and of external debt are high. In 1977 the former was close to 10 percent and the latter was higher than 40 percent of GDP.

It is clear that the public enterprises are not contributing sufficiently to the requirements for development. Not only do they have the above-mentioned problems, but also their investment effort is concentrated in capital-intensive projects. These projects, which could have a positive effect upon growth and exports, contribute very little to the objectives of improving employment and income distribution.

DEVELOPMENT POLICY DURING THE 1960-1971 PERIOD

This section describes and analyzes the development policies that have been advocated by the several governments between 1960 and 1971. Emphasis is placed on the interrelationships between these policies and the structural changes described in the above section.

The Paz Estenssoro Period (1960-1964)

The structural changes undertaken between 1952 and 1956, in addition to the drastic monetary stabilization program undertaken by the government of Hernán Siles Zuazo between 1957 and 1960, provided the necessary elements for development within a framework of financial stability beginning in 1960.

In the early sixties, the National Secretariat of Planning and Coordination was created at the ministerial level and given the assignment to define future strategies for the development of the country. As a result, the Secretariat, with the advice of a distinguished group of foreign experts, concluded the formulation of the *Ten Year Plan* for the 1962-1971 period. The Plan was to be implemented through two-year operational plans.

The Plan envisaged a real annual rate of increase in GDP of 9.2 percent during the first five years and 8.3 percent annually for the entire ten years. These rather optimistic targets were in sharp contrast with negative annual rates of growth experienced during the fifties.

The Plan was mainly concerned with the diagnosis of the problems and bottlenecks existing in the Bolivian economy. Objectives were established based on macroeconomic projections derived from the use of a Harrod-Domar type model and similar techniques. However, very little was accomplished toward the attainment of these goals. Consequently, the Plan only presented the general objectives of a very broad sectoral analysis and little concerning specific projects. This shortcoming was clearly recognized in the Plan itself. "The principal deficiency that will be noted in the formulation of the present plan is the small number of specific investment projects, studied in all their details, which have been included. It is the most urgent task that the preinvestment studies whose economic justification is given at length in the different sections of the plan are now completed, including the pertinent engineering studies, so that the execution may now proceed with the speed that imperative conditions require."[3]

It is well known, however, by anyone familiar with development projects that it takes more than five years for most projects to be initiated and become operational. The gestation period includes not only the preparation of prefeasibility, feasibility, and engineering and design studies, but also the process of obtaining financing either from foreign or local institutions, as well as the actual execution of the project. Consequently, it was rather unrealistic to expect the Bolivian economy to grow at a rate of more than 9 percent a year without having delineated a set of projects that were at least in the feasibility stage at the outset of the planning period.

Assuming that the problem of insufficient projects could have been solved, there was little indication in the Plan of how the country would finance and implement the ambitious investment program which envisaged changes in the annual level of investment of 50 million dollars in 1960 to 164 million dollars in 1971. The policy changes that would be required, in terms of monetary, fiscal, exchange and institutional matters were largely neglected.

In spite of the deficiencies it should be recognized that the *Ten-Year Plan* represented the beginning of a new era for development policy in Bolivia. For the first time there was a philosophy that expressed the view that, within the context of certain structural and financial constraints, it was indispensable to plan for a rational allocation of resources in order to attain economic goals.

The Barrientos Period (1964-1969)

In addition to the problems derived from the macroeconomic orientation of the *Ten-Year Plan*, planning suffered a blow when the government of General René Barrientos came into power in 1964. This regime discouraged the implementation of the Plan since the new government strongly advocated a return to an economic system based on private enterprise and market orientation. Consequently the role of planning was reduced and the Planning Secretariat was attached to the office of the President where its powers and functions were substantially reduced.

Although two-year plans were prepared for the 1963-1964 and 1965-1966 periods, an operational plan was elaborated for 1967 and a three-year plan was prepared for the 1968-1970 period; none of them were effective instruments of action for the lack of preparation of detailed investment projects and of well conceived financial programs. In sum, there was no relationship whatsoever between the plans and the financial programs necessary to carry them out. Because of all of these constraints the *Ten-Year Plan*, the two-year plans and the operational plans were not operable. Consequently, investment did not follow the suggested lines of action. Instead, those projects which had completed feasibility studies, were politically supported, or could obtain external financing, were the ones undertaken.

In spite of the fact that the Barrientos government had no overall development strategy in effect for Bolivia, the government gave high priority, as can be observed in Table IX-8, to the rapid improvement of the transportation network in order to further the economic integration of the country. A major program of road construction between the *Altiplano* and the *Oriente* was undertaken as a move towards this end. In the productive sectors the authorities placed their major reliance on private initiative, although certain activities were reserved for public corporations. Even in these activities private investment in joint ventures was welcomed. The contract signed between the Bolivian State Mining Company (COMIBOL) and a United States consortium for the exploitation of the Matilde Zinc Mine was a first attempt to implement this new policy. In manufacturing, the Investment Incentive Law of 1965 promoted private investment through tax concessions. The government also gave priority to export diversification. The initiation of large-scale oil exports by the Gulf Oil Corporation was a result of such policy, as was the new emphasis placed on the development of Bolivia's large reserves of natural gas for export to neighboring countries. Construction was begun on a gas pipeline to Argentina under a joint venture between the Bolivian State Petroleum Company (YPFB) and the Gulf Oil Corporation.

The development programs in agriculture were of minor importance during the Barrientos government. An exception was the initiation of the Abapó-Izozog integral agricultural development project in the eastern part of the country. The small-farmer colonization program of the *Oriente* which was started in the early sixties met with very limited success due to a lack of comprehensive planning, administrative difficulties and insufficient budget appropriations. Therefore, emphasis was shifted to the development of large-scale farming in the Santa Cruz area and the development of livestock operations in the *Altiplano* and Beni regions.

Investment was directed also towards improving power generation, communications and urban social infrastructure. Notwithstanding, the lack of sound development strategies during the Barrientos administration, good external conditions, including the favorable terms of trade and investment climate--both of which attracted foreign investment--as well as reasonably good internal financial policies permitted the economy to reach the highest rates of growth of its history and to do so with very small increases in the price level. As was shown in Table IX-1, the cumulative growth rate of GDP in real terms for the 1964-1969 period was 6.2 percent. This strong growth was attained with only an annual average of 5 percent inflation.

The Ovando and Torres Governments (1969-1971)

After the death of President Barrientos in 1969, there was a series of shortlived governments under the consecutive direction of presidents Luis Adolfo Siles Salinas, Alfredo Ovando Candia and Juan José Torres. Of these governments, the one headed by General Ovando had the most important repercussions on the behavior of the economy, not only during 1969 and 1970, but also in the 1970-1977 period.

The Ovando government began a policy of eliminating foreign control of natural resources with the nationalization of the assets of Gulf Oil Corporation, which during the Barrientos government had considerably increased its operations in Bolivia. This action was followed in 1971, during the Torres government, by additional nationalizations of the property of the Matilde Zinc Mine and other foreign interests.

The Ovando government placed emphasis on the importance of having an overall development strategy and the benefits of planning. To this end the Planning Office was made a ministry and given enough power to guide development policy. A general perspective plan entitled *Social and Economic Strategy* for the 1971-1991 period was prepared, which set up the main objectives and guidelines for development for the twenty-year period.

This Plan was mainly concerned with the definition of social and economic objectives to be attained in the next twenty years. In this context, policy instruments and goals that were the basic elements in the Plan for development were designed to lessen Bolivia's dependence on the external sector, to integrate the marginal rural population of Bolivia into active economic life, and to assign top priority to the development of the productive sectors of the economy. Following these lines, the strategy of the Plan called for special emphasis on exports of mining, petroleum, agricultural and manufactured goods, as well as the production of mass consumption goods for the domestic market that had a high value added component. The Plan also called for a selective import substitution approach to industrialization in order that only efficient industries would be established to produce for the domestic market, i.e., those having comparative advantage. It envisaged a regional strategy for the location of new industries in order to integrate the national economy, and contemplated supplementary social investments in education, health and housing.

The Plan was very critical of the fact that in the past, great emphasis had been placed on infrastructural projects which have a very long maturity--while little emphasis was directed to projects in the productive sectors, which are the ones that can generate the additional savings necessary for rapid economic development. Furthermore, the Plan suggested an active role for the public sector, not only in the guidance of economic activity, but also in the direct participation of the industrial sector through public and mixed enterprises in order that all profits would be used for new investment. Finally, the Plan was also concerned with administrative efficiency, and included guidelines for reform of the public sector entities.

The Plan was not explicit concerning quantitative matters, however, as it did not present macroeconomic nor sectoral projections to determine how feasible it would be to undertake the ambitious changes in the economy it envisaged. Thus, there were only broad guidelines for specific sectoral strategies and a tentative, but very short, list of projects in different stages of preparation. The document can be considered a plan of necessities without regard to possibilities. It recognized, nonetheless, given the low level of internal savings and the difficulties in mobilizing public and private resources, that massive amounts of external funds would be required to achieve the objectives.

Therefore, from a conceptual viewpoint the Plan represented an improvement over the previous *Ten-Year Plan*, although it could only be considered as a good point of departure for future action. Coherent plans would need to be developed to include projects and the means to implement these projects in order to achieve the broad goals of economic growth, higher employment, better income distribution, national integration and other general objectives. The Plan called for the preparation of future medium-term plans. For example,under these provisions planning was henceforth undertaken by a team of foreign experts to identify priority projects for Bolivia's participation in the Andean Group.

The nationalization of the Gulf Oil assets had immediate negative effects, both internationally and domestically, as it caused a general contraction in economic activity, particularly in the private sector. In the medium-term, however, the nationalization had positive effects upon the public sector's capacity to save,as YPFB was able to receive most of the benefits of gas exports once the pipeline to Argentina was completed in 1972.   Nonetheless, the nationalization created a sense of insecurity for foreign investors lasting several years. This consequence had a negative impact on the economy because of the low domestic savings capacity of the country and the limits that Bolivia's debt servicing capacity imposed on direct external borrowing.

THE BANZER GOVERNMENT

The 1971-1974 Period

The Torres government fell after a coup by the armed forces in 1971 and a coalition composed of the armed forces, the National Revolutionary Movement Party (MNR) and Bolivian Socialist Falange (FSB) soon brought Colonel Hugo Banzer Suárez to the presidency.   There were a number of factors which contributed to the change in government. Among the most important was the lack of confidence, both domestically and internationally, in the Torres government. In part this was caused by serious political problems and the deterioration of the economic performance of the country in 1970 when the rate of growth of GDP fell to less than 5 percent a year, unemployment increased to more than 10 percent, balance of payments difficulties worsened, and public sector finances deteriorated considerably.   These factors combined to lead to a general climate of uncertainty and political chaos.

Between 1971 and 1973 the Banzer government had to concentrate on the solution of short-term problems, mainly those related to restoring financial equilibrium and confidence. Consequently, development planning was secondary among government priorities. This is reflected in the fact that the Ministry of Planning and Coordination became the Secretariat of the Economic and Planning Council (CONEPLAN). Although it was considered to be at the ministerial level it did not enjoy high status in the cabinet hierarchy. Economic decisions were in the hands of the Finance and Commerce Ministries which, logically, were more interested in short-run policies than in development objectives.

The year 1972 marked a turning point for the Bolivian economy. The deteriorating financial situation which had been carried over since the late sixties led to the first exchange rate modification in fourteen years and the adoption of a new set of internal financial policies within a Stabilization Program. Despite the climate of uncertainty generated by the internal financial situation, the real rate of growth of GDP rose from 4.9 percent in 1971 to 5.8 percent in 1972 as a consequence of the initiation of natural gas production made possible by the completion of the Santa Cruz-Yacuiba gas pipeline. However, the growth of real output in most other sectors continued to lag.

In 1973 and 1974 the Bolivian economy reaped the benefits from record high prices for the country's major exports. Following a rise of about 30 percent in 1973, export prices nearly doubled in 1974, resulting in a similar increase in export value. GDP grew at the real rates of 6.9 percent in 1973 and 6.2 percent in 1974. In addition, the real rate of growth in income was much higher due to the effect of a favorable change in the terms of trade. Unfortunately, most of the rise in real income was channeled to consumer spending, which in turn, given the openness of Bolivia's economy, meant a considerable increase in imports.

Between 1971 and 1974 there was continued emphasis on the development of natural resources—mining, petroleum and gas—as well as that of transportation, commerce, finance and urban services. However, no defined development program existed. Budgetary, external financing and monetary allocations were decided within a short-run context. Immediate gains were sought for commercial agriculture in the Santa Cruz area through massive credit allocations, but very little financing was directed to the *campesinos* of the *Altiplano* and the Mountain Valleys. [4]

The 1974-1978 Period—The Institutional Setting

In 1974 the armed forces under the leadership of General Banzer decided to take full control of the government with the advice of civilian, apolitical technocrats. They observed, even though the initial philosophy of the new government after the 1971 revolution had been similar to that of the market-oriented Barrientos government, that the fact of the matter was that the trend towards a larger public sector, started in 1969 during the Ovando administration, had continued during the 1970-1974 period. Furthermore, they believed that this trend would continue in the future and would, therefore, require the definition of clearcut development priorities and the establishment of appropriate controls.

The government recognized the urgency of strengthening the planning mechanisms, since the lack of a medium-term development strategy would mean, as in the sixties, the channeling of most of the surpluses from the favorable external prices for Bolivia's main exports to consumption rather than to capital formation. Also it was recognized that the policies of governments since the 1952 revolution had done very little to solve the problems of the vast majority of the rural population. Further, that a continuation of this policy structure would work against the goals of better income distribution and national integration.

For these reasons in 1974 the national planning and project systems were strengthened by the following actions:

(1) The Ministry of Planning and Coordination was accorded a higher position in the hierarchy within the Cabinet. The Minister of Planning and Coordination was to act as head of the economic team and serve as chairman of CONEPLAN. This council works as an economic cabinet. Ministers involved in economic and social matters, such as finance, agriculture, industry, health, labor and transportation participate in its regular weekly meetings.

(2) Planning offices were created in all ministries and in regional corporations in order to perform planning and supervisory tasks at the sectoral and regional levels.

(3) A specialized pre-investment agency, the National Institute for Pre-Investment (INALPRE) was created to identify, promote, finance and follow-up the preparation of adequate feasibility studies in priority sectors.

(4) A specialized external debt agency, The National Institute of Financing (INDEF), was created to centralize all foreign loan negotiations and to ensure that all external funds are channeled to priority projects.

(5) A National Project's Committee under the chairmanship of the Undersecretary of Planning was established. The Committee, which is composed of the Undersecretary of Finance, the President of the Central Bank, the Economic Advisor to the President and the Executive Directors of INDEF, INALPRE and the National Institute of Investment (INI), has the responsibility of recommending the investment programs to be included in development plans.[5] To this effect, sectoral and regional priorities as well as macroeconomic constraints such as internal savings and external debt-service capacity are considered. Also, as a necessary condition for a favorable recommendation, the specific merits of a given project are analyzed whenever its capital cost exceeds one million dollars. The analysis includes technical, financial, institutional and socioeconomic criteria. For the latter, cost-benefit methodologies, which include shadow pricing, are applied.

(6) A General Law of Regional Development Corporations was approved in order to regulate the performance of these corporations and to integrate them to the national planning and project systems.

(7) A national system of science and technology was created in order to formulate national policies in these fields and coordinate the action of all public and private entities involved.

(8) A follow-up system of plans, programs and projects was created. The system not only includes the central government, but the whole public sector. In addition, for the public enterprises, a high-level board has been recently established and is presided over by

the Minister of Planning and Coordination. The Minister of Finance acts as vice-president and there are six directors. This board is responsible for providing performance guidelines to the public enterprises, for approving their annual budgets and financial statements, for establishing the parameters of comparison among them and for suggesting to the President of the Republic adjustments in management or policy matters.

(9) A general population census was undertaken in 1976 for the first time in twenty-five years. It provided new and recent data on economic and social development in Bolivia. In addition, a national system of information was created to facilitate planning, which integrates sectoral and regional offices with the National Institute of Statistics (INE).

(10) A high-level mission headed by Harvard professor Richard Musgrave was contracted to present specific recommendations concerning the economic setting, with particular emphasis on fiscal matters. Research studies were also undertaken by the Ministries of Planning and Coordination and Finance with the assistance of several local and foreign universities.[6]

The 1974-1978 Period - Development Strategy

In 1975, as a result of the new emphasis on medium-term planning, the President issued Directive No. 1. This document set forth the basic philosophy of Bolivian development and was considered the guideline for the preparation of future plans and policies at the macro, sectoral and regional, as well as project levels.

Within the framework of Directive No. 1, a medium-term plan—the *National Plan for Economic and Social Development*—was prepared for the five-year period 1976-1980. The Plan was conceived as a set of five-year guidelines that were to be revised annually, and then extended over the following year (rolling plans) in the light of actual experience with execution and short-term constraints. To this end, one-year operational plans have been prepared since 1976 which are closely integrated with financial programming in the areas of the public sector budget, the monetary program and the external debt program.

This new planning mechanism was a major step forward for Bolivia. As stated by Professor Musgrave, "The Plan considers both aggregative and sectoral aspects, and seeks to relate projected economic developments to broader social goals. Attention is given to linking specific investment projects to sector goals and to strengthening the institutional basis for project evaluation and implementation. While the planning process and techniques are still in a formative stage, a sensible framework for policy formulation is being evolved, which should contribute greatly to Bolivia's development prospects."[7]

In preparing the development strategy for the medium-term plan it was recognized that, notwithstanding the important changes that have occurred since the 1952 revolution, Bolivia is still one of the poorest countries in Latin America. Yet within this context, the preeminent preoccupation that the main objective of the nation is to reach, as soon as possible, levels of economic development that would permit high levels of well being for the majority of the population. This means, in other words, the existence of employment opportunities for all and the satisfaction of social aspirations in terms of nutrition, health, education and housing standards, cultural and political development and other aspects measuring the quality of life.

One problem that had to be faced in preparing the medium-term strategy was related to the appropriate balance that should exist between economic and social development. As in all developing countries, conflicts exist among the growth, employment, income distribution and financial equilibrium objectives. For example, natural resource based export oriented activities, which contribute to growth and financial equilibrium, are normally capital intensive and, consequently, are in conflict with income distribution and employment objectives. In another example, job creating activities, which are consistent with income distribution and employment objectives, are often in conflict with growth and financial equilibrium criteria. The Plan intends to try to resolve conflicts, such as those mentioned above, by combining purely economic considerations with social aspects. Equity and employment criteria for the selection of appropriate activities, programs and projects, as well as for general economic policy, are included even if this implies that some growth must be sacrificed.

There are seven fundamental global objectives to be achieved over the medium-term in the Plan. First, to accelerate real GDP growth by: (a) concentrating efforts on the development of the productive sectors—agriculture, mining, hydrocarbons and industry—complemented by integrated projects in the economic and social infrastructure; (b) aiming at self-sufficiency in foodstuffs; (c) increasing the domestic value added of traditional exports; (d) promoting non-traditional exports, particularly in agro-industrial activities; and (e) achieving import substitution, whenever economically feasible. [8]

Second, to increase the internal savings capacity of the country by: (a) the elimination of unnecessary consumption; and (b) the improvement of systems and mechanisms to mobilize and channel these resources to development activities. Third, to supplement internal savings with: (a) external loans; and (b) direct investment that is to be directed to priority areas and sectors.

Fourth, to incorporate the marginal population—mostly highland peasants—into the market economy and to increase productive employment by means of better training, especially at the professional levels, of the labor force. Progressive improvements in income distribution are expected through gains in real income and the provision of services enhancing the quality of life, especially of the rural population. Fifth, to continue the process of national integration of the large Bolivian territory both in economic and organic terms, while strengthening Bolivia's participation in the international regional integration schemes.

Sixth, to adopt and diffuse appropriate technologies, compatible with resource scarcities and development objectives. Seventh, to maintain a reasonable internal and external financial equilibrium, in order that inflation is kept low and that an adequate level of international reserves is available to guarantee stable exchange rates.

At the sectoral level the Plan states that agriculture, mining and hydrocarbons are considered the basic sectors for the development of the country and upon which industrial growth should be based. Moreover, that both economic and social infrastructure should be built on the premise that they are not ends in themselves, but rather means to attain development objectives.

At the regional level the major concerns of the Plan are to remedy a number of conditions including the inappropriate dispersion of Bolivia's population, the lack of economic and social integration around a few important urban centers causing the attendant tendency for centrifugal forces to develop, and the tendency of populations along the borders to depend more on the economic and social services provided by neighboring countries than by Bolivia itself. The main thrust of government action is concentrated, therefore, on strengthening the existing ties in the La Paz, Cochabamba, Santa Cruz and Oruro-Potosí-Chuquisaca-Tarija areas and their linkages to the Beni and Pando Departments. The Plan stimulates the promotion and creation of development poles around: (a) the southern Villamontes agro-industrial projects; (b) the Abapo-Izozog livestock and agro-industrial complex; (c) the southeastern Mutun iron, mining and steel project; (d) the northeastern Pando-Beni-La Paz livestock, timber and agricultural development programs; and (e) the southwestern non-metallic mineral complex in the salt lakes region. In the process, ancillary investments are contemplated in the transportation and social infrastructure to provide incentives for internal migration to the main development poles and to organize viable regional commercial markets.

The Plan has special concern for the rural areas, which account for almost two-thirds of Bolivia's total population, but for only one-sixth of domestic output. Except in a few select areas, a traditional style of agriculture predominates. Characteristic of this type of agriculture are: low productivity, extensive underemployment, lack of irrigation facilities (an estimated 3 percent of Bolivia's total farmland is under irrigation), deficient infrastructure in transportation, storage and energy, poor housing, and dependence on monopolies or quasi-monopolies for transportation and marketing services. These factors, together with the lack of complementary agro-industries and social services, have caused the greater part of the peasant population to remain at the margin of the modern economy with low levels of nutrition, literacy, income, and higher than average mortality rates.

The Plan intends to concentrate its efforts on organizing peasants in self-supporting communities that would provide a minimum of economic and social services for their residents, as well as an organic link with local and regional authorities, in order to enhance the process of infrastructural planning. These communities are also to be organized on a scale sufficient to generate enough economic and social activities to support a minimum of commercial relations, not only between themselves, but also with the larger urban centers to which they will be linked up. These efforts will include the installation of both professional training centers and agricultural research stations. They are designed to improve the farmers' technical skills and improve marketing practices. Such a strategy, if applied on a global scale, should be instrumental to: remedy the present isolation of the highland farmers, improve and diversify the supply of agricultural products, raise farm incomes, inject a greater dynamism in the production process, and improve rural health, nutrition and education. The ultimate objective would be the actual incorporation of the *campesino* into national life. The importance of this approach is that integrated rural development permits a reconciliation among the objectives of growth, employment and income distribution.

In quantitative terms the Plan calls for an annual average rate of real growth of GDP for the five-year period of between 7 and 7.7 percent depending on the alternatives chosen. To maintain this growth rate the Plan envisaged a total investment for the period of 3.5 billion dollars measured at 1975 prices. Of this amount 70 and 30 percent were to come from public and private sources, respectively. Table IX-8 presents the planned sectoral composition of investment of the Plan, as well as the actual investments realized during 1976 and 1977 and the projected investment mix for 1978. The composition reflects the above mentioned sectoral strategy. Regional investment also follows the Plan strategy so that La Paz, Santa Cruz, Cochabamba and Oruro, receive more than 60 percent of total investment. To finance the total investment package the Plan contemplated that 69 and 31 percent would be financed from internal and external resources, respectively. One of the main differences between the 1976-1980 Plan and previous plans is that the sectoral and regional targets are well supported by concrete investment projects. In fact, in addition to nearly five hundred projects amounting to 2.3 billion dollars that were already in their implementation phase when the Plan was prepared, there is now a similar number of new projects valued at more than 3 billion dollars with feasibility studies completed or well advanced. It is reasonable to expect that these new projects could begin to be implemented during the Plan period. The other fundamental difference between previous plans and the current one is the careful consideration given in the Plan to the financial possibilities for implementing the planned investment, based upon the assumptions concerning the performance of the envisaged leading sectors, such as hydrocarbons.

The Plan has been very well accepted in the international community. In this connection, Bolivia became the third country in Latin America and among fourteen in the world, for which the World Bank has organized consultative groups to coordinate the industrialized countries and international institutions' channeling of soft funds for development purposes. The first meeting of the group took place in Paris early in 1977. [9]

An evaluation of the *Five-Year Plan* after two years of actual implementation shows that although some of the targets were too optimistic, the results have been satisfactory. In fact, a preliminary appraisal shows that both at the macro and sectoral levels around 80 to 85 percent of the original targets have been accomplished. On the negative side the weak performance of the hydrocarbons sector has had an unfavorable impact upon exports and balance of payments. Moreover, a shortage of internal savings has required additional external financing.

The Plan is threatened by the capacity of certain dynamic sectors to absorb the relative scarce resources with capital-intensive projects for which feasibility studies are already completed or underway. If these projects were to be implemented in the next four years they would seriously affect the development strategy of the Plan by creating serious sectoral and regional imbalances in investment patterns. For example, only taking account of some selected large projects that are in the feasibility stage: the Mutun iron and steel development; the lead, silver and zinc smelters; the gas pipeline to Brazil; and the automobile and petrochemical industries, the total capital cost for these few projects is equivalent to three billion dollars. Assuming a four-year implementation phase, this is equivalent to seven hundred million dollars a year. This amount represents more than 75 percent of Bolivia's annual investment capacity. Obviously, to proceed with all these projects simultaneously would require the postponement of projects in agriculture, transportation, education, health and other sectors with the consequent negative impact upon employment income distribution and social development.

Over the next four years these capital-intensive projects would create only approximately 30,000 new jobs; meanwhile there would be an estimated increase of 160,000 workers in Bolivia's labor force during the same time period.

Were these projects to be implemented the regional balance of investment as prescribed in the Plan would be considerably disrupted. More than 70 percent of such investment would be located in the Santa Cruz area, whereas only 25 percent of the nation's new investment is assigned to that region in the Plan. Moreover, such action would only serve to exacerbate interregional tensions which already exist due to the concentration of investment in the La Paz-Cochabamba-Oruro and Santa Cruz axis.

In order to avoid these potential problems, the Bolivian government has taken important steps during 1977 and early 1978 to try to promote more projects in the northern and southern regions of the country, and to basically accelerate rural development in the *Altiplano* and the Mountain Valleys. The rural development projects are designed to employ an integrated approach. Under this scheme actions related to agricultural research, credit, extension, marketing and the building of economic infrastructure are coordinated along with the expansion of social services and the organization of the *campesinos* at the local level. To this end, a rural development plan will be prepared in 1978-1979. It is expected that the preparation of specific projects, following the integrated approach, would call for greater emphasis on rural development in future plans. The target is an allocation of more than 25 percent of the national investment effort to rural development in the *Altiplano* and the Mountain Valleys, where the majority of the poor live.

Additional efforts should also be made to develop more labor-intensive projects when it is possible to attain, at the same time, reasonable rates of return on investment. In addition to those within the agricultural sector, labor-intensive technologies appear to offer good possibilities for use in integrated rural development, certain types of manufacturing, and construction. These activities would create eight or ten times more employment than the prestigious capital-intensive projects mentioned above, which in many cases, even have a marginal return on investment.

The trend towards the increasing importance of the public enterprises has been previously noted. Another aspect is that the private sector has not been as dynamic as expected. Consequently, the public sector has grown relative to the private sector. This has had serious implications on grounds of equity and economic efficiency. With respect to the former, growth has been concentrated in capital-intensive activities. With respect to the latter, inefficiencies have led to deficits in many public enterprises. A consequence has been an increase in the deficit of the public sector. The public deficit for 1977 represents approximately 10 percent of GDP. Public enterprises also account for most of Bolivia's external debt. Future plans should give more emphasis to private initiative in nonstrategic fields and also to direct foreign investment as a substitute for external loans.

Another undesirable aspect of the economic and social development in recent years has been the unchanging nature of some misconceived policies. Some examples are: the subsidies to consumers of petroleum and some agricultural products such as rice and sugar; the freezing of prices for traditional agricultural products; the concentration of agricultural credit in the eastern part of the country; and the inflexibility of financial policy. The latter, as manifested in the exchange rate, interest rate policies, and liberal investment laws, has tended to favor capital-intensive projects and the importation of unnecessary goods and services. It is imperative that actions are taken to modify such policies, which are in conflict with the attainment of development objectives.

In qualitative terms, the first two years of the *Five-Year Plan* have had a positive impact in changing the outlook of most public institutions. Plans and projects are beginning to be prepared following sound principles. A sense of respect for the planning system has been developed and closer coordination between the Ministry of Planning, the Finance Ministry and the Central Bank has provided the necessary integration of planning with financial programming.

In order to make the appropriate adjustments for development strategies, the Ministry of Planning and Coordination intends to prepare a long-term strategy for development (1980-2000) and a general five year plan (1980-1984) covering 1980 and 1979. Simultaneously it will be important to improve the institutional setting for planning in the planning offices of the several ministries, regional corporations and public entities. Closer coordination with important pressure groups in the private sector, civic organizations, labor unions and universities, will also be important ingredients for future planning. Finally, it should also be recognized that in August of 1978, after fourteen years of military rule, that Bolivia will again have a constitutional government with all the good and bad things that such a form of government brings. It is hoped that the future administration will recognize the significant strides made in recent years under planning and continue to rely on the planning mechanism as a means towards more rational resource allocation for a sound and viable development process in Bolivia.

SUMMARY AND CONCLUSIONS

The Bolivia of today is in sharp contrast to that country in the fifties. At that time the nation imported approximately 35 percent of its foodstuffs, exported only raw minerals, and had limited infrastructure to provide connections between the highlands, the valleys and the tropical areas. The general level of socioeconomic development was low by any standard and a very small minority of the population controlled economic, social and political activities. In contrast, today Bolivia is practically self-sufficient in foodstuffs with the exception of wheat, oils and milk; has export surpluses in cotton, sugar, coffee, rubber, meat, petroleum and gas; and is becoming an established site for tourism. Approximately 40 percent of its tin is now exported in a semi-processed form. The infrastructure of roads, railways, airways and communications network are vastly improved and the indicators of socioeconomic development are considerably higher. Although income distribution patterns are very far from being satisfactory, the Bolivian citizen lives much better today than he did ten or fifteen years ago.

The changes in Bolivia during the sixties and the seventies should not lead to the conclusion, however, that Bolivia's problems have been solved and that its future prosperity is assured. Notwithstanding the significant improvements in the last eighteen years, Bolivia continues to be one of the least-developed countries of Latin America. It relies heavily on exports of primary or semi-processed raw materials. It has low levels of per capita income, savings and productivity. Social indicators for health, education, nutrition and housing are relatively low. The physical and cultural integration is highly deficient. Perhaps most indicative of the situation is the fact that the majority of the rural population, which represents 56 percent of Bolivia's inhabitants, still lives in conditions of poverty and acute underdevelopment.

Furthermore, although relatively high rates of growth have been attained since 1962, and important changes in production patterns have occurred, the Bolivian economy has not yet achieved a self-sustaining process of growth. It continues to be highly dependent on world markets for raw materials and as a consequence gains and suffers with the fluctuations of prices for these products. Moreover, the productive sectors have not been the most dynamic ones in the process of this growth.

There are a number of significant constraints to the process of change in Bolivia. The small population of the country and the low levels of income of the rural population provide serious obstacles to the development of an efficient industrial base oriented towards the internal market. The fact that more than 60 percent of the population is concentrated in the highlands, complicates the problem. The vast mountainous area of the country makes it difficult and expensive to build an adequate infrastructure to provide for regional and economic integration. The relatively low levels of social indicators of the rural population are indicative of the problems of bringing the countryside into the development process.

It is evident that the important changes experienced since 1952 have not had a desirable impact upon the *campesinos*, although, one of the basic objectives of the 1952 revolution was the incorporation of the *campesinos* into national life. The truth is that very little has been done on this account. Investment priorities from the early days of the revolution have been concentrated in building the basic infrastructure, developing the hydrocarbons mining and capital-intensive manufacturing activities, and in encouraging commercial agriculture and urban social infrastructure.

The entire blame for this situation cannot be placed on Bolivia alone. The approach to development utilized in Bolivia was typical of that employed in many less-developed countries as a result of the development models that were in vogue in the fifties and early sixties. These models did not direct much attention to agricultural development. Moreover, the models visualized income distribution as a problem to be solved in a second stage, through appropriate distributional fiscal policies, once the economy had reached a certain level of wealth.

A second outside element influencing the Bolivian situation was the common tendency to import capital-intensive technologies as embodied in imported consumer goods and in direct foreign investment. Foreign aid institutions were often responsible for the choice of capital-intensive techniques, since as a general practice they mainly finance new capital goods of foreign origin and very seldom local costs. Bolivian investment laws facilitated the process by providing incentives and facilities to capital-intensive production facilities.

Another factor influencing the approach utilized by Bolivia was the balance of payments constraint which derived from export earnings being based on one or two raw materials. The consequent need for export diversification dictated that most investment go to activities where easy diversification could be obtained, such as hydrocarbons, mining, and tropical agriculture, in order to avoid balance of payments difficulties.

There were three administrations between 1960 and 1978 when overall development policy and planning was of sufficient concern to be given a high priority by the government. The first was the Paz Estenssoro administration of 1960-1964 when the *Ten-Year Plan* was prepared. The second was the short-lived Ovando administration of 1969-1970, which prepared a long-term development strategy. The third began in 1974 with the second phase of the Banzer government, when medium-term planning was initiated and implemented. In this latter period there was a considerable strengthening of the institutional framework for development planning and policy formulation. Not only has sectoral and regional planning been integrated with macroeconomic, and particularly financial programming, but also a system for the identification, promotion, financing, implementation and supervision of projects has been developed. Thus, it is only since 1974 that investment priorities have started to be established in accordance with a plan. In previous periods little reference was made to development objectives in the context of budgetary, monetary and external financing allocations.

There are several common elements that stand out in the implicit development strategies of all governments since 1960. First is the importance given to the processing of natural resources, mainly minerals, as a means toward political and economic independence. Unfortunately these projects are highly capital intensive and often with relatively low returns and limited effects upon employment and income distribution.

Second, is the relative low priority given to small, traditional agriculture. This trend began to change, however, with the *Five-Year Plan for 1976-1980* and the corresponding 1977 and 1978 operational plans. Finally, all governments, with the exception of the Barrientos government, gave an increasing role to the public sector. The trend toward increased public participation has progressed to the point, however, where not only inefficiencies are widespread but also the actions of the public enterprises have little impact upon employment and income distribution due to the capital-intensive approach that has been traditionally followed. Therefore, a change in this tendency is necessary if development is to proceed within a framework of efficiency, equity and financial stability.

ENDNOTES TO CHAPTER IX

1. The views expressed in this paper are the author's and as such do not necessarily reflect the thinking of the Bolivian government. Sincere appreciation is expressed to Mr. Juan Prado, Adviser to the Office of the Undersecretary of Planning, for assistance in the preparation of the data expressed in 1977 constant prices.

2. The social indicators presented are based on data gathered by the Bolivian Ministry of Planning and Coordination.

3. Junta Nacional de Planeamiento, *Plan nacional de desarrollo económico y social 1962-1971* (La Paz: Editorial Don Bosco, 1961), p. 33.

4. Some of the main projects undertaken during the period include the expansion of the Vinto tin smelter and the installation of tin volatization, preconcentration and low grade smelter plants. In hydrocarbons, the gas pipeline to Argentina was concluded and the expansion of the Cochabamba refinery and the construction of a new refinery in Santa Cruz, which will be concluded in 1978, were started.

    In addition to expanding cement plants in Sucre, Cochabamba, and La Paz, new projects like the cement plant of Santa Cruz were initiated. Also an agro-industrial program in the Villamontes area, where an oil factory has been established, went forward. The feasibility studies for the Mutun iron ore development program, which have recently been concluded, were also promoted.

    In transport, the main projects started included the construction of the La Paz-El Alto highway, the first phase of the paving of the Oruro-Cochabamba and La Paz-Beni highways, the first and second phases of the railroad rehabilitation program, the improvement of the national airline (LAB) and the modernization of the airports of Cochabamba, Tarija, Santa Cruz, Riberalta, San Borja and Santa Ana.

    In communications, the expansion of the long distance telephone network to the central and southern parts of the country as well as the improvement of telephone and telex facilities abroad, should particularly be mentioned.

    In social sectors, projects included potable water and sewerage in urban centers like Cochabamba, La Paz, Sucre and Santa Cruz as well as rural systems at the national level. They also included social housing, vocational education and training, both urban and rural, and hospital building in urban centers.

5. INI is the National Institute for Investment, which is in charge of direct foreign investment matters.

6. Some of the studies performed refer to project evaluation, shadow prices, comparative advantage, to mention a few.

7. Richard Musgrave, *Fiscal Reform in Bolivia, The Economic Setting*, Vol. I (Cambridge, Mass.: Musgrave Mission, 1977), Chapter 1, p. 4.

8. Allocation of resources, as indicated in the Plan, should be based upon the principle of comparative advantage by which the country should emphasize the type of production that can compete interna-

tionally. Also, the achievement of economies of scale through effective use of the new types of production and enlarged markets that Bolivia has been afforded by economic integration schemes, such as the Andean Pact, is an important allocation criteria.

9. Bolivia presented its external financing needs for 1977-1979 connected with more than ninety projects amounting to total investment of 3 billion dollars and external financing of 2.2 billion dollars to be disbursed between 1978 and 1983.

Of the total investment cost of 3 billion dollars for the ninety projects included, 33 percent corresponded to industry, 15 percent to agriculture and rural development, 14 percent to transportation and communications, 13 percent to hydrocarbons, 12 percent to mining, 3 percent to power and 10 percent to social sectors.

The list included important projects in the natural resource sectors such as the Santa Cruz-Corumbá gas pipeline, a lead and silver smelting plant, a zinc refinery, two cement plants, the implementation of the iron ore and steel development project of Mutun, and the creation of a national mineral exploration fund, to mention the main ones.

In agriculture, emphasis was centered in the rural poor through several integrated projects including credit, research and extension, irrigation, storage, and marketing facilities, access roads, rural electrification vocational education, health, nutrition and cottage industries. Those projects are mainly concentrated in the *Altiplano* and the Mountain Valleys.

In transport and communications, a continuation of the program to rehabilitate the railways was included as well as the completion of the second phase of important roads such as the paved Oruro-Cochabamba and La Paz-Beni highways and the improvement of air transportation to areas with great agricultural potential, which at present cannot be reached by other modes of transportation. The list also included social projects in water, sewerage, education and health both at the urban and rural levels.

Chapter X

The Bolivian External Sector After 1964 [1]

Juan Antonio Morales

INTRODUCTION

The Bolivian external sector has undergone important changes since 1964. This paper presents a survey of the role of the foreign sector in the Bolivian economy as well as an analysis of policy affecting foreign trade and the balance of payments since that date. In this context the specific objectives of the paper are to: (a) document the structural changes in the Bolivian foreign sector, (b) analyze the impact of Bolivian foreign trade policies on the balance of payments and economic development, and (c) examine the special problems of Bolivia's participation in Latin American regional economic integration programs. The latter is viewed as a particular development policy option and is examined separately from the general analysis of trade, balance of payments and development. Finally, conclusions are drawn and prospects for the future are set forth. Before beginning with the above analysis, however, it is necessary to put the discussion in the context of historical perspective.

THE HISTORICAL SETTING

Bolivia, in 1977, with 4.7 million inhabitants and a gross domestic (GDP) of about 3.4 billion dollars constitutes a small economy. Furthermore, the small Bolivian economy is very open, or very dependent upon foreign trade, as can be seen by examining the ratios of imports and exports to GDP. Over a long period, 1965-1977, Bolivia's exports and imports have averaged about 22 and 25 percent of GDP respectively. These figures have been quite stable over the period and there is no discernible trend towards more openness or more autarchy. By these measures Bolivia is one of the most open of Latin American economies. Bolivia's land-locked geographical status implies high transportation costs for exports as well as imports. This situation complicates Bolivia's foreign trade and creates additional pressures on the nation's attempt to be competitive in export markets. Thus it is remarkable that the country still exhibits such a high degree of openness

Historically the composition of Bolivian exports has been totally dominated by minerals and more recently, also petroleum and natural gas. At the present time Bolivia is still a primary quasi-monoproduct commodity exporter and an importer of food staples and manufactures. Given the effort that has been expended to promote economic diversification in the past twenty-five years, this situation is somewhat surprising.

Moreover, the Bolivian modern sector has been and still is of the enclave-type with its exports and imports being determined more by the factor endowments of the industrial countries with which it trades and by its natural resources, rather than by its own capital and labor endowments. In some preliminary estimations, Freddy Sanjines found that the direct and indirect labor content in Bolivian exports was proportionally less than in imports. [2] In other words, Bolivia, a surplus labor and capital scarce country, is an exporter of goods which are more capital intensive than its imports. This paradox may be explained by the high capital investments that the extractive export-oriented industries require and the enclave-type modern sector mentioned above.

The first government of the National Revolutionary Movement Party (MNR) led by Dr. Víctor Paz Estenssoro in the 1950s tried to break with the historical model of trade and development. The MNR attempted to implement an inward-looking development strategy based on economic nationalism. To these ends they undertook nationalization of the Big Three mining companies; land reform; high protection for domestic industry through a mechanism of differential rates of foreign exchange along with quantitative controls for foreign exchange reserves; and deficit financing of development projects, especially those intended for export diversification. The MNR strategy was not, however, very successful. [3] In December of 1956 the government set forth an orthodox Monetary Stabilization Plan and by 1957, much of the reformist zeal and populism that had predominated in economic matters in the early years of the revolution had been lost.

In 1961 a *Ten-Year National Economic and Social Development Plan* was introduced. The *Plan* consisted essentially of a set of physical targets in the production of goods and services, that were to be attained, in many cases, by import substitution together with a parallel development of a basic infrastructure of transportation, education and health facilities. [4] According to the *Plan*, most programs were to be financed by foreign savings, especially those from public sources. However, the importance of a substantial expansion of exports was recognized. The main mechanism in the *Plan* to attain import substitution was the selective use of public credit. There was little reliance on exchange controls, tariffs, or quantitative restrictions on imports to foster industrialization.

In November of 1964 the revolutionary experiments of the reign of the MNR were formally ended with a coup which placed a conservative, General René Barrientos, in the presidency. The ensuing development style of fundamentally conservative governments, that began with the Barrientos regime and have continued up to the present, contrasts sharply with the pattern of the revolutionary period. Thus since 1964, with the exceptions discussed below, Bolivia has followed a more "outward-looking" model of development which represents a return to the historical pattern of openness in the modern sector of Bolivia. [5] A feature of the outward look was the liberalization of the foreign sector regulations, especially for capital movements. The amount of trade liberalization is, however, more difficult to assess due to the small but frequent changes in policies since that year. [6]

The return to the outward-looking historical model was interrupted during the short-lived regimes of Generals Alfredo Ovando Candia and Juan José Torres, that lasted from the end of 1969 to the middle of 1971. President Ovando nationalized the Bolivian Gulf Oil Corporation, and his development plans, as set forth in the *Socio-economic Strategy for National Development* (SSND), threw the weight of the development effort on the production and savings of the public sector. Emphasis was placed on public enterprises in order to try to gain more efficiency in production and higher growth rates of exports. The earlier heavy reliance on foreign savings to finance development was lessened.[7] The SSND set forth a plan for selective import substitution that took into account the nation's endowment of natural resources and the enlarged market for domestic production that was to be provided by the Andean Group.

During the Ovando regime the controversial tin smelters were built. These gave Bolivia the capability to export metallic tin, rather than refined ore, and were to have enormous importance in changing the composition of Bolivia's exports. Although the liberalization of the foreign sector that has prevailed in Bolivia since 1964 has caused a return to the historical trend, it is necessary to recognize the important changes in the *nature* of the nation's foreign trade and development which were made possible by the revolution of 1952, and to a lesser degree by the regime of General Ovando. A detailed description of those changes since 1964 is given in the following section.

MAIN FEATURES OF THE BOLIVIAN EXTERNAL SECTOR

Evolution and Composition of Exports

As shown in Table X-1 the annual rate of growth of the value of exports was very high during the 1965-1976 period when it averaged 15 percent. Particularly important was the sharp rise in 1974 when the total value increased almost twofold due to the doubling of the export values of minerals, metallic tin and oil.[8]

Since 1965 there has been a definite change in the composition of exports. Petroleum and natural gas exports were nonexistent in that year but by 1976 they accounted for more than 27 percent of the total value. Moreover, there is a perceptible long-term trend of diversification away from raw materials. Aside from the metallic tin exports—that have replaced the ore exports—there has been a substantial absolute and relative increase in the export of manufactured goods: mainly sugar, wood, shoes and leather products, canned food and alcoholic beverages. Moreover, there has been a significant absolute increase in the export of agricultural raw materials, particularly cotton. Notwithstanding the diversification, the export share of those goods is still very modest.

The above analysis in current dollars greatly overestimates the real value of exports, especially if imports are used as a numéraire. Given the lack of export and import price indexes for Bolivia it is difficult to assess the magnitude and hence the purchasing power of Bolivian export revenues in terms of imports. It is generally recognized, however, that there has been a medium-term improvement in the terms of trade since 1966. The historical evidence shows, however, that export prices fluctuate widely. This fluctuation unfortunately introduces an important element of uncertainty that conspires against the expansion of exports, and more generally, against most economic policies,

TABLE X-1

COMPOSITION OF BOLIVIAN EXPORTS, 1965-1976[a]

(Millions of Dollars)

	1965		1966		1967		1968		1969		1970	
	Value	%	Value	%	Value	%	Value	%	Value	%	Value	%
Raw Materials	131.8	100.00	150.4	100.00	182.5	100.00	170.6	100.00	198.2	100.00	224.7	98.25
Minerals	124.7	94.61	131.5	87.43	131.3	71.95	138.9	81.42	167.2	84.36	204.8	89.55
Petroleum	---	---	6.5	4.32	22.9	12.55	24.3	14.24	23.0	11.60	13.2	5.77
Natural Gas	---	---	---	---	---	---	---	---	---	---	---	---
Other	7.1	5.39	12.4	8.24	28.3	15.51	7.4	4.34	8.0	4.04	6.7	2.93
Manufactures and semi-manufactures	0.0	0.00	0.0	0.00	0.0	0.00	0.0	0.00	0.0	0.00	4.0	1.75
Metallic Tin	---	---	---	---	---	---	---	---	---	---	---	---
Other	0.0	0.00	0.0	0.00	0.0	0.00	0.0	0.00	0.0	0.00	4.0	1.75
TOTAL	131.8	100.00	150.4	100.00	182.5	100.00	170.6	100.00	198.2	100.00	228.7	100.00

(continued)

TABLE X-1 (continued)

	1971		1972		1973		1974		1975		1976		Average Annual Growth Rate %
	Value	%	Value	%	Value	%	Value	%	Value	%	Value	%	
Raw Materials	187.0	86.61	210.8	87.69	284.0	83.95	556.2	85.52	438.0	84.00	494.4	80.69	12.8
Minerals	149.4	69.20	149.5	62.19	193.6	57.23	331.6	50.98	253.1	48.54	292.5	47.74	8.1[b]
Petroleum	23.9	11.07	31.7	13.19	48.9	14.45	163.9	25.20	111.4	21.36	112.6	18.38	33.0[b]
Natural Gas	----	----	9.9	4.12	18.1	5.35	29.2	4.49	42.5	8.15	54.9	8.96	53.5[c]
Other	13.7	6.34	19.7	8.19	23.4	6.92	31.5	4.84	31.0	5.95	34.4	5.61	15.4
Manufactures and Semi-manufactures	28.9	13.39	29.6	12.31	54.3	16.05	94.2	14.48	83.4	16.00	118.3	19.31	75.8[d]
Metallic Tin	23.9	11.07	24.6	10.23	32.3	9.55	55.6	8.55	51.4	9.86	74.3	12.13	25.5
Other	5.0	2.32	5.0	2.08	22.0	6.50	38.6	5.93	32.0	6.14	44.0	7.18	49.1[e]
TOTAL	215.9	100.00	240.4	100.00	338.3	100.00	650.4	100.00	521.4	100.00	612.7	100.00	15.0

[a] CIF value.
[b] Average annual growth rate, 1966-1976.
[c] Average annual growth rate, 1972-1976.
[d] Average annual growth rate, 1970-1976.

Source: Banco Central de Bolivia, *Boletín estadístico*, various months, 1971-1977.

TABLE X-2

COMPOSITION OF BOLIVIAN IMPORTS, 1965-1976[a]
(Millions of Dollars)

	1965		1966		1967		1968		1969		1970	
	Value	%	Value	%	Value	%	Value	%	Value	%	Value	%
Consumer Goods	33.5	25.02	34.7	25.07	35.5	22.92	31.2	20.42	32.3	19.60	32.3	20.29
Durable	13.4	10.01	13.9	10.04	14.3	9.23	12.3	8.05	11.1	6.74	9.8	6.16
Non-Durable	20.1	15.01	20.8	15.03	21.2	13.69	18.9	12.37	21.2	12.86	22.5	14.13
Intermediate Goods	45.7	34.13	47.4	34.25	60.0	38.73	48.9	32.00	49.2	29.85	59.3	37.63
Capital Goods	54.4	40.63	55.8	40.32	58.7	37.90	71.9	47.05	82.7	50.18	66.2	41.58
Other	0.3	0.22	0.5	0.36	0.7	0.45	0.8	0.52	0.6	0.36	0.8	0.50
TOTAL Customs Statistics	133.9	100.00	138.4	100.00	154.9	100.00	152.8	100.00	164.8	100.00	159.2	100.00

(continued)

TABLE X-2 (continued)

	1971		1972		1973		1974		1975		1976		Average Annual Growth Rate %
	Value	%	Value	%	Value	%	Value	%	Value	%	Value	%	
Consumer Goods	34.2	21.52	34.6	20.07	40.8	20.02	90.4	23.18	127.8	22.91	118.7	21.48	12.2
Durable	9.5	5.98	8.1	4.70	9.8	4.81	37.7	9.67	60.3	10.81	56.0	10.13	13.9
Non-Durable	24.7	15.54	26.5	15.37	31.0	15.21	52.7	13.51	67.5	12.10	62.7	11.35	11.0
Intermediate Goods	53.4	33.61	51.0	29.58	61.1	29.98	119.6	30.67	199.2	35.71	193.8	35.07	14.0
Capital Goods	71.1	44.75	84.6	49.07	99.9	49.02	177.2	45.44	223.7	40.10	235.7	42.65	14.2
Other	0.2	0.13	2.2	1.28	2.0	0.98	2.8	0.72	7.2	1.29	4.4	0.80	27.7
TOTAL Customs Statistics	158.9	100.00	172.4	100.00	203.8	100.00	390.0	100.00	557.9	100.00	552.6	100.00	13.8

[a] C F value of imports.

Source: Banco Central de Bolivia, *Boletín estadístico*, various months, 1971-1977.

The Evolution and Composition of Imports

As shown in Table X-2, the average annual rate of growth of the value of imports over the 1965-1976 period was also high, 13.8 percent, as measured in current dollars. In this period there were strong, hardly containable pressures for imports of consumer durable goods and food staples even if a noticeable degree of import substitution had been achieved in agriculture. Imports of intermediate goods also grew at high rates, especially after 1972 with the recovery of the construction and manufacturing sectors. Capital goods imports have exhibited a little more dynamism than intermediate goods; and as in the case of intermediates, a big increase occurred after 1972, whereas the three preceding years were quite stagnant. It should also be noted that prior to 1969, there were also important increases in imports of capital goods primarily due to the expansion of the petroleum sector.

A comparison of export receipts and expenditures on consumer goods imports strongly suggests that consumer goods imports change more than proportionately relative to other imports as export receipts vary. This would mean that in the years of export expansion, the above-normal receipts from exports are likely to be spent proportionally more on consumption goods than on capital goods.[9] This result suggests the inability of Bolivian governments to contain the strong preference of the public for consumer goods rather than for investment-oriented capital goods. It may also suggest a lack of absorptive capacity for investment. For whatever reason it is indeed regrettable that during the years of the export boom there was a great wastage of the windfall foreign exchange receipts in the sense that they were directed to provide short-run benefits for increased consumption rather than for the long-run benefits for economic development to be derived from investment.[10] This suggests the need for a foreign exchange stabilization fund and well-conceived investment programs.[11]

Lastly, no analysis of importation in Bolivia is complete without considering smuggling. This illegal activity takes on large proportions and is a major Bolivian economic problem. Official sources estimate that from one-tenth to one-fifth of all foreign trade is contraband. Therefore, the data reported in the tables underestimate the actual trade. Much contraband is not reported in any form, and another important percentage of smuggling takes the form of underinvoicing the value of otherwise legal imports by accredited importers of the form of deliberate misclassification in the tariff nomenclature. The current tariff structure, with its dispersion of rates and high rates for luxuries clearly invites this form of contraband.

Patterns of Trade

Patterns of trade with Bolivia's trading partners over the 1965-1976 period are presented in Tables X-3 and X-4. The changes over the period lead to three conclusions. The first and principal conclusion is that there has been a major increase in trade with Latin American countries. In 1965 Bolivian exports to the Latin American Free Trade Association (LAFTA) countries formed only 2.6 percent of total exports. Since that time the share increased rapidly until it reached a little more than one-third in 1975 and 1976. Over the same time period Bolivian imports from LAFTA countries rose from 10.5 percent to about 35 percent. Whereas most of Bolivia's trade is still with the industrial world the increases from the semi-industrial LAFTA countries have come about for two basic reasons: First, the bigger Latin American countries—Argentina, Brazil and Mexico—have made important advances in industrialization and they can competitively offer many manufactured goods for export. Indeed, they have found the natural extensions of their domestic markets in the markets of their less-developed neighbors. Second, the world's raw materials and energy crisis have made profitable investment in the Bolivian transportation infrastructure in order to carry oil, natural gas and minerals from Bolivia to neighboring countries. Trade has increased as a consequence.

The second conclusion, which touches on the later analysis of the Andean Group, is that notwithstanding the extraordinary expansion of Bolivia's trade with the LAFTA countries, commerce with the Andean Group countries has not increased at as rapid a rate as trade with other LAFTA countries. In 1974 Bolivian exports to the Andean Group reached a high of 9.3 percent of its total exports; the percentage has been less in other years. Moreover, imports have surpassed 5 percent of total imports in only two years over the 1965-1976 period.

The third conclusion is that imports from the United States and Canada have been growing less rapidly than those from other areas of the world. Meanwhile, Bolivian exports to these two countries have been growing at a good pace, such that in 1976 Bolivia enjoyed a trade surplus with them.

Both imports and exports from Europe and Japan have grown rapidly. However, in each year of the 1965-1976 period Bolivia experienced a trade deficit with the countries of the European Economic Community (EEC).

With the current new world division of labor an increase in manufactured imports from Asian countries is predictable. In fact, in recent years there has been a noticeable inflow of goods from China, Taiwan, South Korea and Hong Kong. These appear under the "other countries" heading in the tables.

The Balance of Payments

Table X-5 presents data on Bolivia's balance of payments over the 1968-1977 period. Over the period there has been a tendency for a slight surplus in the trade of goods, with the notable exception of the years 1968, 1975, and 1977 when deficits occurred. The trade surplus of 1974 was extraordinarily large and was a high for modern times.

The picture for the whole of the current account is, however, not so favorable. The balance for factor and non-factor services was always in deficit. With respect to non-factor services there is no doubt that the freight and insurance costs negatively impact on the current account. In the factor payments ledger, the serious and continuous increase in factor income payments abroad has led to a heavy negative balance for these items. For example, there was a five-fold increase in the net payment of net profit remittances between 1971 and 1977. This phenomenon is basically explained by the debt servicing requirements for the huge increase in foreign debt, especially in the past six years, and in the increasingly harder terms under which this debt was financed.

The chronic deficits in the current account were financed by large inflows in the capital account of foreign direct private investment during the first years of the period of analysis. However, from 1969 onward most of the inflow has been in the form of loans from public foreign sources. There has also been a sharp increase in loans from foreign private banks. Notwithstanding the very liberal hydrocarbons and investment laws enacted in 1972 the foreign direct private investment has been very modest. For example, according to The Bolivian State Petroleum Company (YPFB), the total investment by foreign oil companies from 1973 to 1977 was only 108.6 million dollars. In contrast, private bank loans, especially short-term loans, to the private sector have been important. These and foreign public loans have accounted for most of the sharp increases observed in

TABLE X-3

VALUE AND STRUCTURE OF BOLIVIAN EXPORTS BY DESTINATION, 1965-1976[a]
(Millions of Dollars)

	1965		1966		1967		1968		1969		1970	
	Value	%	Value	%	Value	%	Value	%	Value	%	Value	%
USA & Canada	56.2	42.64	59.0	39.23	72.3	43.48	60.3	35.33	60.8	30.68	78.5	34.80
Western Europe	69.5	52.73	80.5	53.52	79.6	47.87	91.0	53.31	107.9	54.44	104.4	46.28
EEC countries[b]	69.5	52.73	80.5	53.52	79.5	47.81	87.8	51.44	104.2	52.57	102.2	45.30
Other Western Europe	----	----	----	----	0.1	0.06	3.2	1.87	3.7	1.87	2.2	0.98
LAFTA countries	3.4	2.58	7.7	5.12	9.9	5.95	13.9	8.14	17.5	8.83	19.1	8.47
Andean Group[c]	1.2	0.91	3.1	2.06	2.8	1.68	4.9	2.87	4.8	2.42	6.0	2.66
Other LAFTA	2.2	1.67	4.6	3.06	7.1	4.27	9.0	5.27	12.7	6.41	13.1	5.81
Japan	2.7	2.05	2.8	1.86	4.0	2.41	5.3	3.10	12.0	6.05	21.7	9.62
Other	----	0.00	0.4	0.27	0.5	0.30	0.2	0.12	0.0	0.00	1.9	0.84
TOTAL	131.8	100.00	150.4	100.00	166.3	100.00	170.7	100.00	198.2	100.00	225.6	100.00

(continued)

TABLE X-3 (continued)

	1971 Value	%	1972 Value	%	1973 Value	%	1974 Value	%	1975 Value	%	1976 Value	%	Average Annual Growth Rate %
USA & Canada	69.3	32.10	66.4	27.62	92.4	27.31	200.4	30.81	160.9	30.86	210.3	34.31	12.7
Western Europe	80.1	37.10	88.5	36.81	111.3	32.90	176.5	27.13	126.0	24.17	147.5	24.06	2.1
EEC countries[b]	74.2	34.37	83.0	34.53	97.5	28.82	138.1	21.23	97.9	18.78	119.5	19.49	5.1
Other Western Europe	5.9	2.73	5.5	2.28	13.8	4.08	38.4	5.90	28.1	5.39	28.0	4.57	n.a.
LAFTA countries	40.4	18.71	63.2	26.29	103.2	30.51	210.6	32.37	186.9	35.85	204.7	33.39	45.1
Andean Group[c]	20.4	9.45	19.2	7.99	26.0	7.69	60.9	9.36	28.0	5.37	37.5	6.12	36.7
Other LAFTA	20.0	9.26	44.0	18.30	77.2	22.82	149.7	23.01	158.9	30.48	167.2	27.27	48.2
Japan	17.0	7.87	13.1	5.45	19.5	5.76	32.5	5.00	18.3	3.51	20.6	3.36	20.3
Other	9.1	4.21	9.2	3.83	11.9	3.52	30.5	4.69	29.3	5.62	29.9	4.88	n.a.
TOTAL	215.9	100.00	240.4	100.00	338.3	100.00	650.5	100.00	521.4	100.00	613.0	100.00	15.0

a CIF value.
b Includes exports to the nine EEC countries since 1965, even if three of them have joined the community later.
c Includes imports from Colombia, Chile, Ecuador, Peru and Venezuela since 1965.
Source: Banco Central de Bolivia, *Boletín estadístico*, various months, 1971-1977.

TABLE X-4
VALUE AND STRUCTURE OF BOLIVIAN IMPORTS BY ORIGIN, 1965-1976[a]
(Millions of Dollars)

	1965 Value	1965 %	1966 Value	1966 %	1967 Value	1967 %	1968 Value	1968 %	1969 Value	1969 %	1970 Value	1970 %
USA & Canada	60.2	44.99	59.1	42.70	64.1	42.48	68.4	44.76	54.1	32.79	56.1	35.24
Western Europe	36.6	27.35	41.4	29.91	42.9	28.43	41.5	27.16	50.5	30.61	47.5	29.84
EEC countries[b]	32.8	24.51	35.8	25.87	36.3	24.06	35.6	23.30	41.2	24.97	38.4	24.12
Other Western Europe	3.8	2.84	5.6	4.04	6.6	4.37	5.9	3.86	9.3	5.64	9.1	5.72
LAFTA countries	14.0	10.46	15.2	10.98	17.6	11.66	18.9	12.37	26.1	15.82	27.5	17.27
Andean Group[c]	3.9	2.91	4.0	2.89	4.2	2.78	4.5	2.95	4.8	2.91	6.3	3.96
Other LAFTA	10.1	7.55	11.2	8.09	13.4	8.88	14.4	9.42	21.3	12.91	21.2	13.31
Japan	17.5	13.08	15.5	11.20	18.3	12.13	17.0	11.13	27.1	16.42	19.6	12.31
Other	5.5	4.11	7.2	5.20	8.0	5.30	7.0	4.58	7.2	4.36	8.5	5.34
TOTAL Customs Statistics	133.8	100.00	138.4	100.00	150.9	100.00	152.8	100.00	165.0	100.00	159.2	100.00

(continued)

TABLE X-4 (continued)

	1971		1972		1973		1974		1975		1976		Average Annual Growth Rate %
	Value	%	Value	%	Value	%	Value	%	Value	%	Value	%	
USA & Canada	51.7	30.48	45.6	26.45	51.8	25.42	109.5	28.08	146.8	26.31	155.1	27.97	8.9
Western Europe	49.7	29.30	49.4	28.65	56.5	27.72	79.1	20.29	113.4	20.33	119.4	21.53	11.3
EEC countries[b]	40.6	23.94	36.6	21.30	41.6	20.41	62.3	15.98	92.2	16.53	89.3	16.10	9.5
Other Western Europe	9.1	5.36	12.8	7.42	14.9	7.31	16.8	4.31	21.2	3.80	30.1	5.43	20.7
LAFTA countries	39.6	23.35	48.5	28.13	61.1	29.98	135.2	34.68	191.6	34.34	202.2	36.46	27.5
Andean Group[c]	6.0	3.54	7.3	4.23	9.2	4.51	15.5	3.98	29.8	5.34	24.5	4.42	18.2
Other LAFTA	33.6	19.81	41.2	23.90	51.9	25.47	119.7	30.70	161.8	29.00	177.7	32.04	29.8
Japan	18.2	10.73	19.6	11.37	23.2	11.38	55.1	14.13	88.3	15.83	65.2	11.76	12.7
Other	10.4	6.13	9.3	5.39	11.2	5.50	11.0	2.82	17.8	3.19	12.7	2.29	7.9
TOTAL Customs Statistics	169.6	100.00	172.4	100.00	203.8	100.00	389.9	100.00	557.9	100.00	554.6	100.00	13.8

[a] CIF Value.

[b] Includes imports from the nine EEC countries since 1965, even if three of them have joined the community later.

[c] Includes imports from Colombia, Chile, Ecuador, Peru and Venezuela since 1965.

Source: Banco Central de Bolivia, *Boletín estadístico*, various months, 1971–1977.

TABLE X-5

SUMMARY OF BOLIVIAN BALANCE OF PAYMENTS, 1968-1977

(Millions of Dollars)

	1968	1969	1970	1971	1972	1973	1974	1975	1976	1977[a]
USES										
Imports of goods FOB	161.5	173.4	166.2	181.4	195.7	235.3	364.0	514.9	562.3	670.0
Imports of NF services	41.1	41.8	44.5	46.1	64.9	73.9	121.1	152.4	148.9	187.3
Imports of factor services	25.1	32.2	27.1	21.2	22.0	29.7	41.1	38.1	52.6	96.2
External debt amortization	13.2	15.2	20.6	23.4	32.5	35.5	55.5	64.6	71.5	101.3
International reserves (Increases)	----	0.4	5.3	----	18.6	----	111.5	----	63.1	10.4
TOTAL USES	240.9	263.0	263.7	272.1	333.7	374.4	693.2	770.0	898.4	1,065.2
SOURCES										
Exports of goods FOB	157.1	178.6	195.7	181.9	203.1	270.8	578.2	462.3	567.7	647.8
Exports of NF services	13.0	12.2	14.6	16.4	21.6	26.4	49.4	65.5	61.8	72.6
Interest receipts	1.5	1.7	2.1	4.2	0.2	6.8	3.9	6.7	11.4	3.8
Transfers net	6.7	7.8	3.9	7.1	13.4	15.4	13.7	13.1	14.0	15.0
Private and public capital	68.4	65.7	58.7	78.9	130.7	70.8	105.7	201.3	269.3	364.9
Errors and omissions	-6.4	-3.0	-11.3	-26.4	-35.3	-29.7	-57.7	-23.3	-25.8	-38.9
International reserves (Decrease)	0.6	----	----	10.0	----	13.9	----	44.4	----	----
TOTAL SOURCES	240.9	263.0	263.7	272.1	333.7	374.4	693.2	770.0	898.4	1,065.2

[a]Preliminary estimates based on Bolivian Central Bank data.

Source: Banco Central de Bolivia, *Boletín estadístico*, various months, 1971-1977.

the table under the heading of Private and Public Capital. This item takes into account the inflow of capital less the outflow, excluding public debt amortization.

The strong inflow of foreign capital has been an important factor in the government's management of the balance of payments and has provided some flexibility within a system of a fixed exchange rate and the government's reluctance to devalue.

In spite of the generous inflow of foreign capital that covered the financing of current account deficits during the period under consideration, in some years it was necessary for the government to dip into their holding of international reserves in order to meet foreign obligations and to fend off a devaluation of the Bolivian peso. In 1972, however, the situation became unsalvageable when the extremely low reserve position forced a 40 percent devaluation.

The large inflow of capital while contributing importantly to Bolivia's development in recent years has, however, produced considerable worry about the degree of the nation's indebtedness. The economic consequences of high indebtedness bothered government officials and the public alike, especially in view of the experiences of some neighboring countries where the specter of deep recession has appeared as a consequence of their external financial position. The external public debt has become a major issue in the 1978 political campaign.

As shown in Table X-6 the outstanding external public debt increased almost fourfold, measured in current dollars, from 1970-1977. Repayments, however, have not followed at the same pace. There has also been a change in the composition of the foreign debt. Foreign public aid has declined in relative importance and loans from private foreign banks have increased correspondingly. [12] The latter loans carry harder terms with regard to interest, maturity and grace periods. Fortunately the share of the expensive supplier's credit has been lessening, although the level is still high.

The foreign debt going to the public sector has been quite evenly distributed between the central government and the public enterprises (Table X-7 presents figures for 1977). [13] The central government obtains most of its credit on a soft-term basis from international lending institutions, whereas the public enterprises have high proportions of hard-term loans from private foreign banks and suppliers. Finally, according to government officials, the servicing of the external debt is within tolerable limits. The debt service ratio varied between 12.5 and 24 percent during the 1970-1979 period. The ratio was 22.6 percent in 1977. [14]

As a last point, the relative importance of the errors and omissions in the balance of payments should be noted. This may be indicative of unrecorded capital flight. If this interpretation is correct the amount of flight capital may be considerable.

BOLIVIAN TRADE POLICIES SINCE 1965

In spite of the efforts of the revolutionary period and the modest degree of success obtained in import substitution, particularly of some food staples and petroleum derivatives, by 1964 Bolivia was, and still is, heavily dependent on imports. Hence, all governments have been cognizant of the need to have some control over the behavior of the external sector and of the availability of foreign exchange.

Since 1965 Bolivia has continued the earlier policy of fixed foreign exchange rates which has led to frequent pressures on the balance of payments. The government however, has steadfastly tried to avoid devalua-

TABLE X-6

BOLIVIAN EXTERNAL PUBLIC DEBT, 1970-1977

(Debt outstanding as of December 31, in Millions of Dollars)

Source of Credit	1970 Debt	%	1971 Debt	%	1972 Debt	%	1973 Debt	%	1974 Debt	%	1975 Debt	%	1976 Debt	%	1977[a] Debt	%
Public External Loans	458.4	68.3	537.7	68.8	640.2	67.9	671.5	66.0	758.8	63.6	950.2	62.3	1175.9	59.4	1392.1	55.4
Private Foreign Banks	1.4	0.2	25.4	3.2	39.9	4.3	50.2	4.9	128.5	10.8	294.9	19.4	441.0	22.3	690.9	27.5
Suppliers	143.4	21.4	151.7	19.4	194.3	20.6	228.9	22.5	237.1	19.9	212.0	13.9	294.4	14.9	360.3	14.4
Other	67.4	10.1	67.3	8.6	67.4	7.2	67.4	6.6	67.4	5.7	67.4	4.4	67.4	3.4	67.4	2.7
TOTAL	670.6	100.0	782.1	100.0	941.8	100.0	1018.0	100.0	1191.8	100.0	1524.5	100.0	1978.7	100.0	2510.7	100.0

[a]Preliminary estimates.

Source: Bolivia, Ministerio de Finanzas, *Memorandum sobre el financiamiento externo de Bolivia*, (La Paz: enero, 1978), p. 14.

TABLE X-7

BOLIVIAN EXTERNAL PUBLIC DEBT AS OF DECEMBER 31, 1977
ACCORDING TO SOURCES OF CREDIT AND TO BORROWER[a]
(Debt outstanding in Millions of Dollars)

Borrowing Institution	SOURCE OF CREDIT									Total	
	Public External Loans		Private Foreign Banks		Suppliers		Other				
	Debt	%	Debt	%	Debt	%	Debt	%		Debt	%
Central Government	816.7	58.39	252.6	36.58	38.3	10.82	67.4	100.00		1175.0	46.80
Local Governments	41.7	2.89	24.4	3.53	33.4	9.43	----	----		99.5	3.90
State Enterprises	380.9	27.23	349.0	50.54	253.6	71.62	----	----		983.5	39.10
Public Services	77.1	5.51	27.2	3.94	23.7	6.69	----	----		128.0	5.10
Development Banks	82.2	5.88	37.4	5.42	5.1	1.44	----	----		124.7	4.90
TOTAL	1398.6	100.00	690.6	100.00	354.1	100.00	67.4	100.00		2510.7	100.00

[a] Preliminary estimates.

Source: Bolivia, Ministerio de Finanzas, *Memorandum sobre el financiamiento externo de Bolivia*, (La Paz: enero, 1978), p. 20.

tions. Fortunately, a large inflow of foreign capital has helped to mitigate balance of payments pressures and, as observed previously, has allowed the country to run important current account deficits.

Although the active encouragement of foreign investment and economic assistance was a cornerstone of the external sector policies of the conservative governments of the period, it was by no means the only policy. Three other main instruments should be mentioned. First, Bolivia actively participated in the international schemes of price stabilization for its major exports. Second, in order to expand exports, Bolivia established bilateral negotiations with two neighboring countries, Brazil and Argentina, and actively participated in the Andean Group and, to a lesser extent, the Latin American Free Trade Association. Third, a policy of import regulations was implemented. During the whole 1965-1977 period there were controls of some sort, and in some years of that period, the controls were very rigid. Usually the control of imports was sought in a manner to cause the least sacrifice in current output and employment, regardless of the effects on resource allocation. However, many of these short-term policies have had longer-term and unintended effects such as influencing decisions on investment. On the other hand longer-term policies, such as the ones designed for import substitution, frequently have induced balance of payments problems.

In the following two sections the diverse export and import policy instruments are examined, their impact on the economy is presented, and, where appropriate, their short- and long-term effects are treated separately.

EXPORT POLICIES

The distinction between exports of manufactures and exports of primary goods is important to explain the nature of Bolivia's export policies. Since Bolivia has a very small industrial base, the export policies primarily have been aimed to assert its position in the international markets of raw materials rather than to promote exports of manufactured goods. Only recently a system of subsidization has been implemented to encourage the latter.

Price Stabilization Schemes

Bolivia has been characterized aptly as an "export economy," i.e., "an economy with a significant dependence on one major industry selling in an external market."[15] Thus, it is quite natural that Bolivia's policies have been oriented to strengthen the international price and earnings stabilization mechanisms for its major exports.

By far the most important scheme of price stabilization has been provided by the Bolivia's participation in International Tin Agreements (ITA) which were entered into during the 1965-1977 period. Five agreements have been signed: in 1956, 1961, 1966, 1971 and 1976. During this time Bolivia also signed agreements of lesser scope for tungsten and antimony, other important Bolivian exports.

The ITAs are agreed upon by the main tin producing and consuming countries. The main, but not the only, instrument to achieve the price stabilization objectives is a buffer stock of tin metal. Roughly, the attempts to bring about stabilization with the buffer stock work as follows: the manager of the buffer stock sells tin metal—whenever the market price is higher than an agreed upon ceiling price until the market price falls below the ceiling or the tin stock is exhausted, and buys tin when the price is below the agreed upon floor price until the market price rises above the floor or the funds are exhausted. There are also some regulations for a range of prices between the floor and ceiling. The buffer stock is financed by the producing members. The governing body of the ITA is the International Tin Council (ITC). [16]

Bolivia has participated in all the ITAs. In the negotiations for the last three agreements and especially, the fifth, Bolivia, which has the highest production costs among the producing countries, found that the proposed arrangements did not ensure that the floor and ceiling prices, that were to be set by the ITC, would provide a remunerative return for its production. Thus, she argued for higher floor and ceiling prices. The other producing countries did not follow Bolivia in its demands for higher prices since they feared that the upkeep of the buffer stock would be costly, but more importantly, that a long-run policy of high prices would boomerang to the loss of the producing countries. Furthermore, there were hints of a collusion between some of the producing countries and the consumer countries, given that in many instances the same transnational corporations do the extracting, refining and marketing of the mineral. As a final result, the reference prices fixed in the ITAs have not suited Bolivia's interests completely.

Moreover, there is considerable controversy on the workings of the ITC and of the buffer stock. For example, there is a problem with the smallness of agreed upon stock. In fact the buffer stock became irrelevant in the booming market observed after 1973. Moreover, the buffer stock can hardly cope with the most important destabilizing factor in the tin market, namely, the huge strategic stockpile of metal tin held by the United States General Service Administration (GSA). Mere hints of disposals of tin metal by the GSA create a speculative climate that causes important falls in the tin price. Of course, actual sales can depress the market significantly. As an important part of its export policy, Bolivia has tried consistently to influence the U.S. management of the GSA stockpile of tin metal.

Mining Taxes

Besides the problem of price stabilization, the production and export activities of the mining sector are impacted severely by the Bolivian tax legislation. The mining sector is subjected to two main types of taxes: a *regalía*, which was initiated in 1965, and an export tax that was imposed with the devaluation of 1972. The *regalía* is a tax on presumed income, i.e., the nominal base of the tax is given by the difference between world mineral prices in specified markets and a presumed cost set by the Bolivian Ministry of Mines. The *regalía* replaced a complex set of low-yield taxes that were generally earmarked for municipalities, regional development corporations and so forth. Since presumptive costs change infrequently, *regalía* functions as a tax on the gross value of output. According to a study made in 1976 by a consultant group from the Institute for International Development of Harvard University, the *regalía* overtaxes the mining sector, and particularly the weakest enterprises, in years of low mineral prices, whereas it fails to fiscally appropriate the rents that are generated in years of rising mineral prices. Moreover, tax codes do not encourage investment in mineral exploration and development. [17]

There is a great need for new investment in exploration since the mines are becoming exhausted and the metal content of the ore is increasingly lower. If Bolivia wants a more substantial development of its mining sector and to promote exports more effectively, then a reform of the taxes bearing on the production and exportation of minerals along the lines proposed by the Harvard consultants is called for. Such reform should encourage new investment by *both* the public and the private mining enterprises. [18]

Petroleum Policy

In the petroleum and natural gas sector, there has not been a clear-cut policy to expand exports. Bolivia does not belong to OPEC, but follows the pricing policies set up by this organization for its petroleum exports.

Bolivia has a residual petroleum export policy in the sense that only after all domestic consumption has been satisfied, are exports allowed. With the slowdown in production due to the progressive depletion of the petroleum reserves and with the increases in domestic consumption, the amount left for legal exports has decreased substantially since 1973. It is likely that Bolivia will cease to be a net petroleum exporter in the very near future unless some steps are taken. These steps should include provisions for new investment oriented to exploration and for a realistic *domestic* pricing policy for petroleum derivatives. It has been the government's policy to maintain domestic prices on petroleum products far below the world price in order to keep transportation costs low and reduce inflationary pressures. The systematic domestic underpricing of petroleum products has encouraged, however, a demand for both domestic consumption and for *contraband* export, which has hindered a sensible development of petroleum exports that yield appropriate revenues. Petroleum production and exports are also subject to heavy taxation.

While proven reserves of petroleum are small, Bolivia has important deposits of natural gas. In fact, the nation's prospects for energy lie mainly in natural gas. Exports of the latter to Argentina have been an important source of foreign exchange; however, they are marred by controversies on the price, since the pricing principles were not clearly established when the gas pipeline was put in operation in 1971. There are also advanced negotiations to export natural gas to Brazil.

Non-traditional Exports

The Bolivian government has chosen to subsidize non-traditional (or minor) exports—selected agricultural products and manufactures—since the cheapness of the export dollar, in terms of Bolivian pesos, discriminated unduly against them. That is, subsidies were intended to compensate and balance the effects of the overvaluation of the peso.

The 1977 Law of Fiscal Incentives for Non-traditional Exports grants a host of incentives for the promotion of non-traditional exports that include exemption from all export taxes as well as exemptions from import duties for inputs embodied in exports; and a tax certificate granted to the exporters. The certificate, which amounts to between 10 and 25 percent of the FOB value of exports, can be used to pay income, sales and import taxes, and it can be sold freely to others by the exporter. Thus, in principle, the tax certificate can be readily converted into cash by the exporter and as such it constitutes a direct subsidy. [19]

Minor or non-traditional exports that wholly benefit from this law include all agricultural products as listed in the Andean Brussels Trade Nomenclature (ABTN) excepting sugar, cotton, coffee, rubber, coconuts, wood, hides and coca leaves; and all manufactures, as listed also in the ABTN, excepting a handful of goods that enjoy already a favorable treatment because their production is made in the context of the industrial planning of the Andean Group.

Foreign Trade Revenues

The relative importance of revenues from the export sector appear in Table X-8. To have a complete picture of the importance of the tax revenues brought about by exports, however, custom revenues from imports (same table) should be added to the exports since their existence has been made possible by the exports. The weight of import duties in the government tax revenues has been historically important, although they are becoming a declining source.

The share of taxes from the foreign sector in the total government tax revenues is very high as it can be observed in line (7) of Table X-8. This share is highly correlated with high prices for exports. In fact, fluctuations in export prices and hence in tax revenues, particularly in those generated by the mining sector, have considerable consequences in the financing of central government. Thus, the variability in tax collections has important destabilizing effects upon the level of government activity and, more generally, upon the national economy.

Evaluation of Export Policies

Export policies typically have not always been stated very clearly, nor have been their effects appraised fully. However, in regard to the traditional exports, there has been a constant policy of demanding higher prices, either through commodity agreements like the ITAs or through bilateral negotiations like the ones concerning the disposal of the GSA stock, or the sales of natural gas to Argentina. On the other hand, little use has been made of fiscal incentives to expand traditional exports. On the contrary, the fiscal system tends more to expropriate the economic rents—a legitimate objective, of course—than to encourage the opening of new mines or the drilling of new wells.

It is still too early to evaluate the impact of the legal incentives to promote minor exports. However, it is possible to make two conjectures. First, the scheme apparently overcompensates for the effects of the peso overvaluation. While export promotion is basically a sound policy, if carried too far it can lead to such bad results as exaggerated import substitution. The efficiency and equity costs can be very high.

Second, the exportable products that currently benefit from this export promotion policy constitute less than 5 percent of the value of all exports. It is difficult to imagine that a significantly higher share will be obtained through fiscal incentives, however generous they may be. The emphasis on fiscal measures can obscure the fact that domestic firms and industrialists first have to learn how to improve their production and merchandizing methods. Thus, more effective forms to encourage those exports should be sought. Perhaps, part of the subsidy to exporters should take the form of technical assistance and the state purchase payment of patents developed by transnational firms, which are to be exploited publicly.

IMPORT POLICIES

Import Duties and Controls: The Short-term Effects

With the exception of 1972, successive governments employed fiscal and monetary policies to control imports rather than go to the extreme of devaluation. There was frequent use of quantitative restrictions, changes

TABLE X-8

FOREIGN SECTOR TAXES PAID TO CENTRAL GOVERNMENT AS
A PERCENT OF TOTAL CENTRAL GOVERNMENT TAX REVENUES[a]
(Millions of Bolivian Pesos)

	1965	1966	1967	1968	1969	1970	1971	1972	1973	1974	1975	1976	1977
(1) Total Export Sector Taxes[b]	1.1	47.9	7.5	69.7	68.6	174.2	89.6	225.2	849.7	2419.8	1607.9	2244.7	2555.0
(2) Total Import Duties	343.2	342.9	394.0	348.7	361.6	418.0	378.1	418.2	517.4	947.3	1549.8	1455.9	1693.7
(3) Total Foreign Sector Taxes (1) + (2)	344.3	390.8	401.5	418.4	430.2	592.2	467.7	643.4	1367.1	3367.1	3157.7	3700.6	4248.7
(4) Total Government Tax Revenues	613.0	723.5	771.8	836.9	871.4	1070.4	1093.1	1330.1	2469.5	5069.7	5688.8	6840.9	7641.2
(5) Export Taxes as a Percent of Central Government Tax Revenues (1)/(4)	0.2	6.6	1.0	8.3	7.9	16.3	8.2	16.9	34.4	47.7	28.3	32.8	33.4
(6) Import Duties as a Percent of Central Government Tax Revenues (2)/(4)	56.0	47.4	51.0	41.7	41.5	39.1	34.6	31.4	21.0	18.7	27.2	21.3	22.2
(7) Total Foreign Sector Taxes as a Percent of Government Tax Revenues (3)/(4)	56.2	54.0	52.0	50.0	49.4	55.3	42.8	48.4	55.4	66.4	55.5	54.1	55.6

[a]Cash receipts of the Bolivian Treasury. Figures derived from sources of the state enterprises exceed the figures of the Treasury, since the former include payment of taxes with notes and the expenditures of those enterprises in social services rendered by them on behalf of the government.

[b]Includes export tax revenues proper as well as *regalías* from the mining sector and *estimated regalías* on exports of the petroleum sector.

Source: Banco Central de Bolivia, *Boletín estadístico*, various months, 1971–1977.

in import duties, and changes in other indirect taxes, instead of devaluations, to increase the domestic prices of selected non-essential imports.

Prior to 1965, Bolivia did not have a consistent import policy nor an adequate tariff schedule; most of the rates were very low. However, there were some high rates on luxury goods which were more intended to raise revenue rather than to protect domestic industry. Notwithstanding, the system of multiple exchange rates installed during the early 1950s was effectively a system of tariffs. Thus, when this system was abandoned in 1956, the design of a protective tariff schedule was imperative and the Stabilization Plan of that year included a section on import taxes. It should be stressed that the use of tariffs for balance of payments purposes was not of a frequent practice before 1968.

Two thorough revisions of the system of tariffs for imports were undertaken in 1965 and 1973. Those revisions had as their main objective the establishment of a coherent structure of protection.

In addition to changes in the import levies to regulate imports for balance of payments purposes, Bolivia has been using import bans for selected products, including automobiles, as well as other quantitative restrictions since 1976. A new tool in the kit of import controls was introduced in 1976 in the form of import prior deposits. The system of import prior deposits consists of a 120-day deposit in Bolivian pesos and is equal to a given percentage, with a ceiling of 25 percent, of the CIF value of the imported goods to which the private importers were liable. The deposit has to be made, at the moment of clearing from customs, in the Bolivian banking system. These deposits do not earn interest and are subject to a 100 percent reserve requirement in the banking system. The prior deposit proves to be an effective instrument since, besides making imports more expensive and therefore acting like a tariff, it contributes to diminishing the rate of growth of the money supply and hence, of aggregate demand.

A common characteristic of all the restrictive measures is their high degree of commodity discrimination. In every case the number of goods exempted from the regulation is important; a very important feature of the Bolivian import legislation.

The experience of Bolivia since 1965 in the use of the various policies to regulate imports for balance of payments purposes, appears to support the general conclusion, among economists, that those instruments have varying degrees of effectiveness, i.e., they are not perfect substitutes in terms of their effects. However, as a common characteristic, the effects of all the measures are of short duration, as they seem to only last from three-quarters of a year to one year.

Another common characteristic concerns the consequences of easing the trade restrictions. When this happens, imports are encouraged more than intended. This happened, for example, in 1975 when there were substantial reductions in the tariffs for luxury goods, mainly automobiles and domestic electrical appliances. After this unsuccessful experience in "liberalization," the old tariff levels for the above mentioned goods were restored and new measures of import control were established in 1976.

The Devaluation of 1972

The ultimate test of the validity of the policies for balance of payments adjustments that are used instead of devaluation is, of course, given by a comparison of the effects of the former with those of the latter. The evidence from the non-official Bolivian devaluation in October, 1972, is not altogether conclusive, although it is suggestive that devaluation was preferable to the other alternatives, since the latter had already been used to a considerable extent and there were doubts about their further positive effects. Devaluation appeared as quite inevitable. Moreover, the misallocation effects of the import policies were already of a threatening nature, while there was less danger with devaluation on this matter.

The 1972 devaluation and the collateral measures temporarily freezing nominal wages and the prices of nontraded goods, produced a major shock for Bolivia's economy. But, was the devaluation successful? The equilibrating effects of that measure are still being debated as the nation continued to face a balance of payments deficit the following year. It might be asked, however, without the devaluation would not the deficit of 1973 have been even larger? Further, was not the clear improvement of the balance of payments in 1974 a delayed result of devaluation? The answers to these questions are not clear since it is very difficult to separate the effects of the devaluation from the effects of the extraordinary improvements in the Bolivian terms of trade in 1974. There is some presumption to favor this second interpretation since, after the first semester of 1973, Banzer's government was unable to quell the demands, coming from labor, for a more expansionary policy that included wage hikes. But, as it is well known, the effects of expansionary policies check the intended effects of a devaluation.

Long-term and Allocation Effects of Import Controls

The tariff and non-tariff barriers which are employed as instruments for short-run adjustments in the balance of payments are also basic instruments that Bolivia has used for long-run purposes in order to encourage import substitution industrialization by providing protection from foreign competition.

Tariffs and Bans. As indicated previously the Bolivian tariff system has been modified often. The last major modification took place in 1973 but since then, piecemeal changes in that revision have altered the tax rates in the schedule in significant ways. Another important feature of the existing tariff structure is the existence of provisions for preferential tariffs for: (a) commodities, according to the final use to which they will be put; (b) goods that will be used in the northwestern regions of the country; and (c) goods coming from countries with which Bolivia has economic agreements, or bilateral reductions in tariffs.

Examples of preferential tariffs of type (a) are given by the special provisions for imports for the mining and petroleum sectors, and the exemptions accorded by the Investment Law. Type (c) preferences include the Bolivian lists of tariff concessions to the member countries of LAFTA and the Andean Group.

The provisions for preferential tariffs affect an important proportion of Bolivian imports. Depending on the year, the value of imports subject to the preferential rates range between 25 and 35 percent of total imports. The rationality of the existence of several tariff schedules, excepting Type (c) tariffs, has often been questioned, both on grounds of efficiency and those of incentives for the particular industry or geographical region that benefits, given that more direct means exist of fostering production or employment.

The changing nature of the tariff schedule renders the analysis of the effects of tariffs on resource allocation difficult. However, a first and important conclusion can be drawn: the piecemeal changes introduce an unintended high degree of dispersion of the tariffs, which is deemed undesirable. Worse, frequent changes were frequently brought about by the pressures of special interest groups of industrialists and importers.

This way of introducing modifications works against the objective of using tariffs to influence investment decisions. Of course, all governments are influenced by pressure groups, but the military governments of Presidents Barrientos and Banzer had a very pliant attitude to the demands of businessmen.

The current tariff schedule clearly exhibits that high tariffs on final goods are being used to discriminate against competing imports. For purposes of protecting domestic industry they are not, however, the principal policy measure. The main measures for protection are bans on imports and previous import licensing. At the present time bans on imports affect about 2 percent of the some 4,400 items in the customs classification. Previous import licensing affects 5 percent of the items.

Effective Rate of Protection. Domestic industry is also favored by low import duties on capital goods, which are not available domestically, and because of the small local market are not feasible to produce in Bolivia. Surprisingly, however, duties on raw materials and intermediate goods, which are necessary for domestic manufacturing and hence could be treated in a manner like that for capital goods, are quite variable.

The effective rate of protection is a better indicator of the extent to which a particular set of tariffs protects domestic producers than is the nominal tariff rate. [20] Table X-9 shows the effective rates for selected products. It is clear that there is considerable variation among the effective rates.

More specific conclusions can also be drawn from the data in Table X-9. First, the high protection provided by the import bans stands out. Apart from the prohibitions, the most important characteristic that appears in the structure of effective protection is the high effective rates for goods considered luxuries. They are considerably higher than their already high nominal rates. Although the high nominal rate is undoubtedly designed to discourage domestic consumption of these goods the high effective rate on the luxury goods, in the absence of high rates on intermediate goods used in the production, may invite some domestic producers to enter into the manufacturing of the goods.

Second, it is clear that there is high effective protection for domestic production. In the cases of goods subject to import bans there is complete protection, but it is also true in many cases which are only subject to tariffs. Third, most intermediate products for industrial usage have low (or even negative) effective rates which are generally very close to the nominal rates. Fourth, the effective rates for capital goods are close to the nominal rates. In many cases the effective rates are negative. It is not clear, however, that negative effective rates are desirable for Bolivia. If the country were to shift more towards heavy industry, then higher nominal effective rates would be needed than those now prevalent. It is unlikely, however, that this will loom important in Bolivia. More important is the promotion of employment. A rise in the nominal, and therefore in the effective rates of capital goods, would tend to discourage capital-intensive production methods in some industries where the possibilities exist for labor to be substituted for capital.

Evaluation. The successive Bolivian administrations have paid scant attention to the allocation and efficiency aspects of the import policies. Revenue and short-term considerations have prevailed indeed over the view of using tariffs and other import policies as effective tools to foster industrialization. The numerous piecemeal changes have denatured the original intentions of coherent protection in the 1965 and 1973 reforms of the import legislation. This feature is not unexpected since Bolivia had lacked badly of a general industrialization policy. On this point it is interesting

TABLE X-9

BOLIVIAN NOMINAL TARIFFS AND EFFECTIVE RATES
OF PROTECTION BY INDUSTRY
(As of December 31, 1977)

A. Summary statistics for a list of 337 groups of commodities.[a]

	Mean	Standard Deviation
Nominal tariffs	38.9%	28.0%
Effective rates of protection	74.4%	97.5%

Simple correlation between nominal and effective rates = 0.88
Rank order correlation between nominal and effective rates = 0.88

B. Indices for selected items within this list.[b]

	Nominal Tariff	Effective Rate of Protection
Livestock products	0.17	0.14
Chemical and fertilizer mineral products	0.27	0.38
Butter	0.81	4.83
Cheese	0.67	2.33
Canned fruits and vegetables	0.62	1.81
Flour mill products[c]	0.29	0.77
Bakery products	0.42	0.58
Processed tobacco	0.97	4.29
Carpets	1.18	5.83
Lace products	0.91	1.88
Jerseys	0.71	2.15
Products of carpeting	1.13	2.33
Premanufactured wooden structures	1.12	2.36
Papers for sanitary uses[c]	0.67	1.67
Pharmaceutical preparations[c]	0.17	0.19
Paints, inks and dyes	0.36	0.65
Leather	0.65	1.72
Soles and shoe components	0.97	1.89
Machinery for mining	0.07	−0.05
Steel structures	0.32	0.49
Hand tools	0.24	0.30
Farm machinery, except tractors	0.11	0.09
Machinery for the textile industry	0.09	0.01
Industrial furnaces	0.10	−0.05
Business and office machines	0.38	0.53
Domestic kitchen appliances	0.48	1.03
Washers	0.79	2.54
Fans and other domestic appliances	0.76	2.24
Domestic refrigerators	0.37	0.61
Trucks[c]	0.93	2.82
Household radio and TV sets	0.53	0.91
Motorcycles, bicycles and parts	0.43	1.30
Wood furnitures for homes	0.94	1.60
Small trucks[c]	1.48	4.61

TABLE X-9 (continued)

[a]The complete list upon which these summary statistics are based contains 337 groups of commodities. Each group is constituted by several items of the Andean Brussels Trade Nomenclature (ABTN). The 337 groups overlay the complete ABTN list of 4448 items. This grouping of ABTN items is done in *order* to be able to use the Andean Matrix of input-output coefficients to compute the effective rates. The statistics in A overestimate slightly the means as a result of the grouping.

[b]These are selected as representative groups from the complete list cited in note "a" above.

[c]Group contains banned imports. Implicit tariffs have been computed for those imports by comparing their international prices with the domestic prices.

Source:　Juan Antonio Morales, Rodolfo Ulloa, Gloria Jiménez, "Análisis económico de las implicaciones para Bolivia del Arancel Externo Común del Grupo Andino". Informe al Ministerio de Finanzas de la República de Bolivia (La Paz, noviembre 1978) Table N° 7.

to note that the *Five-Year Plan*, enacted by President Hugo Banzer in 1976 does not mention at all the use of tariffs in its chapter on industrial planning.

The shortcomings of the import policies, as well as of the export promotion schemes for that matter, appear also in the weakness of the Bolivian position in the Latin American integration schemes.

BOLIVIAN AND LATIN AMERICAN INTEGRATION

Bolivia is a member of the Latin American Free Trade Association (LAFTA) and the Andean Group. Both of these regional integration programs were designed to provide for an integration of regional markets in order to enhance regional industrialization and, hence, economic development. Bolivia, however, was and is by conventional measures the smallest and most less-developed economy in either organization. Thus in a strict economic interpretation, Bolivia's participation in LAFTA and the Andean Group probably does not mean very much to the other partner countries. But turning the question around: How important is Bolivia's participation in the two integration programs for its own development? In the following sections the Bolivian position in the two economic integration programs is analyzed in this context. Emphasis is given to the Andean Group.

The Bolivian Position in LAFTA

LAFTA was created by the Treaty of Montevideo in 1960, when most of the major South American republics and Mexico joined efforts to promote a progressive complementation and integration of their economies through trade. The stated objectives were to be obtained by the gradual creation of a free trade zone that would come about through a step-by-step elimination of tariff and non-tariff barriers for intrazonal trade. The Treaty of Montevideo recognized the special needs of the relatively less-developed countries in LAFTA, and agreed to grant them preferential treatment.

Bolivia joined LAFTA in 1966 and was designated a relatively less-developed country. The preferential treatment for Bolivia consists essentially in postponing dates for the implementation of tariff reductions and the dismantlement of non-tariff barriers. Furthermore, any of the member nations may grant trade advantages to Bolivia without making similar concessions to the other members.

The direct benefits of Bolivia's association with LAFTA have been virtually unnoticeable. Bolivian exports to the LAFTA countries consist mainly of petroleum, natural gas and minerals. These exports, however important, would have taken place anyway with or without LAFTA membership. The Bolivian tariff concessions to its LAFTA partners have been rather limited; only a handful of items are imported on this basis. Notwithstanding the lack of concessions, Bolivian imports of manufactures from LAFTA countries have grown at a very fast pace. But this expansion can hardly be attributed to Bolivia's participation in the organization.

Perhaps the importance of LAFTA to Bolivia is best noted by the scant attention directed to LAFTA in Bolivia's development planning. The 1976 *Five-Year Plan* barely devotes a quarter of a page to Bolivia's membership of LAFTA. [21]

It is widely recognized that LAFTA has been faltering for years, almost since its establishment. The target date for completely free trade has been repeatedly postponed and the annual negotiations on tariff reductions have slowed down. There has been no perceptible progress in recent years.

Bolivia and the Andean Group

The apparent failure of LAFTA, at least from the viewpoint of the relatively more poor Andean member countries led to the formation of the Andean Group with the signing of the Cartagena Agreement on May 26, 1969. Bolivia was a charter member along with Chile, Colombia, Ecuador and Peru. Venezuela joined in 1973 and Chile withdrew in 1976.

The Andean Group integration scheme had two main instruments: (a) a customs union, and (b) a joint mechanism of investment programming for a list of goods for the Sectorial Industrial Development Program (SIDP). Furthermore, in order to counteract the adverse effects that these instruments could unintentionally carry, the Andean Group countries agreed upon a set of measures to harmonize other policies that affect trade and to fix common policies for the treatment of foreign private investment.

Bolivia and Ecuador were designated relatively less-developed countries in the Group and were accorded preferential treatment for the two main instruments and subordinate policies. With respect to the customs union a relatively important subsection of the list of goods included in the Andean Brussels Trade Nomenclature (ABTN) and produced in Bolivia and Ecuador have had zero tariff status in the other Andean Group countries since 1974. Furthermore, Bolivia and Ecuador have received concessions in postponing the elimination of duties on intraregional imports, while their exports enjoy tariff reductions. The complete reduction in tariffs on intragroup imports for Bolivia and Ecuador is scheduled for 1988, whereas the other partners are scheduled to meet this requirement in 1983. Similarly, Bolivia and Ecuador have longer delays for the implementation of the common external tariff. However, goods considered in the SIDP do not benefit from this preferential treatment.

With respect to SIDP, the preferential treatment provides a priority claim for Bolivia and Ecuador in the planned allocation and the localizations of plants for industrial investments.

Furthermore, exclusivity is to be sought for the investment and plant allocations made to Bolivia and Ecuador. This principle grants exclusive rights to the two countries for the production of goods in the SIDP plants allocated to them, and thus avoids direct competition by other member countries. Moreover, the Group commits itself to provide technical assistance to help the two countries cope with efficiency problems, in order that they may benefit fully from the SIDP.

Economic integration within the Andean Group created considerable hope among Bolivian policy makers, who thought that it would provide the necessary big push for Bolivian industrial development with the incentive of a large market for manufactures. Bolivia, therefore, enthusiastically supported the Andean Group at the outset. Seven years later there is considerable disillusionment with the workings of the Group among government officials and industrialist organizations in Bolivia. From their point of view the benefits of integration seem rather scant and the costs are presumed to be high. The fact that the whole Andean Group has been in a state of crisis, especially since the withdrawal of Chile, has contributed to the problem and has created more concern among Bolivians.

A detailed examination of the main characteristics and policy instruments of the Andean Group integration scheme can shed more light on the Bolivian position within the Group. The remainder of this section is devoted to this task. For expository reasons the joint programs of sectorial industrial development (SIDPs) are examined first.

The Joint Programs of Sectorial Industrial Development. In accordance with the Cartagena Agreement, member countries are to engage in a coordinated and planned process of industrial development. SIDPs play a

key role in the scheme for sector development. A given SIDP states the
goods that are subject to the program, the country location of the plants
producing the goods, the means of financing the investment, the special
schedule of liberalization for the goods in the program and the special common external tariff that will apply to them. Furthermore, every SIDP states
the deadline for its implementation.

By early 1978 three SIDPs were approved for the Group: petrochemicals, the metalworking industry products and automobiles. Bolivia has obtained important allocations in each of these programs. The estimated
required funds for financing Bolivia's allocations for the 1976-1980 period
are about 350 million dollars.   This amount provides an indication of the
importance of the effort. As a result of the SIDP for the metalworking industry, plants for the production of pneumatic drills, compressors and
special wedges for the petroleum industry already have been installed. As
yet, there is not an implementation of SIDP for petrochemicals. An olefines,
e.g., ethylene, propylene, etc., plant will probably be the first to be installed, but the implementation plan is still in the preliminary stage. With
regard to SIDP for the automobiles industry negotiations with multinational
companies for production of trucks and pick-up trucks are very advanced.
Bolivia should be producing those vehicles by 1980.

If the SIDPs are effectively implemented, they will completely change
the current pattern of Bolivia's industrialization. Up to the present time
industry has been of the very light manufacturing nature and mainly consists in the processing of foodstuffs, liquor and tobacco as well as the
fabrication of textiles and shoes.

The implementation of the allocations depends heavily on the use of
foreign savings and foreign technology and know-how.The projects offered
to date have not been apparently sufficiently attractive to foreign companies
and investors. Only a handful of them have installed plans in Bolivia. On
this point it must be said that the lack of basic transportation, energy, and
technical education infrastructure in Bolivia have worked against the attrac-
tiveness of the undertakings.

It is premature to evaluate the full impact of SIDP in Bolivia. From
experience of the program for the metalworking industry, it appears that
the results obtained are well below expectations. It has been very difficult
to obtain the financing and the enterprises willing to undertake the projects.
In the few cases where new industries have been created they have faced
enormous difficulties, including competition in the member countries of the
Group where competing plants have been installed, although the latter do
not enjoy the trade liberalization benefits granted by the Andean Group.

Liberalization of Trade.   This consists essentially in the mutual and
gradual reduction of tariffs among member countries until a zero tariff is
reached for intra-Group trade.   There is a consensus among Bolivian industrialists that the dismantling of the tariff barriers in partner countries is
going to be of very little help in the expansion of Bolivia's exports. According to them, the lower degree of industrialization and the higher transportation costs for Bolivia vis-à-vis the other countries preclude the
existence of substantial sales of manufacturers.

Previously it was shown that Bolivian exports to the Andean Group
increased rapidly since 1970, *but* they consisted mainly of primary goods.
Those exports would have taken place anyway, regardless of the existence
of the Group. Moreover, even in the few cases where an export activity
would be possible, some of the member countries have erected non-tariff
barriers, including safety and sanitation regulations or, more frequently,
limited quotas of foreign exchange for the purchase of Bolivian exportables.
The latter measure was especially common in those member countries that
were experiencing balance of payments problems, and where there were

exchange controls. Many of the exportable Bolivian manufactures are considered luxury goods and receive last priority in any non-price rationing of foreign exchange.

There is merit in the contention of the industrialists that the lower degree of Bolivian industrialization works against any substantial increase of exports when trade barriers are lowered. [22] It is indeed difficult to compete with countries which are very similar in their factor endowments but which have a longer history of manufacturing.

A lowering of Bolivian tariffs for the Andean Group's products is greatly feared by Bolivian industrialists and public officials. They believe that regional competition will cause some industries to close down and that workers will be laid off. These suspicions are probably justified. As noted previously and shown in Table X-8, there are some very heavily protected Bolivian industries, presumably indicating a high degree of inefficiency and weakness. These industries would have to undertake far reaching reforms if they were to survive in a more open market. This is especially the case in the textile and pharmaceutical industries.

Notwithstanding the pessimistic view of the liberalization process, there are some favorable aspects. With greater competition, the affected industrial sectors would be forced to search for specialization in the lines and products where they are more efficient. Those highly labor-intensive industries based on advantages in their natural resource endowments would probably face the competition without problems. [23]

Finally, for those industries that would be forced out of business by the competition, the sacrifice in employment is likely to be low given the low level of industrialization and the small number of people actually employed in the manufacturing industries.

The Common External Tariff. A common external tariff (CET) will be proposed to the Andean Group before 1979 for the goods *not* included in the SIDP. The CET will be fully implemented over a five-year period by Colombia, Peru and Venezuela, and over a ten-year period by Bolivia and Ecuador. The goods in the SIDP bear also special common external tariffs that are determined in each industrial program. Those tariffs are implemented shortly after the industrial program starts.

The CET and the special common external tariffs of the SIDP pose the greatest problems for Bolivia among all the Group's instruments. In particular, the special common external tariff of the approved SIDP, with their high levels are deemed to be very costly to Bolivia.

More generally, the level and structure of the CET will be crucial for Bolivia's participation in the Group. The proposals of the technical staff of the Andean Group indicate relatively high tariff levels as well as a significant dispersion of them. But, if the common tariffs are set too high, given the structure of Bolivian imports where only about 5 percent come from the Andean Group, the trade diversion effects could be very important. A high CET could mean that Bolivia would be forced to buy a substantial volume of its imports at a dearer price from Group members than from present less-expensive sources on the world market. It is unlikely furthermore that Bolivia would compensate the trade diversion effects with a substantial expansion of exports of manufactures.

With high tariffs, the income transfers from Bolivian consumers to the producers of the member countries could be sizeable. For example, David Morawetz estimates that the additional costs caused by the common tariffs to the mining industry are between seven and ten million dollars per year. Moreover, he estimates that the additional costs on capital goods to the Bolivian industry caused by the CET, will be of the order of 42 million dollars per year. [24] The Morawetz estimates can be criticized, both on theoretical and empirical grounds, but the fact remains that the costs of the CET are likely to be very high.

If, on the other hand, the CET is set at low levels, the power of the tariff instrument for the purposes of creating an integrated regional market would be weakened. This probably would be deemed undesirable by the other more advanced countries of the Andean Group. If the Andean Group agrees on a net preference for industrialization, high tariff levels are predicted. Under these circumstances Bolivia would be forced to seek some strategy to compensate for the large income transfers associated with the high tariffs. [25]

Harmonization of Policies. The Andean Group has the long-range target of arriving at a joint and coordinated planning of the development of the region. However, during a transition period the joint planning will rely essentially on tariff policy and the allocation and location of industrial investments. National policies always threaten these efforts during this transition period and need to be harmonized.

There are several fields where policy harmonization is clearly needed and where some advances have been made. Some of the major ones are: export promotion policies; treatment of foreign investment; national fiscal policies; joint regulation of state purchases; joint regulation of technical norms and quality control; and harmonization of foreign exchange and credit policies. Bolivia has directed some attention to these problems. Essentially, action has occurred when Bolivia's direct interests were at stake. The following discussion is limited to an analysis of the Bolivian position on the controversy about the treatment of foreign investment.

The Treatment of Foreign Capital. The Andean Group's rules for treatment of foreign investment has provoked much controversy in Bolivia as well as in other member countries. [26] In fact it was one of the reasons that Chile used to withdraw from the Group in 1976. The main features of the rules as they would impact on Bolivia are, in short, the following:

(1) Each new foreign direct investment project has to be explicitly authorized and registered by the appropriate national authority. Essentially this means that there is a pattern of discrimination among such projects: some of them would not be admissible. The reinvestment of profits that exceed 70 percent of the invested capital also must be authorized.

(2) Domestic enterprises cannot be acquired by foreign investors unless: (a) they are in danger of bankruptcy, or (b) foreign ownership is restricted to a minority share and there is an increase in the capital of the enterprise as a result of such ownership.

(3) Domestic investment credit is reserved for domestically owned or mixed-ownership enterprises.

(4) Foreign enterprises have to be transformed into domestic or mixed-ownership enterprises within a maximum period of twenty years. Foreign companies which do not wish to change their ownership will not enjoy the tariff advantages set up in the liberalization program.

(5) Foreign capital can be repatriated freely, but after tax profits can be exported only up to a limit of 20 percent of the capital.

(6) Tight regulations exist on foreign loans, the purchase of technology and payment of royalties.

(7) Foreign investment on the mining and petroleum industries are exempted from the above regulations.

Bolivian businessmen believe that the rules are unduly restrictive and that they penalize the less-developed countries of the Group. [27] Furthermore, there is the opinion that the treatment accorded to foreign investment contradicts the 1972 Bolivian Investment Law. As of yet there does not exist a thorough analysis of the implications of the rules for Bolivia. It should be noted that Bolivia has never attracted foreign capital in significant amounts for manufacturing and, thus, there is little basis to judge what have been the negative effects, if any, on the inflow of direct foreign investment in manufacturing. Besides, Bolivia has a preferential treatment on this matter as compared with the other countries of the Group.

The third meeting of the Planning Council of the Andean Group, which took place in La Paz in November 1977, found no evidence that the Andean treatment of foreign capital had diminished the inflow of foreign capital to the member countries. On the contrary, they concluded the regulations for foreign investment have brought about the orderly management of such investment and they have set clear guidelines that benefit also the foreign investor. It is better indeed, from their viewpoint, to have a common and clear set of rules for the whole Group than to face a maze of national legal arrangements that also influence investment.

CONCLUSIONS AND PROSPECTS FOR THE FUTURE

The "outward looking" model of development followed by Bolivia since November 1964 under the aegis of military governments supported by the United States, has been a rather mitigated success. Admittedly, the rates of growth of exports and of the national economy have been generally satisfactory during 1965-1977, but there are doubts concerning the degree of self-sufficiency attained and the potential obtained for a self-sustained growth. The shortcomings of the model have appeared conspicuously in the management of the foreign sector. The design of policies was generally poor and as a consequence, little export diversification was attained and gains in efficient import substitution were modest. Little has been left after the bonanza of 1974, and four years later, the national economy faces extreme instability in its export earnings and extreme dependency on imports.

Given that Bolivia has a high degree of indebtedness, it can be conjectured that the balance of payments will be a more serious constraint in the future than it has been the case in the past thirteen years. However, it must be said on behalf of the governments of the period, that it was very difficult to control exogenous shocks, such as the great inflow of foreign exchange in 1974, and even more difficult, to fine tune the economy after taking a few important measures like the 1972 devaluation.

The incursion of Bolivia after 1969 in the international petroleum market explains most of the diversification in the commodity composition of its exports. While there is only a modest degree of diversification in the commodity composition of Bolivian foreign trade in general, the period 1965-1977 has witnessed an important diversification in the trade partners of Bolivia.

The behavior of exports and their fortuitously high international prices have been a key element in explaining Bolivia's development since 1964. It appears, however, that the contribution of exports to growth and development was not as important as could have been expected. The expansion in export earnings was accompanied by a considerable inflow of foreign capital, particularly after 1974. But neither the extraordinary export earnings nor the foreign capital seem to have been put into productive new investments. In fact, much of the export earnings have been used to import consumption items, including luxury goods. And the inflow of foreign funds has been frequently invested in huge undertakings of doubtful profitability.

Prospects for a significant expansion of traditional exports in the next five years are rather dim, unless a higher share of national investment is reoriented to exploration in minerals and hydrocarbons. In particular, it is necessary to open new mines since the old ones are depleted and the metal content in the ores is too low.

The Bolivian demands in the ITC for higher reference prices for tin are justified on economic grounds, and the current behavior of the market is lending support to Bolivian claims. On the other hand, Bolivia has lacked of an imaginative policy concerning the threat of the stockpile of the U.S. General Service Administration. Indeed, an adamant opposition to sales of tin from the stockpile cannot constitute the only policy. A more vigorous pricing policy for the sales of natural gas to Argentina is also needed.

The system of taxation for mineral exports in force since 1965 has worked against an expansion of production and exports but it has not been the only limiting factor. Minor reforms in the *regalía* system as well as the abandonment of the export tax created in the aftermath of the devaluation of 1972 can doubtlessly eliminate the undesirable features of the tax system.

Legislation with incentives to encourage minor exports has come too late and it is inadequate. Yet, there are attractive prospects for an expansion of these exports, particularly for rice, meat, handicrafts, textiles and wood and leather products. Moreover, the importance of the creation of employment in those exporting activities makes them even more attractive.

It is unfortunate that the somewhat uncoordinated efforts since 1964 to industrialize Bolivia have not created the necessary base to face the challenges of the Andean Group. The delays granted to Bolivia by the Group in the adoption of the integration instruments were meant to provide time to catch up with the more advanced countries, but the opportunities have been largely wasted. Given this fact, the costs to Bolivia from its association to Andean Group are likely to be greater than the benefits. Because of the retarded development of Bolivia vis-à-vis the other countries of the Group, the adoption of common external tariffs is going to be particularly costly.

In spite of what has been said above, the Andean Group offers still a feasible policy option for Bolivian development. A reprogramming of the Group's development of the metalworking industry, along more realistic lines, could be of interest to Bolivia. The program for the automobiles industry offers also reasonable hopes. The effective implementation of these two programs calls for an important contribution of Bolivia to the design and, especially, to the procedures of allocating investment in the Group. It is regretful that Bolivia's industrialization plans are poorly coordinated with the plans of the Andean Group.

The saving of much needed foreign exchange through import substitution does not seem feasible in a significant scale over a medium-term horizon. Profound reforms are needed in the import legislation since neither the tariff schedule nor the system of licensing and bans have a clearcut protective intention. In fact, as they currently stand, they result more from the workings of several pressure groups than from deliberate government policy. The frequent modifications in the tariff schedule and in the system of licensing and bans have made the imports arrangements increasingly piecemeal.

Many Bolivian economists as well as policy makers consider that a reappraisal of the policies followed in the last thirteen years is needed. Policies should direct more attention to newer sources of raw materials and energy and they should give the necessary encouragements to exploit them profitably. The long neglected sector of traditional agriculture should also receive more attention, because although there has been some progress in the substitution of imports of food staples, scarce foreign exchange is still used to import considerable amounts.

With respect to industrialization, Bolivia should encourage it more selectively than it has been done in the past. This would require a thorough revision of the actual system of incentives, including the tariff structure, other import controls, as well as policies to promote the export of manufactures.

All those efforts should be conducive to prevent a situation where the lack of foreign exchange obstructs a very needed expansion of the national economy or the full employment of the productive capacity. The key question is: Will the coming civilian governments seize upon these opportunities and be better administrators of the national economy than were the authoritarian military regimes of the period 1964-1977?

ENDNOTES TO CHAPTER X

1. Special appreciation is expressed to Javier Comboni who provided valuable research assistance in the preparation of this paper.

2. Freddy Sanjinés, "Producción y factores de producción que intervienen en el comercio internacional Boliviano," (unpublished M. A. thesis, Universidad Católica Boliviana 1977), pp. 64-70.

3. The economic policies implemented by the revolutionary government of Paz Estenssoro led to incredibly high rates of inflation and to a complete disruption of the monetary and credit mechanisms. However, not all the effects of inflation were bad or even unintended. The income distribution changes that resulted from inflation favored the Santa Cruz area in particular, and laid the basis for its development. The implicit tax levied on the western mining zones through inflation and the complicated system of differential rates of exchange financed the state petroleum industry and the undertakings of the Bolivian Development Corporation for heavy investment in the Santa Cruz area. The economy of the Santa Cruz area has shown the highest rate of growth in Bolivia in the past twenty-five years.

   J. G. Eder correctly asserts that the Bolivian State Petroleum Company and the Bolivian Development Corporation were principally responsible for the inflation from 1952 through 1956. A complete demonstration of this assertion appears in J. G. Eder, *Inflation and Development in Latin America: A Case History of Inflation and Stabilization in Bolivia*, Michigan Business Studies Number 8 (Ann Arbor: The University of Michigan, 1968), pp. 59-65.

4. Bolivia, Junta Nacional de Planeamiento, *Plan nacional de desarrollo económico y social, 1962-1971, Resumen* (La Paz, 1962), pp. 60-82.

5. The prevalent attitude in the last thirteen years has been one of sympathy towards businessmen and foreign capital and toughness towards labor.

6. It is believed, however, that the current structure grants, on the average, less protection to domestic industry, capital and labor than the scheme of differential rates of exchange put into effect in the aftermath of the 1952 revolution.

   It is necessary to mention, however, that the manipulations in the foreign exchange market constituted a great source of corruption in the administration and inefficiency in the protected industries. The abandonment of the system was, in the author's view, inevitable given the popular reaction against the profiteers.

   The current foreign trade mechanisms are explained in detail in the Bolivian trade policies section.

7. Bolivia, Ministerio de Planificación y Coordinación, *Estrategia socio-económica del desarrollo nacional*, (La Paz, 1970), pp. 87-90.

8. Unfortunately, the analysis has had to be carried out in current values since Bolivia does not publish an export price index.

9. This hypothesis was tested by the author by utilizing a simple econometric model. The results showed that in the years of above-trend exports, the proportion of consumer goods increases significantly. Details on the test are available from the author on request.

10. Notwithstanding what has been said it is necessary to introduce the qualification that changes in the structure of imports can be explained partially by changes in relative prices among the several types of imported commodities.

11. The idea of a stabilization fund appears in Peggy Musgrave and Jorge Desormeaux, "Stabilization and Development with Fluctuating Export Earnings," *Fiscal Reform in Bolivia, Staff Papers*, Vol. II, No. 3 (Cambridge, Mass.: Musgrave Mission, 1977).

12. The shift from foreign public aid to loans from private foreign banks reflects a world trend and is not completely imputable to the policies of the Bolivian government. On the credit supply side, the great world credit expansion at the beginning of the 1970s, the recycling of the petrodollars and the relative decrease in foreign public aid also contribute to an explanation of the shift.

13. Investment by the state enterprises represents more than 50 percent of total investment.

14. Bolivia, Ministerio de Finanzas, *Memorandum sobre el financiamiento externo de Bolivia* (La Paz, January 1978). The debt service ratio is given by the ratio of amortization plus interests to exports.

15. This definition of an export economy is due to Walter Gómez in "Mining in the Economic Development of Bolivia 1900-1970,"(unpublished Ph.D. dissertation, Vanderbilt University, 1973), p. 1.

16. The International Tin Council has its headquarters in London. The Council is in charge of making periodic estimations of the probable production and consumption of tin. The Council also undertakes and promotes technical studies on short-term and long-term problems of the tin industry.
    More importantly, the manager of the buffer stock follows the guidelines set by the Council. The Council has also the very important task of controlling the amount of tin which may be exported by producing countries, or to take actions in the event of tin shortages.

17. Malcom Gillis, Meyer W. Bucovetzky, Glenn P. Jenkins, Ubrich Petersen, Louis T. Wells and Brian D. Wright. "Taxation and the Mining Sector in Bolivia," Report prepared for the Ministry of Mining and Metallurgy—Republic of Bolivia, under the auspices of the Institute for International Development. Harvard University. (La Paz, 1976), pp. IV-9—IV-36. (Mimeographed.)

18. The Bolivian State Mining Company (COMIBOL) that regroups the state mines is liable to pay the same taxes as the private mining consortiums.

19. The *tax certificate* for agricultural and handicraft exports amounts to 10 percent of their f.o.b. export value, as verified by the sales of foreign exchange by exporters to the Central Bank. The *tax certificate* for exports of manufactures is a proportion, depending roughly on the domestic value added, of the total sales of foreign exchange to the Central Bank by exporters of those manufactures. The proportion varies from 5 to 25 percent. The latter figure corresponds to an minimum domestic value of 70 percent.

20. The maximum proportion by which the tariff structure permits the domestic value added, in a given productive activity, to exceed the value added at world market prices represents what has been called the *effective rate of protection*. Effective rates are expressed as the percentage excess of domestic value added over foreign value added.

    References to the subject are given, for example, in Bela Balassa and associates, *The Structure of Protection in Developing Countries* (Baltimore: Johns Hopkins Press, 1971); W. M. Corden, *The Theory of Protection* (Oxford: Clarendon Press, 1971); and the review article of R. M. Stern, "Tariffs and Other Measures of Trade Control; A Survey of Recent Developments," *The Journal of Economic Literature*, Volume XL, No. 3(1973), pp. 857-888. The documents on the common external tariff of the Technical Staff of the Andean Group also gives an excellent overview of the problems involved.

21. Bolivia, Ministerio de Planeamiento y Coordinación, *Plan de desarrollo económico y social 1976-1980, Resumen* (La Paz, junio 1976), p. 133.

22. On this point, see, e.g., René Candia Navarro, General Manager of The National Chamber of Commerce, "La Liberación del intercambio y el arancel externo común", (La Paz: Camara Nacional de Comercio, septiembre 1977). (Mimeographed.)

23. There are also reasons to believe that the lower prices for the consumer goods, subject—up until now—to high tariffs or import bans, will be beneficial and that the resulting reallocation of production will have a favorable effect on exports and possibly on the traditional agriculture of the highlands and valley regions.

24. David Morawetz, "Beneficios y costos para Bolivia de su participación en el Grupo Andino". Report to the Ministry of Mining and Metallurgy (La Paz, November 1976), pp. 23-24. (Mimeographed.)

25. In this case Bolivia's strategy would still consist of a search for a compensated trade diversion. That is, Bolivia, or any other country of the Group, would expand its commerce in the region on the basis of comparative intra-Group advantages. This limited withdrawal from world markets implies for Bolivia, or any other country, a trade diversion that should be compensated by an expansion of its exports to the other Andean countries; introducing, by the same token, trade diversions to the partners.

    Morawetz, op. cit., pp. 13-14, criticizes this idea of compensated, or reciprocal, trade diversions. He argues forcefully that Bolivia is not likely to gain anything since: (1) the country has only a handful of higher-than-international priced goods to offer to its partners, and hence, the amount of subsidy that Bolivia will obtain will be less than the amount that the country will pay; (2) the production of the most developed Bolivian industry--mining--is sold principally on world markets, whereas other member countries sell the products of their principal industries in their domestic markets, or in the protected Andean market; (3) the bigger market sizes of other members allow them to invest in similar industries to the ones allocated to Bolivia under the SIDP. They can spare the benefits of regional tariff reductions since they have a large domestic market.

26. An excellent overview of the issues related to foreign direct investment in the Andean Group, appears in Ernesto Tironi, "Políticas frente al capital extranjero en la integración Andina". *Estudios CIEPLAN* 11, (Santiago, June 1977).

27. See René Candia Navarro, "La Decisión 24 en el financiamiento del desarrollo", (La Paz: Cámara Nacional de Comercio, septiembre 1977). (Mimeographed.)

Chapter XI

Bolivia's Agriculture Since 1960: an Assessment and Prognosis [1]

Morris D. Whitaker and E. Boyd Wennergren

INTRODUCTION

In most of the developing countries of the world, traditional agriculture has been largely ignored as a basis for more rapid economic growth. Instead, development programs and policies have emphasized growth via import substitution industrialization, and export of a limited number of raw materials or agricultural products.

The utilization of the "industrialization first" approach to economic growth is rooted intellectually in the growth stage model of Rostow and the dynamic dual sector models of Lewis, Ranis and Fei, and Jorgensen. [2] While such models do identify the importance of agriculture in producing a surplus for economic growth, they assume that such a surplus is somehow automatically produced and focus instead on development of a modern industrial sector as the basis of economic development. By the late 1960s, several countries that had tried these models had experienced disappointing results, as reduced opportunities for import substitution, and the limited capacity of their agricultural sectors to respond to rising demand constrained general economic development. [3]

Bolivia is a prime example. Export of raw materials has been the basis for economic development from colonial times to the present. Since the revolution in 1952, the government has attempted to reduce Bolivia's primary dependence on tin exports by increasing production and exports of nontraditional minerals and petroleum. At the same time, emphasis has been given to domestic production of principal food crops that were previously imported by developing large-scale commercial agriculture in Santa Cruz. Finally, the government has promoted development of domestic industry.

Little has been done, however, toward improving traditional agriculture in spite of rhetoric associated with the land reform of 1953 and more recently with the world food problem. Furthermore, the limited government programs for agriculture, such as colonization, have generally been directed toward the symptoms rather than the causes of agricultural backwardness. At the same time, the government has maintained several general development policies, e.g., low food prices to urban consumers which underwrites the price of agricultural products. Consequently, the performance of the sector has been generally poor with demand growing faster than supply and prices of agricultural products rising relative to prices of nonfarm products.

The critical importance of improving agriculture and increasing its productivity as a basis for fostering overall economic growth has been more widely recognized by economists in recent years.[4] Increased agricultural production and productivity contribute to general economic development in several ways. First, agricultural products become more competitive in the world market resulting in increased export earnings and savings from import substitution. Second, downward pressure on the price of food and fiber from increased production results in increased consumption of agricultural products but a lower food bill because the demand for food is generally inelastic with respect to price changes. Third, the lower food bill effectively increases the real income of all consumers, thus increasing the demand for wage and investment goods produced in the nonfarm sector and strengthening intersectoral linkages. Since agricultural products are among the most important wage goods for most consumers in developing countries, the increase in real income and subsequent impact on demand for nonfarm goods and services can be substantial. Fourth, the distribution of income will tend to shift in favor of the poor because low-income people generally spend a relatively large proportion of their income on food. Fifth, the nutrition of the population tends to improve from consumption of more and better quality food made possible by lower prices and increased real incomes. Finally, the internal terms of trade—the price of agricultural products relative to nonfarm products—tend to decline and owners of resources employed in agriculture are under pressure to transfer them to higher-paying, alternative uses in the nonfarm sector.

While the role that an agricultural surplus can play in promoting general economic development is generally well understood among agricultural economists, relatively few have confronted the difficult question of a general theory of agricultural development, i.e., a theory which explains how a country can set in motion and sustain growth in agricultural production and productivity. Hayami and Ruttan,[5] with their theory of induced agricultural development, which builds on the pioneering work of Schultz,[6] are a notable exception. In their model, technical change in agriculture is induced in both public and private sectors in response to price signals in factor and product markets, and saves the scarce factor of production. For example, if land is scarce, the market will induce public and private sectors to develop biological and chemical innovations such as high-yielding rice varieties and low-cost fertilizers and pesticides which can be substituted for the scarce land, thus raising its productivity. Furthermore, technical change induces institutional modification and innovation so that individuals and groups can internalize the return from technical progress. Finally, technical progress that resolves one constraint often leads to another bottleneck which is subsequently resolved by induced innovation, thus setting up dynamic sequences of technical changes within the agricultural sector and intersectorally in the economy.

The Hayami-Ruttan theory of induced development thus identifies four general areas for focusing public policy or investment to develop agriculture: (a) factor and product markets; (b) industrial inputs which can substitute for scarce land or labor; (c) a scientific base for production of new technical knowledge; and (d) general and technical education for increasing the capacity of farmers to assimilate and adopt new techniques.

This paper presents, in the light of the Hayami-Ruttan theory of induced development, an assessment and analysis of Bolivia's agricultural sector since the 1960s and a prognosis of performance in the future. The first section presents a brief overview of the sector including its geography, people, traditional versus modern components, land use, and markets. The second section contains an assessment of performance of the sector and its contribution to the development process between 1960 and the present. The nature and effect of government support for agriculture are reviewed and analyzed in the third section. In the fourth section, the problems restricting development of the agricultural sector are discussed, while the prognosis for growth in Bolivian agriculture is presented in the fifth section.

OVERVIEW OF THE SECTOR

Geography, Climate, and Principal Products[7]

Bolivia has three distinctive geographic regions with highly varied and diverse climates conducive to the production of a wide variety of agricultural crops and livestock. As shown in Figure XI-1, one is the *Altiplano*, a high plain bounded on the east and west by two chains of the Andes Mountains. The plain between these ridges lies mainly in Bolivia, is approximately 150 miles from east to west, 600 miles long, and is 12,000 to 14,000 feet above sea level. The *Altiplano* has a cool to cold climate with a pronounced rainy season during the spring and summer months of October through February. The climate becomes harsher from north to south with an average temperature of 12° C and annual rainfall of 650 mm in the North *Altiplano* near Lake Titicaca, compared to 8.5° C and 250 mm of rainfall in the Southern *Altiplano*. The principal agricultural enterprise of the *Altiplano* is livestock—sheep, llamas, and alpacas—which are raised on unimproved rangelands. The most important crops are potatoes, barley for grain and hay, forages, a native cereal, *quinoa*, legumes, onions, and other vegetables. Crop production is centered in the Northern *Altiplano* around Lake Titicaca where the climate is milder.

A second region includes the *Yungas* and Mountain Valleys, which are located on the eastern slopes of the eastern chain of the Andes. *Yungas* are steep tropical and subtropical river valleys characterized by a diversity of microclimates and elevations but with generally heavy rainfall and relatively high average temperatures. In contrast, the Mountain Valleys are higher, more open, drier, and have a temperate climate, with a more pronounced rainy season from October to March. The Mountain Valleys also vary greatly with elevations ranging from 3,900 to 7,900 feet above sea level, average temperatures from 17° C to 22° C and annual precipitation from 400 mm to 1200 mm. The most important *Yungas* crops are citrus, coffee, bananas, vegetables and coca, from which cocaine is derived. The temperate valleys produce potatoes, corn, wheat, barley, grapes, deciduous fruits, and a large variety of vegetables. Dairy cattle, poultry, pigs, and goats are the most important livestock.

The remaining geographic unit is the *Oriente* or the eastern lowlands, a great plain extending from the foothills of the eastern slopes of the Andes to the eastern Bolivian border. The *Oriente* contains five easily distinguishable tropical and subtropical ecologic zones. The first zone is a tropical rain forest in the Amazon Basin in Bolivia's northeast, with annual rainfall of 2500 mm and average temperature from 27° C to 30° C. Principal agricultural enterprises are extractive in nature including gathering Brazil nuts, tapping wild rubber, and hunting animals and snakes for their skins, all for the export market. A very limited amount of domestic subsistence corn, rice and black pepper are produced.

Moving south, there is a transition to the second lowland zone, a vast *pampa*, or grassy plain, called the Beni Plains where most of Bolivia's beef cattle are raised. Average temperature is less than that in

Figure XI - 1

GEOGRAPHIC PROFILE OF BOLIVIA

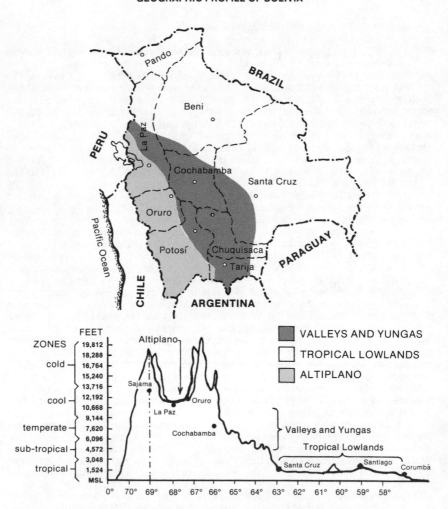

Source: E. Boyd Wennergren and Morris D. Whitaker, *The Status of Bolivian Agriculture* (New York: Praeger, 1975), p. 20.

the northern jungles, annual rainfall is about 1800 mm, and there is a pronounced rainy season from May to August.

South of the Beni Plains is the third lowland zone, a subtropical forest and savannah in the Santa Cruz region, which has become the new agricultural center of Bolivia in the last fifteen years. There is a high percentage of good quality land although the forest must first be cleared. The average temperature is 25° C with annual rainfall of 1150 mm and a pronounced dry season from May to October. The area northwest of the city of Santa Cruz is better adapted for crop production because of more balanced rainfall. Principal crops include rice, sugar cane, cotton, corn, oil seeds, and some beef cattle.

The fourth lowland zone is the Brazilian Shield east of the Santa Cruz zone. Soils are old, highly acid, and leached of nutrients. Rainfall is about 950 mm per year and the zone has a pronounced dry season from May to August with average daytime temperatures of 24° C. Beef cattle are produced by grazing the sparse grasses and shrubs which characterize this zone.

The Bolivian *Chaco*—the fifth lowland zone—which is south of Santa Cruz has a lower average rainfall, 750 mm per year, than either the Santa Cruz or the Brazilian Shield. The climate is semiarid with a prolonged dry season of seven to eight months, April to November, and relatively high temperatures averaging 28° C. Vegetative cover generally consists of thorny, drought-resistant varieties. Beef cattle are the principal agricultural enterprise.

Rural Population [8]

Bolivia's population was estimated to be 5.9 million in 1977, with approximately 69 percent of the total classified as rural. The annual growth rate for the total population is currently estimated to be 2.7 percent, and the age distribution of the population is highly skewed in favor of those fifteen years of age and under. Annual rates of population growth in the urban sector currently exceed those in rural areas and are projected to continue at the higher level.

Approximately 78 percent of Bolivia's rural population is concentrated in the *Altiplano* and Mountain Valley regions with 15 percent in the *Oriente* and the balance in the *Yungas*. The rural population is most dense in the North *Altiplano* with almost fifty-three people for each square kilometer. The next most densely populated rural areas are the Central *Altiplano* and the Mountain Valley regions, which have approximately ten people per square kilometer, while the *Oriente* has less than one person for each square kilometer.

People living in the North and Central *Altiplano* are mainly Aymara Indians, with as many as 40 percent not speaking Spanish. [9] The South *Altiplano* and the Mountain Valley regions are inhabited primarily by Quechua Indians, who are more likely to speak Spanish. The rural dweller of the *Oriente* region, where Spanish is almost universally spoken, is likely to be mixed Spanish-Indian. Miscegenation has occurred to the greatest extent in the *Oriente* and is proceeding among the Quechuas in the Mountain Valley region. The Aymaras have generally resisted such mixing.

Bolivia's people have long been concentrated in the *Altiplano* and Mountain Valley regions. The cradle of the Inca civilization was around Lake Titicaca, and even today this is where the population is most heavily concentrated. The Mountain Valley region is fully accessible from the Altiplano and offers temperate and subtropic climates with their long growing season, which supports a much larger variety of agricultural production.

In contrast, the *Yungas* and *Oriente* regions are relatively inaccessible, and transportation both inter- and intraregionally is a major problem. Although these regions are endowed with fertile soils and a year-round growing season, human diseases, crop diseases and pests, and flooding and erosion increase the risks for a farmer relative to the highlands.

While rural-to-rural migration has occurred in Bolivia, it has not significantly altered rural population densities among areas. The major internal migrations have been from the Mountain Valley and *Altiplano* regions to the *Yungas* around La Paz and Cochabamba and to the lowlands of the Alto Beni, Chapare, and Santa Cruz zones. Since the mid-1950s, an estimated 200,000 persons have migrated to and established permanent residence in these areas of Bolivia. This is an average of less than 10,000 people a year which is only about 15 percent of the estimated increase of the rural population in the *Altiplano* and Mountain Valley regions during 1976. (The rural population of the *Altiplano* and Mountain Valley regions— approximately 2,748,000—was assumed to increase at the national average estimated to be 2.33 percent.) Consequently, the rural population density has been increasing on the relatively small farms in the *Altiplano* and Mountain Valleys.

Rural-urban migration has been occurring at an increasing rate, with an estimated 104,000 such migrants in the 1960s, and a projection of 174,000 in the 1970s. Furthermore, the rate is likely greater than assumed in official estimates of population by the National Institute of Statistics (INE).

Despite the increasing levels of rural-urban migration, average incomes in rural and urban areas have diverged. These data suggest that labor has been dammed up in agriculture, or forced to accept employment in the low-skill personal services sector. In either case, a burgeoning labor force from the relatively young population and extremely limited employment possibilities in nonagricultural activities pose a serious dilemma for future development of Bolivia.

Traditional Versus Modern Agriculture

Bolivian agriculture is comprised mainly of small farms with very traditional production technologies and subsistence consumption. The small-farm sector has over 95 percent of the rural population and produces approximately 80 percent of the value of all agricultural crop production. Most of the population of the small-farm sector—over 80 percent—is concentrated on the relatively limited and depleted soils of the highlands. The remaining are mainly located in the *Yungas* and the Santa Cruz region of the *Oriente*.

Landholdings for farmers practicing traditional agriculture range from one-half hectare in the vicinity of Lake Titicaca and the Cochabamba Valley to fifteen to twenty-five hectares in some of the drier areas of the *Altiplano* and Mountain Valley regions. The relatively small size of farms in traditional agriculture is largely a result of the land reform implemented in 1953 which broke up large estates and parceled them out to landless peasants.

Traditional production techniques are utilized in most of the small-farm sector, with the influence of the ancient Incan civilization and the colonial period still evident. Primitive plows and digging tools, animals or humans for motive power, and *criollo* varieties of seeds and animals are common. Family labor is used intensively in land preparation, seeding, insect and weed control, livestock management, and harvesting, and in domestic activities such as weaving and spinning. Labor is the most

important of all productive factors and is supplied almost exclusively by
the family, augmented by traditional community labor pools. The family
is usually extended, mainly of Quechua or Aymara origin, and adults,
especially women, generally speak little or no Spanish. The level of investment in fixed capital--animals, machines, buildings, irrigation infrastructure, and the like--is relatively low, and much of what does exist
has been created with heavy labor inputs. Only the production that is
surplus to subsistence is marketed. Livestock production is a principal
subsistence activity of much of the small-farm sector but does provide
some income from commercial sales. Livestock is raised on native ranges,
generally with no modern management. The results are depleted ranges
and poor animals. [10]

A more modern agriculture with relatively large-sized holdings has
developed in the Santa Cruz region of the *Oriente* where arable virgin
land is relatively abundant. The large-scale commercial agriculture of
Santa Cruz has had substantial public and private financial support but
comprises only an estimated 5 percent of the rural population. Modern
techniques are utilized with mechanization characterizing the production
of most crops. Markets for both inputs and products are relatively well
developed, and the products of the large-farm sector are all marketed.

Integration of the extensive small-farm sector into the market economy has been limited. Linkages to the rest of the economy are weak and
most are forward in nature, i.e., sale of surplus production for direct
human consumption. Consequently, the majority of rural people live a
subsistence existence only partially involved in the market economy and
have experienced declining levels of productivity and income associated
with the increasing concentration of population on the limited land base.

Land Use[11]

Bolivia's land area totals approximately 110 million hectares. About
27 percent is in forests; 63 percent is classified as natural pastures and
ranges principally located in the lowlands; and about 3 percent is in
wasteland, cities, lakes, rivers, and the like. Approximately 7 percent,
or 7.8 million hectares, is classified as prime land for production or agricultural crops.

About 56 percent of the 7.8 million hectares classified as prime cropland has never produced agricultural crops. A large portion of the land
has not been mapped in detail or formally classified. Another 6.5 million
hectares of more marginal land that is currently classified as pastures,
ranges, and forest are judged as capable of crop production.

Only 12 percent of land classified as prime for crop production is
in annual production. This area, 942,000 hectares, is slightly less than
1 percent of the total land in Bolivia. However, another 32 percent of
prime cropland is in fallow so 44 percent of the prime cropland is in the
production process. [12]

Recent estimates by the Ministry of Peasant Affairs and Agriculture
(MACA) indicate that corn for grain occupies the most land with about
219,000 hectares followed by potatoes with 101,000 hectares and barley
for grain with 97,000 hectares. Wheat, vegetables, barley hay, rice, and
sugar cane also utilize significant amounts of land. New lands areas in
the Santa Cruz region comprise approximately 25 percent of cultivated
land.

Land in crop production has increased by about 9 percent, 65,000
hectares, since 1963-1965. Crops grown exclusively in the agricultural
areas of the lowlands—rice, yucca, sugar cane, bananas and plantains,
coffee, cacao, cotton, citrus fruits, and peanuts—increased in net area

by 67,682 hectares. In the *Altiplano* and Mountain Valley regions, land in crop production decreased by 2,358 hectares. Thus, the increases in cropland during the last decade resulted from the development of new lands in the *Oriente*.

The net decrease in land in cultivation in the *Altiplano* and Mountain Valley regions masks some significant changes in land devoted to various crops. Land in potatoes, wheat, and *quinoa* fell by 37,341 hectares from 1063-1965 to 1970-1972. This was offset, however, by increases in land producing corn, vegetables, barley, dried beans, barley hay, miscellaneous vegetables, miscellaneous tubers, deciduous fruits, and oats that totaled 34,983 hectares. The reduction in cropland devoted to potatoes, wheat, and *quinoa* was possible because of substantial increases in yields. The land released by increased yields was almost completely shifted to production of other traditional *Altiplano*-Mountain Valley crops—corn, vegetables, barley, and the like—that experienced only very modest or no increases in yields during the past decade.

Agricultural Markets

Factor and product markets in Bolivia are generally underdeveloped. However, product markets tend to be more advanced and efficient than are markets that supply agricultural inputs. Markets for most agricultural products are found throughout Bolivia, but tend to be more developed for products of the commercial agricultural sector in Santa Cruz, which are tied to world markets. Factor markets are very regional in nature, and inputs used by the small-farm sector are generally not traded in formal markets.

Factor and product markets are restricted in efficiency by the absence of essential public institutions. The lack of employment services, institutions for increasing skills, and an effective communication network impedes labor market efficiency. Credit markets suffer from government restrictions and bureaucratic processes that complicate lending procedures. The absence of a cadastral survey, farm size limitations imposed by the land reform, and mortgage and transfer restrictions on land are major factors restricting more efficient land markets.

Product market efficiency is also inhibited by the poorly developed communications system, ineffective or nonexistent quality and sanitation standards, inadequate storage facilities, noncollection and reporting of market information, and the absence of homogeneous system of weights and measures.

Highways and trucks are the most important mode of transportation affecting both factor and product markets of the agricultural sector. Considerable use is also made of air transport, especially in beef marketing. Railroads are much less important to Bolivian agricultural production but do transport some imported agricultural products and inputs. Planned improvements and expansion of the primary road system should increase the efficiency of both product and factor markets. However, more resources should be devoted to market access roads, which are seriously deficient.

PERFORMANCE OF THE SECTOR

The performance of Bolivia's agricultural sector during the 1960s and 1970s, while improved over the disastrous years immediately following the 1952 revolution, still has been relatively poor. Demand for agricultural products has grown at a much more rapid rate than aggregate domestic production which has not even kept pace with the modest, for a developing country, rate of growth in population. The consequence has been an increase in the relative price of agricultural products, higher food bills, lower real incomes, decreased food consumption and nutrition, reduced demand for nonfarm products, and a tendency for additional resources to be demanded in agriculture. Thus, the inherent inability of Bolivia's agricultural sector to adequately respond to the increasing demand for food and fiber has constrained the total process of development.

Aggregate Growth[13]

After remaining essentially stagnant in the 1950s, Bolivia's gross domestic product (GDP) in agriculture grew at an annual average rate of 1.9 percent between 1960-1962 and 1970-1972. However, the recovery of the rest of the economy was much more dramatic with rates of growth of 6.6 percent in industry and services, and 7.8 percent in mining and petroleum and an average rate of growth for the economy of 5.4 percent for the same period.

The slow rate of growth in agriculture relative to the average for the economy as a whole has reduced agriculture's share of GDP from 31 percent in 1960-1962 to only 22 percent in 1970-1972. The low share of GDP from agriculture relative to the large share of the labor force employed in agriculture, 65 percent in 1970-1972, partially illustrates the degree of backwardness in the sector.

The generally poor average performance of the agricultural sector conceals some dramatic production increases during the latter 1960s and early 1970s for several crops produced principally on large farms utilizing newly cleared land near Santa Cruz. Between 1963-1965 and 1970-1972, for example, cotton production increased at an annual average rate of 29.4 percent, rice at 6.2 percent, and sugar cane at 4.4 percent. These statistics take on additional significance since increased rice and sugar production has completely replaced imports resulting in substantial savings of foreign exchange, and cotton exports are a new source of foreign exchange when world prices are favorable.

The performance of agriculture appears to have improved somewhat during the decade of the 1970s with GDP in agriculture growing at 3.5 percent during the 1969-1971 to 1974-1976 period.[14] The increased rate of growth in agricultural GDP during the 1970s, however, is principally due to rapid increases in the production of commercial crops on relatively large farms in the new lands area centered in Santa Cruz Department. For example, when cotton and sugar cane are removed from agricultural GDP, the remainder—principally traditional crops and livestock produced on semisubsistence farms in the *Altiplano* and Mountain Valleys—grew at only 2.1 percent during the 1969-1971 to 1974-1976 period, significantly less than the rate of population growth of 2.7 percent.[15] Furthermore, GDP in agriculture declined absolutely in 1977 by 3.2 percent, thus compounding an already difficult situation.[16]

Demand and Prices

The rate of growth in demand for food and fiber has far exceeded that of domestic agricultural production, especially of traditional products. On average, population increased at about 2.6 percent in the 1960s and 2.7 percent in the 1970s, resulting in a direct increase in demand of the same magnitude. At the same time, it is estimated that GDP per capita grew at 2.0 percent per year during the 1960s and early 1970s. The

United Nations Food and Agricultural Organization has estimated the income elasticity of demand for the farm value of all food to be 0.6 in Latin America.[17] Assuming the income elasticity is the same in Bolivia, demand increased by approximately 1.4 percent per year because of increases in per capita income. The total increase in demand from rising population and per capita income was 4.3 to 4.4 percent during the 1960s and 1970s according to these data.

A consequence of greater growth in demand than in production has been an upward pressure on food prices. Relief from food imports was not forthcoming because of chronic balance of payments deficits on current account. Data to measure price changes in agricultural commodities are very limited. There are no published time series of prices or indexes at either the farm gate or at wholesale, and unpublished data that exist for only a few crops and livestock are of questionable reliability. Data are available, however, on the cost of living index for food and other commodities in La Paz, Bolivia's largest city.[18] Based on this indicator, the price of food has increased by almost five times between 1970 and 1976 from an index of 82.5 to 389.4 on a 1966 base. The rise has been rapid in the 1970s. The price of food increased at an average rate of 19.6 percent annually, during 1970-1976 with especially sharp increases between 1972-1973 and 1973-1974. This is compared to an annual rate of increase of 2.1 percent during 1960-1965, and of 7.8 percent during 1965-1970. Furthermore, the price index of food has shown a consistent increase relative to the price index of all other commodities — housing, clothing, transportation, etc. — and by 1976 was 17.2 percent greater than the general index.

The relatively rapid increase in the price of food in the 1970s can be attributed to the world food shortage of 1972-1973 and the devaluation of the Bolivian peso in October, 1972. The peso was devalued from 12 pesos per dollar to 20 pesos per dollar, or by a nominal 67 percent. At the time of the devaluation, the black market rate was approximately 15.30 pesos per dollar, suggesting that the new exchange rate was pegged at an undervalued position. Concomitantly, ad valorem taxes were levied on most export items including many agricultural goods. The effect of these taxes for most items was to decrease the new exchange rate to a level somewhat commensurate with the black market rate.

However, the effect of these taxes on agricultural products was negligible because of the ease with which such products could be clandestinely exported. Consequently, exports of contraband agricultural products increased dramatically in 1973, partly due to rising world prices but accentuated by the maintenance of an undervalued exchange rate for agriculture. The rapid increase in exports reduced domestic supplies dramatically and resulted in rapidly rising prices. Supplies of some products were completely exhausted during 1973 and early 1974, and queues and black market operations were common.

Nutrition

The nutrition of Bolivia's population was substandard in 1962 according to the *Bolivian Nutrition Survey*, hereafter referred to as the *Survey*, and estimates of apparent consumption made in 1970 suggest the situation has worsened.[19] In the *Survey*, diets of members of the military and of civilians were sampled by regions of the country and then evaluated with two different methods to measure nutrient intake. Also, data on population, apparent consumption, and nutritional coefficients were utilized to estimate the average protein and calories consumed per capita during 1958-1962. These estimates were consistent with the results of the sample survey and corroborate the production, import, export, and intermediate use data of MACA.

The *Survey* indicates that in 1962 per capita caloric intake was 12 to 17 percent less than the acceptable level for the average person in the sample, given its age and sex composition, varying by region with the greatest deficit in the high altitude zones. Total protein intake was adequate for the high and medium altitude zones and exceeded the accepted level by 5 and 7 percent, respectively, but was deficient by 8 percent in the low altitude zone. Serious deficiencies were noted in all zones in the consumption of calcium, vitamin A, thiamine, riboflavin, and niacin.

Comparisons between the apparent consumption of food per capita on average during 1958-1962 as reported in the *Survey*, and in 1970, suggest a decline in the average level of nutrition. For example, per capita caloric intake in 1970 was estimated as 1,834 compared to 2,108 in the earlier period, a decline of 13 percent. Similarly, protein intake declined by 26 percent, from 66.1 grams to 48.7 grams. Some dramatic changes also took place in the items contributing to protein intake. Protein from animal sources declined by 35 percent from an average of 20 grams in 1958-1962 to 13 grams in 1970. The reduction in consumption of beef and veal was even sharper, declining by 45 percent. Thus, the average Bolivian in 1970 apparently consumed fewer calories and less protein than in 1958-1962, with a larger proportion of protein coming from vegetable sources.

These data are consistent with trends in agricultural production and prices in Bolivia during the 1960s. Agricultural production has not kept pace with population growth, and relative prices of agricultural products have been rising. The implications are especially serious for most urban consumers who tend to have relatively low, fixed salaries. If average nutrition per capita has declined at the rate and to the extent suggested, the nutrition of low- and middle-income families living in urban areas has probably declined relatively more given their low, fixed incomes. Although data on this point are lacking, most consumers in urban areas of Bolivia have likely suffered decreasing levels of nutrition in the 1970s.

To the extent that the rural sector is a subsistence sector, nutrition levels likely have been little affected. However, the *campesino* has become more and more integrated into modern economic life, and under such conditions price increases for his production represent an increasing opportunity cost.

AGRICULTURE AND THE GOVERNMENT

Since the revolution in 1952, the central thrust of development programs and policies of the government of Bolivia has been to ameliorate balance of payments problems through petroleum and mineral exportation, industrialization, and production of agricultural commodities, previously imported. However, relatively low priority has been attached to public investment in agriculture, especially the small-farm component. The consequence has been undervalued agricultural products and extraction of resources from the agricultural sector in contravention of natural economic forces.

The fact that agriculture has not been considered to be an important source of efficient economic growth is illustrated in the relatively low share of government expenditures for agriculture. For example, the average during 1967-1973, the government spent less than 7.7 percent of total public expenditures on programs for agriculture, not including education.[20]

Furthermore, the majority of public expenditures for the sector has been for credit, processing, and marketing to support development of large-scale commercial agriculture in the Santa Cruz region. One principal program for developing this region has been credit, supplied via the Bolivian Agricultural Bank (BAB), which has gone principally to operators of relatively large farms in the lowlands. A second major program area for agriculture is the processing and marketing of agricultural products, including sugar, rice, milk, and vegetable oils carried out by the Bolivian Development Corporation (CBF). The combined programs of BAB and CBF accounted for 65 percent of all public expenditures in agriculture in 1967-1969, and almost 84 percent during 1971-1973. While some of the resources of these agencies do go to the small-farm sector, most of their budget is directed toward large-scale commercial agriculture, principally in the Santa Cruz region.

The resources expended for technical and social services for agriculture are relatively small compared to those for marketing and credit, and the share has declined significantly in the early 1970s. In the 1967-1969 period social services accounted for 19.6 percent, and technical services for 8.5 percent of total public expenditures in agriculture. However, by 1971-1973, these shares had declined to 7.3 and 6.5 percent, respectively. While the nominal annual average amount for technical services nearly doubled between 1967-1969 and 1971-1973, but remained constant for social services, it clearly declined in real terms for the latter and probably the former due to rapid rates of inflation.

Thus, technical services for agriculture have had the lowest priority of any government programs for the sector, and real expenditures for such services have likely declined over time. In essence, government support for agriculture has not only been extremely limited during 1967-1973 at 7.7 percent of all public expenditures, but it has also been grossly misdirected with less than 7.1 percent of public expenditures in agriculture for critically important technical services.

Another program that is also identified as important for agricultural growth—education—has been given more emphasis by the government. During the 1960s and 1970s, an average of 22.3 percent of the budget has been allocated to education with emphasis on improving primary and secondary schooling in rural areas, although budget data are not at hand for rural areas. [21]

Unfortunately, rural education has contributed little to the development of agriculture despite the effort of the government. Only 28 percent of the rural population of ages six to nineteen years were enrolled in school in 1969, and dropout rates are extremely high starting in the second year of primary school. [22] These estimates suggest primary and secondary education as presently constituted are deemed by a significant number of rural families to have little value as an investment good.

PROBLEMS RESTRICTING AGRICULTURAL DEVELOPMENT

In the writers' judgment, there are six basic problems which have restricted the development of a more modern agricultural sector in Bolivia. Included are: (a) an extremely limited and deficient scientific base for the sector; (b) lack of human capital at both the general and technical-scientific level of training; (c) ineffective administration of public services; (d) ad hoc, uncoordinated foreign donor programs; (e) deficient factor and product markets; and (f) restrictive general development policies.

Absence of a Scientific Base

A prime problem in Bolivian agriculture is the absence of a scientific base. Only such a base, supported publicly, can provide technical knowledge essential to development of a progressive agricultural sector. [23] While the problems associated with traditional technology are more serious in the *Altiplano* and Mountain Valley regions, the lack of a scientific base adversely affects the entire sector.

Research capability in Bolivia is extremely limited because of inadequate budgets. Agricultural experiment stations are seriously underfinanced and have been forced to operate as commercial farms which has severely restricted scientific inquiry and analysis. Supervision and management of the research system and stations are inadequate because of a lack of experienced scientists. The entire research system has not developed a long-run commitment to continuing scientific discovery and innovation, which must underpin a viable agricultural sector. Finally, few, if any, agricultural research programs are associated with the university system.

Extension services are virtually static in most regions. Many vehicles and much equipment were initially purchased under the now defunct Interamerican Agricultural Service (SAI) and are generally worn out. Operating budgets are so low that extension agents have serious difficulty maintaining their vehicles, and travel is restricted. Supervision and management are generally inadequate because of an insufficient number of trained personnel. Other social programs that provide complementary services to encourage institutional and technical change in the agricultural sector, such as community development, also are limited by lack of budget support and qualified scientific input.

The recent creation of the autonomous Bolivian Institute of Agricultural Technology (IBTA), which is comprised of the previous research and extension programs of MACA, is clearly a move in the right direction, since budget support for autonomous agencies is from specific sources and, hence, is much more stable than budget support for ministries. However, in order to be effective, IBTA will require a substantial increase in budget commitment, and for a relatively long time.

The deficiencies in research, extension, and related social services have meant limited adoption of modern techniques of production in most of Bolivian agriculture in the 1960s and 1970s, especially outside the Santa Cruz region. In contrast, research and extension programs developed under SAI in the 1950s and early 1960s had a substantial impact on agriculture. These programs were well developed and viable in the early 1960s and were the foundation for a potentially strong scientific base in Bolivian agriculture. Much of the current deficiency in the research and extension services can be attributed to the premature withdrawal of United States financial and technical support from the SAI programs in the early 1960s before government support was assured. As a result, more than a decade of effort and investment has been lost, and the similar capability must be rebuilt and augmented if the agricultural sector is to achieve long-run viability and growth.

Lack of Human Capital

Extremely limited amounts of human capital at all levels of training is another very serious restriction on agricultural development. [24] This problem is closely related to the deficient scientific base and is treated as a separate problem area in order to emphasize its importance.

The significant government commitment of resources to primary and secondary education in rural areas has been ineffective in facilitating agricultural development. Primary and secondary educational opportunities, as now constituted, have only limited value as an investment good for a large proportion of rural children as evidenced by high dropout rates during early years and a relatively low proportion of the school age population enrolled in school. This suggests that the rural populace sees future earnings resulting from education as being less than earning potentials without education. Much of the resistance to and rejection of formal education probably arises from dissatisfaction with curriculums that are irrelevant to the needs of rural people. In terms of employment opportunities, a large proportion of rural residents entering the labor force is likely to be employed in agriculture for some time to come. Since most of these rural people have no training in agricultural processes or management, they present a serious obstacle to development of a modern agriculture. Lack of communicative and technical management skills seriously restricts their capacity to utilize modern inputs and adopt more modern production techniques.

The current system of university training at both the degree programs and technical levels also does not meet the current needs of the agricultural sector. Considering current demand, the number of agricultural graduates seems to be sufficient. Most are from urban areas, however, and have little or no practical experience in agriculture. A serious problem in attracting qualified students is the substantially lower salaries paid graduates in agriculture compared to those in other disciplines and the limited number of jobs. Agricultural courses are highly philosophical and are taught by academically inbred professors, who most likely have had neither advanced training nor research experience and hold only part-time positions. Emphasis is on the physical-biological sciences. No degree programs are offered in agricultural economics or rural sociology. The reorganization of the university system in 1972 recognized these deficiencies, but programs are yet to be developed.

Finally, there is a critical shortage of senior agricultural scientists and technicians with advanced training or experience to manage research and extension programs and to fill high-level government positions concerned with policy formulation. Personnel deficiencies occur in all physical, biological, and social sciences relative to agriculture. Such scientists and technicians are of primary importance to developing a viable scientific base in the agricultural sector. In the words of Hayami and Ruttan: "Lack of a sufficient stock of scientific and technical manpower in the tropical and subtropical countries . . . imposes a severe constraint on the exploitation of the new technical opportunities for growth." [25]

A major constraint to developing a cadre of scientists working in Bolivian agriculture is the low wages paid for such positions relative to alternatives, especially those available in the international market. [26] This, of course, reflects the low priority accorded by government development programs to agriculture and its related professions. Bolivians who have been educated abroad at the expense of the Bolivian government and donor agencies commonly accept employment in the public sector of other nations which are willing to pay many times more for equivalent training. Failure of the government to support and maintain human capital has seriously restricted progress in the sector.

Ineffective Administration of Public Services

Administration of public agencies and institutions providing support services for agriculture is notoriously ineffective and inefficient. Such agencies are characterized by a complex of overlapping jurisdictions and programs. Planning and implementation of development projects and programs are generally on an ad hoc basis in reaction to immediate short-run pressures and with little or no interagency coordination.

Ineffective administration of public services for agriculture is mainly due to the lack of a critical mass of professionals trained and experienced in managing a public support system for the agricultural sector in the context of a market economy. A critical problem is the lack of a public employment system with descriptions of positions and requisite qualifications, prescribed grades and salaries, merit increases, and a system for competitive employment. Lack of such a system results in nepotism and preferential treatment in hiring; it is not uncommon to find people on the public payroll in name only. Concomitantly, individuals are often employed with scant regard for their technical or professional skills.

In a climate where human capital is extremely limited, the result is a cadre of officials in public agencies serving agriculture that are more inexperienced and less qualified in their areas of expertise than average. These people generally have little or no understanding of the agricultural development problem, or even of the state of knowledge in their various (purported) disciplines. Furthermore, most do not comprehend the processes of scientific investigation and policy formulation, are generally naive concerning the role of government in agriculture, and do not understand that planning the development of socialized versus private sectors involves two very different activities.

Finally, public positions, by tradition, often provide their holders with opportunities for illicit gain in the form of bribes or graft. Consequently, many public administrators have vested personal interest which, when combined with general ineptitude, preclude efficient public sector administration. The final result is little or no policy thrust and superficial palliative reforms that are usually misdirected at symptoms rather than the causes of agricultural backwardness.

Ad Hoc, Uncoordinated Foreign Donor Programs

Foreign donor programs have not contributed, as they could have, to improving the general effectiveness of public services in agriculture. Many foreign donor programs are of the project type. Such programs assume that services will be provided by public agencies of the government, with foreign donor financing and some technical assistance to the agencies during the project. The involved agencies have usually been expected to continue operating the project after the foreign donor assistance has been withdrawn. Unfortunately, they can rarely maintain either the required budget support, because of government fiscal problems, or the level of input from senior scientists provided by foreign donors. Donor-initiated projects also tend to divert public agencies from their central focus. The problem is intensified when several on-going projects require simultaneous support from the same agency--especially research, extension, and community development. Foreign donor assistance directed to institution building generally tends to underestimate the required gestation period. Premature withdrawal of support and periodic shifting in program emphasis by foreign donors have plagued government agencies. As a result, agencies and their programs yet in formative stages have often been left without necessary financial and technical assistance, and foreign donor assistance has been used ineffectively.

A major cause of the ineffectiveness of foreign donor assistance is the failure of the government to coordinate the diverse and relatively large program of foreign aid for agriculture. There is some contact among the more important foreign donors, and excessive duplication has not been a problem. The recent emphasis on sector planning, analysis, and lending on the part of the U.S. Agency for International Development (AID) as well as other donors offers some improvement. But the prevailing lack of central planning and coordination has resulted in inefficient use of the total set of foreign aid to Bolivia. While major responsibility for such planning and coordination must rest with the government, development programs of various foreign donors have often proceeded because of their own sense of political expediency, without sufficient demonstration of program feasibility, and with seemingly little regard for the needs and inherent programs of Bolivia's public agencies providing services to the sector.

Finally, the magnitude of concessionary loans and grants provided by foreign donors to the government for agricultural development programs is, in our opinion, greater than can be effectively assimilated. Key constraints are limited human capital and ineffective administration of public services for agriculture. Since most foreign donor assistance is provided as soft loans, one consequence is an unnecessary increase in Bolivia's already burgeoning external debt.

Deficient Factor and Product Markets

Product and factor markets are generally deficient because of the absence of essential public institutions and services and, in some cases, because of excessive government regulation and interference. Labor markets lack both employment services and the institutions that could provide skill training to facilitate labor mobility. Credit markets are hampered by government restrictions and bureaucratic processes that seriously complicate loan procedures. Land markets are restricted by limitations on land size, mortgages, and land transfers imposed by the Agrarian Reform Law. Furthermore, Bolivia has not had a complete cadastral survey.

Product markets are characterized by nonexistent or unenforced quality and sanitation standards, and there is a general absence of a homogeneous set of weights and measures. Storage and handling facilities are also inadequate. Furthermore, the government has taken over the processing and marketing of several important crops including rice, sugar, and milk.

The efficiency of factor and product markets is restricted by inadequate information and communication systems and transportation networks. The extremely limited information regarding prices and marketing of both factors and products is a serious problem as is lack of primary statistical data on the sector. Communication systems for private and public interchanges of information are also inadequate. Despite substantial levels of investment in surface transportation, farm-to-market access roads are insufficient in both quantity and quality.

The deficient markets restrict the adoption of more advanced production techniques. Changes in relative prices of factors and products may accurately reach only a small share of producers. At the same time, dissemination of educational information on the use of new techniques is also restricted. When farmers cannot perceive the probable direction and magnitude of changes in relative prices and do not understand how to use new and more productive techniques, it is almost impossible for them to determine if adoption of such techniques will be profitable.

Nevertheless, farmers in both the commercial and *campesino* sectors are responding to accessible price signals in organizing their short-run production and longer-run investment decisions. Also, innovations in both highland and tropical agriculture are saving scarce factors of production, and induced technical change in taking place, albeit slowly. This trend is a positive base from which to proceed in improving factor and product markets and developing the agricultural sector.

Restrictive General Development Policies

Several general economic development policies also restrict and limit the prospects for modernizing agriculture. First, the policy of maintaining low, fixed prices for basic food products in order to protect consumers has generally restricted progress in agriculture. Such prices tend to be maintained below scarcity value. The results are reduced incentives to produce, and an even more limited supply of food, which exacerbates the very problem the institutional prices were intended to solve. To the extent that the institutional prices are effective, they contribute to an increasing "deficit" in the sector. Furthermore, when supplies are short, consumers bear added nonfood costs associated with distribution by queueing or rationing.

The impact of low institutional prices imposed on basic food products is somewhat modified by the formation of black markets, with contraband supplies entering from other countries. When prices in the exterior are higher than the institutional price, however, food and supplies tend to leave Bolivia, as they did during 1972 and 1973.

Second, the present system of internal customs posts, the *trancas* and *retenes*, which tax internal movement of agricultural produce, seriously restricts market efficiency. These taxes also tend to be highly regressive as most internal food taxes are paid by low-income consumers who spend much of their income on food and comprise the largest share of the population. Furthermore, the costs of maintaining the collection system must be high, given the large number of public entities involved.

Third, foreign trade policy designed to earn revenues for the government has restricted development of agriculture. Although now at relatively low levels, high taxes have historically been levied on imports of inputs used in agriculture and on exports of some agricultural products. The results are relatively higher factor prices and lower product prices, which convey additional disincentives for farmers to produce.

Finally, the government is placing more emphasis on import-substitution as a basis for economic development. Unfortunately, Bolivia's import-substitution policy has not emphasized, until very recently, the development of industries that manufacture factors of production for agriculture. Yet, domestic production of nitrogen fertilizer and pesticides has offered one of the most attractive possibilities for import-substitution to be found in Bolivia. One of the principal raw materials for these industries-- natural gas--has been produced in the Santa Cruz region since the mid-1960s, which is the major market center for most of the fertilizer and pesticides used in Bolivia, and which has rail linkages to Brazil and Argentina where excess production can be marketed. The failure to develop these vital supply industries imposes one more restriction on the development of a modern agriculture.

PROGNOSIS

The prognosis for improving the performance of Bolivia's agriculture in the next two decades is pessimistic. The writers expect a relatively slow rate of growth in products of the traditional sector—substantially less than the rate of growth of population on average for all products. One exception may be in potato production where a concentrated effort is now underway to improve research, extension, and cooperative organization. If successful, land could be freed to produce other crops. But there will be a continual upward pressure on food prices in general and reduced purchasing power and nutrition for a large proportion of the population. The *campesino* sector will become increasingly concentrated on the limited land base of the Altiplano and Mountain Valleys as colonization efforts will not be sufficient to relieve the population pressures. The consequences will be increased political unrest in rural areas and pressure for greater emphasis on improving traditional agriculture.

In contrast, growth in the output of agricultural products produced in the lowlands will continue at a more rapid rate than for those produced in traditional agricultural areas because of the pattern of past and expected government support in providing marketing, credit, and technical services. Growth in cotton, sugar cane, and rice production will moderate relative to the 1960s and 1970s as internal demand is satisfied, and supply fluctuations will be principally in response to world market prices. However, production and processing of oil seeds should increase substantially as the government attempts to reduce imports of vegetable oils.

There are two basic, interrelated reasons for this pessimistic forecast. First, it is highly unlikely that requisite programs and policies for overcoming the problems restricting development of the agricultural sector will be implemented on a timely basis. Consequently, it is expected that the government will continue at least through the mid-1980s with essentially the same mix of programs and policies among sectors and within agriculture as in the 1960s and 1970s.

This expectation is partially based on the philosophical bias of key Bolivian policymakers, who are generally sympathetic to the "industrialization first" approach to economic growth. More critically, reforms in administration of public services, which must logically precede any genuine reformulation of agricultural development policy, are unlikely to occur. Bolivian public administration is notoriously inefficient and immature in dealing with the complex issues of the economy and of agricultural development. Entrenched and vested interests of public administrators are often in basic conflict with needed reforms. Traditional agricultural programs and policies have not brought perceptible changes in the past ten years despite considerable technical and financial assistance from foreign donors. The current system restricts professionalism, and young scientists and technicians, especially if well trained, encounter frustrations which, when coupled with relatively low salaries, eventually lead them elsewhere. In the absence of scientific knowledge about social, economic, physical, and biologic processes affecting agriculture and its role in the development process, it is unlikely effective policies and programs for agricultural growth will be developed.

Furthermore, foreign donor assistance, particularly that of AID, has been characterized by shifting program emphasis and fragmentation of effort which has seriously limited the effectiveness of the assistance. [27] Here again, there is no reason to expect significant changes in the impact of U.S. technical and financial assistance on Bolivian agriculture based on the experience of the 1960s and 1970s.

The second reason for the pessimistic prognosis for growth of Bolivia's agriculture is the extreme improbability of employing, in the next five to ten years, enough qualified agricultural scientists to manage and carry out adequate research, extension, and related programs. Filling the existing deficit implies some long-term commitment to training and importation of needed scientists from other countries during the interim. AID and other foreign donors are not currently predisposed to involvement with in-country agricultural education programs which require relatively long-run commitments. Past programs to train Bolivians outside their country have proven ineffective in relieving the critical shortage of human capital. Furthermore, political realities in Bolivia, coupled with the extremely high costs of importing foreign technicians, restrict the extent to which Bolivia can staff such programs with outside assistance. Without some source of technical competence, the necessary scientific base for the sector will not be forthcoming. We see very minimal potentials for improving the supply of human capital for agricultural development given the current attitudes within the nation and among foreign donors.

Even if Bolivia tried to implement the reforms necessary to eradicate the problems we have outlined, it could only partially do so because the requisite inputs are not readily available. The gestation period for most reforms is relatively long—five to ten years or more—even if all inputs are available. The fact that some are in short supply suggests that improved performance in agriculture is a long way off. Considering that Bolivia is unlikely to even partially implement the needed reforms before 1985, the prospects for significantly improving the performance of the sector before the year 2000 are dismal indeed. And, of course, a shift in the political situation away from the stability of the last several years could eradicate or further delay any hopes for improvement.

ENDNOTES FOR CHAPTER XI

1. This paper is based on: *The Status of Bolivian Agriculture*, by E. Boyd Wennergren and Morris D. Whitaker (New York: Praeger Publishers, 1975). Copyright 1975, Praeger Publishers, a division of Holt, Rinehart and Winston, CBS Publishing Group. Used by permission of the publisher. In order to minimize endnotes, data and material taken from this book are not footnoted, excepting sources of general interest.

2. Walter W. Rostow, "The Stages of Economic Growth," *The Economic History Review*, XII (August, 1959), 1-15; W. Arthur Lewis, "Economic Development with Unlimited Supplies of Labor," *Manchester School of Economics and Social Studies*, XXII (May, 1954), 139-91; Gustav Ranis and John C. H. Fei, "A Theory of Economic Development," *American Economic Review*, LV (September, 1961), 533-65; Dale W. Jorgenson, "Testing Alternative Theories of Development of a Dual Economy," *The Theory and Design of Economic Development*, ed. Irma Adelman and Eric Thorbecke (Baltimore: The Johns Hopkins Press, 1966), pp. 45-60.

3. For an evaluation in the context of Latin America see Albert O. Hirschman, "The Political Economy of Import Substitution Industrialization in Latin America," *The Quarterly Journal of Economics*, LXXXII (February, 1968), 1-32.

4. For a review of the literature on the role of agriculture in economic development see: Bruce F. Johnston, "Agriculture and Structural Transformation in Developing Countries: A Survey of Research," *Journal of Economic Literature*, VIII (June, 1970), 369-404; and Yujiro Hayami and Vernon W. Ruttan, *Agricultural Development: An International Perspective* (Baltimore: The Johns Hopkins Press, 1971), Chapter 2. Also see William H. Nicholls, "The Place of Agriculture in Economic Development," *Agriculture in Economic Development*, ed. Carl Eicher and Lawrence Witt (New York: McGraw-Hill, 1964), pp. 11-44.

5. Hayami and Ruttan, op. cit.

6. Theodore W. Schultz, *Transforming Traditional Agriculture* (New Haven, Connecticut: Yale University Press, 1964).

7. Data on geography, climate, and principal products were synthesized from unpublished reports of Bolivia's Ministry of *Campesino* Affairs and Agriculture and The National Meteorologic and Hydrologic Service.

8. Data on population are based on unpublished reports of the National Statistics Institute.

9. More information on the native Indians of Bolivia may be obtained from the Instituto Linguistico de Verano in La Paz.

10. See Morris D. Whitaker and E. Boyd Wennergren, "Common Property Rangeland and Overgrazing: Resource Misallocation in Bolivian Agriculture," *Proceedings*, First International Rangeland Congress, Denver, Colorado (forthcoming, 1978).

11. Data on land use are synthesized from Thomas T. Cochrane, *Potencial agrícola del uso de la tierra: un mapa de sistema de tierra* (La Paz: Editorial Don Bosco, 1973).

12. The high proportion of cultivated land in fallow reflects the traditional rotation system of the *Altiplano* and Mountain Valley regions. Fallowing may last from three to ten years and includes from 10 to 85 percent of a farmer's land, depending on local conditions.

13. Estimates of gross domestic product are from Bolivia, Ministerio de Planificación y Coordinación, *Cuentas nacionales 1950-1969* (La Paz: 1970); and unpublished data provided by a successor agency--Consejo Nacional de Economía y Planificación.

14. Estimates of GDP in agriculture and crop production for 1969-1976 are from U.S. Department of Agriculture, *Indices of Agricultural Production for the Western Hemisphere 1967-1976*, Economic Research Service Statistical Bulletin No. 569 (Washington, D.C.: Government Printing Office, 1977).

15. This remainder accounted for over 88 percent of GDP in agriculture on average during 1974-1976.

16. *El Diario* [La Paz], Sunday, January 1, 1978, p. 3.

17. United Nations, Food and Agriculture Organization, *Agricultural Commodities--Projections for 1970*, FAO Commodity Review 1962, Special Supplement (Rome: 1963).

18. Bolivia, Instituto Nacional de Estadística, *Indice de precios al consumidor en La Paz* (La Paz: 1974) for 1966-1974; and Bolivia, Instituto Nacional de Estadística, *Boletín estadístico* (La Paz: 1977) for 1975-1976.

19. U.S. Department of Defense, *Bolivian Nutrition Survey* (Washington, D.C.: Interdepartmental Committee on Nutrition for National Defense, 1964).

20. Statistics on the government of Bolivia expenditures for agriculture and in total are from Bolivia, Ministerio de Finanzas, *Presupuestos generales de la nacion* (La Paz: 1967-1973).

21. Expenditures in education are based on unpublished reports and data in the Dirección Nacional de Planeamiento Educativo del Ministerio de Educación y Cultura.

22. Thomas N. Chirikos et al., *Human Resources in Bolivia*, report prepared for the U.S. Agency for International Development and the Government of Bolivia by Ohio State University (Columbus, Ohio: The Center for Human Resources Research, 1971), p. 59.

23. See Hayami and Ruttan, op. cit., chapter 12.

24. Differences in the stock of human capital explain 35 percent of the differences in agricultural labor productivity between developed and developing countries. Ibid., chapters 4 and 5.

25. Ibid., p. 287.

26. Despite recent increases in salaries of IBTA personnel, salary levels are still not competitive with the private sector or the international market.

27. See, e.g., E. Boyd Wennergren and Morris D. Whitaker, "Social Return to U.S. Technical Assistance in Bolivian Agriculture," *The American Journal of Agricultural Economics*, LIX (August, 1977), 565-69.

Chapter XII

The Public Sector in Bolivian Agricultural Development
José Isaac Torrico

INTRODUCTION

It is widely recognized that the growth and performance of the agricultural sector in Bolivia has lagged behind other major sectors. This has resulted in a relatively high rise in food prices and poorer nutrition. Moreover, agricultural growth has been concentrated in the sparsely populated commercial farming areas of the *Oriente*, or eastern lowlands, to the neglect of the densely populated traditional farming areas of the highlands of the *Altiplano* and the Mountain Valley regions. This has contributed to not only considerable regional inequalities, but also to a worsening in the size distribution of rural incomes.[1]

After the 1952 revolution the land reform program, which began in 1953, made important progress in redistributing land. By 1976 the National Land Reform Council (CNRA) had distributed 79.6 percent of the farm and ranch land area that was in private hands in 1950.[2] Thus, land that was formerly in the hands of large landowners was effectively redistributed to the small farmers or *campesinos*.

This redistribution was not sufficient, however, to foster growth of the agricultural sector at a pace which would permit agriculture to make its most appropriate contribution to development. On the one hand, the land reform has been incomplete because many *campesinos* still do not have titles to their new lands due to the sluggishness of the government bureaucracy responsible for issuing the documents. This condition has seriously impacted on investment in agriculture.

More importantly, on the other hand, agricultural growth and development have been hampered by the lack of adequate institutional structures and appropriate policy measures to complement land reform and foster agricultural development, particularly among small farmers. This is in spite of the fact that between 1966 and 1977 there were substantial increases in government funding for agriculture and the establishment of numerous new public institutions to serve the sector. Therefore, although there was an increase in funding and an institutional structure has been established it appears to have been insufficient to foment wide-scale agricultural development.

The purpose of this paper is to examine the institutional changes, budget expenditures and several major policy instruments undertaken by the government since the mid 1960s and to analyze their impact on the agricultural sector. In this context, first, the growth and changes of the institutional structure of government agencies that have been established to work in the agricultural sector and the allocation of government budgets to these institutions are described. Second, major policy measures that have been employed by the government in agriculture are analyzed. The final section sets forth conclusions, recommendations for a redirection of government agricultural policy and an outlook for the future.

INSTITUTIONS IN AGRICULTURAL DEVELOPMENT

The Bolivian government allocated an average of 9.8 percent of its total budget to the agricultural sector over the 1967-1977 period. In these years there was considerable change in the governmental institutional structure and financial support for the sector over this period. The nature of these changes is illustrated by examining: a) the present overall institutional structure in agriculture, b) the institutional changes and government financial support for the various institutional components of the sector since the mid-1960s, c) the changes in the total government budget for the sector, and d) the changes in the sector's human resource base.

The Overall Institutional Structure in Agriculture

In analyzing the public institutional infrastructure of the agricultural sector, it is important to understand that the executive branch of the Bolivian government is organized at two levels: a) the central administration, and b) the decentralized administration.

The central administration is comprised of the presidency and fifteen ministries. Within the presidency there are the General Secretary, the Economic and Planning Council and the National Board of Social Development. The decentralized administration is comprised of development corporations, public institutions, public enterprises, and mixed enterprises. As shown in Table XII-1, public organizations in the agricultural sector are found at both the centralized and decentralized levels.

A brief description of each institution along with the date that it was established is presented in the table. Most of the institutions were created in the 1970s during the time that the government attempted to establish an institutional infrastructure to service agriculture. The pattern of institutional development and, perhaps more importantly, the funding of same becomes more clear in the following sections. Suffice it to say that prior to 1965 there were only a few institutions in existence.

The Ministry of Agriculture was founded in 1905. It was reorganized in 1974 and its name was changed to reflect its expanded function, e.g., the Ministry of Peasant Affairs and Agriculture (MACA). The Bolivian Agricultural Bank (BAB) was founded in 1942 as a means to finance agriculture but only undertook a major commitment to finance small farmers, campesinos, after 1975. The National Land Reform Council (CNRA) was established in 1953 to carry out the government's land reform program initiated in that year. Apart from these organizations several lesser institutions were established to carry out wool and coffee marketing and meteorological services.

Since 1965, a plethora of institutions have been created. Additional marketing institutions were established for rice and wheat; colonization programs were centralized under the National Colonization Institute; the

National Community Development Service was created; and a number of smaller and specialized institutions were established.

Particularly noteworthy in the 1970s was the rapid expansion of regional development corporations to all nine departments. Initially, these corporations were responsible for urban infrastructure, but now, most are involved with development projects in many sectors including industry, mining, hydrocarbons, and agriculture. They have played an important and expanding role in promoting regional development within each department.

The Bolivian army, in a period of military governments, also has played a lesser, but significant, role in development through COFADENA, the Military Development Corporation.

The Bolivian Development Corporation (CBF), established in 1943, has played a particularly important role in establishing Bolivian industry. In agriculture it has concentrated in the processing of agricultural products. These include the milk processing plants (PIL) in Cochabamba and La Paz, sugar mills in Bermejo and Guabirá, Brazil nut processing plants and a new oilseed processing plant in Villamontes. In addition to these industries CBF also has established several commercial farms.

Budget Commitments to Public Institutions

All public institutions are nominally under the control of a ministry, with the minister having the authority to appoint the director or the president of the institution. However, they are autonomous in their budget and decisions. Table XII-2 shows the budget support for the public institutions in agriculture. For the 1967-1977 period, a total of 221.37 million dollars was committed by the government. Of the total budget, 180.73 million dollars were allocated from national sources and the balance of 40.64 million dollars came from external sources.

In 1967, there were only 2.1 million dollars of support for three public institutions. By 1977, the total number of institutions had increased to fifteen and the budget support in nominal terms had risen by more than one-hundred fold. The average annual rate of growth has been 38.3 percent over the ten-year period.

Of the total budget in 1977, the most funds, 46.6 percent, were allocated to the National Rice Enterprise (ENA), which has been in operation since 1973 and has acted as the monopsonistic rice buyer in Bolivia. However, it encountered financial difficulties and, in 1977, its buying operations declined. In 1978 the government decided to withdraw from rice marketing because of ENA's lack of success in managing the orderly marketing of the crop. Thus, ENA terminated its buying operations and began to sell its remaining stock.

As of 1977 colonization and rural socioeconomic promotion activities appear as high priority in the government sectoral development policies; INC and SNDC had the second and third largest budgets.

Budget Commitments to Public Enterprises

Table XII-3 shows the government budget commitments to public enterprises in agriculture. CBF received 58.9 percent of the total over the 1967-1977 period. Of total commitments to that institution almost 9 percent, 33.58 million dollars, came from foreign sources. Over the same time period, BAB received 40 percent in the total commitments for sectoral public enterprises of which 29 percent came from foreign sources.

TABLE XII-1

PUBLIC ORGANIZATIONS OF THE AGRICULTURAL SECTOR, BOLIVIA, 1978

	Acronym	Year of Creation	Purpose
A. CENTRAL ADMINISTRATION			
1. Ministry of Peasant Affairs and Agriculture	MACA	1905[a]	Monitor whole sector
B. DECENTRALIZED ADMINISTRATION			
1. Development Corporations			
a. Development Corporation of Santa Cruz	CORDECRUZ	1943	Development corporations are supposed to promote regional development by executing specific development plans. They are also responsible for the natural resources conservation and exploitation.
b. Development Corporation of Chuquisaca	CODECH	1967	
c. Development Corporation of Beni	CODEBENI	1968	
d. Development Corporation of Potosí	CORDEPO	1968	
e. Development Corporation of Cochabamba	CORDECO	1970	
f. Development Corporation of Tarija	CODETAR	1971	
g. Development Corporation of La Paz	CORDEPAZ	1971	
h. Development Corporation of Oruro	CORDEOR	1971	
i. Regional Development Council of the Northwest	CORDENO	1967	
2. Public Institutions			
a. National Land Reform Council	CNRA	1953	To issue land titles
b. Bolivian Wool Promoting Committee	COMBOFLA	1962	To promote wool production
c. Meterological and Hydrological Service	SNMH	1963	To develop weather statistics
d. Bolivian Coffee Committee	COBOLCA	1965	To promote coffee production
e. National Institute of Colonization	INC	1965	To promote internal migration
f. National Wheat Institute	INT	1969	To promote wheat production
g. National Community Development Service	SNDC	1970	To promote rural development
h. National Rice Enterprise	ENA	1972	To carry rice marketing
i. Food for Development	ALDE	1972	To provide food assistance
j. Development Corporation for Abapo-Izozog Project	CORGEPAI	1973	To develop Abapo region

TABLE XII-1 (continued)

	Acronym	Year of Creation	Purpose
2. Public Institutions (continued)			
k. Forestry Development Center	CDF	1974	To develop forestry plans
l. Tropical Agricultural Research Center	CIAT	1975	To carry out research programs
m. Bolivian Institute of Agricultural Technology	IBTA	1975	To carry out research programs
n. Ingavi Integral Development Project	INGAVI	1975	To develop Ingavi province
o. National Service of Hoof and Mouth Disease, Rabies and Brucelosis	SENARB	1976	To control livestock diseases
3. Public Enterprises			
a. Bolivian Agricultural Bank	BAB	1942	To implement agricultural credit programs
b. Bolivian Development Corporation	CBF	1943	To develop industrial activities
c. Military Development Corporation	COFADENA	1972	To implement army project

aReorganized in 1974; previously was named Ministry of Agriculture.

Sources: Ministerio de Hacienda, Dirección General de Presupuesto, *Presupuestos generales de la nación* (La Paz, 1967–1970); Ministerio de Finanzas, Dirección General de Presupuesto, *Presupuesto del sector público* (La Paz, 1971–1977).

TABLE XII-2

GOVERNMENT BUDGET COMMITMENTS TO PUBLIC INSTITUTIONS IN AGRICULTURE, 1967–1977
(Millions of U.S. Dollars)

Institutions	1967	1968	1969	1970	1971	1972	1973	1974	1975	1976	1977	TOTAL
CNRA	0.26	0.27	0.24	0.28	1.06	1.39	0.19	1.26	1.22	1.34	1.72	9.23
INC	0.98	3.71	2.52	1.25	0.73	0.94	0.76	0.84	6.68	8.18	7.02	33.61
SNDC[a]	---	2.39	3.02	1.62	1.05	1.92	2.36	2.64	2.74	4.84	5.77	27.35
CORDEPAI[a]	---	0.10	1.30	0.93	0.69	0.64	0.49	0.84	1.30	1.32	1.39	9.00
SNMH	---	---	0.08	0.15	0.45	0.66	0.59	0.54	0.92	0.67	0.87	4.93
COMBOFLA	0.86	1.20	1.20	0.58	0.57	0.52	0.29	0.44	0.64	0.74	1.17	8.21
COBOLCA[b]	---	---	---	0.05	0.19	0.13	0.05	0.07	0.11	0.10	0.13	0.83
ALDES[b]	---	---	---	0.36	0.24	0.20	0.12	0.15	0.16	0.17	0.18	1.58
INT[b]	---	---	---	0.13	0.25	0.88	0.29	1.18	1.71	1.71	---	6.15
ENA[c]	---	---	---	---	---	---	0.17	12.91	33.45	35.13	21.60	103.26
CDF[d]	---	---	---	---	---	---	---	---	1.64	1.55	2.29	5.48
IBTA[e]	---	---	---	---	---	---	---	---	---	---	3.68	3.68
SENARB[e]	---	---	---	---	---	---	---	---	---	---	3.60	3.60
CIAT[e]	---	---	---	---	---	---	---	---	---	---	0.72	0.72
INGAVI[e]	---	---	---	---	---	---	---	---	---	---	3.74	3.74
TOTAL	2.10	7.67	8.36	4.35	5.23	7.28	5.31	20.87	50.57	55.75	53.38	221.37

[a]CORDEPAI and SNDC began their operations in 1968.
[b]COBOLCA, ALDES and INT began their operations in 1970.
[c]ENA was created as a public institution in 1973, but it began operations in 1974.
[d]CDF began its operations in 1975.
[e]IBTA, SENARB, CIAT and INGAVI began their operations in 1977.

Sources: Ministerio de Hacienda, Dirección General de Presupuestos, Presupuestos generales de la nación (La Paz, 1967–1970); Ministerio de Finanzas, Dirección General de Presupuestos, Presupuestos, Presupuestos del sector público (La Paz, 1971–1977).

TABLE XII-3

GOVERNMENT BUDGET COMMITMENTS TO PUBLIC ENTERPRISES IN AGRICULTURE
(Millions of U.S. Dollars)

Enterprises	1967	1968	1969	1970	1971	1972	1973	1974	1975	1976	1977	TOTAL
CBF	8.01	10.49	8.42	13.59	12.96	15.46	24.87	47.27	61.95	73.46	97.68	374.16
National	8.01	10.49	8.42	10.34	12.96	15.46	16.00	38.23	56.44	66.88	96.75	340.58
Foreign	----	----	----	2.65	-----	-----	8.87	9.04	5.51	6.58	0.93	33.58
BAB	1.08	6.37	5.80	12.89	14.07	28.30	21.36	11.62	38.05	37.46	77.43	254.43
National	1.08	2.61	4.38	8.20	10.39	16.62	10.24	5.82	20.27	31.36	69.58	180.55
Foreign	----	3.76	1.42	4.69	3.68	11.68	11.12	5.80	17.78	6.10	7.85	73.88
CORADENA[a]								1.69	1.91	1.65	1.48	6.73
TOTAL	9.09	16.86	14.22	26.48	27.03	43.76	46.23	60.58	101.91	112.57	176.59	635.32

a Includes the budget commitments related only to agricultural sector.

Sources: Ministerio de Hacienda, Dirección General de Presupuestos, *Presupuestos generales de la nación* (La Paz, 1967-1970); Ministerio de Finanzas, Dirección General de Presupuestos, *Presupuestos, Presupuesto del sector público* (La Paz, 1971-1977).

Although small in comparison to other entities, since 1974, COFA-
DENA has increased its activities in different fields of agricultural production and agro-industry.

The average annual rate of growth in total budget commitments to
public enterprises in agriculture over the 1967-1977 period was 34.5 percent. The average annual rate of growth for CBF and BAB has been
28.4 and 53.3 percent respectively.

Budget Commitments to Development Corporations

Since 1973, development corporations and committees have become
increasingly important in regional development in Bolivia. Prior to that
time these institutions and these fundings were not significant.

Total budget allocations to development corporations over the five-
year period of 1973-1977 have increased substantially and allocations to
agricultural projects of the corporations have approximated 12 percent of
the total. Table XII-4 presents the percentage share of the total budget
to each department. As would be expected that for Santa Cruz, CORDE-
SAC, received 61 percent. The second highest, the CORDECH (Chuquisaca) received only 10.4 percent. The rest of the development corporations and committees shared the remaining 28.6 percent. The lowest
percentages were allocated to CORDENO (Pando) and CORDECO (Cochabamba) 2.4 and 2.6 percent respectively.

It is noteworthy that foreign assistance has been available to selected development corporations. Over the five-year period, 36 percent
of the total budget support for the corporations--132.67 million dollars--
came from foreign sources.

Government Budget Commitments to the Agricultural Sector

As shown in Table XII-5 the total budget commitments of the Bolivian government to agriculture for the 1967-1977 period totaled 947.78
million dollars which represented only 9.8 percent of the total national
budget. Of the sector's budget 39.5 and 26.8 percent were allocated to
CBF and BAB respectively. Thus, these two enterprises received two-
thirds of the total sectoral budget. Public institutions received another
23.4 percent of the total and MACA 4.9 percent.

It should be noted, however, that in spite of the low average percentage of the total government budget received by the agricultural sector, there was a trend to increase the proportion of the Bolivian government's general budget directed to the sector. In 1967, agriculture
received a share of only 4.8 percent but in 1977, the sector received
10.4 percent. The highest allocation occurred in 1975 with 13.5 percent.
The increase in agriculture's share in the general budget is more due to
the expansion of the number of institutions and programs and does not
generally reflect increments of the budget support for each institution.

Human Resources in the Agricultural Sector

The trend in the number of public employees serving the agricultural sector has increased sharply since 1967, but more or less in relation to the increase in the total budget. As shown in Table XII-6, in 1967
public employees in agriculture numbered 3,026 and in 1977, 9,267. This
represents an average annual growth rate of 11.8 percent. The average
annual increase in CBF employment has been most dramatic, at a rate of

TABLE XII-4

GOVERNMENT BUDGET AND FOREIGN AID COMMITMENTS FOR ALL SECTORS TO THE DEVELOPMENT CORPORATIONS AND COMMITTEES, 1973-1976

(Millions of U.S. Dollars)

	1973		1974		1975		1976		1977		TOTAL		TOTAL	SHARE
	Budget	Aid	Budget	Aid	Budget	Aid	Budget	Aid	Budget	Aid	Budget	Aid		
CODECH	12.59	----	4.67	0.51	7.85	0.73	5.42	0.98	5.18	----	35.71	2.22	37.93	10.40
CORDEPAZ	0.62	----	1.93	----	3.25	----	4.13	1.43	4.88	0.76	14.81	2.19	17.00	4.70
CORDECO	0.10	----	0.25	----	0.56	----	1.64	1.80	3.19	1.80	5.74	3.60	9.34	2.60
CORDEOR	0.29	----	1.69	----	3.47	----	3.42	----	5.90	1.03	14.77	1.03	15.80	4.30
CORDERFO	2.44	----	3.78	----	7.61	----	4.05	----	6.82	0.03	24.70	0.03	24.73	6.80
CORDESAC	7.66	2.69	19.35	12.71	23.11	45.77	23.59	17.18	27.44	42.36	101.15	120.71	221.86	61.00
CODEBENI	0.56	0.10	0.91	----	0.72	----	2.40	----	2.38	----	6.97	0.10	7.07	1.90
CORDENO	0.88	----	1.17	----	1.27	----	1.97	----	3.27	----	8.56	----	8.56	2.40
CODETAR	0.18	2.79	3.54	----	3.19	----	6.62	----	5.20	----	18.73	2.79	21.56	5.90
TOTAL	25.32	5.58	37.29	13.22	51.03	46.50	53.24	21.39	64.26	45.98	231.14	132.67	363.81	100.00

Sources: Ministerio de Hacienda, Dirección General de Presupuestos, *Presupuestos generales de la nación* (La Paz, 1967-1970); Ministerio de Finanzas, Dirección General de Presupuestos, *Presupuestos del sector público* (La Paz, 1971-1977).

TABLE XII-5

GOVERNMENT BUDGET COMMITMENTS TO THE AGRICULTURAL SECTOR, 1967-1977

(Millions of U.S. Dollars)

	1967	1968	1969	1970	1971	1972	1973	1974	1975	1976	1977	TOTAL
MACA	2.79	2.40	2.56	6.42	3.20	3.74	2.61	4.69	7.19	4.35	6.74	46.69
Public Institutions	2.10	7.67	8.36	4.35	5.23	7.28	5.31	20.87	50.57	55.75	53.88	221.37
BAB	1.08	6.37	5.80	12.89	14.07	28.30	21.36	11.62	38.05	37.46	77.46	254.46
CBF	8.01	10.49	8.42	13.59	12.96	15.46	24.87	47.27	61.95	73.46	97.68	374.16
COFADENA[a]	----	----	----	----	----	----	----	1.69	1.91	1.65	1.48	6.73
Development Corporations and Committees[a]	----	----	----	----	0.35	0.84	2.19	4.10	18.88	11.82	6.19	44.37
TOTAL	13.98	26.93	25.14	37.25	35.81	55.62	56.34	90.24	178.55	134.49	243.43	947.78
TOTAL Government Budget	293.67	368.00	414.00	496.38	467.22	540.22	645.85	876.65	1319.65	1883.51	2331.73	9636.88
Sector and Share	4.76	7.32	6.07	7.50	7.66	10.30	8.72	10.29	13.53	9.80	10.44	9.83
Sector without CBF	5.97	16.44	16.72	23.66	22.85	40.16	31.47	42.97	116.60	111.03	145.75	573.62
Share without CBF	2.03	4.47	4.04	4.77	4.89	7.43	4.87	4.90	8.84	5.89	6.25	5.95

[a]Includes the budget commitments related only to agricultural sector.

Sources: Ministerio de Hacienda, Dirección General de Presupuestos, Presupuestos generales de la nación (La Paz, 1967-1970); Ministerio de Finanzas, Dirección General de Presupuestos, Presupuestos del sector público (La Paz, 1971-1977).

TABLE XII-6

HUMAN RESOURCES OF THE AGRICULTURAL SECTOR
GOVERNMENT INSTITUTIONS

Institution	Number of persons 1967	Number of persons 1977	Annual Change (percent)
MACA	1,013	798	-2.4
Public Institutions	932	3,953	15.5
BAB	205	397	6.8
CBF	876	4,119	16.7
TOTAL	3,026	9,267	11.8

Sources: Ministerio de Hacienda, Dirección General de Presupuestos, *Presupuestos generales de la nación* (La Paz, 1967-1970); Ministerio de Finanzas, Dirección General de Presupuestos, *Presupuestos del sector público* (La Paz, 1971-1977).

16.7 percent. Personnel in the public institutions and BAB have expanded at annual growth rates of 15.5 and 6.8 percent respectively.

In contrast, the number of persons employed by MACA decreased from 1,013 in 1967 to 789 in 1977. The average annual decline of 2.4 percent reflects the decentralization of the activities of this ministry as other sector public activities were developed.

The number of persons serving the agricultural sector in public institutions is probably more than sufficient for the present level of program development. A problem arises, however, in the levels of training and capacity of the personnel. Table XII-7 summarizes the qualifications of the personnel in the sector in 1977. Only 11.3 percent of the employees were university graduates. Moreover, most of the university graduates only have degrees at an undergraduate level, mostly in agronomy, economics, or law. As of February 1978, there were only twenty agriculture public employees in agricultural institutions with the masters degree and three with the doctorate.

In part, the low level of education and professional training in the public institutions serving agriculture is undoubtedly due to the relatively low salaries in those institutions compared to similar institutions in other ministries. In particular, as shown in Table XII-8, the salaries of MACA employees are low. It is readily apparent why the more qualified persons prefer to work in the decentralized public enterprises, the private sector, or prefer to work abroad where salaries are higher.

Summary

There has been a significant increase in the number of government institutions that deal with the agricultural sector in the 1970s. This has resulted in an increasing share of the Bolivian government's general bud get going to the sector and reflects an increase in the government's commitment to assist agriculture. But within this context, the large number of new institutions shows the restructuring of the governmental struc-

TABLE XII-7

QUALITY OF HUMAN RESOURCES IN THE PUBLIC
AGRICULTURAL SECTOR, 1977

	MACA	Public Institutions	CBF	BAB	TOTAL	Percent Share
Executive Personnel[a]	15	47	13	19	94	1.0
University Graduates	217	574	71	182	1,044	11.3
Middle-grade Technicans	56	479	130	34	699	7.5
Administrative Personnel	281	1,218	255	141	1,895	20.4
Service Personnel	113	1,278	206	21	1,618	17.5
Laborers	116	357	3,444	---	3,917	42.3
TOTAL	798	3,953	4,119	397	9,267	100.0

[a]Executive personnel may have a university degree.

Sources: Ministerio de Hacienda, Dirección General de Presupuestos,
Presupuestos generales de la nación (La Paz, 1967-1970);
Ministerio de Finanzas, Dirección General de Presupuestos,
Presupuestos del sector público (La Paz, 1971-1977).

TABLE XII-8

AVERAGE GROSS SALARIES OF DIFFERENT GOVERNMENT
AGENCIES BOLIVIA, FEBRUARY, 1978
(U.S. Dollars Per Year)

Position	MACA	IBTA	CBF	Ministry of Finance	BAB
Director	9,100	10,500	22,950	12,800	21,000
Department Head	8,400	9,000	17,000	9,600	16,000
Division Head	5,950	7,000	13,600	8,000	12,000
University Graduate	4,550	5,600	7,650	6,000	6,370

Source: Derived from MACA, IBTA, CBF, and Ministry of Finance
payrolls.

ture away from activities centralized in MACA towards more decentralized and autonomous institutions. The pattern also reflects the rapid growth of the government in agro-industries through the CBF and the expansion of the regional development corporations.

The sheer establishment of institutions and a corresponding payroll is not sufficient, however, on several grounds to foster agricultural growth. First, although it can't be denied that many such institutions may be necessary to provide an infrastructure in support of agricultural and agro-industrial development, it has to be recognized that many of these institutions lack the budget, the quality personnel, and the firm commitment of the government to enable them to carry out their tasks. In their present form, there exists considerable lack of orientation, inefficiency and enthusiasm to carry out their respective tasks. Political factors often override economic facts and considerations in the decision making process.

Second, the institutions cannot operate effectively in an ambiance of non-policy or inappropriate policy for the development of the agricultural sector. Appropriate policies must be utilized in order to not only properly allocate resources at the farm level, but also to assist the institutions in carrying out their tasks. Unfortunately, in Bolivia, there has been no grand scheme for agricultural policy and the selective agricultural policies have not been well conceived. Most were developed with a political orientation. In the next section, several of these policies are discussed to illustrate this situation.

PUBLIC POLICY FOR AGRICULTURE

In the previous section the substantial increases in government expenditure and public employment in the agricultural sector institutions were noted. These changes undoubtedly represent an attempt by the Bolivian government and foreign donors to expand the institutional base in order to try to foster agricultural growth and development.

Each institution was created and designed to work in a specific problem area. For example, much of CBF's resources have gone to the construction of food processing plants, the development corporations address the problems of regional development and the numerous public institutions treat a multifarious set of activities. Whereas the priorities may be questioned, the establishment of the broader institutional base is certainly a step in the right direction and many of these programs have been successful in their own right.

The overall success of these institutions' programs has been hampered, however, by the absence of a well-integrated set of government goals and policies aimed at agricultural development.[3] This in combination with shortages of highly trained personnel, the failure of the government to provide adequate funding and excessive fragmentation of the institutional structure has limited the success of the various programs in solving Bolivia's agricultural development problems.

This is illustrated by the government's goals for the agricultural sector and the financial allocations to the institutions. First, the goals for the agricultural sector were fundamentally established in the context of non-agricultural sector ends. Balance of payments and inflation considerations were foremost. There was a clear government goal of reducing food imports through import substitutions and later, when it was recognized that Bolivia could compete in certain world markets, to promote exports. There was also the goal of keeping down the prices of wage goods in order to reduce inflationary pressures and to benefit the urban working and middle classes. In addition there was a continued thrust by the government to develop the *Oriente*. This is not to say that there was not considerable rhetoric about the need for developing agriculture and especially the *campesinos*. Yet the type of policy measures adopted and the government expenditures strongly suggest these were words with little content. For economic and political considerations the policies worked for the rapid expansion of commercial agriculture and agribusiness in the *Oriente* and to a much smaller extent in the Mountain Valleys and *Altiplano*.

The budget figures from the previous sections are an indication of the orientation of government policy. As noted previously, over the 1967-1977 period, BAB received 26.8 percent of the agricultural sector budget. This demonstrates the prominent role of government-financed credit. CBF and public institutions received 39.5 and 23.4 percent of the budget respectively, which shows the government's orientation to develop food processing facilities and marketing structures for selected products.

There was no goal for integrated agricultural development neither in terms of a well thought out plan nor in terms of budgeted resources. To be sure efforts were directed to research, extension and marketing but the shortcomings of the institutions mentioned above, in combination with the lack of a centralized and coordinated direction from the government, did not permit them to perform their assigned functions in the scheme of agricultural development. Political considerations played an important role in policy formulation and, as a consequence, policy measured reflected a bias in the favor of the politically powerful commercial farming and agribusiness interests.

Thus, in spite of the rapid development of an institutional structure, the government fundamentally relied on three policy instruments for agricultural growth and political objectives. First, through CBF and some public institutions they developed a capacity for food processing. Second, the government utilized pricing policies for many agricultural products. Depending upon the product these were devised to benefit the producer and/or the consumer. Third, the government utilized control over credit to allocate resources in agriculture. In the following sections of this paper we examine the policies of the latter two instruments in terms of the content of the policy and its impact on the agricultural sector. It will be clear that the policies employed did not benefit a large portion of the Bolivian farmers and as a consequence contributed little to the broad development of the agricultural sector.

Price Policy

In establishing a system of price supports it is argued that in order to provide a producer with sufficient incentive, the support price of a given crop has to be established relative to prices paid for other crops as well as the costs of production.[4] In Bolivia, however, little consideration has been given to these criteria because support prices have been heavily influenced by political factors and have been employed to benefit mainly the urban classes and some large- or medium-size farmers. The following sections on coffee, wheat, sugar and rice pricing policies are illustrative.

Coffee. Bolivian coffee is grown by small farmers in the mountainous subtropical areas of the *Yungas*. The Bolivian Coffee Committee (COBOLCA) was established in 1965 to promote coffee production and control marketing of the product. Little, however, has been done to promote production. There are no special programs to provide techincal assistance, to expand land devoted to coffee nor to improve coffee quality. Rather COBOLCA has been concerned mainly with pricing policies.

Bolivian coffee exports are in good demand. There is also a strong domestic demand because coffee is a mainstay in the Bolivian diet. In order to try to maintain low prices for the domestic consumer, the government has established a two-tier price system, one for exports and another for imports, as well as the use of export quotas to limit the amount going abroad. The result has been that average price of coffee has been below the external price and, therefore, coffee producers have been harmed to the benefit of the domestic consumer. This is illustrated by comparing price indices. In the 1966-1976 period, the percent change in the world market coffee price index was 597 percent, whereas the change in the price index for prices paid to farmers was 244 percent. [5]

The low domestic price for coffee plus export restrictions that are less than those set forth by the International Coffee Agreement have led to an excess demand for coffee in both internal and foreign markets. However, in spite of the demand, the price incentive to the Bolivian farmer has not been sufficient to encourage increases in production. The dearth in public programs to encourage coffee production is another contributing factor.

In order to increase coffee production and producers' incomes, higher prevailing domestic coffee prices should be allowed. However, to date, the philosophy of the government has been that "bread and coffee prices cannot be raised without social consequences." Thus consumers have benefited to the detriment of producers and foreign exchange earnings.

Wheat. Bolivian wheat is mostly grown by small farmers in the Mountain Valley regions of Cochabamba, Chuquisaca, Potosi, and Tarija. By international standards the yields per hectare are low. For example in 1975, the average national yield was 803 kilograms per hectare. The relatively low yields are attributable to the poor quality of land, use of traditional technology, unimproved varieties of seeds and unfavorable climatic conditions. [6] The limited production has led to the need to import considerable amounts of wheat; currently domestic production satisfies only about 20 percent of the national demand.

Another important factor that has limited domestic wheat production has been the government's pricing policy. The Ministry of Industry, Commerce and Tourism fixes wheat prices at the farm, wholesale and retail levels. As mentioned previously, the government's philosophy has been to maintain low prices for bread, and consequently wheat, in order to benefit the working classes and to thus avoid what they perceive to be undesirable social consequences. A result of this policy, however, has been to discourage domestic wheat production, increase imports, and to reduce the income earning potential for the small farmers who grow wheat. A comparison of fixed domestic wheat prices with those of imported Argentine wheat, CIF La Paz, demonstrate this effect.

From 1966-1972 the price of imported Argentine wheat and the fixed price for domestic wheat were comparable with only slight differences. In 1973, however, there was a major change when the price of Argentine wheat rose to 142 pesos per hundredweight compared to a fixed price of 100 pesos for domestic wheat. In 1974 the government raised the fixed price to 190 pesos but Argentine wheat sold for 333 pesos. For the next three years the fixed price remained constant and Argentine wheat sold for as much as 302 pesos. [7]

According to government regulations Bolivian wheat mills are obligated to buy all the domestic wheat when the fixed price is less than the imported price. However, since the early 1970s, when this price structure held, wheat production fell and imports rose it is clear that the domestic fixed price was not a sufficient incentive to encourage production. As in the case of coffee a more realistic price structure in combination with programs of technical assistance should serve to increase wheat production, reduce imports and save foreign exchange.

Sugar. Bolivian sugar cane is grown in the *Oriente* by mostly large- and medium-sized farmers. The Center for Research and Improvement of Sugar Cane (CIMA) and the National Commission for Sugar Cane Studies (CNECA) are responsible for coordinating all aspects relative to sugar production and marketing.

The pricing policy for sugar and sugar cane production is completely different from that for coffee and wheat. The government fixes quotas for the domestic markets, sets domestic prices for sugar and sugar cane and establishes export quotas for sugar mills. For many years the Bolivian retail price has been higher than the world price, which suggests that Bolivian sugar production is not competitive on the world market. For the 1966-1976 period, the percent change in the Bolivian retail price index for sugar was 187 and the percent change in the world sugar price index 186, i.e., the two indices increased at about the same rate. However, over the same period the index of prices paid to cane producers increased 283 percent due to large price increases beginning in 1972.[8] Therefore the price paid to cane growers has been fixed at a level higher than the market equilibrium price. Meanwhile, government quotas have limited production to avoid an excess supply and sugar mills have been forced to export some of their output at lower prices and negative returns. Clearly the domestic consumer has been subsidizing the producer and also sugar exports.[9]

Sugar cane growers appear to have strong political power that they can use to influence government decisions. Each year price negotiation meetings are held with cane producers, government officials and sugar mill representatives. In these meetings the cane producers, most of them large farmers, use political pressure to obtain prices above market levels. Moreover, the government allocates a great deal of resources to sugar production; for example, substantial amounts of credit have been utilized in sugar cane production, marketing and sugar processing.

Sugar pricing policy contrasts with that for coffee and wheat. The small farmers producing coffee and wheat are penalized in favor of consumers, whereas in the sugar cane pricing policy, consumers are subsidizing the inefficient production of large farmers.

Rice. Bolivian rice is also grown in the *Oriente* by small- and medium-sized farmers. In 1972 the government established the Bolivian Rice Enterprise (ENA) to provide more orderly marketing of the crop, to fix farm, wholesale and retail rice prices and to eliminate the middleman in favor of the farmer by buying directly from the farmer at more favorable prices. In practice, however, the latter has not been achieved as ENA regularly buys from middlemen.

Under the pricing policy ENA has built up large excess stocks of rice that cannot be sold on domestic nor foreign markets. Between 1966 and 1976 the average retail price of rice in Bolivia has exceeded what would be the effective price of Brazilian rice delivered to Santa Cruz. This relatively high price has encouraged production, but discouraged domestic consumption and exports. Moreover many middlemen have been able to market rice to the consumer at less than the official price. All of these factors have contributed to excessive ENA stocks and caused serious financial difficulty for the institution. The rice pricing policy has penalized the consumer, [10] benefited the middlemen and has not favored the farmer as was intended.

Credit Policy

Bolivian credit policy and substantial foreign assistance were major factors contributing to the nearly five-fold increase in annual flows of agricultural credit from Bolivian banking institutions over the 1966-1975 period. The Bolivian Agricultural Bank (BAB) has been the major lender, but since 1967 the commercial banks, particularly the government-owned State Bank, have become increasingly important such that by 1975 they accounted for almost 43 percent of the loans to the sector in contrast to their contribution of less than 10 percent in 1967. [11]

The rise in bank lending is in part due to a stronger demand, especially in the *Oriente* where there was a boom in agricultural and livestock production. It was also due to policy factors influencing credit supply. Very important was the increase in domestic and foreign aid resources that were channeled to BAB. Moreover, beginning in 1967 the Bolivian Central Bank imposed requirements on the commercial banks' loan portfolios in order to direct more credit to production activities (construction, industry, mining and agriculture). At present 75 percent of their portfolios must be loans for these purposes. Simultaneously this policy was reinforced by sharp increases in the amount of funds held by the Central Bank designated for refinancing loans made by BAB and commercial banks for agricultural production.

Foreign assistance played a major role in financing agriculture, through major credit programs for BAB and several important refinancing lines for the Central Bank. From 1965-1975 at least 42 percent of bank loans to the sector were estimated to have been financed by international aid institutions. [12]

In spite of the large nominal increases in the amount of agricultural credit the evidence about the use of the credit strongly suggests that there were a number of deficiencies in the policy structure. Several of the more important indicators are briefly discussed.

First, relatively high rates of inflation since 1972 considerably reduced the real value of the amounts loaned. In fact, in 1975 the real value of the total amount loaned was less than in 1973, in spite of an increase in nominal value of about 20 percent over the three years. [13]

Second, most credit was channeled to the *Oriente* with the consequences of seriously impacting on regional and personal income distribution in favor of that region. From 1964 to 1976 almost 79 percent of BAB credit and almost all commercial bank credit went to Santa Cruz, mostly to the benefit of the large- and medium-sized farmers of that region. In sharp contrast the highly populated regions where traditional and small-sized farmers are located received considerably less credit. Fortunately in recent years foreign assistance has been redirected to working with small farmers in these traditional regions. A number of new credit programs have been designed for this purpose.

Third, loan delinquency was very high. By 1975, 47 percent of BAB's portfolio was in arrears mostly due to the heavy delinquency experienced in cotton, soybeans and beef cattle in the *Oriente*. [14] The State Bank also experienced heavy delinquency. A consequence was that the credit institutions lost considerable income and lending capacity, a situation that does not lead to long run financial viability for the institutions. In fact, after 1976, the State Bank decided to virtually eliminate agricultural loans because of these problems.

In summary, Bolivian agricultural credit has been an important element in the government's policy package to develop the sector. It appears, however, that the policy measures employed were designed to mostly benefit the large-farming interests of the *Oriente*. Only since 1975 has the government, with pressure and financing from foreign assistance, made a major effort to finance small farmers.

CONCLUSIONS AND RECOMMENDATIONS

Even though there was a rapid expansion of public institutions between 1967 and 1977, agricultural development has been hampered by the lack of support for these institutions and ill-conceived and inadequate policy measures. Budget support for the institutions has been insufficient and, in most cases, only enough to cover the low salaries of the numerous staff and to pay some limited operating expenses. This has seriously limited the effectiveness of public institutions providing research, extension, marketing and social infrastructure.

In the new institutional structure there has been a trend towards more decentralization, in the sense that more autonomous public institutions are being created, but, at the same time, activities that could be attractive to the private sector are being taken under the control of government public enterprises, such as the agro-industries owned by CBF. Many, however, are inefficiently run. The losses appearing in the income statements of most CBF enterprises are well known in Bolivia.

Decentralization is also occurring at regional levels with the creation of regional development corporations. Whereas this appears to be an appropriate policy two factors warrant comment: (1) the unequal distribution of the budget among regions could cause internal problems and increase regional rivalries if the government does not define criteria for more equitable distribution of resources; and (2) some of the development corporations are undertaking risky investments and operations which could create social costs that worsen the poor economic situation of this country.

The stock of human resources in agriculture needs to be improved. Sectoral development requires more qualified people, higher salaries and some criteria for salary distribution.

Apart from the development of the institutional structure the major policy instruments for the sector have been those of product prices and credit. In both instances these policies have had the effect of enhancing the development of the *Oriente* and its larger commercial farmers to the neglect or even the harm of development in the Mountain Valleys and *Altiplano* and their tradition-oriented small farmers. The urban consumer has benefited at the expense of the small farmer in the cases of coffee and wheat pricing policy but has, in turn, subsidized the farmers of the *Oriente* who produce sugar and rice.

Given that about 60 percent of Bolivia's population is engaged in semi-subsistence farming the allocation of such a large proportion of the government's agricultural resources to the *Oriente* as well as a policy structure that favors the larger farmers of this region would appear to be in error. The government's strategy for agricultural development needs to be carefully examined. It would appear that the following changes would be called for. More emphasis should be given to the private sector to finance the large commercial farmers in order to permit the government to direct its resources towards credit for small farmers. The government's institutional structure should be strengthened to more widely and better serve the small farmer. Pricing policies should be redesigned to encourage small-farmer production and not to favor the urban consumer. Pricing policies designed to support inefficient production of large farmers should be eliminated.

To undertake such changes would require a major commitment by the Bolivian government. Considerably more funding and the upgrading of personnel are required. Moreover, existing policies would have to be modified, a difficult process. However, unless this is done the future for Bolivian agricultural development the large numbers of small farmers is indeed very gloomy.

ENDNOTES FOR CHAPTER XII

1. The first part of the discussion is to a large extent based on E. Boyd Wennergren and Morris D. Whitaker, *The Status of Bolivian Agriculture* (New York: Praeger Publishers, Inc., 1975) and Musgrave Commission, "Report to GOB on Reforma Fiscal en Bolivia", *La política presupuestaria y de gasto*, Vol. II (1977), (Mimeo-graphed.)

2. CNRA, "Diagnóstico de actividades agropecuarias del Consejo Nacional de Reforma Agraria, formulación histórica". Report submitted by CNRA to Mr. Boris Marinovic, Undersecretary of Agricultural Affairs, (La Paz, 1977).

3. Wennergren and Whitaker, op. cit., p. 297.

4. B. Delworth Gardner, *Agricultural Price Policy in Bolivia*. (La Paz: USU Series, No. 8, 1975), p. 61.

5. The figures for the price indexes were calculated from unpublished data available in the Ministerio de Industria, Comercio y Turismo, División de Comercio Interno, La Paz, Bolivia.

6. Ministerio de Agricultura y Asuntos Campesinos, División de Estadísticas, *Estadísticas agropecuarias*, Boletín No. 2. (1961-1975).

7. Unpublished data available in the Ministerio de Industria, Comercio y Turismo, División de Importaciones Expeciales, La Paz, Bolivia.

8. The price index figures were calculated from data available in the *Comisión de estudios de la caña y del azúcar*, La Paz, Bolivia.

9. Gardner, op. cit., p. 46.

10. Ibid., p. 54.

11. Jerry R. Ladman, Ronald L. Tinnermeier, and Isaac Torrico, "Agricultural Credit Flows and Use in Bolivia," Report submitted to USAID/Bolivia (La Paz, March 15, 1977), p. 23.

12. Ibid., p. 63.

13. Ibid., pp. 23 and 36.

14. Ibid., p. 131.

Part Five

Social and Economic Change

Chapter XIII

The Move to the Oriente: Colonization and Environmental Impact

Ray Henkel

INTRODUCTION

One of the principal goals of Bolivian domestic policy in recent years has been the settlement and development of the *Oriente*. [1] Two events have contributed significantly to the formulation of this policy: the Chaco War of 1931-35 and the revolution of 1952. The Chaco War alerted Bolivia to the fact that the sparsely populated *Oriente* could be lost to a foreign power if it were not integrated politically, economically, and socially with the core regions in the highlands. [2] As a means of achieving this integration, the Bolivian government began to construct roads from the main highland centers of Cochabamba and La Paz into the lowlands.

The revolution of 1952 created a number of social and economic problems. The land reform program carried out as an aftermath of the revolution was unable to provide land for every peasant in the highlands, especially in the densely populated Mountain Valley and *Altiplano* regions. [3] Moreover, many of those receiving land found their holdings much too small to support their family. The disruption of traditional tenure relationships and methods of farming also led to a severe decline in food production in the highlands. The ability of the government to offset this decline through the purchase of food items on the world market was greatly restricted by the loss of foreign exchange brought about by economic disruptions caused by the nationalization of the tin industry.

As one means of solving these problems, the Bolivian government began to promote the colonization and agrarian development of the *Oriente* by extending and improving the roads begun in the Chaco War, the construction of processing plants for agricultural products, the development of agricultural experiment stations, and the establishment of government-directed colonization projects. [4] As a result of these efforts some 50,000 families have moved eastward and taken up land in areas undergoing colonization, while numerous others have migrated eastward to work on farms of the colonists or large commercial farms created during the agrarian development process.

The purpose of this paper is to assess the recent colonization efforts of the Bolivian government in the *Oriente*. More specifically the paper will be concerned with a description of the regions undergoing colonization, the nature of the colonization efforts being carried out, the systems of agriculture being created, and the impact of colonization on the environment.

THE AREAS OF COLONIZATION

As shown in Map XIII-1 and in Table XIII-1 the three main areas of colonization in the *Oriente* are the Alto Beni, Chapare, and Santa Cruz regions. Other areas where colonization is occurring to a much lesser extent are the Tarija region near the Argentine border, the Robore-Matun area near the Brazilian border, and the Casarabe-San Borja area of the Beni plains in north central Bolivia.

The Alto Beni Region

The Alto Beni is a subtropical forest-covered land of low hills and narrow valleys lying along the base of the Andes some 220 kilometers northeast of La Paz. Significant migration to this region began in 1958 when a road was completed from Coroico to Caranavi.[5] The completion of this road encouraged a number of peasants to move down from the *Altiplano* and settle in the hills and valleys around Caranavi.[6] Additional settlement occurred when government-directed projects were initiated along the Alto Beni River during the 1960s.[7] There were approximately 17,000 families residing in this area in 1977.[8]

The Alto Beni colonization area is the main source of tropical products for towns, cities, and rural areas of the *Altiplano*. Large quantities of rice, maize, bananas, and citrus are shipped to highland markets while coffee and cacao are produced for the national market and export. Farms are small, averaging eight hectares in size in areas settled by independent farmers and twenty hectares in size in government-directed projects.[9] The major problems of the farmers are soil erosion, soil impoverishment, and insufficient land.[10] Most of the colonists have remained at the subsistence level with annual farm incomes averaging less than 500 dollars per family.[11]

The Chapare Region

The Chapare is a low-lying plain covered by tropical rainforest located about 120 kilometers northeast of the city of Cochabamba. Settlement of the Chapare began in 1920 when General Frederico Román established a colony along the banks of the Chapare River at Todos Santos.[12] The initial colony consisted of some fifty Yuracare Indians, a few soldiers, and five families from the uplands.[13] Migration to the Chapare region increased significantly upon the completion of a road from Cochabamba to Todos Santos in 1940.[14] Further expansion occurred in 1952 when many peasants moved to the area after being freed from their obligations to the large estates in the Cochabamba Valley but were unable to make a living on the small plots provided by the government through land reform.[15] By 1966 the population had increased to 7,300 families.[16] Further colonization was brought about by the initiation of a government-directed project along the Chimore River east of Villa Tunari in 1963 and the construction of a tarmac road from Cochabamba to the Chapare in 1971. By 1977 approximately 10,000 families, mostly Quechua speaking Indians from the Cochabamba Valley, had moved to this region.

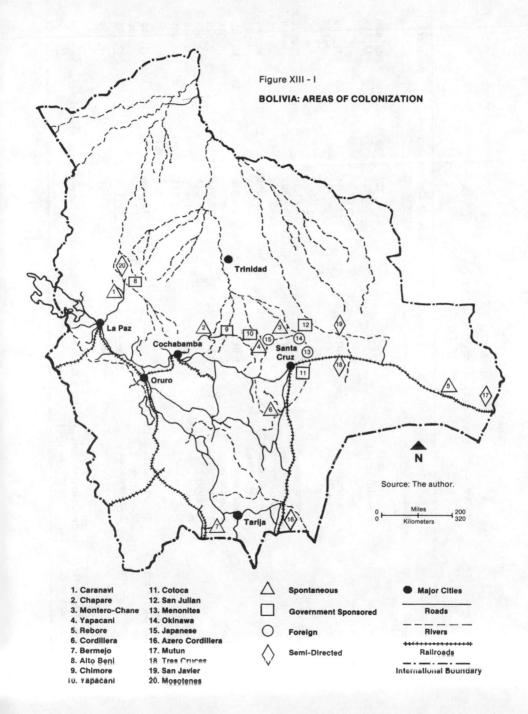

Figure XIII - I

BOLIVIA: AREAS OF COLONIZATION

Source: The author.

1. Caranavi	11. Cotoca
2. Chapare	12. San Julian
3. Montero-Chane	13. Menonites
4. Yapacani	14. Okinawa
5. Rebore	15. Japanese
6. Cordillera	16. Azero Cordillera
7. Bermejo	17. Mutun
8. Alto Beni	18. Tres Cruces
9. Chimore	19. San Javier
10. Yapacani	20. Mosotenes

△ Spontaneous

□ Government Sponsored

○ Foreign

◇ Semi-Directed

● Major Cities

Roads

Rivers

Railroads

International Boundary

TABLE XIII-1

STATISTICAL SUMMARY OF COLONIZATION IN BOLIVIA
AS OF 1977

Areas of Colonization	Type	No. of Families	Size of Concession (Hectares)	Population
Alto Beni Region				
Caranavi	Spontaneous	14,372	144,707	57,480
Alto Beni	Gov-directed	4,565	66,032	18,268
Chapare Region				
Chapare	Spontaneous	7,812	122,051	31,266
Chimore	Gov-directed	1,816	36,120	7,224
Santa Cruz Region				
Yapacani	Spontaneous	2,518	79,580	10,076
Yapacani	Gov-directed	1,986	99,300	7,944
Buen Retiro	Gov-directed	794	39,700	3,176
San Pedro-Chane	Semi-directed	8,887	268,690	35,548
Cotoca	Gov-directed	53	7,650	212
Robore	Spontaneous	2,369	84,950	10,216
Cordillera	Spontaneous	2,689	140,850	10,516
San Julian	Semi-directed	581	29,059	2,324
Mennonites	Foreign	339	44,838	2,954
Okinawans	Foreign	714	81,872	4,714
Japanese	Foreign	371	35,288	1,451
Other Regions				
Casarabe-San Borja	Spontaneous	860	13,940	3,440
Tarija	Spontaneous	674	13,480	2,696
Uncontrolled Areas	Spontaneous	11,000	110,000	40,000
Totals		62,000	1,418,108	230,105

Source: Instituto Nacional de Colonización, *Resumen de colonias y familias asentadas en zonas de colonización*, 31 octubre 1977 (La Paz: 1977), p. 1.

The settlers of the Chapare produce large quantities of rice, bananas, citrus, and coca leaves for sale in the Cochabamba Valley. Coca is the main cash crop with over 2,000,000 kilos of leaves being sold throughout Bolivia each year.[17] Because of increasing quantities of coca leaves being used for the illegal manufacture of the narcotic cocaine, the Bolivian government, with assistance from the United States Agency for International Development (AID), has endeavored to find crop substitutions. However, the extremely high annual rainfall of over 4,000 mm has greatly restricted the possibilities for producing other cash crops.

The main problem of the Chapare has been the rapid decline in soil fertility due to erosion and leaching. Soil impoverishment has led to widespread land abandonment in the older settled areas with many farmers returning to the highlands or moving to the constantly expanding edge of the frontier to take up new land.[18]

The Santa Cruz Region

The Santa Cruz region is located about 500 kilometers east of the city of Cochabamba around the town of Santa Cruz. This region has considerably more physical diversity than the Chapare and Alto Beni regions and offers better possibilities for agriculture. Areas to the south and east of Santa Cruz receive 500 to 700 mm of rainfall each year, have sandy soils, and are covered by a scrub forest. In contrast, the areas to the north and northwest receive 1,500 to 2,200 mm of rainfall each year, have alluvial soils of recent origin and tropical forest vegetation.[19]

Santa Cruz was largely isolated from highland Bolivia until the primitive road connecting it to Cochabamba was widened and paved during the early 1950s. The completion of this project combined with heavy investments by the Bolivian Development Corporation (CBF) in agricultural processing plants, experiment stations, and other infrastructure provided the stimulus for rapid agrarian development while the construction of roads northward from Montero opened vast areas of virgin forest to settlement.[20]

The colonization that followed was quite diverse. Spontaneous colonists occupied land along the road leading to Cochabamba west of Santa Cruz. Mennonites from Paraguay and Canada settled on lands purchased from the Bolivian Cotton Corporation to the east and south of Santa Cruz. The government-directed projects of Huaytu, Cuatro Ojitos, and Aroma were initiated in the forested area to the north and northwest of Montero. Toward the northeast, small groups of spontaneous settlers from the highlands and immigrants from Okinawa established themselves along the banks of the Rio Grande, while immigrants from Japan and families from the highlands formed colonies northwest of Santa Cruz along the Yapacani River.[21]

Much of the internal migration, most of the directed resettlement, and all of the foreign colonization in Bolivia since 1954, has taken place around Santa Cruz. This migration largely reflects the greater potential for agriculture of this area in comparison to the Alto Beni and the Chapare. It also reflects the favored position this region was given with respect to government investments in infrastructure to support agriculture.[22] By 1977, approximately 20,000 highland families and 1,500 foreign immigrants had settled in the Santa Cruz region. Many other immigrants from the highlands were working as laborers on large commercial farms devoted to the production of sugar cane and cotton or engaged in commercial and other activities in the rapidly expanding urban centers of Santa Cruz, Warnes, and Montero.[23]

THE FORMS OF COLONIZATION

Four kinds of colonization exist in the Bolivian *Oriente*. These are spontaneous, government-directed, semi-directed, and foreign. Each of these was important during a specific time period. Prior to 1955, most of the colonization was of a spontaneous nature. Government-directed and foreign projects tended to dominate between 1955 and 1970; while semi-directed colonization has become the most common form since 1970.

Spontaneous Colonization

Spontaneous colonization occurs when settlers move to the frontier with little or no assistance from the government. This form of colonization has been most common in the Chapare around the town of Villa Tunari and in the Alto Beni around the town of Caranavi. It has been of less significance in Santa Cruz due to the distance of this area from centers of highland Indian populations and because of the widespread resentment of the *Cambas*, or persons from Santa Cruz, to the incursions of the *Kollas*, or the highland Indians. [24]

The procedure for establishing spontaneous colonies is rather simple. Most are begun by a small group of adventurous people from a single highland community who move eastward and occupy land on the tropical frontier. They are soon joined by friends and relatives. Nearly all of the colonists know someone in the settlement before arriving and they often live with that person while their house is constructed, land is cleared and crops are planted. [25] The new settler will help plant and harvest the crops of his friend or relative who in turn teaches him the techniques of farming in the tropics and provides him with room and board.

Spontaneous settlements usually evolve along navigable rivers or along roads built into the forest to extract timber. Lots are generally rectangular, but with an elongated depth and a narrow frontage on the road or stream. [26] The settlers clear the land, build their homes, and plant their crops with no financial or technical assistance other than possibly some road building and road improvement carried out by the government. [27] *Sindicatos*, self-governing peasant unions, are organized to voice their demands and to serve as an administrative unit for the colony. [28] Administered by a secretary and a committee, composed of six to eight members who are elected annually by and from its membership, the *sindicato* collects a monthly tax from each colonist and some labor for community improvement projects. The *sindicato* also petitions the government for land and allots parcels to new members who are promised titles after residing on and utilizing the parcel for two years. Few titles are ever granted, however, and conflicts over landownership are common, especially in those *sindicatos* where surveys were never made to establish property boundaries. [29] The lack of capital, absence of technical advice, poor connections to highland markets, and limited knowledge of the tropical environment have greatly hindered productivity in the spontaneous settlements. [30] Most farmers are never able to lift themselves above the subsistence level. The greater part of them farm the land for only a few years and then move on as the soil becomes impoverished. [31]

Government-Directed Colonization

The limited number of highland families moving eastward to areas of spontaneous settlement during the early part of the 1950s and the low productivity of these settlements caused the Bolivian government to assume that colonization of the lowlands could best be achieved by government-directed colonization. [32] The first attempt at government-directed colonization occurred in 1955 at Cotoca near Santa Cruz. Here CBF, in cooperation with the Andean Mission of the United Nations, attempted to settle thirty-two Quechua families from the *Altiplano* near Potosí. Most of these people soon abandoned the project in spite of extensive financial and technical assistance. [33] The Cotoca experiment was followed by the efforts of the Bolivian Army and CBF to assist colonists settling in the Cuatro Ojitos, Huatu, and Aroma settlements established in the forests north of Montero in 1957. [34] These settlements were also plagued by a high rate of abandonment. The causes most often given for abandonment were the inability of the colonists to adjust to the tropical environment; outbreaks of diseases, especially yellow fever; distance of the settlements from other centers of Quechua population; lack of knowledge of farming practices suitable for the tropics; and absence of social amenities. [35]

The next efforts at government-directed colonization came in 1961 when CBF, with the assistance of AID, settled 600 families from the *Altiplano* in a project in the Alto Beni. [36] Although the costs were high, averaging 2,500 dollars per family, the abandonment rate was low. [37] The favorable results obtained here led to the beginnings in 1963 of the Alto Beni, Chimore, and Yapacani projects whereby 8,000 colonists were to be settled by CBF in the lowlands over a ten-year period. [38] The land chosen for these projects was located in areas immediately adjacent to existing areas of spontaneous colonization. It was assumed by locating the directed projects near these areas that: (a) incoming settlers would find work on farms in the spontaneous areas, (b) seed and plants could be obtained from these areas, and (c) the cost of extending roads from the spontaneous settlements to the directed projects would not be excessive.

A loan of nine million dollars was obtained from the Inter-American Development Bank (IDB) to finance the program. The money was to be used to construct roads to and within the projects, to purchase plants, seed and tools for the colonists, to survey the land, to provide schools and other facilities, and to provide administrative and technical assistance. [39] In spite of the extensive assistance provided, few colonists were willing to enter these projects. The lack of willing applicants was attributed to the reluctance of highland families to move to the lowlands, the absence of information about the program in the highlands, and most of all, the unwillingness of prospective settlers to assume the estimated financial obligation of 1,200 dollars associated with settling in these projects. [40] Few were willing to assume financial obligations of this extent when they could settle in a nearby spontaneous colonization area without incurring any costs.

These projects never achieved the success expected of them. The abandonment rate among the colonists was extremely high, averaging 42 percent during the initial five years of their existence. [41] The main causes of abandonment were poor access roads to highland markets, problems of disease and insects, the psychological feelings of loneliness associated with life on the remote frontier, and the hard work involved in carving a farm out of the forest. [42] In addition, per family costs of settlement were very high averaging 1,831 dollars for the Alto Beni project, 1,970 dollars for the Chimore project, and 1,301 dollars for the Yapacani project. [43] Furthermore, the expectations that productive systems of agriculture could be readily developed never materialized. Most of the colonists remained at the subsistence level, unable to sell the products they produced because of poor transportation connections to highland markets. Moreover, many were unable to compete for those markets with farmers from the spontaneous zones who possessed more skill and experience in tropical agriculture. [44]

Semi-Directed Colonization

The limited success and high cost of the government-directed projects caused Bolivia to turn to a semi-directed program of colonization during the 1970s. The semi-directed program tended to combine the most desirable elements of both the spontaneous and government-directed colonization. Efforts were made to give direction to and exercise control over areas undergoing spontaneous colonization. [45] Under these programs the government provides the necessary infrastructure such as roads, credit, lot delimitation, and technical advice but does not provide funds for food, tools, seed, and plants. Also, there is no restriction on the kinds and amounts of crops to be planted. The settlement of groups of people, rather than individuals, is encouraged. It is assumed that settlement of homogeneous cultural groups from upland villages will result in the transfer of cultural institutions and be conducive to greater cooperation among the colonists. [46]

A varied pattern of farm size has also been adopted. Small plots of the most desirable lands located near transportation routes are given to small-scale farmers while larger grants in more remote areas are given to colonists with the capability of carrying out large-scale, commercial agriculture. It is assumed that given the necessary technical advice, credit, and access to markets, the small farmer would be able to compete successfully with the large-scale, commercial farmer. Much more concern is also given to ecological conditions. Areas deemed not suitable for agriculture are reserved for forestry or livestock ranching. The San Julian project northwest of Montero and the Chane-Piray project north of Montero are examples of semi-directed colonization now in progress. The San Julian project is financed with funds from AID while the Chane-Piray project is being developed with government funds.

Foreign Colonization

During the 1950s several hundred Japanese, Okinawan and Mennonite families were permitted to settle in the Santa Cruz region. It was assumed that these immigrants would not only contribute to the food supply of the nation but also bring agricultural skills that could be readily transferred to Bolivian farmers. The Okinawans and Japanese came to Bolivia under an agreement between Japan, Bolivia, and the United States. [47] The Bolivian government agreed to accept Japanese and Okinawan families, which were displaced from their land by American airbase construction. The first contingent of Japanese arrived in 1953 and were settled in the colony of San Juan northwest of Montero. [48] These were soon joined by others and by 1966 some 300 families had immigrated to Bolivia. [49] There has been very little Japanese immigration since 1966 due to restrictions imposed by the Bolivian government. [50] The first group of Okinawans, composed of 269 families, arrived in 1954. These were joined by others and the colony grew to 628 families by 1965. Since that time there has been a slight decrease in the population as some families have moved to towns in Bolivia while others have moved to Argentina and Brazil.

The Mennonite migrations to Bolivia occurred in stages. The first group arrived from Paraguay in 1954. [51] These were followed by other groups from Paraguay, Canada, and Mexico. The Mennonites migrated to Bolivia to escape religious persecution and to practice their way of life without governmental interference.

The total number of foreign immigrants entering the *Oriente* has been small. There were only 339 Mennonite, 714 Okinawan, and 371

Japanese families residing in the lowlands in 1977. Although small in numbers, they have established productive farming systems and contributed significantly to the food supply of Bolivia. The Okinawans and Japanese produce large quantities of rice, wheat, and poultry for the Bolivian market while the Mennonites produce large quantities of livestock, poultry, and dairy products. [52]

Comparative Analysis of Types of Colonization

A comparative analysis of the different forms of colonization in Table XIII-2 shows that the foreign colonies have achieved the greatest degree of economic viability. The higher degree of prosperity achieved by these colonists has been attributed to the greater amount of capital and technical assistance available to them in the settlement process, their skill in organizing productive systems of agriculture, the larger size of their holdings, the high degree of cooperation within each group, and their skill in marketing their products. [53] The limited viability of the spontaneous colonies has been attributed to lack of capital, absence of technical assistance, poor access roads, high cost of transportation, and insufficient land. [54] The lack of prosperity among colonists settling in the government-directed projects can be attributed to poor access roads, poor planning, the absence of capital, and excessive control exercised over the activities of the colonists. [55] Although the income levels of settlers in the lowlands appear to be rather low, they are well above the average income of peasant farmers in the highlands. [56]

TABLE XIII-2

COMPARISON OF DIFFERENT FORMS OF COLONIZATION

	Average Farm Size (Hectares)	Average Land in Cultivation (Hectares)	Percent Abandoning Colony (Percent)	Average Annual Income (Dollars)	Average Income per Hectare Cultivated (Dollars)
Foreign					
Okinawan	50	22	5	2,960.00	134.50
Japanese	50	18	6	2,280.00	126.60
Mennonites	40	16	2	1,975.00	122.20
Spontaneous					
Chapare	10	6	16	660.00	110.00
Caranavi	8	4	12	310.00	77.50
Govt.-directed					
Alto Beni	20	4	52	310.00	77.50
Chimore	20	7	46	405.00	58.00
Yapacani	30	6	32	330.00	55.00
Semi-directed					
Chane-Piray	30	12	8	1,026.00	85.50

Source: Hernán Zeballos-Hurtado, "From the Upland to the Lowlands" (unpublished Ph.D. dissertation, University of Wisconsin, 1975), pp. 60, 63, and 88; and Bolivia, Instituto Nacional de Colonización, *Proyecto de colonización*, p. 33.

THE STAGES OF AGRARIAN DEVELOPMENT

All settlements in the *Oriente* appear to undergo similar stages of agrarian development regardless of their form of integration. These are: (a) a pioneer stage, (b) a commercialization stage, (c) an abandonment and consolidation stage, and (d) a revitalization stage.

The Pioneering Stage

During this stage the settlers are concerned primarily with occupying the land and bringing it into production. The forest is cleared, the vegetation burned, crops are planted, and a house is constructed. Agriculture is primarily of the subsistence type with rice, maize, manioc, and bananas being the principal crops. The farmer derives what little income he receives from the sale of small quantities of rice or from work on farms of colonists who are already established in the region. The system of agriculture is one of "shifting cultivation." Two or three hectares of virgin forest are cleared, farmed for a year or two, and then abandoned with a new area being cleared from the forest. Such a system is ecologically sound in that it permits the soil to be rejuvenated, restricts significantly the build up of insect and disease infestations, and restricts the loss of soil fertility by erosion and leaching. However, it does not generate a high level of productivity and can be highly destructive if areas are farmed too frequently to permit the soil to recover. During this stage of development there is much sharing of labor among the settlers who appreciate each others company as a means of alleviating the deep feelings of loneliness and isolation associated with life on the frontier. [57]

The Commercialization Stage

The commercialization stage begins with the attainment of access to markets through the construction or improvement of transport linkages. There is no definite time period when this will occur, but usually a road materializes within 5 to 10 years due to the insistent demands of the settlers. [58] In those areas where roads have been constructed prior to settlement, commercialization begins almost immediately with the only delay being the time required to bring the farm into production. The accessibility to markets stimulates the farmer to bring into production as much of his land that his access to labor will permit. [59] The remaining areas of virgin forest are quickly cleared and usually placed into rice production while other areas of the farm are most often devoted to the cultivation of bananas, maize, citrus, coca, sugar cane, or soybeans. [60] Since the land most farmers have available for cultivation is limited due to the small size of their holdings, they usually resort to a "short fallow" system of shifting cultivation which soon leads to a rapid decline in soil fertility. [61]

The Abandonment and Consolidation Stage

The decline in soil fertility combined with an increase in plant diseases, insects, and weed invasions results in lower yields. At the same time that yields are declining, labor requirements to keep the fields free of weeds are increasing. Faced with this situation, many colonists abandon their land and move inland in search of more fertile areas of virgin forest. [62] Others remain permitting the greater part of their farms to revert to fallow since the return in yields with respect to labor expended is very low. In those areas where continuous burning of the vegetation has created savanna grasslands, some farmers sell their holdings to cattlemen entering the area or to neighbors with sufficient capital to initiate livestock operations. [63] The land remains devoted to livestock production, or at the subsistence level of crop production, until market demand for products increases to such an extent that it cannot be supplied by bringing new land into production. [64] The higher transportation costs associated with the increasing distance of new land settlements on the frontier may also provide the stimulus for the revitalization of older, farmed-out areas. [65]

The Revitalization Stage

Revitalization generally requires considerable inputs of capital, fossil fuels, chemical fertilizers, insecticides, improved varieties of plants and labor-saving machinery or combinations of these. Since these items are not readily accessible to the ordinary peasant farmer, revitalization is usually carried out by large-scale commercial farmers or agro-corporations. This has been the case in the Santa Cruz region where large-scale commercial farming devoted to the production of sugar cane and cotton has developed on lands formerly occupied by subsistence farmers or cattle ranchers. [66] An exception may be occurring in the Alto Beni region where the Bolivian government has introduced high-yielding varieties of coffee and cacao. [67] It appears that this area may undergo an economic resurgence based on a change from field crops to tree crops. [68] The constraints imposed by the physical environment, especially excessive rainfall, have greatly restricted the revitalization of the old farmed-out areas in the Chapare. However, the continued strong demand for coca leaves for internal consumption and the illegal manufacture of cocaine assures some degree of prosperity for the farmers living in this region. [69]

ENVIRONMENTAL IMPACT

Colonization has had a significant impact on the environment. Removal of the forest has led to severe problems of soil erosion, seasonal flooding, loss of wildlife habitat, and destruction of genetic material of significant scientific value.

Erosion, Sedimentation, and Flooding

Soil erosion, resulting from land clearing, is particularly severe in the foothill zone at the base of the Andes in the Chapare and Alto Beni. The clearing of steep slopes in these regions has led to numerous landslides. The resulting debris from these slides is often deposited in rivers causing huge dike-like impoundments. When the dikes break, high walls of water known as *turbios* move rapidly downstream destroying everything in their path. Such a *turbio* destroyed the old settlement of Todos Santos on the banks of the Chapare River in 1940, while another turbio destroyed the bridge being built across the Yapacani River in 1967. [70] The *turbio* on the Chapare also resulted in a change in the course of the river which left the settlement of Todos Santos isolated. Most of the colonists abandoned this area and moved elsewhere as a result of the isolation.

The increase in volume and rapidity of run-off and the resulting sheet erosion causes streams to become clogged with silt and overflow their banks. Widespread flooding also occurs because tributary streams cannot discharge their load into the main channels that have experienced a rise in base level and volume of water being carried. Other changes brought about by the clearing and cultivation of the land include a rapid drying out of the soil and a drop in the water table during periods of low rainfall. Wind erosion has also become a major problem in the Santa Cruz region. Large dust storms now form during the dry season and sweep across the barren plains causing severe discomfort for man and beast. The loss of soil from wind erosion is most severe in the Mennonite and Okinawan colonies to the east and northeast of Santa Cruz. There is a definite need for government policy that would prevent or greatly reduce the problems created by wind and water erosion in the colonization areas. Ultimately, some consideration will have to be given to the construction of flood control systems since this represents the only effective solution to seasonal flooding in the colonization areas.

Changes in the Soil

During the clearing and burning process much of the nitrogen, phosphorus, and organic matter that is stored in the natural vegetation is lost. [71] These losses, however, are partially offset by nutrients added by the accumulation of ash from the fires, the most important being phosphate. The accumulation of phosphate in the ashes at the surface level results in a significant rise in the pH factor and a marked acceleration of the rate of decomposition of organic matter. This causes alterations in the biological processes such as nitrogen fixation, nitrification, and *mycorrhizae* development. In the mineralization of the humus that follows, the vital nutrients of nitrogen, phosphorus, and sulphur are released. These are then taken up by the plants or lost through leaching.

Chemical changes have a minor effect on the loss of soil fertility in comparison to erosion, leaching, and cropping. Once the soil is exposed to high rainfall, there is much loss of nutrients through erosion and leaching. The fine soil material and much of the rich top soil is removed. Once this happens, there is always the danger that lateritic material will be drawn to the surface causing a hard crust to form.

Virtually all crops grown in the colonized areas--such as rice, maize, and bananas--are heavy users of nutrients. There has been no effort to plant nitrogen-fixing legumes on fallow land to restore soil fertility as well as to protect against erosion and leaching. The result is a rapid loss in soil nutrients. Crop yields decline by as much as one-third to one-half during the first three years the land is in cultivation. [72] Most land can be cultivated only three to five years without letting it return to fallow. The rapid decline in soil fertility resulting from short-fallow cropping systems must be regarded as the primary cause of land abandonment in the colonization zones.

Wildlife

The destruction of the forest and the resultant vegetation change has had a devastating effect upon wildlife populations. [73] Few original tropical forest species--be they reptiles, birds, or other animals--have been able to survive the changes created in their habitat.

Many animal species such as the tapir, manatee, deer, capibara, wild turkeys, and peccary are eliminated by settlers hunting for food. Other species that have been hunted for their hides, such as the jaguar and caiman, have become virtually extinct. Hunting has also eliminated geese and ducks from the rivers. Game is seldom seen near the older settlements. Some species of fish and turtles have also disappeared from the rivers. In contrast, certain undesirable rodents that feed off crops, such as the jochi and large cave rats, have increased.

Insects

Significant changes have occurred in insect populations resulting from the breakup of predator-prey relationships. Ant populations appear to have increased while mosquitoes, sand flies, and tick populations have tended to decline. Perhaps the most significant change affecting man has been an increase in the population of leaf cutter ants which are highly destructive to crops.

Climatic Change

There is no way at present to determine what climatic changes are occurring as a result of land clearing in the Bolivian *Oriente*. No long-term weather observations are available that could be utilized to support or refute theories of climatic change. It is known; however, that where extensive deforestation has taken place in tropical areas of West Africa, the results have been increasing aridity and desertification. [74] There is some evidence of increasing aridity in the Santa Cruz region as evidenced by the greater frequency and intensity of dust storms. There is also speculation that the clearing of vast areas of virgin forest in Bolivia and elsewhere in the Amazon Basin of Latin America will dramatically alter climatic patterns over vast areas. However, there is no basic agreement among scientists as to what these alterations will be. Some common assumptions are that there will be a decrease in rainfall, an increase in temperature, and a decrease in oxygen. [75]

Genetic Material

Perhaps one of the significant losses brought about by colonization is that of genetic material. There is a tremendous diversity of life forms in the tropical forests of the *Oriente*. Many species, especially of flora and insects, have not yet been identified. With the present rate of destruction of tropical forest here and elsewhere in the Amazon Basin, there is the significant danger of extinction of thousands of species. Their extinction will be a significant loss to science. Much of what we know about the evolution of plants and animals was learned by naturalists working in tropical forests. If these forests are destroyed, along with the species that inhabit them, the loss to the scientific community will be incalculable.

Aesthetic Values

The aesthetic loss is particularly evident to anyone who has seen the extensive areas of tropical forest prior to their being destroyed by man. Regardless of how picturesque a landscape of cultivated fields and open savannas may be, it does not have the same pleasing qualities to man as the original varied and complex tropical forest. The basic tendency, however, since the development of civilization, has been for man to alter the environment to satisfy his needs. The diversity that exists in the natural landscape is constantly replaced with a limited number of species of plants and animals. The basic reasoning behind this is that man can manipulate this limited number to more effectively produce the food he needs. Therefore, regardless of its aesthetic qualities and inherent genetic value, the natural landscape of the Bolivian *Oriente* will be transformed into a man-made one. The short-term effect will result in an increase in available food supply. One can only ponder what the long-term effect will be.

CONCLUSIONS

Migration and Integration

More than a half million people have migrated to the *Oriente* from the Bolivian highlands since the 1952 revolution. It is estimated that immigration to Argentina and other countries has been of equal significance. This migration to the *Oriente* and other countries has alleviated some of the pressures of population growth in the highlands, but natural increases in population in the highlands have kept continual pressures on the resource base in these parts of the country.[76] Rural-urban migration in the highlands has been of far greater magnitude and has created a number of urban-related problems in this part of the country.[77] Therefore, colonization of the *Oriente* must be viewed as only one alternative as a means of alleviating population pressure in the highlands and further solutions to this problem must be sought elsewhere.

The colonization of the eastern lowlands since the early 1950s has contributed significantly to the social, political, and economic integration of the country. Prior to 1954, much of the trade, commerce, and other activities of the *Oriente* were directed toward Brazil, Paraguay, and Argentina. The construction of roads into the lowlands and the considerable investment of the Bolivian government in colonization and agrarian development have contributed to stronger economic ties between the lowlands and the highlands. Colonization has also contributed significantly to the integration of the highland *Kolla* and lowland *Camba* cultures. The entry of highland Indians and *mestizos* into the lowlands has modified significantly the ethnic and cultural composition of the *Oriente*. The increased contacts between the upland *Kollas* and lowland *Cambas* have led to greater appreciation and understanding of each other's culture and has resulted in a lessening of the social and political tensions that have long existed between these different cultural groups.

Increased Food Production

Colonization resulted in significant increases in the food supply for Bolivia. The colonists have been most successful in the production of rice, bananas, manioc, citrus, maize, coffee, cacao, and sugar. The abundance and low cost of these products has resulted in dietary changes among the population of the uplands. Rice, bananas, manioc, and a variety of tropical fruits have now become common staples in the diets of many of the people of the uplands. Rice is perhaps the most important crop produced in the settlements. It has assumed considerable more importance as a food item and serves as a valuable substitute or supplement to the traditional mainstays of wheat and potatoes in the Bolivian diet. Rice production increased from 14,925 metric tons in 1955 to 84,000 metric tons in 1974.[78] Approximately 83 percent of the rice produced in Bolivia comes from the areas of colonization.[79]

Efforts to settle and develop the *Oriente* have also led to a reduction in agricultural imports and an expansion of agricultural exports with resultant increases in foreign exchange on these accounts. The decision to settle highland Indians in the Santa Cruz region indirectly led to an increase in sugar cane, cotton, and soybean production. The land reform law of 1953 created fears of land invasion and subsequent expropriation among the large land owners in the area. Many of them began to convert their idle holdings to the production of sugar cane and cotton in order that they would qualify as agricultural enterprises and not be expropriated. The incentives provided by the MNR to diversify the economy and promote the development of agriculture by building roads and constructing large sugar cane mills in the Santa Cruz region also motivated large landowners to engage in commercial production of this crop. The result was that domestic sugar output increased from 4,500 metric tons in 1954 to 1,400,373 metric tons in 1972.[80] The increase in sugar production not only supplied the domestic market but led to significant exports. In 1976 Bolivia exported over 19 million dollars worth of sugar.[81] Further investment in infrastructure to support agriculture also facilitated the production of cotton and soybeans; two crops that were not cultivated commercially in Bolivia prior to the land reform. Domestic cotton requirements were satisfied by 1970, and since that time a significant surplus has been exported. Cotton exports amounted to 17,800,000 dollars in 1976 and were expected to increase in the future.[82]

The recent increase in cotton production attracted a number of vegetable oil and seed concentrate manufacturers to Santa Cruz. This has added valuable products to the domestic market and provided additional agricultural exports. Approximately one million dollars of cotton seed and seed by-products were exported from the Santa Cruz region during 1975.[83] As a response to the construction of seed processing plants and an oil mill, Japanese settlers in the colony of San Juan began to plant soybeans on a commercial scale. Their example was soon followed by a number of other farmers in the region. As a result, Bolivia is rapidly moving toward self-sufficiency in vegetable oils. The construction of sugar refineries, cotton gins, oil mills, rice mills, saw mills, and a petroleum refinery to process the oil from nearby deposits has contributed to Santa Cruz becoming the most rapidly growing industrial center in Bolivia.

Continued Poverty

Although colonization and agrarian development in the *Oriente* has provided large quantities of low-cost food for the upland populations and reduced foreign exchange expenditures, it has not brought prosperity for most of the settlers. A number of factors have contributed to the low level of economic achievement. Among these have been the small size of the farms, the poor quality of the road network, the inadequate marketing structures, the limited market for the products produced, the high cost and limited availability of technological inputs, and the restrictions imposed by the tropical environment.

The small size of the holdings has greatly restricted the creation of viable systems of commercial agriculture in many colonies. The average size of the farms **in** most spontaneous settlements is ten hectares while farm size averages twenty hectares in the government-directed projects. This is insufficient land to establish either viable systems of agriculture, based on ecologically sound long-fallow methods of shifting cultivation, or more intensive agriculture based on the use of fossil fuels, labor-saving machinery, and other technological inputs. It is only in the Okinawan, Japanese, and Mennonite colonies, where most farms average fifty hectares or more, that sufficient land exists for the creation of viable systems of commercial agriculture. The size of land grants should be increased in future colonization projects to fifty or more hectares if commercial agriculture is to be a desired goal of colonization efforts.

Roads and inadequate markets, perhaps more than any other factors, have hindered production in most of the settlements. Most roads are impassable during the long wet season and are in poor repair during the short dry season. Even when bananas, rice, citrus, manioc, and other crops are shipped to the market, they are often in over supply and must be sold at depressed prices.

Some Solutions

One solution would be to place more emphasis on export crops even though market potentials are somewhat limited by the interior location of Bolivia, poor transportation linkages to neighboring countries and to ocean ports, poorly organized marketing structures, and an often limited demand on foreign markets for the products that could be produced. The increasing amounts of coffee, cacao, cotton and sugar that have been sold on the international market indicate that these restrictions can be overcome and that possibilities exist for increasing agricultural exports. The advantages that Bolivia possesses that could offset some of these restrictions are abundant land resources, an expanding agricultural labor force, and a low internal market demand which results in a surplus of agricultural products.

A concentrated effort needs to be made to integrate the colonists, most of whom are small-scale subsistence farmers, into the export process. Agricultural exports to date, with the exception of cacao, have been produced by large-scale commercial farmers and agro-corporations in Santa Cruz. The ordinary colonist cannot compete with these people because of the small size of his holdings; his limited access to capital, credit, and technological inputs; and his undeveloped entrepreneurial abilities. Many of the benefits of government investment in agriculture in the *Oriente* have been derived by large-scale commercial farmers rather than the colonists. There is a definite need to restructure government investment in agriculture in such a way that the colonists and small farmers will benefit if they are to survive. The moderate success achieved by the Bolivian government in its efforts to introduce cacao into the Alto Beni settlements as an export crop indicates that there are possibilities for developing tree crop exports from the colonization areas. The advantages of emphasizing tree crop cultivation would be that it is an ecologically sound system of agriculture for regions of high rainfall, it can be carried out on small farms, and would not place the colonist in competition for foreign markets with the large-scale commercial farmer whose emphasis has been on sugar cane, cotton, and soybean production.

While many crops are being overproduced and cannot be sold on either the domestic or export market, Bolivia continues to import considerable quantities of vegetable oils and wheat each year. In an effort to reduce dependence on foreign sources of wheat, Bolivia has conducted experiments designed to adapt selected varieties of wheat to the tropical conditions in an area north of Santa Cruz. These experiments show

promise but as yet have not yielded significant results. Other possibilities for producing wheat in the *Oriente* lie in the development of the
Abapo-Izozog irrigation project in the dry Chaco region to the south of
Santa Cruz. It has been argued for a number of years that both wheat
and vegetable oils could be produced here and that government investments should be directed toward this project rather than the creation of
more colonization projects in humid tropical regions. [84]   An increase in
soybean production in Santa Cruz and the introduction and adaptation of
African oil palm varieties in the Chapare and Alto Beni offer other possibilities for increasing vegetable oil production.

There is a definite need for a regional assessment of agriculture in
the *Oriente*. At present, the three regions of colonization are competing
with each other. Effort needs to be directed toward ascertaining the
types and kinds of agriculture systems that can best be created in each
of these regions in accordance with market opportunities and the constraints imposed by the natural environment. One of the main deficiencies of colonization efforts in the *Oriente* is that there has been little
effort directed toward regional planning. Each project has been designed
and carried out independently with little consideration given to how it
fits into the total development of the *Oriente*.

Impact on the Environment

One of the most devastating aspects of colonization has been its impact on the tropical environment. The tropical forest has been destroyed
at an alarming rate. The agricultural systems replacing the forest have
not been stable and have generated a low rate of return to the farmers.
Most have also resulted in the destruction of valuable soil, vegetation,
and wildlife resources. There is a pressing need for establishing sound
conservation and land use practices in the colonization areas. There are
a number of ways the present situation could be improved. Detailed
land use capability studies need to be carried out prior to settlement.
All lands deemed not suitable for agriculture should be placed in permanent forest reserves. Tree crop cultivation should be encouraged in
the Chapare, Alto Beni, and those areas of high rainfall northwest of
Santa Cruz where the dangers of soil erosion and leaching make field
crop cultivation inadvisable. In the semi-arid regions to the east and
northeast of Santa Cruz, livestock ranching and dry farming methods
should be encouraged as a means of reducing wind erosion. It is only
through the initiation of land use practices that are compatible with the
environment that more permanent forms of agriculture can be created in
the settlements.

Future Prospects

The relentless movement to the *Oriente* will undoubtedly continue.
Road building into new areas will continue to be the key to opening new
lands for settlement and development. Priority in government road construction in the *Oriente* in the future will likely be directed toward connecting the Beni and Pando regions to highland Bolivia. Since colonization is inevitably tied to road construction, the areas most likely subject
to settlement in the future are those lying along the path of the proposed
routes from the Alto Beni and Santa Cruz regions to the Beni and Pando
areas of northern Bolivia. Other areas that will probably receive increased attention are the tropical forests lying along the base of the
Andes between the Chapare and Alto Beni and extending north of the

Alto Beni to the Pando. One would expect a number of changes in government policy regarding the development based on the experience gained in developing other areas. There will most likely be an increased emphasis on semi-directed colonization projects in that they offer the opportunity for government control of the development process while utilizing the motivational forces inherent in spontaneous colonization. Since the small size of the holdings was found to be one of the most significant deterrents to commercialization of agriculture and the creation of viable land use systems, the size of the grants is likely to increase. There probably will be a tendency to allocate land in accordance with the ability of the grantee to utilize it in a productive manner. Whereas land has been granted in the past only to landless peasants, grants in the future are more likely to be made to individuals with the experience and capability of becoming productive commercial farmers. Future colonization efforts will probably be directed more toward obtaining economic rather than social goals. If this be the case, a much greater emphasis will be placed on creating commercial systems of agriculture in the *Oriente* rather than settling peasants in the *Oriente* as a means of alleviating social and economic problems in the highlands. Efforts will undoubtedly be made to increase agricultural exports by expanding tree crop cultivation in the Chapare and Alto Beni and increasing soybean, cotton, and sugar cane production in Santa Cruz.

The most disturbing possibility posed by government policies emphasizing economic rather than social returns to colonization could be that much of the wealth of the *Oriente* might become concentrated in the hands of a few people much as it was in highland Bolivia prior to the revolution of 1952. Although this would perhaps be compatible with the economic needs of Bolivia, such an outcome would not be compatible with the social needs of the country. Virtually the only way to ensure that this does not happen is for the government to invest heavily in the necessary social, economic and technological inputs that would enable the small farmer to compete with the large-scale commercial farmer for internal and foreign markets. Another alternative would be to create a dual economy in the *Oriente* by allocating certain lands for large-scale commercial agriculture while reserving other areas for small-scale commercial agriculture and subsistence farming. Such an economy has already evolved in the Santa Cruz region but is unlikely to persist unless there is increased intervention on the part of the government to improve the viability of the small farmer.

Summary

The agrarian development of the *Oriente* is inevitable given the present day need of Bolivia to increase agricultural production for internal consumption and export. Migration to the *Oriente* will undoubtedly continue until there is no more virgin land to develop. Inevitably, this process will result in the destruction of significant forest and wildlife resources as the land is cleared and brought into agricultural production. Hopefully, the benefits gained from development will offset these losses. The settlement and agrarian development of the *Oriente* will continue to be one of the paramount challenges facing the Bolivian government in the immediate future. This challenge is not one of just settling people on the land but ensuring that the development process that follows results in the maximum social and economic benefits to the people of the nation.

ENDNOTES FOR CHAPTER XIII

1. The *Oriente* is the region lying east of the Andes in Bolivia. It is a vast plain that slopes gently eastward and northward toward the Brazilian border. It contains about two-thirds of the national territory and less than one-sixth of the population and is considered to be a frontier region.

2. Bolivia lost approximately 55,000 square miles of territory in this war. The Bolivians attributed this loss to the fact that few Bolivians were living in the Chaco, and transport connections to highland core regions were very poor. In recent years, the Bolivians have become very concerned about Brazil penetrating into the *Oriente*.

3. The Mountain Valleys refers to a physiographic region along the east side of the Andes where tectonic movements and erosional forces have formed broad valleys at elevations of 2,000 to 3,000 meters. This region contains 14 percent of the country and is inhabited by approximately 30 percent of the population. The *Altiplano* is the term given to the high plateau lying between the eastern and western branches of the Andes in Bolivia. The plateau covers 16 percent of the territory of the country and is inhabited by approximately 55 percent of the population.

4. The desire to develop the *Oriente* became a major goal of the National Revolutionary Movement Government (MNR) almost immediately after the revolution and continued to be a goal of the party as long as it was in power. AID supported this policy and provided considerable loans and grants to finance infrastructural and agricultural development in the *Oriente*.

5. Alexander T. Edelman, "Colonization in Bolivia: Progress and Prospects," *Inter-American Economic Affairs*, XX (Spring 1967), 39-54.

6. Kelso Wessel, "An Economic Assessment of Pioneer Settlement in the Bolivian Lowlands" (unpublished Ph.D. dissertation, Cornell University, 1968), p. 35.

7. Bolivia, Corporación Boliviana de Fomento, *Reseña histórica del proyecto Alto Beni* (La Paz: 1965), pp. 28-35.

8. Bolivia, Instituto Nacional de Colonización, op. cit., p. 1.

9. John W. Marus and Rada J. Monje, *Estudios de colonización en Bolivia* (La Paz: 1962), p. 269.

10. Michael Nelson, *The Development of Tropical Lands: Policy Issues in Latin America* (Baltimore: Johns Hopkins Press, 1973), p. 160.

11. Hernán Zeballos-Hurtado, "From the Upland to the Lowlands" (unpublished Ph.D. dissertation, University of Wisconsin, 1975), p. 197.

12. Don Alberto Letellier, *La colonización del Chapare* (La Paz: Editorial Universal, 1939), p. 53.

13. Ibid., p. 54.

14. Wessel, op. cit., p. 45.

15. Ibid., p. 48.

16. Raymond E. Crist and C. Nissly, *East From the Andes,* Monograph Series, No. 50 (Gainesville: University of Florida Press, 1973), p. 140.

17. Robert B. South, "Coca in Bolivia," *Geographical Review,* LXVII (January, 1977), 30–31.

18. Ray Henkel, "The Chapare of Bolivia: A Study of Tropical Agriculture in Transition" (unpublished Ph.D. dissertation, University of Wisconsin, 1971), p. 19.

19. Mario Hiraoka, "Pioneer Settlement in Eastern Bolivia" (unpublished Ph.D. dissertation, University of Wisconsin-Milwaukee, 1974), pp. 45–53. Provides an excellent discussion of the physical environment of the Santa Cruz region.

20. Zeballos-Hurtado, op. cit., p. 16.

21. For excellent descriptions of recent pioneer colonization in Santa Cruz see Hiraoka, op. cit., and Allyn Maclean Stearman, "The Highland Migrant in Lowland Bolivia: Regional Migration and the Development of Santa Cruz" (unpublished Ph.D. dissertation, University of Florida, 1976).

22. Cornelius H. Zondag, *The Bolivian Economy, The Revolution and Its Aftermath* (New York: Frederick A. Praeger, 1966), pp. 153–157.

23. Crist and Nissly, op. cit., pp. 151–152.

24. Dwight B. Heath, Charles Erasmus, and H. Buechler, *Land Reform and Social Revolution in Bolivia* (New York: Frederick A. Praeger, 1969), p. 274.

25. Edelman, op. cit., p. 20.

26. Henkel, op. cit., pp. 139–140.

27. Ibid., p. 142.

28. Crist and Nissly, op. cit., p. 140.

29. Henkel, op. cit., p. 92.

30. Nelson, op. cit., pp. 160–161.

31. Henkel, op. cit., p. 253.

32. The official policy statement of the MNR government with regard to government-directed colonization projects in the *Oriente* can be found in Bolivia, Servicio Nacional de Planificación y Coordinación, *Plan nacional de desarrollo económico y social, 1962-1971, resumen*

(La Paz: 1961), pp. 51-56. This statement tends to emphasize the strong commitment of the MNR government to directed colonization projects.

33. Crist and Nissly, op. cit., p. 134.

34. A comprehensive description and analysis of the CBF projects in Santa Cruz can be found in Wolfgang Schoop "Vergleichende Untersuchungen zur Agrarkolonisation der hochlandindianer am Andenabfall und in Tiefland Ostboliviens," *Aachener Geographische Arbeiten* Heft 4 (1970), 89-127.

35. Zondag, op. cit., p. 160.

36. For a detailed description of this project, see Bolivia, Corporación Boliviana de Fomento, *Reseña histórica*, op. cit., pp. 1-41.

37. Ibid., p. 14.

38. Bolivia, Servicio Nacional de Planificación y Coordinación, *Plan nacional,* op. cit., pp. 88-91.

39. An accounting of the financing of these projects is provided in Bolivia, Instituto Nacional de Colonización, *Proyecto de colonización Puerto Villarroel-Km 21, Chane-Piray, ampliación de San Julián,* Vol. 1 (La Paz: 1974), pp. 35-43.

40. Henkel, op. cit., p. 103.

41. Bolivia, Instituto Nacional de Colonización, *Programa de colonización INC-BID Informe Final* (La Paz: 1970), pp. 30-32.

42. Henkel, op. cit., p. 103.

43. Bolivia, Instituto Nacional de Colonización, *Proyecto,* op. cit., p. 28.

44. Zeballos-Hurtado, op. cit., p. 138.

45. The goals and purposes of the semi-directed projects are given in *United States Agency for International Development Report LADR-SAEC/P-74-76, Bolivia-Subtropical Lands Development* (La Paz: 1974), pp. 1-59.

46. Allyn Maclean Stearman, op. cit., pp. 331-332.

47. Casto Ferragut, *Principal Characteristics of the Agricultural Colonies of Bolivia and Suggestions for a Colonization Policy* (Rome: FAO, 1961), p. 6.

48. For a discussion of Japanese settlement in Santa Cruz see Mario Hiraoka, "Structural Variations Among Dwellings in the Japanese Colony of San Juan de Yapacani," Yearbook, *Association of Pacific Coast Geographers,* 34 (1972), 138-52.

49. Wessel, op. cit., p. 65.

50. The Bolivian government imposed these restrictions largely because of complaints of Bolivian colonists living in the region. The main complaint was that the Japanese so monopolized the rice market that the Bolivians were unable to compete with them.

51. Wessel, op. cit., p. 57.

52. Ibid., p. 69.

53. Zeballos-Hurtado, op. cit., pp. 92-95.

54. Ibid., p. 98.

55. Ibid., p. 98.

56. Ibid., p. 92.

57. The system of shared labor known as the *ayñe* is one of the main institutions brought into the settlements from the highlands. It tends to disappear when commercial agriculture replaces the subsistence system of agriculture.

58. Nelson, op. cit., p. 73.

59. Since the maximum amount of land most farmers can handle with family assistance is 3 to 5 hectares, there is a tendency to expand production by hiring *peones* or working out sharecropping arrangements with new families entering the colonization areas at this stage of development.

60. Henkel, op. cit., p. 253.

61. The exception is the foreign colonies where farm sizes average 50 hectares or more.

62. Stearman, op. cit., p. 373.

63. Henkel, op. cit., p. 309.

64. Ibid., p. 310.

65. For an excellent assessment of the influence of transport costs on income in a colonization area, see Boyd Wennergren and Morris D. Whitaker, "Investment in Access Roads and Spontaneous Colonization: Additional Evidences from Bolivia," *Land Economics*, 52 (January 1976), 138-52.

66. Stearman, op. cit., p. 384.

67. Zeballos, op. cit., p. 84.

68. Ibid., p. 85.

69. The Bolivian government with financial assistance provided by AID has been attempting to find substitute crops for coca in the Chapare. These efforts have yielded limited results to date primarily because no other crops have been found that can generate a level of income return equal to that of coca.

70. Henkel, op. cit., p. 23.

71. For excellent studies of changes in tropical soils under cultivation see Arnold Finck, "The Fertility of Tropical Soils Under the Influence of Agricultural Land Use," *Applied Sciences and Development* I (January-February, 1973), 17-32; and David R. Harris, "The Ecology of Swidden Cultivation in the Upper Orinoco Rain Forest, Venezuela," *Geographical Review*, LXI (October, 1971), 487-492.

72. Henkel, op. cit., p. 251.

73. For an excellent study of the effects of forest clearing on the environment see William Denevan, "Development and the Imminent Demise of the Amazon Rain Forest," *Professional Geographer*, XXV (January, 1973), 217-222.

74. Oladipo Adejuwon, "The Human Impact on African Environmental Systems," *Contemporary Africa*, ed. C. J. Knight (Englewood Cliffs: Prentice Hall, 1976), pp. 140-159.

75. Hermann Flohn, "Some Aspects of Man-Made Climate Modification and Desertification," *Applied Sciences and Development*, X (August-September, 1977), 44-59.

76. United States Superintendent of Documents, *Area Handbook for Bolivia* (Washington: Government Printing Office, 1974), p. 65.

77. Ibid., p. 62.

78. Bolivia, Ministerio de Asuntos Campesinos y Agropecuarios, *Diagnóstico del sector agropecuario*, 1974, Vol. 2 (La Paz: 1975), pp. 531-536.

79. Ibid., p. 767.

80. Ibid., p. 531.

81. Bolivia, Banco Central de Bolivia, Gerencia Técnica, *Boletín estadístico*, (March 1976), p. 55.

82. Ibid., p. 55.

83. Ibid., p. 55.

84. The Abapó-Izozog project was proposed in the early 1960s by a German consulting firm, Engineer Global, as an alternative to colonization of tropical areas as a means of increasing the food supply of Bolivia and providing products for export. In a major policy decision, Bolivia decided to continue colonization efforts in the humid tropics rather than develop irrigation projects in the Chaco. The arguments for and against these two approaches to development are presented in Bolivia, Ministerio de Economía Nacional, *Deutsche Projeckt Union GMBH Ingenieria Global, Informe No. 39, Análisis económico de los proyectos de colonización y de riegos* (La Paz: 1965).

Chapter XIV

The Role of the State in the Rural-Urban Configuration[1]
Salvador Romero Pittari

INTRODUCTION

A grasp of the relationship between rural and urban sectors is one of the most significant factors in understanding the dynamics of a society, particularly in those societies which have been dominated by the rural sector, as is the case in Bolivia. This may surprise those who think of the rural areas as an almost fixed adornment in a drama whose principal actors are urban. Nonetheless, the peasant has been linked to all the fundamental changes in Bolivian society from before the time of Bolivian independence up to the present. His actions, expressed through different types of movements, have contributed to new societal orientations.

It is inadequate to approach the rural-urban relationship from a purely quantitative point of view. Such an approach virtually reduces the entire phenomenon to the ratio between rural and urban populations, or to some other combination of isolated figures which have little reference to the underlying system of social relations. This paper considers the rural and urban sectors not as two autonomous and closed extremes, but rather as components of a unified structure whose fundamental characteristics are derived from the interaction of the two sectors. Therefore, after first setting forth some quantitative dimensions of the two sectors, focus is placed on explaining their observed differences. In particular, the role of the state is carefully examined in the context of the socio-economic structure of rural and urban areas. Bolivian history since the 1952 revolution has been marked by an increase in the degree of power centralized by the state. Thus, the emphasis of this paper is placed on an examination of the role of the government, both in its form and in its policies, as it has influenced rural and urban changes.

POPULATION GROWTH

In comparison with many other countries, the population of Bolivia in the last half-century has grown moderately. In the first half-century the average annual rate of increase was only 1.1 percent.[2] In the last several decades the rate of growth has increased substantially; measured between the 1950 and 1976 censuses the average annual rate of growth was 2.1 percent. Stated in other terms, between 1950 and 1976 the population increased 73.4 percent.

This relatively low growth rate, by Latin American standards, can be partially attributed to a high mortality rate. Even though the birth rate during recent years has held steady at 46.6 per thousand, mortality was 15.5 per thousand in 1958 and 18.0 per thousand in 1975.[3] Infant mortality in 1975 alone accounted for 157 deaths per thousand infants born alive. As a consequence, the life expectancy for males and females is among the lowest of the continent, 45.6 and 50.9 years respectively.[4]

The efforts undertaken by the state in recent years to improve the conditions of hygiene and health have been of little help to the great masses of rural inhabitants. In 1975, less than 20 percent of the resources of the Ministry of Social Planning and Public Health, the institution which provides almost all of the rural health and medical services, were directed to rural hygiene and health. Indices of health, without exception, are lower in the countryside than in the cities.[5]

Between 1971 and 1975, the risk of death was very high for rural children two years or younger; the mortality rate was 224 per thousand.[6] The fact that Bolivia is a predominantly rural society helps to explain why the country has such a high mortality rate.

Another reason that the Bolivian population has grown relatively slowly has been the heavy flow of international emigration, especially toward Argentina. It is estimated that between 10 and 15 percent of the total Bolivian population has moved to that country. However, this tendency appears to have diminished recently, partly because of economic and social difficulties in the surrounding South American countries and partly because there is an increased seasonal demand for laborers in the modern agricultural activities in Bolivia. Emigration for the 1970–1975 period has been roughly estimated to be –1 percent per thousand.[7]

INDICES OF THE RURAL-URBAN SHIFT

Table XIV-1 indicates the rural and urban increases in population at fifty year intervals over a hundred-year period. It considers urban centers as those with 10,000 or more inhabitants. Although in the last twenty-six years the rural population increased at a higher rate than in the previous fifty years, the rate of growth of the urban population was even more marked. In light of the above figures, there is no doubt that the Bolivian population is progressively losing its peasant character.

This phenomenon is illustrated in Table XIV-2 by the proportion of rural inhabitants in relation to the total population. Until 1900 the rural inhabitants, as a proportion of total population, remained almost constant at about 91 percent. Between 1900 and 1950, it decreased to less than 80 percent; however, by 1976 only 64 percent of the total population was considered rural. Stated another way, from 1950 to 1976 the urban population grew from approximately 20 to 36 percent of the total population. In this twenty-six year period the total increase in urban population was 206.5 percent.

THE EVOLUTION OF THE STATE AND THE RURAL-URBAN SHIFT

Bolivian development since the 1952 revolution has been marked by the increasing role of the state, not only in the ownership and production

TABLE XIV-1
ANNUAL RATES OR POPULATION GROWTH
(Percentages)

Year	Total Growth	Rural Growth	Urban Growth
1847[a]-1900[b]	0.20	0.20	0.40
1900 -1950[c]	1.10	0.90	2.60
1950 -1976[d]	2.14	1.30	4.30

Sources: [a]J.M. Dalence, *Bosquejo estadístico de Bolivia* (La Paz: Ed. Universitaria, Universidad Mayor de San Andrés, 1975).

[b]Bolivia, *Censo demográfico de 1900* (Cochabamba: Ed. Canelas) 1973, 2nd ed.

[c]Bolivia, *Censo de 1950* (La Paz: Ministerio de Hacienda y Estadística) 1953.

[d]Bolivia, *Resultados provisionales censo 1976* (La Paz: Instituto Nacional de Estadística) 1976.

TABLE XIV-2

PERCENTAGE OF TOTAL POPULATION LIVING IN RURAL AREAS

Year	Total Population	Urban Population (Percent)	Rural Population (Percent)
1847	1,373,896	8.74	91.26
1900	1,696,400	9.50	91.50
1950	3,019,031	20.36	79.64
1976	4,687,718	36.00	64.00

Sources: Same as Table XIV-1.

of goods and services, but also in policies that were designed to affect the economic and social structure. These changes have taken the state into managerial activities that were previously almost exclusively reserved for private enterprise or not attended to at all. Thus the influence of the state has widened considerably and has penetrated almost all aspects of the social structure.

The 1952 revolution constituted a social movement in which there was a merging of the peasants, laborers and urban middle class sectors and in which the latter assumed the leadership role. This movement crystallized in a social reorganization in which the peasant and labor groups were progressively weakened while the middle class consolidated its power.

The increasing role of the state, in combination with a burgeoning public payroll, meant that the state rapidly assumed a bureaucratic-authoritarian character. [8] The new social organization was dominated by the presence of large public organizations which had a hierarchical system of responsibilities, operational rules, and technical criteria for decisions. The growth of these public organizations was paralleled by a concentration of power in the executive branch of government and a reduction in the political power of citizens, especially since the coup of 1971.   This move was justified by recourse to the "cold ideologies" which were articulated in the context of the necessity for development and which were considered the ultimate foundation for the legitimacy of social power. These "cold ideologies" emphasized the cooperation between social classes before their fights, rational decisions for development that were impregnable in relation to private interests, and a peaceful social atmosphere as a condition for determining national objectives and programming strategies. Moreover, the participation of the private sector was reduced, in order to create the indispensable climate of predictability in which government programming could function. It should be noted, however, that this did not eliminate the recognition of the emergence of a new managerial group in the private sector who could compete for control of the initiative in the country's development.

In spite of the frequent references to the "cold ideologies," the fact remains that the selection of development goals is not solely a technical and rational process. While the degree may vary, goal selection is always sensitive to pressure groups and to the special interests of the decision makers themselves.

With the state's increased political power and direct control over economic activity, the state and its policies have become the arena where social conflicts—whether of class, region, or culture—are expressed. This means that such conflicts have taken on a more indirect character since 1971 because they are mediated in areas defined by government activity.   What general characteristics does the rural-urban relationship reveal in relation to the evolution of the power of the state? What specific forms do the social actors assume? What kind of claims do they impose?   These are the questions which are addressed in the following analysis.

THE RURAL SECTOR

Between 1952 and 1972, agriculture's share of the gross national product declined from 22.2 to 15.6 percent. [9] Moreover, average productivity did not increase as rapidly in the agricultural sector as in the urban sector; the urban-rural per capita income ratio shifted from 7.1 in 1960 to 12.1 in 1972. [10]

The peasant movement played an important role in the 1952 revolution that resulted in a land reform program under which the majority of the landless rural population obtained land. Once the land redistribution had been accomplished, however, the peasant movement lost its unity. It became fragmented, not only in the upper levels of its organization, which were more susceptible to political manipulation, but also among its masses, which were more oriented to local problems. This fragmentation meant a loss of power for the rural population in the society as a whole and strengthened the power of the cities even more.

Although the rural sector has always been characterized by heterogeneity, this trait was accentuated after the land reform. In the period preceding the reform there were two basic types of rural establishments-- the hacienda and the village community, *comunidad*. In the eastern lowlands, the *Oriente*, there was also the plantation, but its importance, on a national level, was minimal. The two major types of establishments differed less in the characteristics of their ecotype than in their manner of participating and relating to the larger society. The differences in the way that both major types of establishments related to the larger society was not an obstacle to the unification of the peasant movement since they-- the people from the communities as well as the hacienda--both opposed the large land owners.

Rural Zones

Today there are three distinguishable rural zones in Bolivia: (a) where subsistence farming predominates, (b) where subsistence farming is mixed with market-oriented farming, and (c) where market-oriented farming dominates.

Each zone is defined in terms of population: density, productive organization, patterns of crop specialization, and relationships to the dominant systems in the society. In each of these zones peasant organization and action varies according to local economic and social values. Also there are differences as to the peasants' relationship to the state and to other social groups as well as to their social demands upon, and their orientation to, society as a whole.

Subsistence Farming Zone

The first zone consists of various small communities and ex-haciendas located principally on the southern and central high plains or *Altiplano*. The small size of farms, poor quality of land, rudimentary technology of production, and difficulties of communication have contributed to a very low level of productivity in this zone.

Few of the farm families are completely self-sufficient; the majority are oriented, in varying degrees, toward some production for the market. The major efforts of these peasants are directed to the bare survival of the family unit. Their extreme marginality often means that collective peasant action takes the form of a withdrawal from modern society. The result of this decision is the abandonment of all efforts to learn in terms of the larger social medium, and the limitation of aspirations to the narrow community framework. The maintenance of traditional values and roles works against economic advancement for these peasants and for their participation in the national society. In fact it tends to lead to an increase in their marginality.

The Subsistence-Commercial Farming Zone

This second zone includes the majority of the peasantry located in the regions of the Mountain Valleys and *Altiplano*, where land reform was widely undertaken with the exception of some few areas where the political influence of the old landowners limited the redistribution of lands.

The predominant crops in this second zone are traditional: potatoes, barley, quinoa, wheat, and corn. Livestock and poultry production is also common. Production techniques, which continue to be quite archaic, are labor intensive and most often utilize only animal power. In the mid-1970s, it was estimated that 90 percent of the power used in the *Altiplano* came from animal sources. The corresponding figure for the Mountain Valleys was 70 percent. In sharp contrast, in the *Oriente*, the third zone, the production was the inverse; 90 percent of the power came from motorized sources, and 10 percent from animals. [11]

In the second zone, the family is the principal unit of production. Except on rare occasions, salaried help is not employed, and the traditional forms of labor sharing and cooperation are sufficient to satisfy farm labor requirements even in periods of high demand. Crop yields are relatively low. Production, however, often covers the needs of the national market for many basic foodstuffs.

Market-Oriented Zone

The third zone, a modern market-oriented agriculture, is found mainly in the *Oriente* in the departments of Santa Cruz and Beni. In contrast to the other two zones, agricultural activity in this zone is characterized by more capital-intensive and modern technologies. The predominent products are cotton, sugar cane, rice, soybeans and beef cattle.

This thriving agriculture is of recent origin. It has been developed in those regions where land reform had limited applications due to the abundance of land and the scarcity of men. Since 1952, the state has strongly encouraged its growth via credit policies and infrastructural development. Favorable export markets for agricultural products and petroleum development in the *Oriente* have further supported the growth of commercial agriculture in this zone. A result of these developments has been the privileged access to the centers of policy decisions for the large agriculturalists from the *Oriente*. This, in turn, has influenced government policy in favor of the third zone relative to the traditional and colonized areas.

The existence of dual agricultural sectors, traditional and modern, has created a problem for the government in that both sectors must compete for productive resources which are channeled to agriculture through government policies. The record clearly shows, however, that the government has opted to direct most resources to the modern sector of the *Oriente*.

The new commercial farmers and agricultural businessmen, especially those in the *Oriente*, have played a major role in this process. They are tightly linked to other business sectors by a network of interests that form, on a national level, a new bourgeoisie with activities extending throughout the country. This group differs from the traditional bourgeoisie, which is more fragmented in its interests and more geographically localized. In the last few years because of their economic power base, the new bourgeoisie has been able to participate in or influence the government's techno-bureaucracy in developing national policies, many of which have been for their direct benefit. This, in no small part, explains the heavy flow of resources to the *Oriente*.

PEASANT AGRICULTURE

Land Reform and Marketing

The *Altiplano* and Mountain Valleys, which comprise the first two zones, together contain 86 percent of the rural population of the country. Farms are small; approximately 55 percent of the properties in these zones have fewer than five hectares, and more than two-thirds of them have fewer than ten. However, it is premature to use these figures to assert, as some critics do, that the most important consequence of the land reform has been the *minifundio,* e. g., farms that are too small to adequately support a farm family. In characterizing the *minifundio* one must include not only the man-land ratio but also the type of technology utilized, the products produced, and the specific peasant culture. As several studies have indicated, the peasant farmer in many regions received more land than he can work utilizing his present technology, given the prevalent social guidelines for organization and work. The redistribution of lands has not solved the peasant's needs, even those established by tradition, which on all sides are being displaced by the omnipresence of other more modern lifestyles. Moreover, the economic and political system in which the peasant must operate often serves to his disadvantage and keeps him in an economic situation which inhibits the growth of his income and level of living.

An example within this system is the typical marketing system for basic foodstuffs in rural areas. Here the peasant is subjected to middlemen and low product prices, both of which contribute to the exploitation of the peasant, with its consequent negative influence on the conditions of peasant life. This exploitation exists because of the conditions of production in which the peasants of the *Altiplano* and the Mountain Valleys work, and because of the minimal pressure which the peasants are able to exert on the political decision centers. The fact that the middlemen virtually control local markets is not, in itself, a sufficient explanation of the mechanism by which part of the peasant wealth passes to other sectors of the society. In many cases the middleman has been replaced by cooperatives or other kinds of marketing structures. The low product prices, however, have been maintained. The level of prices for traditional products reflects not only the market supply and demand but also, in large measure, the government's policy of keeping food prices low in order to benefit the urban consumer. The weak position of the peasant in the power structure has not enabled them to effectively counteract the urban pressures on the government to maintain low prices.

Rapid Population Growth

Rapid population growth in rural areas has worsened the problem in the two zones by increasing the man-land ratio. Even though the proportion of the population living in rural areas has been decreasing, fertility in the rural areas is much higher than it is in the cities. In 1975, in the city of La Paz, there were 4.8 children per adult woman and in other urban areas there were 5.8. In rural areas there were 7.8 children per adult female. The same differences can be observed by considering the fertility in relation to language spoken. Women who spoke only a native language, doubtless mostly of rural origin, had an average of 7.6 children; by contrast, among those who spoke only Spanish, presumably mostly urban dwellers, the figure was 5.7. [12]

Underemployment

The high rural birth rate in combination with small parcels of peasant land, contributes to underemployment and open unemployment in rural areas. It is estimated that only 15 percent of the manual labor of the central *Altiplano* receives the prevalent salary of the region. For the entire rural area, this percentage was 47 percent.[13] These figures reflect low productivity and inefficient employment of human resources.

Education and Migration

The plight of the peasant is exacerbated by the rise in his expectations that was generated, in large part, by the enormous increase in basic education in rural areas since the land reform. In 1950, 15.3 percent of the peasant population between the ages of 6 and 14 attended school whereas by 1975, that percentage has risen sharply to 79.4 percent.

Knowledge of the Spanish language has become widely generalized in the Indian speaking areas of Bolivia, which facilitates better communication throughout the country. In 1975, 6.7 percent of the population spoke only Aymara while 13.7 percent spoke only Quechua. These were mostly people of old age or ones very young.[14] Furthermore, the penetration into the countryside of various mass communication media such as radio, as well as increased frequency of travel, have prompted the peasants to consider lifestyles and values different from those which formally dominated the rural community. These changes have created conditions under which the desire for migration from rural to urban areas acquires greater importance. Until recently, newly acquired land, displacement toward the old towns, internal colonization, and limited opportunities for work in the city would appear to have been strong factors keeping the peasant in the rural areas. But the combination of factors discussed above indicates that the moment for an extensive rural exodus toward the city is arriving.

Government Policies

Without denying the great importance of the changes that have taken place on the *Altiplano* and in the Mountain Valleys since 1952, it is clear that the rural sector has been damaged by government policies which have favored the cities and the commercial agricultural areas, particularly those in the *Oriente*. All of the available indicators related to income, consumption, housing, access to culture, and health demonstrate a strong disparity between the traditional rural and urban sectors. There are also inequalities in productivity, in the use of modern technologies, and in access to credit. In spite of the preponderant concentration of rural population on the *Altiplano* and in the Mountain Valleys, the major flow of agricultural credit has been to the *Oriente,* whereas the traditional areas have only received information about new production techniques. Consequently, government policy has created a situation in which a large portion of the peasant population has not received the necessary credit to put the new knowledge into practice. Furthermore, the situation has been exacerbated because the bulk of the investment in the infrastructure of roads, bridges, etc., also has been directed toward market-oriented agricultural regions.

Government-directed migration programs and spontaneous migration have not solved peasants' problems in either the areas of origin or destination. The more than 350,000 peasants in the *Oriente*, who migrated basically from the Mountain Valley region, should be considered as members of the traditional rural population discussed above. It is common that they not only have their new lands but also that they maintained their plots in the traditional areas. Although the geographical conditions are different, they tend to continue their traditional cultural practices in the *Oriente*. Thus in their region of origin pressures on the land were maintained while at the same time peasant economic practices were transferred to the areas of colonization. This is not to say that some changes did not take place. There were the inevitable changes in their attitude and behavior that occur as a result of the migratory process.

Briefly summing up what has occurred in recent decades, the outstanding factor has been an increasing state intervention in a peasant society. The government fixes the framework of the markets, establishes the infrastructure, provides technical assistance and determines credit policy, thereby deciding in large measure the limits to, and levels of, social-cultural participation of the peasant. Parallel to this growth of governmental action, in the peasant world there have been cultural forces at work that have led to the fragmentation of rural society and a resultant differentiation in the rural orientation of society as a whole. This phenomenon has brought about the emergence of more localized and specific social demands in the rural sector. These changes are evident in the increasing diffusion of rural assistance organizations supported by government policy and focused on the satisfaction of functional or productive needs of the communities. Also there has been a gradual receding of the political organizations dedicated to the incorporation of peasant interests in the decision centers.

The Peasant Movement and The Future

Given the rise of the state and the associated techno-bureaucratic rationality and authoritarian posture it is clear that the peasants' possibilities for access to power and information are very limited. Moreover, it tends to reduce them to the role of a producer, or perhaps that of a consumer, who presents demands only in reference to these positions. It would be an error, however, to conclude that all peasant action is localized and has lost its dynamism. Today, as in the past, many forces which contribute to the modeling of the future Bolivian society are generated in peasant society. This is due not only to the sheer numerical weight of the peasantry, but also to the significance of their claims. The most salient inference that can be made from the peasant movement since land reform is, as indicated previously, the change in the movement's orientation as a result of the modifications in the nature of the domination exercised over the peasant. Prior to land reform the domination came directly from the landlord. Today, it is a more subtle form that comes from the state via economic, social, and educational policies—or lack of same—and market action. In traditional agricultural regions, although technology has not undergone fundamental innovations, the strong penetration of exogenous forces is breaking up the homogeneity and isolation of the peasant world and is bringing about changes in the peasant lifestyle. Without doubt, considerable subsistence farming still persists, as does poverty and limited access to the advantages of modern culture. The changes to which the increasing presence of the larger society contributes, however, are giving a new content to peasant action. The peasants' new demands are placed principally against the government. They are seeking not only better market policies, but also better conditions of life. Apart from the particular interest that these groups express, they carry a more general sense of opposition to the predominant government policies and a review of the role of the peasant in the general society. Some conflicts have already been manifested. For example, in 1972 in the Valley of Cochabamba, peasant protests were made against the policy of monetary stabilization. [15] In other traditional rural areas, where the slowness of change in the models of work organization and of life in general tend to make the rural culture seem immobile, the claims tend to be based exactly on differences from the techno-bureaucratic apparatus centered in the city. Thus, the peasants' sense of cultural identity confronts the domination exercised in the name of general progress and shaped by the interest of power groups. [16]

Racial and cultural conflicts are not unique to Bolivia. Around the world, social movements are being nurtured by such conflicts. The influence of these other social conflicts on Bolivia can not be denied. However, it must be emphasized that the conflicts in Bolivia have historic domestic roots and are not a result of worldwide influences.

The indigenous movement, *el indigenismo,* has a precept that Pre-Columbian man and his culture still exist in the rural areas and that a resurgence in his basic values is taking place. These beliefs have always constituted an important element of national life and have been influential on political ideologies. Paradoxically, the movement has been more influential in urban areas than in the rural areas as might otherwise be assumed. This situation, however, is changing. Recently these beliefs have been gaining acceptance in the rural areas where Aymara and Quechua are spoken since it is assumed that a common language forms the basis of a pure culture and also defines racial identity.

In a diffuse way, the indigenous movement accuses the technical-bureaucratic structure of destroying its cultural identity. As a defense against government policies, which place the real needs of man second to economic gain, this reaction is justifiable. However, the movement overlooks the fact that its cultural and racial identity have already been broken. Historically, biological and social mixing have significantly altered the "pure" race and languages spoken in various regions. These languages —Aymara and Quechua—have become integrated into a predominantly mestizo culture.

This cultural battle places the forces of cultural identity in opposition to directed social change. By substituting the superstructural aspects for the social base of the conflict, however, it ends up incapable of revealing the true causes of the battle. Therefore, the cultural battle possibly reinforces the mechanisms of peasant domination and exploitation. In other societies, conflicts of this nature place communities that present characteristics of a viable global society in opposition to another viable global society. In Bolivia, the linguistic identity groups constitute only one segment of a global society, into whose mechanisms of domination they were incorporated more than 400 years ago. The movement's emphasis on the particularities of the peasant sector limits the effectiveness of peasant action. Without neglecting the violence and pain that these fights can cause in a society, their major defect lies not in their aspiration for justice, but rather in their identification of that aspiration with a past moment in history. Some of the peasant values doubtlessly deserve to be preserved, but the refusal to recognize the present dynamics deprives the proposed utopia of real force.

The two types of peasant claims examined—one being basically economic and the other basically cultural—represent different forms of resistance that share their opposition to the dominant bureaucratic-authoritarian power and that at any given moment could join forces. Should this occur, the peasant movement would become more powerful.

Another type of peasant movement exists in the colonized rural areas. The peasants in these areas, especially those in Yapacaní, find themselves in a situation where conflicts tend to take the traditional form of opposition between rich and poor or between large producers and peasantry for the scarce and necessary resources of production. As a result of these conflicts, there is an awakening of the peasants' sensitivity to the Marxist themes of class struggle, which leads to a search for a redefinition of society and the political apparatus. The latter is considered to be the instrument necessary to create a new and dominant privileged class. This helps explain why peasants in the rural colonized areas are able to join forces with political movements which originate in the city. Such a merging of urban and rural concerns could eventually become the basis for a national movement.

It can therefore be concluded that the current peasant movements in Bolivia are a reaction to national policies which have benefited the urban areas and have perpetuated a social structure which exploits the peasants.

THE URBAN SECTOR

The process of urbanization in Bolivia has not yet reached the alarming characteristics of other Latin American countries. Throughout the continent rural migration to the cities has created rings of poverty around the urban centers and inequalities between the countryside and cities have become more extreme, as have the inequalities between certain cities.

Inter-urban Growth

Until the middle of the twentieth century, the cities of La Paz, Oruro, and Cochabamba experienced rapid growth and formed a social, political, and economic system with La Paz as the epicenter. The policy of geographic and economic diversification introduced after the 1952 revolution was characterized by the move of the focus to the *Oriente*. This was accomplished through government investments in infrastructure, the flow of domestic and foreign capital towards commercial agriculture and the migration of professional businessmen and peasants to that region. The strength of this movement has produced a rearticulation of geographic, social, and political space, with two focal points—La Paz and Santa Cruz. The change is illustrated in Table XIV-3.

Clearly the city of Santa Cruz has grown very rapidly compared to La Paz. In 1950, La Paz was 6.5 times larger than Santa Cruz but by 1976, it was only 2.5 times larger. The city of Santa Cruz has had the fastest average annual rate of growth in the country; between 1959 and 1976, it grew 7.3 percent annually while La Paz and Cochabamba only grew at average annual rates of 3.51 and 3.94 respectively. The major cities in the more traditional areas—Oruro and Potosí—grew only slightly more than the average rate of population growth.

Major urban centers have grown relative to smaller urban centers and towns. In 1950, La Paz was almost twelve times larger than the next urban center in the department of La Paz, and Cochabamba was almost nine times larger than any other urban center in that department. In 1978 these differences had become 66.5 and 10.5 respectively.

Bolivian urbanization has been linked principally to the expansion of the service sector and, in a lesser but no small degree, to the survival of craft activities. Industrial growth has played a limited role. The in-

TABLE XIV-3

GROWTH OF THE PRINCIPAL BOLIVIAN CITIES (1950–1976)

City	1950	1976	Annual Growth Rate (Percent)
La Paz	267,008	654,713	3.51
Cochabamba	74,819	204,414	3.94
Santa Cruz	41,461	255,568	7.25
Oruro	58,558	124,121	2.93
Potosí	43,306	77,233	2.25

Source: Bolivia, Instituto Nacional de Estadística, *Boletín No. 20*, La Paz, 1976.

dustrial sector employs only 9 percent of the Bolivian labor force, and 90.5 percent of all industrial labor is located in the cities of La Paz, Cochabamba and Santa Cruz.[17] Almost two-thirds of national manufacturing is concentrated in La Paz, and 80 percent of it consists of small industries and craft shops which typically employ manual labor. Modern, large-scale industry plays a very small role in industrial employment. The slow industrial expansion has created limited employment opportunities and consequently a significant percentage of the urban labor force is employed in relatively low-productivity type jobs in the tertiary sector or are unemployed. There is an appreciable number of underemployed persons such as street vendors, domestic servants, and part-time workers.

The rapid development of the public sector in the last several decades is one of the factors that explains the growth of the cities. Approximately 10 percent of the total population depends directly or indirectly on work distributed by the state.

Urban and Town Growth

Large-city urban development has taken place at the expense of the smaller cities and the towns and to a lesser extent, the rural areas. After the land reform many former landlords moved to the cities and the rural towns lost their most dynamic human elements. The result has been an increasing concentration of wealth and power in the larger urban sites. The town remains, however, as the crossroads between rural and urban lifestyles and serves as the base for commercial operations, but the characteristics which formerly made town life similar to life in the urban centers have generally disappeared. The towns now give a painful impression of abandonment, with their old dignified houses in ruins, their streets in disrepair, and their public services both precarious and limited.

The process of growth experienced in the last five years in Bolivian society, directed primarily by an elite of the middle class and, later, shared in some measure by the new bourgeoisie, has produced a concentration of wealth and social services in the cities of La Paz, Cochabamba and Santa Cruz.[18]

Regional and Distributional Inequalities

This trend has been accompanied by a relative decline in the investments undertaken in other areas; which often forms the basis for interregional jealousies and disputes. Simultaneously, wealth has become concentrated in the upper and middle classes. In 1970 Bolivia had one of the most asymmetrical income distributions in Latin America. The ratio between the per capita income of the richest 5 percent and the poorest 20 percent was 50 to 1, whereas the figure for the rest of the region was 31 to 1.[19] Observers agree that since that date the situation has worsened. The small portion of the population with wealth undertake ostentatious consumption, as is readily observed in the relatively rapid rise in prices of urban land, houses, and rents in the principal cities. This situation heavily influences the flow of investment to these activities and away from industries of popular consumption. Therein lies another reason for the survival of crafts and for urban unemployment.

Close to 44 percent of the work force of the cities of La Paz, Cochabamba and Santa Cruz have occupations with unstable and, hence, fluctuating incomes.[20] Difficulties in obtaining employment, low wages, and lack of job information means that a considerable portion of the urban population are relegated to a marginality similar to that of the rural peasant. Like their rural counterparts, the capabilities of these urban dwellers to remedy their situation is not very high because, not only do they lack an organizational structure to represent their interests, but also they lack information which would permit them to actively participate in the social arena alongside the other interest groups. Their action, up to now, has been centered more on the search for participation through the channels offered by already established organizations or agencies.

Class and Inter-class Action

The other urban groups, factory workers and crafts workers, have maintained their traditional forms of organization, but since 1971 the Banzer government's progressively restrictive policies toward union activity have severely limited their capacity to incorporate their interests in the larger society. As a result, they have become sensitized to the urban middle-class themes of urban and regional progress and have jointly voiced their concerns with that group.

On the other hand, the labor movement made up of workers from the larger industries have been better organized and consequently stronger. The unions oppose many of the policies of the authoritarian-bureaucratic state and seek to demonstrate in public forum how such policies are part of special national and international interests and not in the interest of the working class.

Regionalism

As a consequence of both of these developments, new styles of action are appearing and are accompanied by forms of populism in which the demand for urban and regional protection constitutes the predominant element. The local character of these demands corresponds to the loss of power by interest groups, political parties, and labor unions on a national level and has created important new lines of tension. Such pressures have provoked serious distortions in national programs designed by the techno-bureaucratic apparatus of the government. Although regionalism is not a new phenomenon in Bolivia, its present manifestations are giving specific content to previously diffuse sentiments, which have coalesced into action forces with a strong regional orientation.

In regions of recent development, this phenomenon is mostly and strongly impacting on a pattern of modern urban life. The middle- and upper-class groups are pushing for urban progress. However, other social groups, among them the lower level townspeople are also expressing demands for betterment. At the present, however, improvement in well-being has been realized principally by upper- and middle-level groups, which has had the effect of separating even further the lifestyles of the privileged and the poor.

In addition to the above-mentioned causes, the new combined urban and regional movements have been made possible by the diffusion of urban values within the systems of social stratification, which barely have been penetrated by the tensions of industrialization. In many cases, however, the participants in these movements have viewed their situation completely in the context of their local situation and have failed to recognize that their movement is only one manifestation of a larger social change.

There have been considerable differences among regions in their capacity to influence change not only through local action but also in gaining support from the state. The consequent uneven regional development has been a factor in breeding conflicts among the regions. These are not new phenomena, but rather have become more visible through the expansion of networks of communication.

Non-Homogeneous Middle Class Group

The middle-class groups do not constitute a homogeneous group. It is purely arbitrary to speak of them as a single group. The diversity and hierarchies of the various functional components of the middle class have become obvious in relation to power and privilege. Yet, even those groups farthest from the centers of decision, due to their apparently more neutral organizations in relation to power, have had sufficient survival capacity and influence to achieve advantages beyond their economic sphere. For example, they have gained advantages in better public services, health, and general living conditions superior to those of the poorer classes. In part, this can be attributed to the use by the middle-class systems of social communication to generate currents favorable to their interests.

It is these middle-class groups, together with the upper classes, who monopolize the advantages of urban development. Almost all the housing with running water, electricity, and public sewers is located in the principal cities, and, within these cities, in the downtown and residential areas with middle and higher income levels. Moreover, the various urban sectors have, in general, better living conditions, as measured by these standards, than those of the rural population. This has occurred and has been maintained by the state's constant directing of resources to urban rather than rural areas in an effort to contribute to the political and economic stability in urban centers.

CONCLUSIONS

There is considerable inequality within and between the rural and urban sectors in Bolivia. The patterns and forms of these inequalities stem, to a large degree, from the state's authoritarian-bureaucratic policies. Instead of eliminating or lessening the demands on society emanating from the class structure, this situation encourages the expression of ethnic, cultural or regional demands by the people. These demands constitute, through their specificity, a starting point for opposition to a political power which tries, by means of its actions on national and international levels, to determine what will be the orientation of the social development in the country. This political model of social development, which has become increasingly important in the 1970s, has brought with it: (a) the exclusion of important sections of the society in the process of modernization, (b) the concentration of work and wealth in some areas of the country, and (c) the monopolization of information and decision making.

The increasing intervention of the state has led to the marginalization of the peasants and urban working classes and has benefited the urban middle class and commercial farmer. Government policies favored urban areas relative to rural areas which made rural-urban migration more attractive to the numerous peasants who strongly cling to traditional values. However, the urban worker has benefited more than the rural peasant, not only because of the urban-oriented government policy but also because it has affiliated itself with the middle class in its demands for betterment.

Government policy has also favored certain regions, especially the *Oriente*. The resultant growth of this region, particularly in the private sector, has led to the formation of the new bourgeoisie that, in combination with economically powerful groups from other regions, has had an increasingly important role in influencing government policies. The success of the *Oriente* has caused a reaction in the rest of the nation which has been manifested in an increasingly regional orientation in order to attempt to obtain the benefits of more government resources for the other regions. In this scheme there has been a loose unification of the various groups and classes in the regions.

In the future there is little reason to expect major changes in this system and its consequences under a continuation of the authoritarian-bureaucratic style of government. Regional development efforts will cause some change in the flow of government resources within the nation but intra-regional inequalities will continue to exist. Should future democratic governments attempt to incorporate the peasant and urban working classes into the political coalition there will be possibilities for major change as the benefits of government policies would be directed to these groups and thus permit them to make relative gains in comparison to the rest of the society. Such policies should build up agriculture, develop stronger rural communities and reduce the rate of rural-urban migration as well as enhance living conditions among the poor in urban areas. Without these actions the prospects for broad-scale Bolivian economic and social development are dim.

ENDNOTES FOR CHAPTER XIV

1. The author is grateful to Bina Breitner and Robert Vitro for assistance in translating the paper from Spanish.

2. See *Censo general de populación, 1900* (Cochabamba: Ed. Canelas, 1973) 2° edición and Ministerio do Hacienda y Estadística, *Censo demográfico: 1950* (La Paz: Ed. Inca, 1953).

3. J. Somoza, *Encuesta demográfica nacional de Bolivia.* (La Paz: Instituto Nacional de Estadística, 1976), p. 48.

4. Ibid., p. 37.

5. Some examples:

    Population served with drinkable water (1974):
    Urban: 24.5%
    Rural: 0.6%

    Medical services (1974):
    Urban: 6   beds and 3 medical hours per 10,000 patients.
    Rural: 0.5 beds and 1 medical hour per 10,000 patients.

    J. Albó, "Bodas de plata o requiem para una reforma agraria", *Revista paraguaya de sociología* 35 (1976): 32.

6. K. Hill et al. *La situación de la mortalidad en Bolivia* (La Paz: Instituto Nacional de Estadística, 1976), p. 9.

7. J. Somoza, op. cit., p. 44.

8. G. A. O'Donnell, *Modernización y autoritarismo* (Buenos Aires: Paidós, 1972), p. 162.

9. Ministerio de Asuntos Campesinos y Agropecuarios, *Diagnóstico del sector agropecuario* (La Paz, Mimeographed, 1974), p. 45.

10. Ministerio de Planificación y Coordinación, *Estrategia Socioeconómica del desarrollo nacional* (La Paz: Ed. Ministerio de Planificación y Coordinación, 1970), p. 58.

11. Ministerio de Asuntos Campesinos y Agropecuarios, op. cit., p.229.

12. C. Arretz, *Análisis de la fecundidad en Bolivia.* Basado en los Datos de la Encuesta Demográfica Nacional de 1975 (La Paz: Instituto Nacional de Estadística, 1976), pp. 28 and 30.

13. Banco Interamericano de Desarrollo, *Prioridades de inversión en el sector agropecuario de Bolivia* (Washington, D.C., Mimeographed, 1973), pp. 6-7.

14. Ministerio de Planificación, *Resultados anticipados por muestreo* (La Paz: Instituto Nacional de Estadística, 1977), p. 69.

15. See J. P. Lavaud, *L'opposition a L'etat fiscal en Bolivie*, (La Paz, Mimeographed, 1976).

16. On this subject see A. Touraine, *Pour la sociologie* (Paris: Ed. du Seuil, 1974).

17. Ministerio de Trabajo y Desarrollo Laboral, *Estadísticas laborales 1970-1975* (La Paz: 1976), IV. (Mimeographed.)

18. Throughout the country, only 14.4 percent of all urban housing has running water, 33 percent has electricity and 12.4 percent has access to public sewers. Most of these services are concentrated in these cities. See Ministerio de Planificación, op. cit., pp. 75-77.

19. S. Romero, "Notas sobre la estratificación social en Bolivia," *Estudios sociales* 5 (1975): 119.

20. Ministerio de Planificación y Coordinación, Instituto Nacional de Estadística, *Encuesta de empleo* (La Paz, Mimeographed, 1977), p. 11.

Part Six

The End of an Era and Prospects for the Future

Chapter XV

The Political Economy of the "Economic Miracle" of the Banzer Regime

Jerry R. Ladman

INTRODUCTION

On August 21, 1971, Colonel Hugo Banzer Suarez led a successful conservative-backed, civilian-military coup—the 182nd change of government in Bolivia's 146 years since independence. The coup toppled the leftist leaning government of General Juan José Torres and the Banzer government became the third in a succession of military regimes to rule the country since the National Revolutionary Movement Party (MNR) government of Víctor Paz Estenssoro was overthrown in 1964 by General René Barrientos. Banzer's reign was to last almost seven years, an unprecedented length of term in office in modern-day Bolivian history. It was marked by an aura of economic progress—the "economic miracle"—and political stability that transcended foreigners and middle and upper class Bolivians alike, albeit in a repressive environment in which the political opposition and the peasant and working classes were increasingly marginated to positions of little influence.

It is the contention of this paper that the economic miracle was indeed not a miracle, but rather a myth based on unfounded prospects for petroleum and fortuitous events in the international petroleum and minerals markets, both of which were not of Banzer's doing nor were under his control. Further, that Banzer was able to remain in power by riding the crest of the wave of the myth and by astutely marginalizing the opposition and dissident elements in society. His regime was to be a continuation of the legacy of the 1952 revolution, which had favored the middle class elements and had not substantially improved the lot of the peasant and working classes. When it became apparent, however, that the economic miracle was indeed a myth and that harsh unpopular measures would be necessary to correct this situation, it was clear that the government would need a popular mandate in order to effectively deal with these problems as well as the resurfaced thorny question with Chile over Bolivia's outlet to the sea. Elections were called for July 1978, and from all appearances Banzer was the leading candidate to become a popularly elected president. However, when the government was forced to decompress to allow opposition to have a voice, previously bottled-up pressures against Banzer surfaced within most elements including the military. Thus, not only did he decide not to run, but also his government began to crumble and he had to fight for survival until the elections. At the polls the peasants and workers voiced their dissatisfaction with Banzer and his lackluster hand-picked successor, General Pereda. Fraud, employed to save the government's candidate, became so obvious that the elections were nullified in a strange sequence of events. Soon thereafter Pereda staged his successful coup.

In the following sections this paper first describes the economic myth, how it was maintained up to the zenith of the Banzer regime in 1976 and how it began to dissolve in the regime's last two years. Second, it discusses how Banzer came to power. Third, it describes how Banzer negotiated the difficult years through 1974, by means of consolidating power and marginalizing the opposition, to ride the crest of popularity through 1977. Fourth, it examines Banzer's quest for a popular mandate, and last, it reviews the elections of 1978.

THE ECONOMIC MYTH, 1971-1978

Economic Growth

The Bolivian economy grew at a robust pace between 1971-1978. There were four basic factors responsible for this growth. First, this was a time when the economic boom of the *Oriente* peaked. The active development of the *Oriente* had begun almost twenty years earlier after the 1952 MNR-led revolution. Yet it wasn't until the late 1960s that the area began to take off, as petroleum production rapidly expanded and agriculturalists began to widely produce for world markets. By the mid-1970s this boom had peaked.

Second, rising world prices for Bolivian exports favored the balance of payments. Petroleum exports were expanding at a time when the OPEC action fortuitously raised petroleum prices. The substantial rises in world tin prices sharply increased revenues and foreign exchange earnings from the troubled Bolivian tin industry. Favorable world prices for agricultural products encouraged the export of these products.

Third, although the above factors were largely not of his doings, President Banzer was able to combine astute politics with the favorable economic conditions to remain in power. The resultant political stability reinforced the growth by creating an atmosphere of certainty and confidence. In particular, this was manifested in foreign lending to Bolivia, which enhanced the balance of payments. Domestic investment in agriculture, private mining, manufacturing and construction also increased in this atmosphere.

Fourth, intertwined with the above was the growth of the public sector and of state enterprises. To a large extent this was made possible by the economic growth that generated substantial government revenues and foreign exchange, which permitted an expansion of public activity and, in the case of the state enterprises, an importation of capital and intermediate goods. Banzer's desire to build a large and loyal base of support in the middle class government bureaucracy undoubtedly contributed to the heavy allocation of resources to this sector.

The growth over the 1971-1978 period was not continuous. As shown in Table XV-1 the real rate of growth peaked in 1976 when it reached 6.5 percent. In 1977 and 1978 it fell to 4.8 and 4.0 percent respectively. Between 1971 and 1976 it averaged 5.7 percent. The decline after 1976 is explicable in terms of the problems that grew out of the economic myth of the earlier years. An explanation of the important factors follows.

TABLE XV-1
ANNUAL REAL RATES OF GROWTH OF BOLIVIAN
GROSS DOMESTIC PRODUCT, 1971-1977
(Percent)

	1971	1972	1973	1974	1975	1976	1977
Growth Rate	5.9	6.9	6.1	5.5	6.5	4.8	4.0

Sources: Banco Central de Bolivia, *Boletín estadístico*, No. 230, junio 1978, and *Presencia* [La Paz], 11 de febrero, 1979.

Petroleum

Although tin is by far the major export commodity, the "economic miracle" of the 1970s was fundamentally based on petroleum. Not only did the petroleum activity in the *Oriente* serve as an engine of growth in that region, but also the prospect of large foreign exchange earnings and government revenues provided the basis for confidence in an otherwise unpromising Bolivian economy. Such prospects played an important role in attracting foreign capital and in encouraging public and private investment in other sectors of the economy. The truth of the matter, however, is that the prospects were not realized and the miracle became a myth.

Petroleum was first exported in 1966. By 1969 petroleum exports had reached 11.6 percent of total exports.[1] In that same year the petroleum industry was nationalized by President Ovando and predictably production and exports fell. It wasn't until 1972 that production again exceeded the 1969 level, as shown in Table XV-2.

Official estimates of petroleum reserves in the early Banzer years were very encouraging. In 1973 Bolivian production was 47,300 barrels per day. In 1974 the estimates were that by 1977 Bolivia would be producing 100,000 barrels per day and that by 1980 the output would rise to 250,000. As late as 1976, the *Five-Year Plan* estimated 1980 production to be 280,000 barrels per day. The fact is that in 1973 production peaked and then declined at an average annual rate of 7.5 percent through 1978 when only 30,000 barrels per day were produced.[2]

Not only did this outcome impact on the domestic economy because of unrealized plans for direct employment and income, but also through the lesser indirect effects that would have been brought about through multipliers. Perhaps equally as important was the impact on the balance of payments. In this context there were two forces at work. First, domestic consumption of petroleum rose at an unanticipated rate of about 15 percent per year such that by 1978 the country was consuming 25,000 barrels per day.[3] Second, this in combination with the decline in production meant that petroleum exports fell drastically. In 1978 only one-third of the production was exported. The outlook is even more dim. One reliable source estimated that Bolivia would be importing petroleum by 1980.[4]

On the more sanguine side, Bolivia's reserves of natural gas have proven to be larger than estimated. Production rose from 376.8 thousand cubic meters in 1969 to 4,232.2 thousand in 1977.[5] Exports began in 1972 with the completion of the gas line to Argentina. There are controversial plans to sell gas to Brazil in the future. Should this come to pass, the prospects of natural gas as a major source of foreign exchange are promising. In fact, beginning in 1977, earnings from natural gas began to exceed those of petroleum.[6]

TABLE XV-2

PETROLEUM PRODUCTION, EXPORTS AND DOMESTIC USE,
1969-1978

	1969	1970	1971	1972	1973	Year 1974	1975	1976	1977	1978[a]
Annual Production (million cubic meters)	2349	1402	2138	2539	2744	2640	2342	2362	2015	938
Percent exported	67.9	52.9	62.8	68.5	68.6	65.0	56.2	54.3	35.4	33.4
Percent Consumed Domestically	32.1	47.1	37.2	31.5	31.4	35.0	43.8	45.7	64.6	66.6

[a]First six months.

Source: Banco Central de Bolivia, *Boletín estadístico*, No. 230, junio 1978.

Tin and Other Minerals

Over the 1971-1977 period Bolivia was the second largest tin producing country in the world in spite of its high costs of production. The combined sales of concentrated tin ore and metallic tin accounted for over 61 percent of the value of total mineral production; zinc, wolfram, and silver were the other major products.[7] As shown in Table XV-3 there was only a slight increase in the volume of tin produced between 1970 and 1977, but the world price rose steadily such that the foreign exchange earnings more than tripled by 1977. The pattern for other major minerals was similar. Were it not for the mineral exports Bolivia's balance of payments would have been in serious trouble when petroleum exports began to decline, especially in 1977 and 1978.

Balance of Payments

Between 1971 and 1974 Bolivia maintained a favorable balance of trade, had moderate increases in foreign debt, and experienced a debt-servicing ratio well within the acceptable limits. As shown in Table XV-4, after 1974 the situation began to change drastically. Imports increased rapidly, whereas exports declined sharply in 1975 to rise again in later years, but the tendency was for a negative balance of trade. In 1978 it was reported to have reached a staggering 117 million dollars.[8] In 1975 the level of foreign borrowing almost doubled over the 1974 level. Much of the increase was from the private sector to finance the rapidly expanding state enterprises. In the following year the increased borrowing is

TABLE XV-3

INDICES OF TIN EXPORTS, 1972–1978
(Base Year of 1970 = 100)

	1972	1973	1974	Year 1975	1976	1977	1978[a]
Value of Exports	106	122	215	160	202	305	370
Quantum of Exports	109	102	104	90	103	111	121
Price of Exports	98	121	207	179	196	273	307

[a]First six months.

Source: Banco Central de Bolivia, *Boletín estadístico*, No. 230, junio 1978.

TABLE XV-4

SELECTED BALANCE OF PAYMENT DATA, 1971–1977
(Millions of U.S. Dollars)

	1971	1972	1973	Year 1974	1975	1976	1977
Exports	181.9	201.3	270.8	578.2	462.3	567.7	647.8
Imports	181.4	195.7	235.3	364.0	514.9	562.3	670.0
Capital Inflow	78.9	130.7	70.8	105.7	201.3	269.3	364.9
Debt Service	23.4	32.5	35.5	55.5	64.6	71.5	101.3
Debt Service Ratio (percent debt service of exports)	12.9	16.1	13.1	9.6	14.0	25.9	19.0

Source: Juan Antonio Morales, "The Bolivian External Sector After 1964," in Jerry R. Ladman, ed., *Modern Day Bolivia: The Legacy of the Revolution and Prospects for the Future* (Tempe, Arizona: Arizona State University, Center for Latin American Studies, 1982), Table X-5.

reflected in the debt service ratio of 25.9. Although the ratio fell again in 1977, by 1978 it was reported to be 30 percent, which required that Bolivia remit 250 million dollars to meet its foreign obligations. [9] The outlook was bleak. Clearly refinancing was necessary in order for Bolivia to survive without a devaluation.

The Public Sector

Between 1970 and 1977 the government's annual deficit rose from 296 to 3,313 million pesos. As shown in Table XV-5 there were very substantial increases in 1972, 1973 and 1975, and gigantic increases in 1976, 1977. The main reasons for this rise were that the government payroll expanded rapidly beginning in 1972 and that government transfer payments to state enterprises and payments on the public debt increased rapidly beginning in 1974.

TABLE XV-5

BOLIVIAN CENTRAL GOVERNMENT ANNUAL DEFICIT
(Millions of Pesos)

	1971	1972	1973	1974	Year 1975	1976	1977	1978[a]
Deficit	296	738	413	455	707	1399	3313	1455

[a]First six months.

Source: Banco Central, *Boletín estadístico*, No. 230, junio 1978.

Clearly the public sector figured more importantly in the Bolivian economy in the Banzer years. García reported that it accounted for 75 percent of the total investment between 1970 and 1975 in comparison to 52 percent for the 1964-1969 period. [10] Much of this increase corresponds to the growth in decentralized agencies and state enterprises. García reports that 72 percent of the national budget in 1977 went for the eighty-nine decentralized agencies and sixty state enterprises and ... "The state enterprises play an important role in the Bolivian economy. They account for 13 percent of GDP, 3 percent of total employment, 40 percent of external public debt, and for 37 percent of central government revenues... and almost 50 percent of the total national investment." [11]

The state enterprises, however, have run considerable deficits. Overinvestment as well as poor management are principal reasons for this trouble. García reports a government subsidization to the fifteen major entities by about 200 million dollars from 1975 to 1977. [12] In January 1979, the general director of Public Mixed Enterprises reported that 65 percent of the seventy entities that were supposed to generate incomes were running deficits. [13] To illustrate, the Bolivian State Mining Company (COMIBOL) ran a deficit of 60 million dollars in 1978, in spite of high tin prices. The projected deficit for 1979 was 80 million dollars. [14] The Bolivian Development Corporation (CBF) expected a deficit of 41 million dollars in 1979. [15] The Bolivian State Petroleum Company (YPFB) was in serious trouble, a deficit of 70 million dollars was expected in 1979. [16] Part of this problem came from the government's unwillingness to raise the price of petroleum on the domestic market, a policy which was carried over since the establishment of OPEC. Also important was the high degree of excess capacity, especially in refineries. In mid-1979 domestic prices were about one-third the level of prices on the world market. It was estimated that the total deficit of the state enterprises and decentralized agencies in 1979 would reach 500 million dollars, which means that the consolidated public debt for the year would exceed 10 percent of GDP. [17]

Although most of these grave figures are for 1979—their magnitude was not available to the public in earlier years—it is clear that they are symptomatic of problems that began to occur in earlier years with the rapid expansion of public enterprises. Clearly, emphasis was on the expansion of the public sector with little regard to efficiency. Tax revenues from exports and foreign exchange earnings were to be used to cover deficits and foreign borrowing in the short run, with the hope that in the long run the enterprises could become self-sufficient. Political considerations also came into play, not only to build up a large and loyal public sector, but also to subsidize the populace, for example, with low gasoline prices.

Summary

When Banzer came to power in August 1971 he inherited an economy that had built-in growth elements basically due to the petroleum-agricultural boom of the *Oriente*. There were, however, troubles, for example with the balance of payments, which required that he direct his attention to short-run matters. The decision was made to devalue the peso in October 1972 when the rate of exchange with the dollar went from 12.5 to 20. The predictable result was high inflation in 1973 and 1974. With the ensuing stability of 1975 and 1976 prices again stabilized but began to rise again in 1977 and 1978 when the severe imbalances in the economy surfaced.

TABLE XV-6

ANNUAL RATE OF INFLATION, 1970-1978:
AS MEASURED BY THE CONSUMER PRICE INDEX OF LA PAZ
(Percent)

				Year				
	1970	1971	1972	1973	1974	1975	1976	1977	1978[a]
Inflation Rate	3.8	3.7	6.5	31.5	62.8	7.9	4.5	8.1	15.0

[a]Annual rate based on first six months.

Source: Banco Central de Bolivia, *Boletín estadístico*, No. 230, junio 1978.

It is clear, that by the time Banzer left the presidency in July of 1978, the economy was in serious trouble. The turning point was after 1976 when the rate of growth slowed, balance of payments problems became apparent and the government deficit soared as the numerous state enterprises began to run huge deficits. Were it not for fortuitous rises in tin and other minerals and extensive foreign borrowing, the problems would have been much worse.

These are only symptoms of the problems,however. The actual problems developed much earlier. Even their symptoms did not become immediately apparent or, if they did, they were easy to neglect in the euphoria of economic growth and political stability. Actually, many of the problems were masked over by the government since much data and information on the true state of petroleum and the state enterprises was not made available. The next sections tell how a combination of political measures and economic events caused the "economic miracle" to occur and to keep Banzer in the presidency. This discussion is followed by one in which the myth of the economic boom is elaborated as an important element in Banzer's fall from power.

BANZER'S RISE TO POWER

When a military coup led by General René Barrientos overthrew the MNR and Paz Estenssoro on November 4, 1964, the stage was to be set for the Banzer government seven years later. Barrientos believed in the value of private enterprise and market forces. During his regime the conservative business and commercial agricultural elements, particularly in the eastern lowlands , the *Oriente,* and in the medium- and small-sized mining sectors, began to flourish and to become major sources of political strength in the economy. Foreign investment was encouraged. Petroleum exports began in 1966 and construction of the gas pipeline to Argentina was initiated. Barrientos was not a friend of organized labor, but did work to gain the allegiance of the peasants with his frequent forays into the countryside. His own peasant background, his fluency in Quecha and his establishment in 1966 of the Military-Peasant Pact enhanced his cause. Under the latter, the military agreed to assist the peasants by providing socioeconomic services and infrastructure in the countryside in exchange for their allegiance and support. In this manner he was effective in courting the peasants and using them to counterbalance the strength of the middle class factions.

When the president met his tragic death in a helicopter accident in April 1969, Vice-president Luis Adolfo Siles Salinas came to power only to be ousted on September 26, 1969 by a military coup led by a friend, General Alfredo Ovando Candia. President Ovando tried desperately to swing the pendulum left of center by building a broader coalition patterned on the Peruvian model, whereby not only peasant, but also labor and reformists were integrated with the military and middle class elements. In a bold move he nationalized Gulf Oil on October 17, 1969, only to lose the support of private business, the military, and foreign investors. After not having been able to bring an effective coalition together, he was deposed by another military coup on October 4, 1970, which elevated General Juan José Torres to the presidency.[18] Torres, a progressive and liberal army officer with leftist inclinations, tried to form a coalition with labor and the ideological left. Immediately the more mainline and conservative elements in the military, private business, and the middle class became very alarmed. Torres also had difficulty in forming an effective coalition with which to rule. He resorted to frequent changes of commands in the armed forces to keep the military in line but he was never able to control the middle class. Regional discontent with government policies in Tarija and Santa Cruz provided the opportunity for manifesting middle class discontent. For example, in Santa Cruz the new central government was viewed as ". . . a band of reckless radicals which attacked the new oil industry, allowed obligations such as pensions in arrears and permitted peasants to run landowners off their farms."[19] Within a time span of only a few months, in January 1971, the conservative military and civilian factions led by Colonel Hugo Banzer attempted an unsuccessful coup. Undaunted, Banzer fled to Argentina to regroup and await a more propitious moment. On August 20, beginning in his native state of Santa Cruz and with the strong backing of the middle class and the private business interests, he again launched a coup attempt against Torres. Rapidly the garrisons fell such that by August 22 Torres was overthrown and Banzer was installed as head of the government. Thus the pendulum had swung back to the right to continue the Barrientos-type military-private sector alliance after" . . . Torres and his predecessor had failed in their search for a workable political coalition going beyond the confines of the middle class."[20]

THE CONSOLIDATION OF POWER 1971-1976

Banzer's reign can be conveniently divided into three periods 1971-1974, 1975-1976 and 1977-1978. The first was a period marked by the consolidation of political power by an increasing marginalization of the opposition, labor, and the peasants; and the survival of some disturbing economic events, such as the devaluation of 1972. The second period was a time when Banzer rode the booming economy to what seemed to be wide-spread popularity and political stability, having successfully neutralized the opposition. The third period was a time when the myth of the economic boom was beginning to be recognized. There was an attempt to return to democracy and Banzer's power crumbled. This section treats the first two periods; the third is discussed in the following section.

Banzer's Base of Power

Banzer came to office with the support of a coalition of three main middle class constituencies that had been threatened by Torres: the military, private business, and factions of the MNR and the Bolivian Socialist Falange (FSB). Later he was to build a beholden support within the government bureaucracy by rapidly expanding not only government activity but also employment in the public sector; from 1970 to 1977 the central government's payroll increased 5.6 times.[21] Banzer made little effort to bring the peasants nor students into his power base and increasingly debilitated organized labor.

The middle class coalition supporting Banzer was named the National Popular Front (FNP) and early established goals of normalizing the situation and returning the country to democratic rule with elections suggested as early as 1975. Banzer was soon to find, however, that apart from organized labor, even within the FNP he did not have total allegiance. He was thus forced to take the path of increasingly assuming personal power and neutralizing the opposition such that on November 9, 1974, he declared a military dictatorship. Elections and the return to democratic rule were postponed until 1980. Key elements of the dictatorship were the banishment of political parties, the repression of labor unions, and compulsory civil service under a new law which allowed the government to draft people for a wide variety of jobs to promote socioeconomic development. The following sub-sections describe Banzer's interactions with the FNP coalition, peasants and labor.

The Military

The military, uneasy under the very liberal Torres, was quick to rally behind Banzer who clearly represented their traditional and more conservative interests. As usual, however, there was some division within the ranks. In particular, the younger generation of officers were especially eager for a return to democratic rule and better conditions for the working classes. When they saw the pendulum moving in the opposite direction they began to organize opposition to Banzer and the older military establishment. The pressure had built up to the point that on June 4, 1974 an attempted coup led by the younger officers had the troops of the Tarapaca Regiment circulating around the presidential palace and the Murrillo Plaza in armored cars. For some reason they lost their nerve and did not follow through on the coup. [22] Clearly all was not well for Banzer. The next time a coup was attempted he was better prepared. On November 7 of the same year there was an attempted civilian-military coup in Banzer's home territory of Santa Cruz. Banzer personally commanded the loyal troops to put down this rebellion, called a state of siege and, on November 9, declared a military dictatorship with himself as head and postponed elections until 1980. [23]

Private Business

From the outset Banzer had the solid backing of the agricultural, commercial, and petroleum interests of the *Oriente*. He quickly gained the support of the small and medium-sized mining companies who had begun to flourish under Barrientos.

Banzer maintained the allegiance of these groups by carefully providing a favorable economic environment to them with the result of increased output that contributed to the economic boom of the country. There were modest annual increases in petroleum production and a sharp increase in the production of natural gas in the early Banzer years. Gas exports to Argentina began in 1972. There was a 238 percent increase in the value of agricultural exports between 1971 and 1974. [24] Most of this increase was due to sharp increases in sugar, cotton and mahogany exports, all of which come from the *Oriente*. Mineral production from privately owned mines gained increasing favor. [25]

A major means used by the Banzer government to assuage the interests in the *Oriente* was credit. The real amount of agricultural credit in Bolivia increased 50 percent over the 1971-1974 period of which an estimated 80 percent went to the *Oriente*. [26] Moreover, this credit was loaned at concessionary interest rates that were 6 to 15 interest points below the rate charged for commercial loans. This clearly resulted in a substantial transfer of income to the large commercial farmers of the *Oriente*. The unwillingness of the government to enforce collection of delinquent loans increased the income transfer substantially as did the rather severe inflation. With these bargains, it was little wonder that much agricultural credit found its way into other activities such as construction and foreign investments. Clearly, this was a policy that favored the large-scale farmers and businessmen of the *Oriente* who in turn provided political support for the government. [27]

Banzer's courting of this group is also illustrated by his support of the cotton growers in 1973 when they were in dispute with international cotton buyers with whom they had forward contracts to sell their cotton at a predetermined price. When the world cotton price rose substantially above this level they refused to sell and the buyers refused to pay more than the contracted price. The government backed the growers with the result that many cotton loans went into default and had to be absorbed by the Bolivian Agricultural Bank. This created a tremendous hardship on the bank and eventually led to its bankruptcy in 1979, when it had to be rescued by a tremendous government subsidy of nearly 41 million dollars.[28] Although the handwriting of bankruptcy was clearly on the wall at a much earlier date, Banzer continued to use his credit cum income transfer to curry support in the *Oriente*. He would not permit the bank to pressure the cotton farmers for repayment and in late 1977 extended these debts up to 12 more years.[29]

Private business was undoubtedly Banzer's strongest element of support. It helped bring him to power and he utilized policy measures that directly benefited them. His staunchest support came from the *Oriente* and business interests in the private sector elsewhere in the country. It was fortuitous that Banzer's rise to power came at the zenith of the *Oriente's* growth in agriculture and petroleum. This growth pole provided Banzer with the economic strength that was necessary to be in a good position to undertake the repressive measures that were to neutralize the opposition and permit him to remain in power. Without the economic growth of this region and the consequent economic prosperity in the nation, as well as the backing of the agriculturalists and businessmen benefiting from this growth, it is questionable whether Banzer would have been able to remain in power in these early years.

The MNR and FSB

For lack of alternatives more suitable to their political persuasion, the Paz Estenssoro wing of the MNR and the FSB under Mario Gutierrez joined forces with Banzer. They were clearly secondary members of the FNP and soon found they had little voice. By November of 1973 Paz Estenssoro was sufficiently disgusted that he resigned his token cabinet post; on January 8, 1974, he went into exile.

After the attempted coup, November 9, 1974, Banzer extinguished all political opposition when he banned all political parties and forced all of the opposition leaders into exile. Having eliminated all the opposition, he announced a military dictatorship with himself as head of the government.

The Peasants

Banzer did not cater to the traditional agricultural areas and their massive peasant populations. The absolute and relative amounts of government spending for agriculture sharply increased in his administration going from 6.8 percent in 1967-1971 to 10.2 percent for the 1971-1977 period;[30] most, however, went to the *Oriente*. Compared to his predecessors Banzer made few visits to the rural areas. Except for marked improvements in rural educational facilities and some roads he did little to rally peasant support for his administration. He did, however, name some very reliable spokesmen who could be counted upon to say the proper things on cue. The peasants, like labor, were restricted in their organized activities. Restless and neglected peasants were not to remain quiescent. In January 1974, a group of peasants set up roadblocks on arteries leading into Cochabamba in protest of higher food prices. The government, eager to put down this show of opposition, sent in the troops. Firing broke out and an estimated 100 peasants were killed in what was to be known as the Massacre of Tolata.[31] In an effort to appease the angry peasants Banzer renewed the Barrientos' Military-Peasant Pact on February 12, 1974, but with little enthusiasm relative to its founder. This marginalization of the peasants and labor was to come to haunt Banzer and his candidate, Pereda, in the 1978 elections.

Organized Labor [32]

Labor viewed the Banzer coup as a threat to the favored position they had acquired under Ovando and Torres. In fact, the Bolivian Workers Central (COB) organized security squadrons and pickets to protest the coup. Their suspicions of Banzer were justified, evidenced by his move against the major elements in Bolivian organized labor to neutralize their influence. He quickly banned the Popular Assembly and the COB; the powerful Bolivian Federation of Miners' Unions (FSTMB) was forbidden to hold congresses. Banzer survived the October 1972 devaluation, which had impacted hard on labor, and in November of that year eased his stand against labor by announcing that unions could operate so long as they remained apolitical. FSTMB promptly held a national congress, but the COB was not permitted to reorganize. Inflation in 1973 and 1974 caused considerable unrest among labor and protest strikes became common and were troublesome for the government. Thus on November 9, 1974, Banzer reacted by announcing a plan to reorganize labor that would put the unions under the virtual control of the government. A main feature of the plan was to employ the new compulsory civil service law to place hand-picked government representatives to lead the unions in the newly created positions of labor union coordinators after existing labor union leaders were dismissed. Other features were the banning of all strikes and lockouts, and the suspension of union dues and assessments. [33] On November 11, the FSTMB and Textile Workers Union called a forty-eight hour hunger strike in protest. The following day Banzer reacted with vigor. Troops were sent into the mines and textile mills, where they were to remain for four years to ensure order. Union leaders were arrested and strikers threatened with dismissal. Labor had been neutralized.

University Students

In a similar fashion Banzer quickly repressed and marginated the potentially volatile students. When Pro-Torres students occupied the main building at San Andres University to protest the Banzer coup, infantry stormed the edifice while aircraft strafed its roof to quell the protest. [34] In 1974 the students again protested, this time over the appointment of an FSB party stalwart as rector. [35] The government rescinded the appointment; the students had made the point that they would oppose the government if provoked.

In June 1976 the students had their big opportunity. After Torres had been mysteriously assassinated in exile in Buenos Aires his widow wanted to bring his remains to La Paz for a state funeral and a lying in state befitting an ex-president. Banzer, fearful that this could serve to rally the opposition, would not give permission. Predictably the students protested and again the military riot squads and tear gas had to be utilized to quell the disturbances.

The Stable Years of 1975-1976

Throughout 1974 the Banzer regime can be succinctly characterized as a time when the military, in coalition with private business, rapidly asserted itself as a reactionary, conservative, and authoritarian government. The incipient petroleum boom and the agricultural boom of the *Oriente* provided the country with the economic strength to sustain the government and to tolerate its authoritarian and repressive ways. It also meant that there was a distinct shift in the power base to the *Oriente*.

There were several foreign-related matters that further called for a strong government resolve to quiet the opposition. First was the devaluation of 1972. Second was the initial recognition of relatively enormous reserves of natural gas. The Bolivians, wishing to capitalize on their additional foreign-exchange earning possibilities, looked increasingly to Brazil as a customer to add to the sales to Argentina which began in 1972. Thus in 1973, ministers of the two countries negotiated an agreement whereby Bolivia would sell natural gas to Brazil for twenty years at the prevailing international price. In return, Brazil was to provide loans to Bolivia for the construction of a gas pipeline as well as the development of the Bolivian iron ore deposit in Matun, near the Brazilian border. On May 22, 1974, Presidents Banzer and Geisel met in Cochabamba to sign the agreement. Cries of a sell-out to Brazilian expansionism arose in Bolivia as a result. [36]

Third, in 1974, neighbors Chile and Peru were building up armies on the common border and sabers were rattling. Although Banzer did not want to get his nation involved in the conflict, should war have occurred, Bolivia would likely have to be drawn into the conflict. Their historical dispute with Chile over a right to an outlet to the sea would have seen to this.

Thus in 1974, when Banzer was threatened by the young military, labor, peasants and students, as well as the potentially disturbing foreign-related events, he decided to take complete charge under the military dictatorship. In the next two years with the opposition eliminated and the working and peasant classes marginated, Bolivia embarked on an era of remarkable political stability. There were outward signs of economic prosperity and the economy continued to grow at an increasing rate. The seeds for the deterioration of the economy were, however, growing. The new engine of growth, petroleum, was faltering, but the myth surrounding it had not yet been uncovered. The quick gains of the agricultural export boom in the *Oriente* had been realized and the boom was beginning to taper. Meanwhile banking institutions, which had heavily financed cotton, were in serious trouble. Tin production was not increasing, but this was masked by rising world prices. The public sector was expanding apace with the consequences of an increasing public debt, large deficits in the state enterprises, and heavy borrowing abroad by the state enterprises. The latter, in combination with rapidly increasing imports, was setting the stage for balance of payments problems. The combination of all of these factors was to prove to be a key to the deterioration of the Banzer regime in its last two years of government.

The issue of an outlet to the sea, which played an important role in the solidarity of the government in 1975 and 1976, like the economy, was to be an important factor in unhinging hostility and opposition in 1977 and 1978. [37] After the quiescence of the saber rattling in Peru and Chile in 1974, Banzer removed attention from the repressive events of November by rallying the nation in an offensive in February of 1975. He did this by reestablishing diplomatic relations with Chile in order to be in a position to negotiate a solution to the outlet to the sea problem. In August Bolivia made a proposal for this solution to Chile and Banzer threatened to resign if the negotiations were unsuccessful. In December Chile made a counter offer that asked Bolivia to give up territory in exchange for the outlet to the sea. Banzer appointed a Maritime Commission to study the problem. Meanwhile, Peru, which had to approve any treaty, made its proposal in November. Banzer, in his 1976 Christmas message, called upon the other two nations for a solution. An impasse was soon reached, however, when Chile refused to consider any outlet without the compensation of some Bolivian territory. Thus, at the end of 1977 the matter was laid to rest until after the 1978 elections.

THE QUEST FOR A POPULAR MANDATE

On January 25, 1977, Banzer, riding a wave of apparent popularity, began a conciliatory posture toward the opposition when he announced a return to normal political activity. Most observers took this measure of decompression as a step to prepare the country for democratic elections. Immediately, the repressed opposition took him at his word. The MNR announced plans to celebrate the twenty-fifth anniversary of their revolution on April 9 and the FSB announced plans to hold a national convention. Banzer, however, squelched both when he said he had referred more to labor union activities, not political activities. However, he did allow political activity after delimiting its scope. Further, he announced that elections would be held in 1980, but that he would hand over the power to a civilian government only if it could guarantee ". . . unity, well being, peaceful coexistence and political stability for every citizen, without exception."[38] Clearly, this would be a tall order for any government. Simultaneously, the labor minister announced plans for new labor legislation to provide a "new dimension" for trade unions to complete democratization later in the year.[39] Moreover, in an attempt to win over the students, the government asked the National Council for Higher Education to survey university students to discover ways of reestablishing communications between students and government.[40] Thus in one fell swoop, Banzer had made a commitment to hold elections and made conciliatory gestures to the previously marginated students and labor. Clearly, however, the game plan was to decompress and conciliate on Banzer's terms; labor was to be reorganized on the basis of the government's plans and the political opposition was quickly informed it was too early to begin to organize.

Meanwhile the outlet to the sea question was still kindling. The government was awaiting the Peruvian and Chilean response to Banzer's plea in his Christmas 1976 speech. In September, Presidents Banzer, Bermúdez and Pinochet met in Washington after the Panama Canal Treaty ceremonies. It was clear that an impasse had developed; Chile insisted that Bolivia exchange territory and Bolivia and Peru opposed this solution. Banzer did not believe he was in a position to negotiate a territorial trade without a popular mandate. Thus the issue was laid to rest until after the elections.[41]

The delicate and deteriorating state of the economy was becoming increasingly apparent. Petroleum production was falling, internal consumption of the product was rising rapidly, and oil export revenues were declining at a greater rate. To try to correct this trend the government made another attempt to attract foreign firms to explore for oil by sweetening the terms of the exploration contracts. In 1973 and 1974 some eighteen firms had signed contracts, but to date only one, Occidental, had struck oil. As Cariaga pointed out, this would have grave consequences for the Bolivian economy.[42]

Fortunately, high tin prices saved Bolivia from extraordinarily severe balance of payments problems. Tin revenues were considerably above projected levels whereas petroleum and gas exports were 41 million dollars below projections. To worsen the situation agricultural exports were 15 million dollars below projected levels.[43] Because imports continued to rise it was obvious that a serious debt servicing problem was imminent.

With the balance of payments problems and decline in oil revenues the impact of the large deficits and foreign borrowing of the state enterprises was emerging. Thus the delicate state of the Bolivian economy on a number of fronts was becoming more apparent to the government. The gravity of the situation was, however, glossed over for the public. It was not until 1978 that the true situation was to become clear. Meanwhile Banzer's popularity continued to ride high.

Elections Announced for 1978

In a surprising move on November 9, 1977, Banzer formally announced that elections would be held in July 1978, two years earlier than his previously announced date of 1980. There are several possible explanations of his decision.

First, it was possible that he was responding to pressure from the United States for improving human rights. While this is very plausible, officials who were posted in the Bolivian embassy in Washington and U.S. embassy in La Paz at that time state that the United States did not exert direct pressure on the Bolivian government. Undoubtedly, there was some indirect pressure. Once the elections were announced, however, the United States strongly supported the decision, a factor that may have had important influence in causing their scheduled occurrence.

Second, perhaps Banzer philosophically believed that the country should return to democratic rule and that this was the propitious time for such a move. This argument is doubtful for he clearly was in a position of strong control at this time, and there was no apparent need to relinquish power.

Third, Banzer probably realized the gravity of the economic situation and the consequences of a stalemate with Chile. Therefore, he wanted to succeed himself under a popular mandate that would have given him the authority to undertake the harsh and unpopular measures that would be necessary to properly cope with these problems. His previous inability to invoke harsh economic measures was demonstrated in January 1978, when he was forced, under popular pressure, to revoke a government decision to raise electricity prices. Meanwhile, time was running out and 1980 would be too late. By then the petroleum myth and the sad state of the economy would be very apparent and it was unlikely that he would be able to maintain the popularity needed to succeed himself in office.

The Government's Candidate

It was almost certain that Banzer would try to succeed himself given the current state of his apparent popularity and an environment where the opposition had been neutralized. The question was, how would it be done? According to the Constitution, Banzer had to be out of office for at least six months to be considered a candidate. Yet, if he vacated the presidency would he be able to maintain control? The solution was to select a controllable replacement. He chose Air Force General Juan Pereda Asbún, preferring not to give the nod to an army general who would have a much stronger power base.

The President then sought support for his plan, but much to his surprise, found that he had miscalculated his own strength. He learned he did not have solid backing. In a November meeting with leaders of the FSB and the Paz Estenssoro Wing of the MNR he was not received well. [44] In a tour of the barracks in the same month he was surprised to find that he did not have the solid support of the military. It was becoming apparent that there were cracks in his base of military support. In particular the younger officers resented the control of the military by the older generals. In an apparent conciliatory move to patch up the cracks, Banzer announced on November 26 his retirement as well as that of twenty-five other generals at the end of the year. [45]

After having attempted to maintain his military support, it was blockbusting news on December 2 when he announced that he would not be a candidate. [46] This may have been a ploy to force a rally of the fragmented support to draft him, but when an overwhelming groundswell of such activity was not forthcoming, Banzer stuck by his decision. Perada was announced in mid-December as the government's candidate. Although Banzer had received a blow, he still had strong support among the military, the middle classes and private business. It was a common belief that with this backing, and with the government's ability to orchestrate the election process and to give Pereda abundant exposure, that Pereda was a virtual shoe-in to replace Banzer.

There remained, however, the thorny problem of how to handle the opposition. It was hardly possible to hold a meaningful election without their active participation. The obvious strategy was to allow political parties to regroup but to delay this as long as possible in order to not allow sufficient time to effectively organize a strong anti-government campaign. The matter, however, was largely taken out of the government's hands by the events of January 1979.

Trouble For The Government

On January 5, a small number of persons began a hunger strike in La Paz to protest the government's policy on political exiles and the presence of troops in the mines, as well as to seek the reinstatement of workers that had been dismissed for trade union activities. By January 17 the strike had spread to all the major cities and the number of strikers had grown to an estimated 1,200.[47] The government, confronted by this dramatic and symbolic show of opposition, attempted to demoralize and break up the strike by harassing the strikers with troops and selective arrests. The strikers were persistent, however, in face of the government's determination. Finally, in frustration, the government overplayed its hand when troops entered the sanctity of churches in Santa Cruz and Oruro to arrest troublesome strikers.[48] The enraged outcries of the church authorities and the public against such action finally forced the government into a position of acquiescing on January 24—twenty tense days after the strike had begun.[49] Public support of Banzer and Pereda began to falter and now that there was a crack in the armor, the opposition and marginated sectors began to take advantage of the situation.

A Scramble to Remain in Power

The FSB proposed a military triumvirate to replace Banzer until the elections. The Tupaj Katari peasant party began to speak out against the government, in spite of the sycophantic support that the Banzer mouthpieces provided in the countryside. Moreover, Banzer had been forced to give in to many of labor's demands. Unions and federations were to be permitted to hold elections.[50] The government's previously proposed labor legislation was dropped.[51] Labor quickly set about to reorganize and it would only be a matter of time before they would push the government for higher wages.

The President was now in a position of having to scramble to remain in power. Having acquiesced to the strikers' demands, Banzer's administration adopted a policy of slowing down the implementation of the required changes in government policy. Exiled political leaders encountered delays in obtaining visas to return. Labor unions encountered bureaucratic hang-ups in their reorganization efforts.[52]

Pereda proved to be a lackluster candidate and was not received well in his public appearances. There were rumors of a split between him and

Banzer. There were even threats within the military that was growing increasingly fearful of the outcome of the elections. Banzer attempted to both divert the public's attention from internal squabbles and to avoid a coup when on March 17 the government brought up the always nationalistic issue of the outlet to the sea and broke diplomatic relations with Chile. Only a few weeks later, on April 2, the President called a four day meeting of troop commanders in La Paz in order to avoid a coup scheduled for April 4. [53]

Banzer, at this time, strongly considered delaying the elections, but the forces in favor of holding elections were too strong. For example, reports indicate that he tried to persuade the troop commanders during the April meeting to postpone the elections but they would not agree. [54] Perhaps their decision was influenced by the simultaneous announcement from the World Bank that "external financing will be easier if elections are in July." [55] Earlier, in February, the United States Agency for International Development Mission director had stated, "President Carter believes that the Bolivian electoral process in 1978 is very important, not only for Bolivia but for the whole of Latin America." [56]

Thus, Banzer had little choice but to continue with plans for the July 9 elections. Pereda continued to have electioneering troubles in spite of government support. Sensing Banzer's weakness he tried to stay at arms length from the president, but he remained an unconvincing candidate. Moreover, he declared his true colors as being decidedly conservative. Opposition parties began to form. Four leftist parties decided to join in support of ex-president Hernán Siles Zuazo. Paz Estenssoro was due to return from exile and a big question was how he would use his support.

To make matters worse, in a completely unrelated event, the United States government began to create pressures for Bolivia by threatening to sell off part of its stockpiles of tin, an action that would undoubtedly cause world tin prices to fall, and raise havoc with Bolivia's fragile balance of payments.

The government was dealt another damaging blow by the United States. A confidential report prepared by the U.S. Embassy on the Bolivian petroleum situation somehow found its way into the press. [57] The consequence of the publication was that the bubble of the petroleum myth was burst.

Meanwhile, organized labor was reexerting itself. The venerable Juan Lechín Oquendo returned from exile to be reelected executive secretary of the FSTMB when it held its Seventeenth Congress in May. The labor coordinators had finally been replaced by elected representatives. Unions pushed for what they claimed to be long overdue wage increases to bring them up to pre-devaluation levels. The government agreed to 20 percent, but labor held out for much more. [58] In summary, as the elections approached, the government and its candidate were in trouble. In spite of this state of affairs, most observers thought that Pereda would be the victor come July 9.

THE 1978 ELECTIONS

This was not to be the case, however, for the National Electoral Court was to annul the disputed elections on the account of fraud. Thus, what had begun in November of 1977 to return Bolivia to democratic rule, ended on July 21, 1978, with a military coup led by the government's candidate, General Juan Pereda Asbún. This was a horrible blow to the plucky Banzer. How did it happen?

The Candidates

There were thirteen parties or coalitions on the ballot from which there were seven candidates for president and vice-president. [59] The presidential candidates were: Pereda, Hernán Siles Zuazo, the Democratic Popular Coalition (UDP) candidate; [60] René Bernal, a Christian Democrat; Víctor Paz Estenssoro, who represented the center-left of the MNR; Cassaro Amurrio, the Leftist Revolutionary Front (FRI) candidate; Luciano Tapia Quisbert, the Tupaj Katari candidate; and Luis Adolfo Siles Salinas, an independent candidate.

Fraudulent Elections

Fraud had been anticipated; it was customary in Bolivia, especially by a ruling party that could exert its power to influence the outcome. Siles Zuazo quickly put the government on notice when, in his first campaign speech, he said that the National Revolutionary Movement of the left (MRNI) would take up arms and go to the streets if the elections were fraudulent. [61] Plans were made to bring in an international team of election observers.

Nevertheless, in the month before the election, the government used the irregular tactics of intimidation and confiscation of materials against the opposition, especially Siles Zuazo who was viewed as its major threat. In Ucureña, for example, a Siles rally was cancelled because of threats of government supporters. In response to protests, Banzer virtually shrugged his shoulders. [62]

In June the FSB candidate, José Patiño Ayoroa, withdrew from the race after charging the government with fraud. Public opinion had it that most of his support would go to Pereda. Meanwhile, the open rift between Banzer and Pereda was healed as the government pulled out all the stops to garner support. Major efforts were made to register voters. Long lines existed at registration booths in the countryside and urban centers alike. Government units and equipment were used to campaign for Pereda. [63] In defiance of election laws, Banzer went on national television on the eve of the election to urge the populace to vote for Pereda. [64]

The early official count showed Pereda with a comfortable lead, but later returns from rural areas and the working class sections of the highland cities showed that Siles Zuazo, Paz Estenssoro and Bernal were gaining support. It appeared that the elections might have to be decided under the constitutional provision governing a situation in which no candidate receives a majority of the votes. In this case the election would be decided in the Chamber of Deputies in a run-off election among the top three vote-getters.

By July 11 Siles was crying "fraud" only to be denounced by Pereda a few hours later as an agent of "international communism." [65] UDP claimed victory in La Paz city and department, Potosí, Sucre, and many mining areas. The miners and peasants had supported Siles, obviously, a protest against their repression and margination under Banzer and fear of more of the same under the ultra-conservative Pereda.

Meanwhile, the international election observers were quick to say that fraud was prevalent on both sides. Robert Goldberg, a United States lawyer, said that routine violations were so prevalent that every result in La Paz could have been challenged and nullified. Further, that there were reports that troops had removed ballots at gunpoint. [66] Lord Avebury, from England, said the elections were "fraudulent from beginning to end."

He described instances of votes in some places exceeding numbers in the recent population census, forged identity cards, switching of ballot boxes, and the removal of opposition voting slips from voting booths. [67] In another disclosure the Catholic Radio Station in La Paz played a tape recording of La Paz Prefect, Mario Oxa, giving rural authorities instructions to swap ballot boxes if the results were unfavorable to Pereda. [68]

The Annulment

In a surprise move on July 20 Pereda called on the National Electoral Court to nullify the elections and to hold new elections in 120 days. At this time he supposedly was ahead by a very thin majority and Siles Zuazo was second with about 20 percent of the votes. The court quickly took this opportunity to annul the elections within a very few days on grounds that the final vote count exceeded the already inflated number of registered voters by 50,000. [69]

It is not certain why Pereda took this action but several factors were undoubtedly important and permit conjecture. First, Banzer had announced on May 18 he would hand over the government on August 6, but if there was no clear successor he would hand it over to a military junta. The way the elections were going this may have been the situation. Second, if this occurred, Pereda feared the potential loss of support and the possibility that Banzer would become a candidate himself, thus shutting out Pereda's future opportunities. Third, he did not expect the court to make a quick decision and the prolonged deliberation would abrogate the need for the junta. Pereda could have then run again in the orderly elections in 120 days.

Thus, when this strategy was shut off by the quick court decision, Pereda apparently decided to take the matter into his own hands. On July 20 from Santa Cruz, he announced that "communism will not triumph" and asked Siles Zuazo to leave the country. [70] Siles's response was that he would not leave "under any circumstances." The following day the Pereda uprising began in Santa Cruz when a military-civilian group seized Santa Cruz radio stations in a "nationalist rebellion" aimed at fighting communism. [71] Soon thereafter the Santa Cruz military airbase fell.

Banzer quickly dispatched two cabinet ministers to go to Santa Cruz to try to persuade Pereda to change his mind. He then went on national television to appeal to the populace to be calm in view "of the dangers that exist in the moment for the nation." [72] This was to no avail. On that same evening of July 21 President Banzer again went on live television from the Hall of Mirrors in the National Palace to announce his resignation and to swear in a military junta. It was a very emotional time, Banzer giving the traditional *abrazo* to each officer. [72] His successful regime of nearly seven years had come to an ignominious end. He had lost control and was forced to turn over the government to his general friends, who promptly named Juan Pereda as president.

Within two days, the former president was again walking the streets very much as an ordinary citizen. [73] However, his desire to regain control of the country would soon become apparent. In the meantime, he left the office with a legacy of such difficult economic conditions that were only to get worse during the reign of the powerless transitional governments over the course of the next two years.

ENDNOTES FOR CHAPTER XV

1. Juan Antonio Morales, "The Bolivian External Sector After 1964," in Jerry R. Ladman, ed., *Modern Day Bolivia: The Legacy of the Revolution and Prospects for the Future* (Tempe, Arizona: Arizona State University, Center for Latin American Studies, 1982).

2. "Bolivia on the Verge of Becoming Net Oil Importer," *Latin America Economic Report* April 6, 1979, p. 108.

3. Ibid., p. 108.

4. Asociación de Bancos e Instituciones Financieras de Bolivia, *Boletín informativo ASOBAN*, September 15, 1978, p. 3.

5. Banco Central de Bolivia, *Boletín estadístico*, No. 230, June 1978, p. 53.

6. Ibid.

7. Ibid., pp. 50, 51.

8. *Presencia* [La Paz], February 11, 1979.

9. Ibid.

10. L. Enrique García-Rodríguez, "Structural Change and Development Policy in Bolivia," in Ladman, *Modern Day Bolivia,* p. 167.

11. Ibid., p. 167.

12. Ibid., p. 167.

13. *Presencia* [La Paz], January 10, 1979.

14. *El Diario* [La Paz], March 22, 1979.

15. *Presencia* [La Paz], March 22, 1979.

16. Private communication to the author from United States Embassy in Bolivia, March 28, 1979.

17. Asociación de Bancos e Instituciones Financieros de Bolivia, *Boletín informativo ASOBAN*, March 22, 1979, p. 1.

18. This section draws heavily on the analysis of Christopher Mitchell, *The Legacy of Populism in Bolivia, From the MNR to Military Rule* (New York: Praeger Publishers, 1977), pp. 114-118.

19. Ibid., p. 117.

20. Ibid., p. 118.

21. Banco Central de Bolivia, op. cit., p. 47.

22. David Wingeate Pike ed., *The Latin American Yearly Review*, vol. III, The Events of 1974 (Paris: The American College in Paris, 1975), p. 76.

23. Ibid., p. 77.

24. Banco Central de Bolivia, *Boletín estadístico*, No. 219,   December 1975, p. 55.

25. Mitchell, op. cit., p. 122.

26. Jerry R. Ladman, Ronald L. Tinnermeier and José Isaac Torrico, "Agricultural Credit Flows and Use in Bolivia," Report submitted to RDD/USAID (La Paz: United States Agency for International Development, March 15, 1977), p. 36.

27. Jerry R. Ladman and Ronald L. Tinnermeier, "The Political Economy of Bolivian Agricultural Credit," Paper presented at the Latin American Studies Meetings, April 6, 1979 (Mimeographed).

28. *El Diario* [La Paz], March 17, 1979.

29. Bolivia, Presidencia de la República, Decreto Supremo, No. 14707, June 28, 1977.

30. José Isaac Torrico, "The Public Sector in Agricultural Development," in Ladman, *Modern Day Bolivia*, p. 264.

31. Mitchell, op. cit., p. 127.

32. This section draws heavily on Robert J. Alexander, "The Labor Movement During and Since the Bolivian Revolution," in Ladman, *Modern Day Bolivia*, pp. 59-80.

33. Bolivia, Presidencia de la República, Decreto Supremo No. 174780, as reported in Alexander, op. cit., p. 24.

34. Mitchell, op. cit., p. 125.

35. Pike, op. cit., p. 76.

36. Ibid., pp. 78-79.

37. This section draws heavily on E. James Holland, "Bolivian Relations With Chile and Peru: Hopes and Realities," in Ladman, *Modern Day Bolivia*, pp. 123-144.

38. "Bolivia Back to Normal," *Latin American Political Report*, March 25, 1977, p. 90.

39. Ibid., p. 90.

40. Ibid., p. 90.

41. Holland, op. cit., pp. 137-138.

42. Juan L. Cariaga, "The Economic Structure of Bolivia After 1964," in Ladman, *Modern Day Bolivia*, p. 158.

43. "Tin Prices Save the Day for Bolivia's Balance of Payments," *Latin American Economic Report*, December 2, 1977, p. 226.

44. "Bolivia: Who Needs a Coup?" *Latin America Political Report*, December 16, 1977, pp. 386-387.

45. *The Wagner Latin American Newsletter*, December 21, 1977, p. 1.

46. "Bolivia: Change of Tack," *Latin America Political Report*, December 9, 1977, p. 377.

47. "Bolivia: Collision Course," *Latin America Political Report*, January 20, 1978, p. 22.

48. Ibid., p. 22.

49. "Bolivia: Balancing Act," *Latin America Political Report*, February 3, 1978, p. 34.

50. "Bolivia: Delaying Tactics," *Latin America Political Report*, February 10, 1978, p. 6.

51. "Bolivia: Balancing Act," op. cit., p. 34.

52. "Bolivia: Delaying Tactics," op. cit., p. 6.

53. "Bolivia: Banzer's Tightrope," *Latin America Political Report*, April 21, 1978, p. 116.

54. Ibid., p. 114.

55. "News in Brief: Bolivia," *Latin America Political Report*, April 7, 1978, p. 104.

56. "Bolivia: Delaying Tactics," op. cit., p. 6.

57. "Gloom Gathers Over Bolivian Oil Prospects," *Latin America Political Report*, April 28, 1978, p. 126.

58. "Miners Declare Wages Against Bolivian Government," *Latin America Economic Report*, June 9, 1978, p. 176.

59. "Bolivia: Wheat and Chaff," *Latin America Political Report*, June 9, 1978, p. 173.

60. The UDP coalition was formed of Siles Zuazo's own party the National Revolutionay Movement of the Left (MRNI); the Communist Party; the National Liberation Alliance (ALIN); and one of the two Tupaj Katari peasant groups.

61. *The Wagner Latin American Newsletter*, May 10, 1978, p. 2.

62. "Bolivia: Rights and Wrongs," *Latin America Political Report*, June 23, 1978, p. 190.

63. Information obtained by author from employees working in these government entities.

64. "Bolivia: The Faking of a President," *Latin America Political Report*, July 14, 1978, p. 1.

65. "Bolivia: Brazening It Out," *Latin America Political Report*, July 21, 1978, p. 222.

66. "Bolivia: The Faking of a President," op. cit., p. 1.

67. Ibid.

68. *The Wagner Latin American Newsletter*, August 2, 1978, p. 1.

69. "Bolivia: Cesarean Birth," *Latin America Political Report*, July 26, 1978, p. 225.

70. *Arizona Republic* [Phoenix], July 22, 1978, p. A-4.

71. Ibid.

72. Ibid.

73. "Bolivians, Thankful for the Calm, Accept Latest Coup With a Shrug," *New York Times*, July 26, 1978, p. A3.

Chapter XVI

The Failure to Redemocratize
Jerry R. Ladman

INTRODUCTION

For two years, following the failure of the July 1978 elections, Bolivia was immersed in what was almost a singular goal: to obtain a democratically elected government. In this period, which culminated in the military coup of July 17, 1980, led by General Luis García Meza, Bolivia experienced six different governments. The country was constantly in a state of crisis as it was increasingly confronted with the difficult economic and political legacies of the Banzer years while simultaneously trying to elect a government. The faltering economy rapidly worsened, but the short-lived governments could not take the necessary measures to right it for lack of a broad base of support and with the fear that the military would forceably intervene if there were excessive domestic disturbances. It was a time during which new forces had to be reckoned with as the country emerged from the strong repression of the previous military governments; for the first time in many years organized labor, political parties, and an elected congress played important roles alongside the military in determining the course of events. Moreover, the military went through a period of soul searching about its role in society as younger, liberal officers began to exert influence. The plan for an elected government was strongly supported by the United States as an important element in President Carter's human rights policy. In the end, however, as many predicted, it was the Bolivian military that held the trump card and prevented Bolivia from being governed by the apparent victor of the June 29, 1980, general elections, Hernán Siles Zuazo, the candidate of the Democratic Popular Coalition Party (UDP).

This chapter briefly chronicles the events of these two years and analyzes why Bolivia was unsuccessful in its attempt to return to a democratically elected government.

THE PEREDA GOVERNMENT

The government of General Juan Pereda Asbún, which came to power with the overthrow of the Hugo Banzer Suarez government on July 21, 1978, began under a cloud of disillusionment and resentment.[1] The

Bolivian public, although accustomed to military rule, genuinely was disappointed at the failure to elect a president. After years of repression under Banzer, political parties and organized labor considered the Pereda coup a setback in their efforts to reorganize. The early reported arrests of some 100 persons, including student and labor leaders and human rights activists, were alarming as were the new president's comments in a nationally televised speech on July 24 when he said that he would govern a democracy under which the popular decisions would be ratified by the armed forces. Moreover, he offered that he did not see the need for congress in the near future. He let it be known that his government was committed to holding elections but he did not specify when they would be held. In naming his cabinet he selected eleven civilians who were identified with the Banzer policies, and four from the military. [2] From all appearances it looked as though the Pereda administration would be cast in the same mold as its predecessor.

Many foreign countries voiced disapproval of this turn of events. Particularly outspoken were the United States and the neighboring Andean countries that were simultaneously returning to democracy after an interregnum of military governments.

Pereda, confronted by internal and external opposition, declared his government to be an interim administration but went on to say on July 28 that elections would be postponed until 1980 on the grounds that 1979 was the centennial of Bolivia's loss of its corridor to the sea. As such, it was not appropriate to have the political divisiveness of an election campaign that would distract from the nation's united effort to regain an outlet to the sea in that year. [3] It was clear that Pereda had decided to try to remain in power either to promote his own cause or to prevent early elections that might send Siles Zuazo and his leftist coalition to the presidency, a prospect that put fear in the hearts of the military and rightist elements. Predictably, Siles protested and threatened strikes and work stoppages if elections were not held soon. The United States also let it be known that it looked very unfavorably upon any long interruption of the electoral process.

The shaky Pereda government, in moves to mollify the opposition and the U.S. government, took a series of measures to disassociate itself with the Banzer regime. This included granting absolute freedom to the press and the repeal of the 1967 National Security Law that had been used by Banzer to repress the opposition. To gain support in the armed services Pereda granted promotions to younger officers who had been held back under Banzer in favor of the ex-president's supporters.

These measures were successful in gaining more credibility with the opposition as well as the full recognition of the new administration by the U.S. government. However, the demands for early elections did not cease, but Pereda adroitly avoided making a definite commitment as to the date. Meanwhile, the right, Pereda's main source of power, displayed serious displeasure with the president's concessions to the opposition as well as his open criticism of Banzer policies. Talks of a rightist coup to restore Banzer to power were rife. In an effort to mend his fences, Pereda named Banzer as ambassador to Argentina in early October, a move that could be interpreted as incorporating the ex-president into the regime but at the safe distance of the friendly Argentine capital city. Predictably, this concession to the right raised the suspicion of the opposition about the sincerity of the earlier Pereda reforms.

Meanwhile, the economic situation continued to deteriorate. The balance of payments worsened as foreign petroleum sales declined and the U.S. threatened to sell stocks of tin on the world market. This sale of tin certainly would lower the price of Bolivia's principal export should it come to pass. Domestically, the huge foreign debt was looming as a large burden, and the excessive losses of many of the decentralized government agencies were beginning to become known. Pereda, however, was not in a position to take the necessary steps to begin to correct these problems. Such actions would have been suicidal because the certain strong repercussion from affected interest groups would have required a response by his fellow officers, and his fragile government was in no position to withstand such an intervention.

By mid-October, when the ineffectiveness of his government became abundantly clear, rumors of an impending coup circulated ever more strongly. On October 30 the government announced that it had uncovered plans for a plot against the president by a coalition of right and opposition members with the suggestion that a coup to return Banzer to the presidency had been imminent.[4]

Bolstered by his claim to have prevented the alleged coup, Pereda reorganized the cabinet, dismissing many of the pro-Banzer civilians and replacing them with younger military officers of the *grupo generacional* who were not sympathetic to the former president[5] and who represented the liberal, progressive elements of the armed forces. By breaking away from the conservative right and joining with the more progressive elements of the armed forces, Pereda tried to form a centrist base of support that would allow him to remain in office. In a bold move to be convincing about the strength of his government, the president defended its legitimacy in a November 6 speech to make long-run economic decisions while the country continued its return to democracy.[6] The following week he announced that the elections would be held in May 1980,[7] sufficiently far enough in the future to allow him to undertake the harsh measures necessary to try to straighten out the economy.

Neither the left nor right was satisfied, nor convinced, that the Pereda government was up to these tasks. The late election date angered the UPD and other leftist groups. A component of the government's proposed economic policy, a crackdown on the highly profitable contraband industry, threatened an important element of Pereda's support, the Santa Cruz business community. Moreover, the necessary economic measures would, at best, be unpopular across broad segments of society. Pressure was being placed on the government by the International Monetary Fund (IMF) to undertake severe austerity measures, including the raising of domestic fuel prices and a wage freeze. Neither these nor the alternative of devaluation could be implemented without widespread opposition. It was clear that Pereda's strategy had not gathered the necessary support and his regime continued in a precarious state. Should his government fail to remain in power, the most likely alternative would be a forceful return to power by Banzer, an outcome that would be unacceptable not only to the left, but also to many of the younger military officers who had recently gained influence under Pereda.

Convinced it was time to act, a military junta led by the head of the army, General David Padilla Arancibia, and supported by the younger military officers of the *grupo generacional*, toppled the Pereda government in a quiet and bloodless coup on November 24, 1979. Siles Zuazo and the opposition openly welcomed this change and likely lent their support to the coup.

THE PADILLA GOVERNMENT

The Padilla-led junta represented the "institutionalist" faction of the armed services: those officers, including the *grupo generacional*, who viewed the military in its traditional defense role and not as a governing unit. This was in contrast to the two previous administrations of "constitutionalists" who believed that the military should govern when the civilians proved incapable of properly leading the country. Indeed, Padilla, named as president by the junta, quickly established that the main goal of his administration was to hold elections on July 1, 1980, in order that a civilian government could be installed on August 6, Bolivian Independence Day. Furthermore, this time members of congress would be elected in order to reestablish the legislative branch which had not existed since 1969.

The Commitment to Elections

Padilla's first task was to convince all that these were indeed his true intentions. He did this by maintaining a firm middle-ground position. To neutralize the threat from the Banzer forces he immediately removed the ex-president from his ambassadorial post, retired the Banzer supporters from the army, and allowed Colonel Rolando Saravia, minister of Agriculture and Peasant Affairs, to openly criticize the Banzer government under which he claimed atrocities had occurred.[8] To compensate, the president warmed up to the right by promising his support to private business, but indicated they should not expect any special favors. Simultaneously, while offering reassurance to organized labor and other elements of the opposition, he would not go so far as to remove the soldiers from the mines or dissolve the military-peasant pact. To directly assert control over the military he assumed the additional position of head of the armed forces.

The Deteriorating Economy

Padilla's second task was to determine how to handle the pressing matters of the deteriorating economy. By this time there was an increasing awareness of the limitations of relying upon petroleum as an engine of growth, and the recognition that in the near future Bolivia likely would become a net importer of petroleum. The prospects for increased sales of natural gas to Argentina and Brazil offered some hope to offset the decline in oil export revenues. Indeed, in October Pereda had signed a letter of intent to sell gas to Brazil. However, the proposed sale gave rise to considerable opposition. Many Bolivians viewed this as a loss of sovereignty over a natural resource and as a deal that would certainly be unfair to Bolivia and favorable to their giant eastern neighbor. Padilla decided to leave the resolution of the matter to the next government.[9]

The Bolivian tin industry was in a precarious state. Faced with high costs of production resulting from low-grade ore and antiquated equipment, the sale price barely covered costs. The situation was aggravated in January when Padilla acquiesced to miners' demands and agreed to a 35 percent increase in the wages of miners employed by the state and about a 25 percent increase to those employed by the private sector. Production was declining; were it not for increasingly high prices on the world market the value of export sales would have declined. The possibility of U.S. sales from its strategic stockpiles threatened to lower prices. Taking account of all these factors, the outlook for Bolivian tin was gloomy.

In spite of these adverse factors, exports were growing slowly; in sharp contrast, imports rose rapidly as the Bolivian peso became increasingly overvalued and foreign-made products became relatively cheap. These trends created pressures on the balance of payments. Another pressure was the need to service the large foreign debt accumulated by the decentralized public agencies during the Banzer years. The true story of these agencies' financial problems was becoming known. Revelations showed their high degree of inefficiency and, in some cases, the outright squandering of funds financed with foreign borrowing. The resultant losses and unproductive investments had not generated the promised import substitutes and export sales, with the result that there were few gains in foreign revenues to offset the debt service requirements. The pressures on the balance of payments threatened a devaluation. This in turn encouraged consumers to hasten their purchases of imports and to make investments out of the country, both of which were facilitated by sharp increases in the supply of domestic credit.

In face of the worsening situation, the IMF recipe for corrective measures became increasingly more severe and austere. Although the IMF did not recommend an immediate devaluation of the peso, they said that if the measures were not implemented right away, such action would be required in the near future. The major IMF measures called for an increase in domestic fuel prices, raises in taxes on coffee and cigarettes, and a drastic cutback in government spending. [10]

In mid-January, Padilla attempted to take measures to correct the economic problems when the cabinet approved the IMF recommendations. Predictably, there was considerable protest by the various interest groups that would have been affected by the proposed policies. Indeed, most of the population would have been affected. The government and military got cold feet and Padilla temporarily backed away from raising fuel prices and taxes, measures which, if implemented, were sure to cause a popular uprising. [11] Such an outcome could easily have jeopardized the elections, serving as a good excuse for a right-wing, civilian-military coup.

Meanwhile, in January the controversy over the proposed large Potosí-based lead and silver smelter, Karachipampa, reemerged in full. The plant, costing an estimated 160 million dollars, had been in the works for sometime, beginning under Banzer. Based upon a feasibility study, the Pereda administration had made the decision to proceed with construction under West German financing. Padilla appointed a study commission to review the feasibility analysis. The commission's report, made public in mid-January, found numerous faults with the analysis and recommended that the project be reconsidered using more thorough and correct procedures. [12] Debate raged on the topic. However, on February 9 the government announced its decision to proceed with the earlier approved plans. The decision was questionable not only on technical grounds, but also because it was directly contrary to the immediate needs for financial restraint. Again, political factors appear to have played an important role. Padilla was under considerable pressure from influential persons not only to honor the commitment of previous governments, but also to permit them to gain from the project. [13] Were the project turned down or restructured it might have threatened Padilla's government and the electoral process.

In sharp contradiction to their actions on Karachipampa, only a few days later in mid-February the government announced that it would invoke strong austerity measures in order to reduce the government deficit, a measure calculated to enhance the chances for an IMF loan. The budget for government salaries was frozen at December 1978 levels and all other spending was to be carefully scrutinized. [14] This was the extent of Padilla's economic measures until May when discussion about raising petroleum prices and taxes again surfaced.

The Election Campaign

The election campaign of 1979 contrasted sharply to that of 1978. This time there was no government candidate and, in the open political process established by Padilla, candidates and political parties were quick to get organized. The country was abuzz with political activity. The leading presidential candidates were obvious. Siles Zuazo of the left-of-center UDP was anxious to build upon his demonstrated appeal to the voters in the last election. The veteran National Revolutionary Movement Party (MNR) leader, Victor Paz Estenssoro, who had only returned to his country from exile shortly before the 1978 election and consequently did not make a strong showing in the balloting that year, was now organizing strong support as a centrist candidate. In addition there were one or more right-wing candidates. There were other candidates from some of the fifty-seven groups claiming to be political parties, but by-and-large their role was to voice a minority position, represent a protest against the establishment, or use their strength to negotiate favorable treatment for their constituency by aligning with one of the major parties, or all three. Minority negotiating was advantageous to both Paz and Siles as they could form coalitions of parties that represented their positions but at the same time provide sufficient diversity and breadth in order to enhance their vote-getting potential.

To try to avoid the unscrupulous tactics of the previous year's elections, Padilla undertook electoral reforms, including measures to eliminate very marginal parties from appearing on the ballot and simplified single ballots to avoid stuffing the election urns. An early deadline for voter registration where voters had to present official documentation to identify themselves was established. The system worked well: some 90 percent of the eligible voters registered, eight presidential candidates appeared on the ballot, and there was little hint of irregularities in the voting process.

The UDP coalition was headed by Hernán Siles Zuazo and his vice-presidential running mate, Jaime Paz Zamora, a progressive, youthful representative of the Revolutionary Movement of the Left Party (MIR). This UDP coalition consisted of eleven political parties, including four leftist parties: the Nationalist Movement of the Left (MNRI), the National Alliance of the Left (ALIN), and the Bolivian Communist Party (PCB). The UDP was formed as an antiestablishment party to appeal to the working classes and the intellectual community, as well as to the middle classes who might see it as an alternative to the old center-right coalitions, but less extreme than the Number One Socialist Party (PS-1) headed by Marcelo Quiroga Santa Cruz.

Victor Paz Estenssoro headed the National Revolutionary Movement Alliance Party (MNR-A), a coalition of seven parties including the Christian Democrats (PDC), the National Revolutionary Movement Historical Party (MNRH), and the Authentic Revolutionary Party (PRA). Whereas the bulk of their strength lay in the centrist parties, the Leftist Revolutionary Front (FRI), a Maoist organization, was brought into the fold to add some leftist appeal.

Retired General René Bernal Escalante of the Santa Cruz Popular Alliance for National Integration Party (APIN) was the first rightist to declare his candidacy. General Banzer later attempted to work out an arrangement to share this ticket, with himself at the top. [15] When this failed Banzer announced his candidacy on the National Democratic Action Party (ADN) ticket.

The other candidates and their parties on the ballot were: Ricardo Catoira of the Workers Vanguard Party (VO), Marcelo Quiroga Santa Cruz of the PS-1, Luciano Tapia of the Indian Movement Tupaj Katari Party (MITKA), and Walter González Valda of the Bolivian Union Party (PUB). The race rapidly settled on the two leading candidates with Bernal and Banzer as dark horses. Active campaigning took place throughout the republic. Virtually no wall was void of campaign posters or handwritten slogans and an air of excitement reigned as the populace gathered in the spirit of an open election.

Although many thought that Paz Estenssoro would be able to gain considerable support because of his moderate position, it became clear that there was a large sentiment in favor of Siles. The right, which could probably have developed a *modus operendi* with Paz, was concerned with these trends and on several occasions tried to disrupt the electoral process. On May 20, a paramilitary group occupied the Santa Cruz airport to prevent Siles from landing for a campaign speech; in the ensuing scramble one person was killed. [16] Later, in early June, editorials in *El Diario* and *Los Tiempos* called for a return to military rule, arguing that the populace did not want elections. [17] Padilla, however, was committed to holding the elections and doggedly resisted these efforts to undermine them and untrack Bolivia's attempted return to democracy.

Organized Labor Regroups

During the Padilla administration, organized labor received a big boost in its efforts to regain lost ground. In early January, the government agreed to hefty wage increases for miners, who had had their wages frozen for seven years. Although the teachers' union was not successful in its bid for wage increases in March due to the freeze on government salaries, the labor movement rapidly reorganized. In early May, the Bolivian Workers Central (COB) held its first congress since 1970. The long-time union leader, Juan Lechín, was elected secretary. Paz Estenssoro and Siles Zuazo fought hard for representation on the directorate; UDP won 80 percent of the seats [18] thus ensuring strong labor support for the party in the presidential campaign. Much to the concern of the rightist elements, labor was again a force to reckon with in Bolivian politics.

Petroleum Prices

In the meantime, the economy continued to deteriorate. There was continued pressure by the IMF and World Bank to take the necessary austerity measures. Padilla, fearful that such action would jeopardize the elections, did not want to move and would not consider devaluation, leaving that decision for the incoming government. In early May, however, the president agreed to raise domestic gasoline prices, albeit in a hidden manner by discontinuing the cheaper grades of fuels and introducing better quality, but higher priced, substitutes. Both Paz and Siles supported this action and agreed to keep down the protests; both thought this a good way for one of them to avoid doing it after the election. [19] The decision, however, was not carried out.

The Election

Some 62 percent of the eligible voters cast 1.169 million votes.[20] This was 803 thousand fewer than the previous year, which clearly shows the extent of irregularities in the first election. When the final count was in Siles Zuazo and Paz Estenssoro were in a virtual dead heat with 35.98 and 35.88 percent of the votes respectively. Banzer ran third with 14.87 percent. The only other two candidates to receive more than 2 percent of the votes were Quiroga Santa Cruz (PS-1) with 4.82 percent and Bernal Escalante (APIN) with 4.10 percent.

The key to the race was the two populous departments of La Paz and Cochabamba. In La Paz Siles Zuazo gained 54.76 percent of the votes compared to Paz's 16.38 percent and edged him in Cochabamba by 1.3 percentage points. The Chuquisaca race was a virtual dead heat. Otherwise, Paz Estenssoro easily won in the less populous departments of the country. He took a majority in Santa Cruz, Banzer's home territory. Siles's narrow margin was due to his success in appealing to the urban masses in the cities of La Paz and Cochabamba as well as the peasants in the mountain valley regions, ironically the latter are those who had received land under the land reform program initiated by Paz in 1953.

The Selection of a President

Under the Bolivian Constitution, a presidential candidate must earn a majority of the votes to be elected outright, otherwise the names of the three candidates receiving the most votes are submitted to congress. Congress then elects a president from among these three, however, the person named must receive a majority of the votes.

The newly elected congress, the first in Bolivia in ten years, met on August 3 with the task of selecting the next president of Bolivia from among Banzer, Paz Estenssoro, and Siles Zuazo. The results of the popular vote could now be thrown out the window; what counted was the number of votes in Congress. The salons of the congressional hall were a caldron of politics. The fact that Paz's party had won many more seats than the UDP gave him an edge. Yet it was clear that horsetrading would be necessary to determine who would be president. The leading representatives of leftist parties, with the exception of PS-1, threw their support to Siles Zuazo and those of the right supported Banzer, but this still left an impasse because no one could obtain a majority. It appeared that Paz Estenssoro would be the victor as various supporters of Siles and Banzer would break from the left and right coalitions to support the centrist candidate. It was clear that after the decision was made that the loser would have to throw his support behind the winner in order to have the national unity necessary to implement economic measures. However, neither candidate was willing to make this commitment. Both parties held the line and Siles Zuazo and Paz Zamora went on a hunger strike to protest the happenings that might deny them the presidency that they believed they had won on the basis of the slim margin in the popular vote. On August 5, after five ballots in the Congress, Paz Estenssoro had sixty-eight votes but seventy-two were needed to be elected.[21] As the going got tough most thought that some bargain would be struck whereby Banzer and Bernal would release some of their votes to Paz, but that did not occur. After seven votes the congress was at an impasse.

Time was running out; ceremonies had long been planned to inaugurate the new president on August 7. Dignitaries from many nations had been invited to attend the ceremonies. Rosalyn Carter, the wife of the U.S. president, was in route to attend after attending the inauguration of the newly elected Ecuadorian president. The second much heralded election in Bolivia in the span of less than a year was coming to an ignominious end. Since no compromise among the candidates was in sight another solution was sought. The ceremonies were postponed one day and congress decided to name an interim president until another presidential election could be held in May 1980. They elected the president of the senate, Walter Guevara Arce, a well-respected former MNR leader, founder of the Authentic Revolutionary Party (PRA), and distinguished civil servant. He was sworn into office on August 8.

THE GUEVARA GOVERNMENT

Walter Guevara Arce, the first civilian to hold the presidency in fifteen years, with the exception of the brief term of Luis Siles Salinas in 1969, came to office under difficult circumstances. He was a compromise, interim president who lacked a power base and who inherited a rapidly faltering economy that left him little choice but to try to undertake severe corrective measures. However, in order to do this it would require that he gain a broad base of support.

This was a large task for anyone, let alone an interim president. His initial approach was to try to form a conciliatory government by gaining the support of both Paz Estenssoro and Siles Zuazo and forming a cabinet with experienced representatives of both parties. Whereas both candidates were in accord that Guevara should take the strong economic measures in order to make the job easier for the victor in the next election, they could not agree to collaborate, especially the UDP. [22] Therefore, the president was forced to select a cabinet comprised of younger and inexperienced ministers who, although capable, did not have the prestige to serve as strong leaders in the administrative branch.

Guevara was also faced with a new problem, congress. Both houses were composed largely of inexperienced legislators representing many political parties. As such, it was difficult to form meaningful coalitions and, moreover, the idealistic new legislators lost valuable time arguing matters that had been debated for years to the neglect of the urgent issues of the day. The president, without a political constituency, was unable to exert much control over this legislative body.

The military, although now out of government, was another threat. It was well known that the constitutionalist generals were waiting for the civilian government to stub its toe in order to justify intervention by the armed forces. It did not take long. In late August, Socialist Party leader, Marcelo Quiroga Santa Cruz, now a member of the Chamber of Deputies, initiated a congressional inquiry into the Banzer administration on grounds of its corruption, mismanagement of the economy, violations of basic human rights, and treason (due to relations with Chile and Brazil). [23] There were mixed reactions within the military. The *grupo generacional* saw this as Banzer's due. Many of the older officers viewed it as a threat of an exposé of wholesale corruption that would certainly involve many high-ranking military figures. Both elements saw it as damaging to the military establishment and they vociferously protested stating that they would not tolerate any attacks on the military as an institution. By careful diplomacy Guevara was able to temporarily diffuse the matter, obtain the affirmation of the military for the democratic process, and put off the threat of a coup.

Simultaneously, the president was forced to contend with the increasing power of organized labor. In August, COB announced it was preparing a package of economic policy measures to present to the government. Certainly such a package would be problematic for the president because it would contain measures to protect the workers' purchasing power, many of which would conflict with the government's measures necessary to strengthen the economy.

The economic crisis worsened. On September 17 the United States announced its decision to sell tin reserves from its stockpile of strategic materials. Although this has been in the offing since early 1978 it was a blow to the Guevara government and its attempt to maintain stability since the high world price for tin had been about the only bright spot in Bolivia's export picture. The IMF and World Bank continued to press for strong economic measures. Now, however, they had added devaluation to their recipe, a measure that would hurt almost all segments of the heavily import-dependent economy.

Congress continued to be an obstacle. It demanded a role in decisions taken by the executive branch and openly questioned the actions by Guevara and his cabinet. In particular there was a right-wing MNR group in congress led by Guillermo Bedregal Gutierrez, José Fellman Velarde, and Agapito Feliciano Monzón who were strongly opposed to Guevara and worked hard to foil his efforts. [24]

Meanwhile the military was growing restless, especially with the Banzer inquiry and the inability of the Guevara government to consolidate the various political interests and launch an economic program. On October 11, the Sixth Army Division rebelled and took Trinidad, the capital of the department of Beni and a common place for coups to begin, in protest of the official sanction of October 8 being designated as a "Day of Homage to che Guevara." Among the rebels' demands were the resignation of the president and the installation of a military government. [25] However, this trial balloon was not able to gather sufficient support from the rest of the military and the siege was called off the following day.

The president had his best success on the international front where he obtained considerable support for Bolivia's claims for an outlet to the sea. In late September, while in Panama along with other heads of Latin American states for the signing of the Panama Canal Treaties, he was able to engender considerable support for Bolivia's cause. In October, Bolivia's plea to the United Nations was also well received. The culmination of the president's efforts came with the strong support given Bolivia at the IX General Assembly of the Organization of American States (OAS) held in La Paz from October 22 to 31, 1979. During that meeting twenty-six member countries signed a resolution in support of Bolivia's position. The only negative vote was cast by Chile. [26]

The IX General Assembly also took the opportunity of its meeting site to praise Bolivia for its efforts to return to democracy. Although accolades came from many fronts, especially noteworthy was that of the speech of U.S. Secretary of State Cyrus Vance. The Declaration of La Paz, the final document of the assembly that was signed by all twenty-seven member nations, had fifteen points. One directly supported the redemocratization movement in Latin America; it said "it is important that all member states [of the OAS] re-establish or improve democratic systems of government, under which the exercise of power will come about as the legitimate and free expression of the populace." [27]

While the OAS was holding its meetings and praising Bolivia, the domestic situation began to deteriorate rapidly. A coup was threatened. Guevara worked hard to hold the pieces together. In a last ditch effort on October 31 he made a strong appeal to Paz Estenssoro and Siles Zuazo to form a cogovernment, but was unsuccessful. [28]

On the evening of the same day Guevara and his cabinet joined with the OAS representatives for the final event of the session, a festival of traditional Bolivian dances and music in the Plaza of the San Francisco Cathedral. As the ceremonies were ending, Guevara and his cabinet slipped away to a hiding place with knowledge of an impending coup. At 2:00 a.m. on November 1, while some of the visitors were returning to their hotels, tanks, armored cars, and troops were taking control of downtown La Paz. At 6:00 a.m. radio stations announced that Colonel Alberto Natusch Busch, commander of the Military College, former minister of Agriculture and Peasant Affairs in the Banzer regime, and leader of the coup, had assumed the presidency. The next sixteen days were to be one of the darkest periods in Bolivian history.

THE NATUSCH BUSCH INTERREGNUM

For sixteen days, until November 16, Bolivia had two governments, that of Natusch Busch who occupied the National Palace, and that of constitutional interim president, Guevara Arce, who was holding forth from a hideout in the outskirts of La Paz. It was a period of great bloodshed, shame, embarrassment, and anxiety for Bolivia.

Blood was shed as the result of the military using heavy and small firearms to "clean" the streets of La Paz of civilian dissidents. This lasted for the first seven days. When it was over the Bolivian Assembly of Human Rights reported 208 civilians dead, 207 wounded, and 124 missing. [29]

Shame and embarrassment came not only from the heavy-handed tactics of the military and the consequent deaths, but also from the threat of losing an opportunity for returning to democracy. After all, only a few days prior Bolivia had been given the center stage at the OAS assembly as an example of redemocratization. Virtually no one could understand the rationale of staging the coup as the OAS visitors were still in town along with a large retinue of international journalists who were sure to paint Bolivia black in their home newspapers.

Anxiety mounted in the first seven days with armor and troops in the streets and indiscriminate shooting. Families even felt uneasy in their own homes. Information was limited as newspapers ceased publication and all radio and television stations were closed except those operated by the Natusch government. Martial law and a curfew were quickly put into effect. To compound this a work stoppage led by COB virtually shut down all businesses, banks, and public services. Supplies were short, especially food. After the seventh day, when the troops retired to their barracks and the work stoppage was lifted, the anxiety took another form, that of how the government situation would be resolved, an unknown until November 16.

There were a number of factors that caused Natusch Busch to attempt the coup which he called a political-civilian-military movement. Fundamental was the widespread dissatisfaction with Guevara's inability to provide effective leadership. Natusch found civilian support from certain elements of the MNR and MNRI parties. Guevara's enemies in congress, led by Bedregál and Fellman, lent their support to the coup and promised to keep that body in line. The military was growing restless not only with the ineptness of the government, but also with the congressional hearings about the Banzer administration. These factors in combination with healthy doses of personal ambition by Natusch and his conspirators led to the decision. Plans were laid several weeks be fore the act, a factor that may have contributed to the quelling of the October 11 uprising in Trinidad.

In the beginning the coup appeared to be in the pattern of the typical Bolivian military intervention: take charge of the National Palace, send out radio and press releases that all is under control, and within a short time have a functioning government. This, however, was not to be the case. COB, tipped off by Guevara about the possibilities of the forthcoming coup, had prepared an immediate work stoppage that virtually shut down La Paz and the mines and affected other parts of the country. By mid-morning of November 1, students and workers were verbally attacking and throwing stones at the troops around the palace, protesting the loss of redemocratization. After first firing into the air, the soldiers then began to fire directly into the unintimidated protestors. Natusch declared the dissidents to be terrorists inspired by communists and set about to "clean up" the city of these elements. [30] Tanks, armored cars, and troops roamed the streets. More encounters occurred as the protestors blocked roads by tearing up streets and lighting fires. Later the troops moved into the working class districts where they again encountered roadblocks and protestors. Airplanes and helicopters strafed areas indiscriminately. [31] This was to continue for seven days.

Natusch could not get a firm hold of support. Internationally, only two nations, Egypt and Malaysia, recognized his government. The United States cut off economic assistance. Domestically, Guevara transmitted radio messages from his hideaway saying that he would not resign from the presidency. Natusch's emissary, General Padilla, was sent to talk to the COB leader, Juan Lechín Oquendo, but came back empty-handed. [32] Contrary to plans, congress did not fall in line and shortly after taking power Natusch dissolved the congress. Later, on November 5, he reinstated it in hopes of gaining their support but was without much success. Despite the implications of the MNR, as well as his own involvement, Paz Estenssoro took to the airwaves to deny this. [33] Except for the military, there was no support for the would-be president. Even within this institution the support was fragmented and many officers fell in behind Natusch only because they believed that if they did not and the regime crumbled that the armed forces would sustain a major blow. As time passed, however, this support began to disappear. For example, General Padilla, who had earlier made a public statement in support of the coup, had second thoughts on the situation, voiced opposition to the movement on November 6, and went into hiding. [34]

Although much of Natusch's support was marginal, the major factor leading to the failure of the coup was labor. The COB-orchestrated work stoppage lasted for seven days and paralyzed La Paz. Labor was not to be intimidated in spite of the fact that the COB office was dynamited on November 3, many labor leaders were imprisoned or forced into hiding, and working class areas of the city were under military fire. Indeed, the rough tactics of the military appear to have reinforced labor's will to resist.

Clearly an agreement had to be negotiated between the different elements. The Catholic Church initiated this effort soon after the coup and reported on November 7 that an agreement had been reached to get COB, the armed forces, and congress together to discuss a solution. [35] On this day COB lifted its work stoppage, troops returned to the barracks, and a sense of partial normality returned. The following day, Guevara sent a message to congress stating emphatically that he would not resign, but implied if congress saw it necessary to take action to replace him that was their responsibility. [36]

By this time it was clear that Natusch Busch would not be able to remain in power since he did not have the support of the populace, congress, COB, or the armed forces. Negotiations continued for a week. Possibilities of a tripartite government of the military, COB, and congress were discussed but were discarded when it was clear that the military and COB would not resolve to work together. The solution was for congress to select the next interim president, but one that would be satisfactory to all three elements. COB and the military retired from the negotiations. On November 15 Natusch Busch announced he would step down. The decision was finalized on the next day when congress selected the head of the Chamber of Deputies and veteran MNR politician, Lydia Gueiler, as the first female president in Bolivian history. She was sworn in that evening and cordially dismissed Colonel Natusch Busch from the National Palace. After sixteen days of sadness, shame, and disillusionment, euphoric relief passed over Bolivia as the crisis had been resolved in a commendable manner and Bolivia was apparently now back on the road to a democratically elected government in 1981. For the moment the gravity of the economic situation was forgotten by the populace, but it was very much on the minds of those parties who had played a role in naming the new government.

THE GUEILER GOVERNMENT

The new president faced two immediate and enormous tasks. The first was to take the economic measures that were now widely recognized as absolutely necessary but at the same time were certain to evoke considerable protest and unrest. The second was to simultaneously form a representative government that could lead and survive to turn over the reins to the elected government on August 6, 1980. Clearly the success of the second task depended heavily on the outcome of the first. The president was successful in remaining in office for a seven-month period, until after the elections, but it was a time during which her regime was increasingly threatened by a coup of the constitutionalist faction in the armed forces. The constitutionalists were anxious to restore the military to its former status after their considerable loss of face in the bloodshed of the Natusch Busch rebellion and were threatened by the increasing power and influence of the left-leaning political parties and organized labor.

Economic Measures

It was fact that severe economic measures were necessary and forthcoming. IMF standby financing and much foreign assistance were contingent upon these decisions and Bolivia could not afford to delay much longer. In contrast to previous governments, the coalition of forces that placed the new president in office was aware of this and lent her their support to take action. The only points in question were what would be and how extreme would be the measures? The president was faced with two options. The first was to follow the recommendations of the IMF and World Bank that called for a healthy devaluation of the peso, large increases in domestic petroleum prices, tight controls on government spending, and small increases in wages. The second was the economic package proposed by COB that emphasized measures to restore the purchasing power of the working class by placing controls on prices, limits on imports of luxury goods, government promises to reduce inflation, and, most importantly, significant wage increases. [3] In fact, there was little choice. The IMF plan had to prevail but there was some room for negotia tion as to the magnitude of the changes. The government agonized over the measures for nearly two weeks and on Sunday, December 2, policies were announced in order to try to provide a day of calm while most businesses were closed. The peso was devalued 25 percent, going from twenty to twenty-five to the U.S. dollar. Many thought this to be insufficient, but perhaps it was as much as was politically feasible in the heavily import-dependent Bolivian economy. Prices of petroleum-derived products were to rise 30 to 100 percent, transportation fares about 60 percent, but prices on rents and many basic food products were frozen. There were provisions to provide income adjustments for those persons earning between 5,000 and 10,000 pesos per month and a special council was created to advise the government on management of the economy. [38]

The foreign reaction was favorable, nearly 500 million dollars in bilateral and multilateral aid were immediately committed. [39] The domestic reaction was predictable. Organized by COB, protestors hit the streets as they saw their real incomes threatened by the small authorized wage increases and direct price increases as well as indirect price increases associated with both the devalued peso and the rapid inflation that was almost certain to follow. The COB-organized national protest virtually paralyzed the country and during which some government offices, stores, and buses were attacked.

Simultaneously, the peasants had another complaint. Not only would the prices of the goods they purchase in the market rise, but also the government's price ceilings meant the prices for most of their products would not rise. Led by the Union of Peasant Workers, they set up roadblocks leading to the major cities to shut off the flow of foodstuff. The blockages and stoppages lasted until December 14 and placed tremendous pressures on the government. However, after making concessions to the dissidents by promising to raise wages and prices of basic commodities, the blockades were lowered and workers returned to their jobs. The government had accomplished this first task and survived.

The Military vs. the Left and Labor

The armed forces came out of the Natusch Busch rebellion badly scathed, a concern to the constitutionalist *golpistas* (those who had participated in the Natusch attempted coup) as well as the institutionalists and *grupo generacional* who had opposed the coup. All groups wanted to restore a favorable image for the military but, being divided in philosophy about the role of the military in society, differed in opinion of how it should be done. Within the groups there was dissension and it would take some time before they would consolidate around specific leaders. This was fortunate for the Gueiler government because the several months it would take for the military leadership to regroup and consolidate gave the president time to implement her economic measures and reorganize the government without a serious threat of a military takeover.

The *golpistas* were not long in beginning to regroup and began to call in their chips for having agreed to the resolution of the Natusch rebellion and in naming Gueiler president. General Luis García Meza, former head of the army and a powerful figure in the short-lived Natusch interregnum, head of the Military College under Guevara and the present government, and cousin of the new president, led a movement to ensure that a *golpista* was named as head of the army rather than an institutionalist. [40] The president reluctantly agreed, a decision that ensured the *golpistas* would have a key position in controlling the armed forces.

Meanwhile, in congress and the executive branch the MNR party was in control. Not only was the president an MNR veteran, but the party also held a significant majority of congressional seats and cabinet posts. The president had tried to form a representative cabinet but was thwarted when the important UDP and ADN parties refused to participate. [41] However, over time the influence of the MNR in the Gueiler administration was to slip when its main base of support, the middle class, begun to shift left as it became disenchanted with the worsening economy and political strife. Moreover, the party lost some of the luster of its leadership as the populace became increasingly convinced that Paz Estenssoro was somehow involved, at least tacitly, in supporting the Natusch rebellion.

In contrast, the left was ascending. The UDP was increasingly more attractive to a citizenry disillusioned with the military and conventional politics. The working classes were better organized and had demonstrated their power during the protests and work stoppages. The peasants, traditionally considered a malleable group, had shown in the recent blockades that they could exercise influence and were reorganizing. Moreover, COB and the Union of Peasant Workers were now beginning to collaborate. Indeed, there was talk of a ticket with Lechín as president and Genaro Flores, the peasant leader, as vice president in the next election. In addition, the socialist, Marcelo Quiroga Santa Cruz, was gaining popularity as he demonstrated his oratorical skills and intellectual capacity in leading the congressional hearings against ex-president Banzer.

The growing influence of the left and labor was worrisome to the right and hastened the consolidation of the military. Paramilitary actions began to occur. There were bombings that could be blamed on the left and other actions designed to put the left on notice. On March 22, the left-leaning Jesuit journalist and movie critic, Luis Espinal, was kidnapped and the next day was found dead. Was it a signal to the left or was it a testing of the waters to measure public reaction? It served both ends. When 70,000 persons turned out in the streets of La Paz to demonstrate on the day of his funeral, clearly there was strong support for the role that Espinal had performed in Bolivia and indignation at his high-handed murder. [42]

Only a few days later COB and numerous other organizations announced the formation of the National Committee to Defend Democracy (CONADE) to show the military and the right that there was strong and widespread sentiment to hold the elections and to threaten any attempt to take over the government by force.

The convergence of these events, the Banzer hearings and the rise of the left and labor, were important in hastening the consolidation of the military. Internal divisiveness had to come to an end. The faction led by General García Meza, who had earlier staked out a position as a *golpista* leader and enemy of the left gathered support among the La Paz commanders, and on April 14 the strong-willed, right-wing general was named head of the army. Upon assuming office he clearly enunciated his position of defending the integrity of the armed forces when he warned the politicians to not slander the military without expecting consequences. [43]

From this point forward the military became an important element in the Gueiler reign. Under the leadership of García Meza the constitutionalist faction became champions of the conservative cause and used their power to try to diffuse the support for the left by threatening the elections with intervention by force if the situation became too unwelcome for the military to accept. For example, in a May Day speech García Meza warned that "extremists" in the labor movement were threatening peace and that this would not be allowed. [44]

As the elections drew nearer and the UDP was clearly gaining strength, the right and the military became more nervous; were Siles Zuazo to be elected both would certainly suffer. Clearly, labor and the peasants would have a strong say in the course of events. Moreover, the left-leaning UDP coalition included the Bolivian Communist Party and it was easy to imagine that were UDP to assume power that the communists would have considerable influence in the government. In any event, the right and private sector community was certain to lose and in all likelihood there would be a big shake-up in the military and its current leaders would be retired. In the extreme, as occurred with the 1952 MNR revolution, the military would be disbanded. Fighting for their existence, the right and military stepped up their tactics to thwart the Siles movement, hoping that an opportune moment for a coup that would have popular support would present itself or could be created.

In early June, the armed forces were placed on full alert based on evidence that extremists were threatening Bolivian democracy. García Meza blamed recent bombings of the Argentine embassy, ADN offices, and a military supply depot on the left, and stated that the Banzer hearings were a "slur on the military." He went on to say "those responsible for bringing these charges will themselves be tried by military tribunal."[45]

Paramilitary terrorists stepped up their attacks on the left. The home of Paz Zamora was bombed on June 2. Later that day the UDP vice-presidential candidate saved his own life by hurling himself in flames from a small plane that exploded while taking off on a campaign trip from the La Paz airport. He was immediately sent to the United States for treatment of the extensive burns. The pilot and five UDP leaders perished; Siles Zuazo would have been on the plane had he not stayed home to attend a funeral. Whether it was an accident or sabotage is not clear, but it served to further gird popular support against the right. CONADE again took the offensive and accused García Meza of trying to destabilize the country and told the population to be ready for a general strike should a coup occur.

The military also saw the United States as an obstacle in its attempt to thwart the elections and did not hesitate to attack Bolivia's principal benefactor when the North American government intervened to try to ensure that the elections would take place. On May 30 the U.S. ambassador, Marvin Wiseman, worked throughout the night to try to avert a coup. This was followed on June 4 by an article in the *Washington Post* stating that a coup had been averted because of U. S. influence and because García Meza could not gather sufficient support for a coup among lower ranking officers.[46] The following day the high command responded indignantly saying, "The decadent imperialists of the North have begun to invent myths and fantasies to justify their intervention in the affairs of the developing nations of Latin America," and demanded that the U.S. ambassador be withdrawn.[47] On June 6, the leaders of the conservative Bolivian Socialist Falange Party (FSB) lent their support by going on a hunger strike.

To make the situation worse, the military received another black mark when, in the early hours of June 7, the commander of the Presidential Guard, in an apparent drunken stupor, attempted to enter the president's bedroom in order to assassinate her. He was foiled as she telephoned for help. Realizing that they had spoiled their opportunities to provoke a coup and that popular sentiment was against them, the military backpedaled and on June 9 called for a postponement of the elections for at least a year saying that they wanted the president to remain in power. The political parties and congress refused their proposal.[48]

In a last attempt on June 17 there was another sally by the right, this time in Santa Cruz. Paramilitary forces attacked the city hall and the U.S. consulate, wounded the mayor in gunfire, seized radio and TV stations, and led a demonstration against the Gueiler government and the intervention of the United States. They demanded the expulsion of the U.S. ambassador and a postponement of the elections. They expected the populace in this department, long recognized as a center of conservatism, to back their cause but were dismayed when they found little support as large numbers of citizens, students, and workers took to the streets to protest and forced the rebels to back down. Again the message was clear, the people wanted elections.

The Elections

The elections were scheduled for June 29. There were twelve presidential candidates on the ballot representing various alliances, some of which had formed since the elections of the previous year. Those candidates appearing on the ballot were: Hugo Banzer Suárez of the National Democratic Action Party (ADN); Guillermo Bedregal of the Nationalist Revolutionary Movement Unity Front Party (FMNR-U); Walter Gonzalez of the Bolivian Union Party (PUB); Walter Guevara Arce of the Authentic Revolutionary Party (PRA); Roberto Jordán Pando of the Alliance of the National Leftist Forces Party (AFIN); Constantino Lima of the Indian Movement Tupaj Katari Party Number One (MITKA-1); Victor Paz Estenssoro of the National Revolutionary Movement Alliance Party (MNR-A); Marcelo Quiroga Santa Cruz of the Number One Socialist Party (PS-1); Luis Adolfo Siles Salinas of the New Alternative Democratic Revolutionary Front Party (FDR-NA); Hernán Siles Zuazo of the Democratic Popular Coalition Party (UDP); Luciano Tapia of the Indian Movement Tupaj Katari Party (MITKA); and Carlos Valverde Barbery of the Bolivian Socialist Flange (FSB).

The leftist National Revolutionary Party Alliance (PRIN-A) headed by Juan Lechín Oquendo withdrew from the ballot in support of Siles. In total, there were thirty-nine political parties represented in the various coalitions appearing on the ballot, eleven more than in the previous year, indicating a further opening up of the political process. The ballot also included more interest groups, as well as the appearance of enterprising politicians hoping to make a place for themselves in the new government if they could gain enough votes to justify their inclusion. Among the candidates were five former presidents.

Campaigning was more sophisticated than in previous elections. Not only were there the numerous public appearances, newspaper ads, a plethora of posters and handwritten slogans on virtually all walls and fences, but also there was an extensive Madison Avenue type TV advertising campaign.

There was a large turnout at the polls; 1.442 million votes were cast representing 72 percent of eligible voters,[49] a sharp improvement over the previous year when only 62 percent of the eligible voters cast ballots and another indicator of the populace's commitment to the elections and the ability of the political parties and interest groups to get out the voters.

It was apparent from the early returns that Siles Zuazo would win the popular vote. In the final count, UDP had 38.5 percent of the votes, an improvement of nearly 3 percent over the previous year. What was most notable was the decline of support for Paz Estenssoro; he received only 20.5 percent of the vote. Banzer attracted some 16.9 percent of the votes and his arch-opponent, the socialist, Quiroga Santa Cruz, rose to 8.7 percent of the votes. No other candidate received more than 3 percent. As in the previous election, UDP received the support of the working classes. They received over 45 percent of the vote in La Paz and had large leads over the other candidates in Cochabamba and the mining departments of Oruro and Potosí. [50]

The selection of the president was again turned over to congress. There was little doubt that Siles would be named and take office on August 6. In contrast to the elections in the two previous years, the UDP had a commanding lead in the popular vote. All combined, the parties of the left had a majority of the vote and there was little chance that Paz Estenssoro could manage to put together a threatening coalition to counter it.

The outcome was not to the liking of the conservative military and private sector who viewed the election as a victory for communism, or at least socialism. They forecasted that the UDP leadership would take drastic reforms to benefit the working class which would completely upset the *modus operendi* of the strong rightist military and private sector coalition to which Bolivia had become accustomed since 1967. It was time to act. Those in control of the armed forces could not wait for the new government to make an error and then intervene, for in all likelihood these conservative, right-leaning officers would by then have been retired by Siles and the power of the armed forces significantly reduced.

THE GARCIA MEZA COUP

On July 17 the military struck. A three-man junta led by General Luis García Meza toppled the Gueiler government in a well-organized operation designed to quickly assume power and snuff out the left. The junta, whose other members were General Waldo Bernal and Rear Admiral Ramiro Terrazas, heads of the air force and navy, named García Meza president. An all military cabinet was appointed. That a coup occurred was no surprise but its timing was impeccable.

Early in the morning of the seventeenth the troops in the garrisons at Trinidad and Santa Cruz rebelled. The president and her cabinet went into an emergency session at the National Palace. While assembled the rebels struck. All but a few of the ministers who escaped were caught. The president was forced to resign and was held in a nunnery until she could be deported. The ex-ministers were placed under house arrest.

Simultaneously labor, left, and CONADE leaders were holding a meeting at COB headquarters located in an historic building on the Prado in downtown La Paz. Paramilitary forces, firing weapons, barged into the meeting taking prisoners. Some thirty leaders including Lechín were captured, some wounded. [51] In the shooting the socialist Quiroga Santa Cruz was killed, allegedly as he was resisting capture. More likely he was singled out for his role in leading the criticism of the military during the congressional hearings of the Banzer administration.

In these two moves the Gueiler government and the key leaders of the opposition were rendered ineffective. Siles Zuazo, again denied the presidency, went into hiding. To seal the fate of organized labor, in a symbolic move, the new government ordered the COB headquarters building be demolished to make room for a parking lot.

There was resistance in the streets of La Paz and in the mining towns. The fanatic disciplinarian, Colonel Luis Arce Gómez, was named minister of the Interior and immediately established a harsh martial law that quickly brought the capital city under control. The government made the prisoner Juan Lechín appear on television to quell rumors of his death and to implore the strikers to go back to work. Early curfews were invoked and persons caught out after hours ran a big risk of being roughed up or jailed by the military who patrolled the streets. A favorite punishment was to put these persons in the La Paz soccer stadium to do calisthentics for the night. Criticism of the new government in the local press was throttled and foreign correspondents who wrote stories unfavorable to the new government were harassed or deported. [52]

The tin miners were not so readily subdued. They continued to strike in protest long after the rest of the country was back to work. It was not until early August that a compromise was reached. In the meantime there was alleged bloodshed. It was reported to Amnesty International that the mining city of Caracoles had been bombed and strafed before the foot soldiers went in. In the process miners were killed and others deported to unknown parts. [53]

The international reaction to the coup was highly unfavorable. The United States withdrew its ambassador, began to reduce its embassy personnel, announced a cutoff of most foreign assistance, and threatened to block economic assistance from other sources. The outcry from the neighboring democratic Andean countries was equally vociferous.

Many Bolivians, long accustomed to coups and military leadership, begrudgingly accepted the coup and saw it as an end to the difficulties associated with the long and tumultuous attempt to return to democracy. Of course most of those on the right welcomed the change. Persons recognized as leftist leaders who had not been captured found it prudent to go into hiding.

Bolivia had come full circle. Its attempt at redemocratization had failed after three successive attempts. The country had reverted back to an authoritarian military government not dissimilar to that of the early Banzer years.

WHY REDEMOCRATIZATION FAILED

Had the Banzer government not failed in its orchestrated elections, Bolivia would have had a "democratic" government in 1978. Its form likely would have been a slightly weaker version of the authoritarian-bureaucratic Banzer regime. Whether it would have survived by avoiding military intervention is conjecture. What is clear, however, is that once those elections were bungled that forces were unleashed to force Bolivia to go ahead with the attempt to redemocratize.

Strong internal pressure exerted by left-leaning political parties and organized labor developed sufficient strength to form an opposition that had to be reckoned with, and they were not about to give up easily the precious ground they had recently gained. Divisiveness within the military surfaced and the *grupo* officers favored a civilian government. The populace genuinely wanted a try at democracy. Externally, there was strong pressure from the United States to continue the electoral process.

Yet, after two more elections, three military, and two civilian interim governments, the transition from the authoritarian-bureaucratic Banzer government to democracy had failed. There were four fundamental, but interrelated, factors that were responsible. First, the economy deterio rated rapidly which led to instability and uncertainty. Second, with the hitting of repression, a system of fragmented and polarized political par ties emerged. Therefore, it became impossible to develop coalitions which had sufficiently broad support and wide appeal to win an election outright. Moreover, the polarization did not allow the necessary compromises once the decision was placed in the hands of congress, nor permit the major parties to jointly collaborate with the interim governments. Third, there was a fundamental and growing conflict between the conservative military and private sector interests that had been the mainstay of the authoritarian bureaucratic government, and the left and organized labor, that had rapidly gained power with the lifting of repression and which exerted increasing influence on the successive governments. Fourth, the military, although suffering from discreditation and internal dissension, never lost its power to forcefully intervene. Its sheer presence kept order but limited the actions of the successive governments. Finally, when the military's conservative elements and the private sector interests were vitally threatened by the left, the military did not hasten to act to preserve itself and return Bolivia to an authoritarian-bureaucratic form of government. The following sections elaborate the interrelationships between these four factors.

The Economy

As shown in Table XVI-1, there was a serious deterioration of the Bolivian economy between 1978 and 1980. The rate of growth of real gross domestic product declined sharply, from 3.1 percent in 1978 to 0.8 percent in 1980. In part, the decline was due to the large postdevaluation increase in the rate of inflation. The government deficit rose sharply in 1979 and again in 1980, as did external debt. Debt servicing problems were substantial. The net holdings of foreign reserves in the banking system were negative and declining. The current account deficit rose sharply in 1979 as petroleum production and exports declined but became smaller in 1980 due to favorable silver prices and the natural gas exports. The volume of tin exports declined substantially but this was compensated by an increase in world tin prices. The decentralized government agencies continued in dire straits.

Vicious Circle of Instability

The worsening economy was of widespread concern and led to uncertainty and instability. A problem was that the measures required to correct the decline likely would provoke even greater instability as they would cause organized labor, whose members were certain to be hurt by the measures, to protest by street demonstrations and work stoppages. Given the antipathy of the military for organized labor and their leftist orientation, this could be sufficient cause for military intervention to bring order and peace. Hence the transition governments, military and civilian alike, were caught in a vicious circle of instability. In this circle the deteriorating economy led to instability, but corrective measures would lead to greater instability, at least in the short run, and the threat of military intervention. As a consequence, the measures were not taken because to do so would risk not only the current government, but also a foreclosure on the coming elections and democracy. The result was that the economy continued to deteriorate and instability heightened, factors which led to increasing support for the left among the workers, peasants, and disenchanted middle class.

TABLE XVI-1

INDICES OF THE BOLIVIAN ECONOMY 1978-1980

	1978	1979	1980
Percentage Rate of Real Growth of Gross Domestic Product, (Base Year, 1970)	3.1	2.1	0.8
Central Government Annual Deficit (Millions of Pesos)	3002	6665	7665
Annual Rate of Inflation (As measured by La Paz Consumer Price Index)	10.4	19.7	47.2
External Debt, End of Year (Millions of U.S. dollars)	1762	1941	2220
Current Account Balance: Balance of Payments (Millions of U.S. dollars)	-279	-340	-118
Net Foreign Reserves in Banking System (Millions of U.S. dollars)	61.3	-69.8	-128.3
Petroleum Production (Million Cubic Meters)	1883	1617	1384
Index of Value of Tin Exports (1970 = 100)	349	370	353
Index of Price of Tin Exports (1970 = 100)	327	386	436
Index of Quantum of Tin Exports (1970 = 100)	107	96	81

Source: Banco Central de Bolivia, *Boletín estadístico*, No. 242, junio 1981; No. 236, diciembre, 1979; No. 240, diciembre, 1980.

Fragmented Political Parties

The only way to break the circle was to have a government that was strong enough to take the economic measures and weather the consequences. But with the highly fragmented political structure, none of the political parties were able to form a coalition that had the broad base necessary to undertake major changes. In 1979, the centrist MNR-A, under Paz Estenssoro's leadership, came the closest, but the unwillingness of the parties of the right or the left to align with Paz, either for the elections or when congress was deciding the outcome, destroyed the possibility of electing a civilian government in that year.

Conflict Between Left and Right

In the 1980 campaign and elections fragmentation remained. By this time, however, the UDP had gained increasing support, mostly by a crossover of MNR supporters. Meanwhile, labor had demonstrated its power during the Natusch coup and, in combination with peasants, had again shown its strength in the aftermath of the Gueiler economic measures.

Thus the predominate coalition was among the leftists; workers and peasants in the UDP. This posed a serious threat to the conservative military and private sector. Were the UDP to be elected, it was almost certain there would be a major restructuring of the Bolivian society and economy under which the conservatives were bound to lose considerably.

The Military

The armed forces, badly discredited and divided following the Natusch Busch debacle, rose to the occasion. General García Meza assumed the leadership of the conservative forces in the military. When all other attempts to keep Siles Zuazo from taking office failed, the military, with strong right-wing support and financial aid from Argentina, stepped in to stop the redemocratization process. They full well realized that this would mean strained relations with the United States, which could have serious economic consequences since the North American nation is Bolivia's principal trading partner and source of external financing. They believed, however, that this was a consequence they would have to suffer, at least temporarily, for it looked like Ronald Reagan, who had a much softer position on human rights than Jimmy Carter, was likely to be elected president in November.

ENDNOTES FOR CHAPTER XVI

1. See Chapter XV for a discussion of the 1978 elections and how General Pereda came to power.

2. "New Bolivian Chief Installs a Cabinet," *New York Times*, July 25, 1978, p. A-3.

3. "Bolivia: Tin Soldier," *Latin American Political Report*, August 11, 1978, p. 242; "Bolivia: Cleft Stick," *Latin American Political Report*, August 18, 1978, p. 252.

4. "Bolivia: Hallowed Rite," *Latin American Political Report*, November 3, 1978, p. 342.

5. The *grupo generacional* are the officers from the first generation of graduates from the Bolivian Military College after it had been restructured following the 1952 revolution. These officers were thus indoctrinated with the revolutionary ideals of the MNR governments. In contrast, previous generations of military college graduates were schooled in the philosophy of prerevolution Bolivia, where a major function of the armed forces was to defend the interests of the private sector, especially those of the large tin mines. Within the armed forces the older officers and those of the *grupo* were often at odds in terms of social philosophy. Banzer was of the older generation and many of his conservative policies were challenged by the *grupo* early in his presidency. He countered by quickly marginating the younger officers by not allowing them influential and important command positions, and keeping them so during his entire administration.

6. "Bolivia: Rallying the Political Forces," *Latin American Political Report*, November 10, 1978, p. 348.

7. "Bolivia: A Hornet's Nest," *Latin American Political Report*, November 24, 1978, p. 364.

8. "Bolivia: Coup de Grace," *Latin American Political Report*, December 1, 1978, p. 370; "Bolivia: Realignment," *Latin American Political Report*, December 8, 1978, p. 383; and "Bolivia: A Regular Soldier," *Latin American Political Report*, December 22, 1978, p. 399.

9. "Próximo gobierno definirá la venta de gas a Brazil", *El Diario* [La Paz], December 12, 1978, p. 1.

10. "Bolivia: Uneasy Compromise," *Latin American Political Report*, January 19, 1979, p. 17.

11. Ibid.

12. "Comisión recomienda reformular el proyecto de fundición Karachi pampa", *Presencia* [La Paz], January 15, 1979, p. 1.

13. "Bolivian Government Divided Over Austerity Measures," *Latin American Economic Report*, January 26, 1979, p. 25.

14. "Será aplicada severa política de austeridad", *El Diario* [La Paz], February 16, 1979, p. 1. and "Bolivia solicitará que refinancie su deuda externa", *Presencia* La Paz, February 24, 1979, p. 1.

15. "Bolivia: Kaleidoscope," *Latin American Political Report*, April 27, 1979, p. 122.

16. "Bolivia: Admonition," *Latin American Political Report*, June 1, 1979, p. 167.

17. "Bolivia: Press Campaign," *Latin American Political Report*, June 8, 1979, p. 175.

18. "Bolivia: Trouble Ahead," *Latin American Political Report*, May 18, 1979, p. 151.

19. "Bolivia: Nasty Medicine," *Latin American Political Report*, May 11, 1979, pp. 142-43.

20. Calculated on basis of number of registered voters was obtained from "1,877,193 Bolivianos votarán el domingo", *El Diario* [La Paz], June 29, 1979, p. 1 and the data on the election results from "Cómputo oficial de la Corte Nacional", *Presencia* [La Paz], August 1, 1979, penultimate page, not numbered.

21. "Sigue la expectación en Bolivia: congreso no ha electado presidente", *La Nación* [San José, Costa Rica], August 6, 1979, p. 22-A.

22. *Quarterly Economic Review of Peru, Bolivia*, 3rd Quarter 1979, p. 22.

23. "Bolivia: Exorcising Banzer," *Latin American Political Report*, September 7, 1979, p. 278.

24. "Viñetas de una pesadilla Boliviana", *Semana de Ultima Hora* [La Paz], November 23, 1979, p. 5.

25. "Bolivia: Ghost of Che," *Latin American Political Report*, October 19, 1979, p. 324.

26. "América dió unánime respaldo a la causa marítima boliviana", *Presencia* [La Paz], January 1, 1980, p. 12.

27. "En La Paz se definieron las pautas para nuevas relaciones hemisféricas", *Presencia* [La Paz], January 1, 1980, p. 12.

28. Nataniel Alvarez A., "Del 'empantanamiento político' al golpe de noviembre de 1979", *Presencia* [La Paz], June 29, 1980, p. 9.

29. "De la Asamblea Permanente de los Derechos Humanos", *Semana de Ultima Hora* [La Paz], November 23, 1979, p. 6.

30. Jaime Moreno Laval, "La guerra de La Paz", Hoy [Santiago, Chile], November 14, 1979, reprinted in *Semana de Ultima Hora* [La Paz], November 23, 1979, pp. 3-4.

31. Ibid.

32. Raúl Gonzáles A., "Siete días que conmovieron a Bolivia", *Semana de Ultima Hora* [La Paz], November 23, 1979, p. 11.

33. "Bolivia: A Coup that Boosted the Loser," *Latin American Weekly Report*, November 9, 1972, p. 20.

34. Ted Córdova-Claure, "Gabinete parlamentario busca Natusch en Bolivia", *Semana de Ultima Hora* [La Paz], November 23, 1979, p. 20.

35. "Declaración de la comisión mediadora de la Iglesia", reported in *Semana de Ultima Hora* [La Paz], November 23, 1979, p. 7.

36. "Mensaje del presidente constitucional interino Dr. Walter Guevara Arce al honorable congreso nacional", *Semana de Ultima Hora* [La Paz], November 23, 1979, p. 8.

37. "Bolivia: Between the IMF and COB," *Latin American Regional Report— Andean Nations,* November 30, 1979, p. 3.

38. "Bolivian Unions React Strongly to Economic Medicine," *Latin American Weekly Report,* December 7, 1979, p. 1. Note this article incorrectly states the devaluation to be 20 percent rather than 25 percent.

39. Ibid.

40. "Warring Military Factions Threaten the Fragile Truce in Bolivia," *Latin American Weekly Report*, November 30, 1979, p. 1.

41. "Bolivia: Cabinet Shuffle Solves No Problems," *Latin American Weekly Report*, February 22, 1980, p. 2.

42. "Bolivia: Coup Forestalled for the Moment," *Latin American Weekly Report*, April 4, 1980, p. 2.

43. "Bolivia: García Returns with a Warning," *Latin American Weekly Report*, April 18, 1980, p. 2.

44. "Bolivia: Army Agrees to Temporary Truce," *Latin American Weekly Report,* May 9, 1980, p. 3.

45. "Bolivia: Tension Mounts as Right Steps up Terrorist Campaign," *Latin American Weekly Report*, June 6, 1980, p. 2.

46. Charles A. Krause, "Military Coup Looms as Election Nears in Jittery Bolivia," *Washington Post*, June 4, 1980, p. A-33.

47. "Uncle Sam's White Charger Rides Into Bolivian Melee," *Latin American Weekly Report*, June 13, 1980, p. 1.

48. Ibid.

49. Calculated on basis of number of registered voters reported in "Electores inscritos para 1980 y sufragantes de 1979", *Presencia* [La Paz], June 29, 1980, p. 1, and "Computo nacional oficial", Presencia [La Paz], July 10, 1080, p. 1.

50. Ibid.

51. "International Outcry Against Military's Seizure of power in Bolivia," *Latin American Weekly Report*, July 25, 1980, p. 1.

52. Ibid., p. 2.

53. "Miners' Resistance Bloodily Crushed," *Quarterly Economic Review of Peru, Bolivia*, 3rd Quarter 1980, pp. 18-19.

Chapter XVII

Prospects for the Future
Jerry R. Ladman

INTRODUCTION

In one fell swoop with the García Meza takeover, Bolivia halted the redemocratization process, reverted to an authoritarian-bureaucratic government, destroyed many of the gains made by the populist sector in influencing the government, and chilled external relations with many countries, most notably the United States and the Andean states that had recently redemocratized. The coup, however, received a favorable reception by the military governments in the Southern Cone countries and Brazil. They had been concerned about the possibility of a leftist government in the heart of the continent that might easily serve as a launching ground for subversive activities in their countries. With the addition of Bolivia there was a complete block of military governments across the southern portion of the continent which lent support to the legitimacy of this form of government.

With this sudden change in the course of events, what are the prospects for Bolivia's future? In the near term will the García Meza government survive? Will the military governments continue in power in the future or will the governments be democratically elected? Will populism resurface? What are the long-term prospects for economic development? The answers to these questions fundamentally lie in the interplay between economics and politics. The papers presented here provide a background and insight to many of the answers. I will draw upon their wisdom and add my own perspectives to make a prognosis for the future course of Bolivia. The chapter first addresses the near-term prospects for the survival of the García Meza government. Second, prospects for long-term economic growth are examined. Third, the long-term prospects for military or democratically elected governments are set forth. Finally, conclusions are drawn with a prognosis for the long-term economic outlook and the form of government that might rule Bolivia.

PROSPECTS FOR THE GARCIA MEZA GOVERNMENT

Tenuous Support

From its beginning, the García Meza government has confronted many obstacles that seriously jeopardize its ability to survive. Although it had quickly and successfully neutralized the leadership of the civilian opposition, it did not have the enthusiastic support of the populace. There was hope that the military government would provide order and straighten out the economic mess, but it had to prove itself capable of the task. Within the military the new president had only tenuous support. He had assumed the leadership of the armed forces without the enthusiastic backing of many of his fellow officers, and in some cases, against their opposition. There was immediate talk of a countercoup within the military and the new president had to devote considerable effort to shoring up his support and building a coalition within the armed forces. Many civilians and members of the military resented the employment of paramilitary forces, strong-arm tactics, and repression to silence the opposition and bring order.

Administrative Ability

The new administration's ability and expertise in managing the government and correcting the economic situation received serious questioning. The first cabinet was composed entirely of military officers, many of whom had little experience in government. It appeared necessary that experienced and qualified civilians be brought into the cabinet and that stronger liaisons be established with the private sector.

The Economic Situation

The near-term economic outlook was grim. Bolivia faced a foreign exchange crisis, had an overvalued currency, and confronted another devaluation and the ensuing inflation unless means could be found to solve its balance of payments deficit. The possibilities of immediately increasing exports of its traditional products were not optimistic, indeed it was thought they might decline. The world tin market showed signs of softening, oil production increasingly was going for domestic use, and there were few prospects for significantly increasing agricultural exports in the short run. The bright spot was the growing sales of natural gas. Imports, both legal and contraband, continued to increase. Bolivia has seldom shown a willingness to cut back on imports and the current inflation and threat of another devaluation hasten both the purchasing of goods as well as the exodus of capital to foreign investments.

In the meantime, Bolivia is saddled with the need to service its huge foreign debt. The worsening economy, recent political instability, and the military takeover have significantly reduced the inflow of foreign loans and financial assistance. The decision by the Carter administration to drastically cut back the U.S. foreign aid program, followed by many other nations, has made the situation worse. Bolivia faces a foreign exchange crisis and another devaluation.

Simultaneously, the García Meza government must deal with the domestic economy and its problems of a large government deficit, inflation, and inefficiency. The remedial prescription calls for government austerity, higher taxes, tighter money supply, increased prices on basic goods, and control of the decentralized public agencies.

The Drug Connection

As if these problems were not enough, the matters were soon to be compounded by the allegations that several high level members of the new administration and key military officers were involved in the production and trafficking of cocaine, which was conservatively estimated to be a 600 million dollar business in Bolivia in 1980. [1] If this was true, it is alarming that the fate of Bolivia is in the hands of a government linked to the international narcotics market. The implications of this are uncertain, and it is disquieting to many Bolivian civilians and military as well as foreign nations, especially the United States which is undertaking a major effort to crack down on cocaine trafficking in its own country.

Prospects for Survival

Confronted with all these obstacles it will be difficult for the García Meza government to survive. The key factor will be the economic situation. If his administration can make progress in correcting the immediate economic problems, the chances for survival will increase very significantly.

It is doubtful that the government is up to the task. The unfavorable economic legacy of the Banzer administration, which was compounded by inadequate policy measures during the two-year hiatus of the attempt to redemocratize, has saddled the García Meza government with a tremendous and immediate economic burden. The withdrawal of U.S. foreign aid and the stringent preconditions for financial assistance imposed by the International Monetary Fund (IMF) have made the situation more difficult. The combined tasks of eliminating the foreign exchange crisis and dealing with the domestic economy would be herculean for a strong government, let alone for one that is fragile and spending much of its energy to solidify its position.

The Near-Term Prospects for Democracy

If the García Meza government falls it will almost certainly be replaced by another conservative military government. It is unlikely that Bolivia will make another attempt to redemocratize within the next few years. The conservative elements will want to maintain control at least until they straighten out the economic situation and they are reasonably certain that the leftist pressures have subsided. Neither is likely in the near term.

The leftist movement gained considerable momentum during the two-year redemocratization attempt. Although the leadership has been neutralized, there is considerable residual support that would be relatively easy to mobilize were the bans on political parties and organized labor lifted. The removal of these bans would be a precondition to elections; therefore, the conservative elements now in control will not be disposed to lift them until they are confident that leftist support has dwindled.

The solution of the current economic problems may take several years or more. Because the economy is highly dependent on world markets, the solution to the economic situation is not completely in the hands of the government. The current trend towards a world-wide recession is foreboding of a softening of the minerals market which would be very disadvantageous to Bolivia's major source of export revenues.

Almost every economic decision taken by the Bolivian government is heavily laden with political considerations. The ability of a government to survive is dependent upon its capability to make decisions that favor its sources of support and keep down domestic unrest. Thus, the gov ernment is faced with certain parameters that constrain its decision making, for to exceed the limits is to run the risk of destabilization and an overthrow. Since the required measures to solve the current economic situation, as specified by the IMF, run counter to the interests of the ruling coalition and can create instability as they impact on the working classes, there is a built-in resistance within the government to take the measures and they are therefore postponed. If the economic sanctions of the U.S. are continued, the situation will be made more difficult.

Although it will experience difficulties in coming to grips with the economic situation, and it may take several governments before the right combination of external factors and leadership emerge to cope with the economic situation, the fear of the left will give the conservative military and private sector coalition the resolve to remain in power. The presence of many other military governments in Latin America, the threat of communism in Central America, and the election of Reagan to the U.S. presidency should reinforce their tenacity.

Whether or not the military government will remain in power in the long run will depend upon a number of factors, of which the most important is the performance of the economy and the government's ability to engineer longer-term economic developments.

PROSPECTS FOR ECONOMIC DEVELOPMENT

There are two salient features of Bolivia's economy that will have a very important influence on long-run economic development. First, Bolivia will continue to be highly dependent upon the foreign sector. However, history has shown, reliance on exports as an engine of growth will be insufficient to create wide-spread economic development for lack of sufficiently strong backward linkages to the rest of the economy. Second, Bolivia has a small and weak domestic economy. The following sections examine the long-run economic problems that Bolivia faces in the external and domestic economies, broadly suggest the necessary requirements for their solutions, and examine the prospects for their implementation.

The Foreign Sector

Bolivia will remain inextricably dependent upon foreign trade for many years in the future. In the near term, the nation does not have the potential for a sufficiently large domestic market to look inward for the principal sources of growth. The domestic market is limited by the small population, the low level of per capita income, and the unequal distribution of that income. Consequently, Bolivia cannot follow the lead of many Latin American nations and look to the growth of wide-scale industrialization to substitute for imported manufactured consumer and capital goods. To be sure, selected opportunities exist for manufacturing some goods that are presently imported and, as economic development occurs, others will present themselves. However, these will be insufficient to provide major poles of growth. The most promising prospects for import substitution are in basic foodstuffs and processed agricultural goods.

Until the domestic economy is capable of supporting import substitution industries, Bolivia will need to expand exports to maintain the wherewithal to import capital goods and many types of consumer goods. Moreover, exports will be needed to service the foreign debt that will be necessary to finance development. Fortunately, Bolivia's biggest wealth is its natural resource base which lends itself to the production of exports.

Minerals. Minerals will continue to be the major source of export revenues. However, Bolivia's mining industry, especially tin, experiences high production costs relative to most producers because the most accessible and highest grade ores have been mined, its machinery is obsolete, taxes are high, and the State Mining Company (COMIBOL) is inefficient. It is clear that new programs and policies are needed to reduce costs, taxes, and the drain of the COMIBOL subsidy on the federal budget.

Bolivia must be prepared to deal with fluctuations in revenues and foreign exchange earnings from mineral exports that result from changes in world demand and supply conditions. The International Tin Agreement provides a buffer against strong fluctuations but can not eliminate all of them.

Petroleum. There are indicators, and hopes, that more petroleum will be found in the *Oriente*, but, to date, the results have been disappointing. At this time Bolivia cannot count on being a net exporter of petroleum. The rise in domestic demand will likely consume all foreseeable increases in production. Natural gas offers much better prospects with sales to both Argentina and Brazil.

The limited amount of nonrenewable mineral and hydrocarbon resources will eventually impose constraints on how much longer Bolivia can count on them for export revenues. Bolivia must seek ways to become less dependent on them by diversifying exports and reducing imports.

Agriculture. Agricultural products have become important exports since the mid-1960s and offer good prospects for continued growth. In contrast to minerals, these products do not use nonrenewable resources and offer opportunity for continuous exports into the distant future. Moreover, the foreign markets for these products are typically more stable than those for minerals. The rapid increase in the world's population should lead to growth in the market. Bolivia's growing conditions lend to the production of a wide variety of exportable crops and livestock products, particularly in Santa Cruz. The potential for exports from the recently opened areas of the Beni and the Chapare has yet to be realized. There are possibilities of wool production for export in the *Altiplano* and Mountain Valley regions.

Bolivia's agricultural exports suffer from two major problems. First, the high transportation costs make many Bolivian products less competitive. Bolivia is distant from external markets on the continent and from seaports for shipment abroad. This can be counteracted by lowering production costs and, for some products, establishing processing industries to lower weight and bulk. This, however, is the second problem. Bolivian agriculture and food processing suffers from the lack of human capital, infrastructure, and government policies that lead to low-cost, efficient production of export quality products. It is important that Bolivia undertake the public expenditure and initiate the policies necessary to make Bolivian agriculture more competitive.

Manufactures. There are limited opportunities for Bolivia to increase its exports of manufactured goods. Processed agricultural products offer some promise. Membership in the Andean Group will produce limited opportunities for manufacturing of automotive products and other goods, but they will be slow in coming. To date, the members have been bogged down in decisions about the allocation of the industries to the several countries. It is doubtful that Bolivia can expect the benefits from the Andean Group it had hoped for.

Reducing Imports. Simultaneously, Bolivia can gain foreign exchange by reducing imports. There are two means that offer immediate promise: first, increasing domestic production of basic foodstuffs and some manufactures to substitute for food imports, and second, reducing contraband imports. Were contraband effectively controlled, Bolivia would gain foreign exchange, government revenues from import duties would rise, and the production of domestic substitutes would be stimulated.

Limits to Export-Propelled Growth. Bolivia will need exports to help finance development. However, the limited nonrenewable minerals and hydrocarbons impose a long-run constraint and suggest a timetable by which alternative sources of export revenue must be well developed or else the economy will be jeopardized for lack of foreign exchange.

The export sector, although accountable for considerable production and foreign exchange, cannot be expected to provide sufficient impetus for long-run economic development. The mining and hydrocarbon sectors directly employ relatively few persons, and, because most of their capital goods are highly specialized and imported, they do not create strong linkages to the industrial sector nor the rest of the economy. Compared to minerals, export agriculture offers greater potential for linkages. Industrial production for export will be limited and cannot be expected to provide sufficient employment to have a major impact on the economy. Therefore, Bolivia must look inward to other sources of growth in the domestic economy.

The Domestic Economy

To provide the basis for long-term development, it is imperative that Bolivia create a strong domestic economy that will in turn create increasing opportunities for employment, domestic investment, and import substitution activities. Up to the present there have been limited incentives for private investment in production-oriented activities due to the small domestic market, restrictive and inadequate government policies, and the presence of more attractive returns to invest in real estate and construction as well as in opportunities abroad. The lack of a strong domestic capital market has discouraged savings in financial intermediaries and has encouraged investment abroad and in domestic real goods, many of them speculative. With inflationary pressures the tendency would be further enhanced as demonstrated by the recent instability which has encouraged investment abroad.

The state has attempted to pick up the slack in productive investment by creating decentralized agencies such as those of the Bolivian Development Corporation (CBF). This has met with very limited success. Many of the CBF industries suffer from the lack of an internal market, the lack of supplies of raw materials, bad initial planning, poor administration, and inappropriate government pricing policies which affect the markets for their products and raw materials.

The key to creating employment and productive investment opportunities is the development of a domestic market. Tight controls on contraband will create a market for goods that can be produced domestically but were previously imported. Most important, however, is the expansion of purchasing power among the masses by increasing their employment and incomes. With more than 60 percent of the population living in rural areas, the countryside must be the major target for long-run domestic development. More specifically, to create a large domestic market much of this thrust must be directed to the peasants of the *Altiplano* and

Mountain Valleys regions, as well as the new small-farming areas such as the Chapare and the colonized areas of the *Oriente*. Such a strategy would require a major reorientation of policy since previously the bulk of government resources for agriculture has flowed to the large-farming interests in the *Oriente*.

The strategy would require the urban bias of government programs be reduced by eliminating the maximum prices on foodstuffs to improve the terms of trade for agriculture with the rest of the economy. Also, by directing more resources for public services to rural areas and under-taking major public investments in rural infrastructure—such as roads, irrigation, research, extension, and credit—production and markets would be improved. The strategy should also emphasize development of small industries in rural areas that are designed to provide services to farmers or use locally produced inputs to manufacture products while simultaneously providing employment and incomes to families living in the areas. A consequence of the policies should be reduced rates of rural-urban migration.

A secondary target should be increased productive employment in urban areas. Programs promoting industrialization in small-scale indus-tries should be developed. A key to the success of this program would be elimination of contraband.

The Role of the State

The state would need to continue to play a major, but greatly modi-fied, role in future development. In its present form it is a heavily laden, inefficient bureaucracy that more often than not makes decisions on political criteria rather than rational economic grounds. Reforms are necessary to minimize these effects and enhance rational economic deci-sions. The Bolivian state planning mechanism has become refined in re-cent years and is a good means to assess needs and resources and to help establish priorities for development. The planning process can be used to try to identify new export products, new urban or rural industry, and to specify the policy measures that will be necessary to obtain the goals. The regional development corporations are good vehicles to ad-dress local needs.

More emphasis should be given to encouraging the initiative of the private sector. The Bolivian government's eagerness to fill in the in-vestment vacuums of the past is commendable, but has created a set of decentralized agencies that have placed a severe burden on the state be-cause of their inefficiencies stemming from poor planning, ineffective management, and incorrect incentives. When government subsidization is readily available there is little incentive to become more efficient. The problem of the decentralized public agencies must be dealt with directly. The entire system and each of its units needs to be examined thoroughly. Some units might be eliminated or transferred to the private sector. Many need a thorough reorganization with the objective of putting them on a solvent basis. To avoid undue pressures on the balance of pay-ments, their ability to enter into foreign debt needs to be controlled.

The government must develop policies that will be more effective in controlling inflation and mobilizing domestic savings. Financial reform is necessary such that monetary and credit policies offer attractive rates of interest to savers and charge interest rates of borrowers that are commensurate with the opportunity costs of capital. Fiscal reform is necessary to raise government revenues and create a tax system that encourages more investment and reduces deficit spending.

Prospects for Change

The need to look inward and the development of the domestic economy will require a major reorientation of Bolivian economic policy. Since colonial times, the driving force behind the economy has been exports. Government policy has been oriented towards export production. Even after the 1952 revolution, the primary emphasis was on developing export production in the *Oriente*; the domestic economy has been of secondary importance.

The political structure has reinforced this position. Historically Bolivia has been influenced heavily by a small elite of the wealthy, many of whom derive their wealth from export. Therefore, government policies have favored this elite. The 1952 revolution made some inroads in changing this orientation with land reform, creating benefits for organized labor, nationalizing the Big Three mining companies, and opening up the *Oriente*. Yet, fundamentally the situation did not change. Apart from getting land, the peasants' lot improved very slowly and an urban bias developed. Government decentralized agencies supplanted those of the private sector and with the rise of state capitalism they became another element of the elite. With the development of the *Oriente* the Santa Cruz large-farming and business interests were also incorporated into the elite. Government policies reflected these events. Consequently, the required inward-looking policies run against the tradition of outward-looking economic policies and, more recently, those favoring the *Oriente* and their supportive political structure. Whether or not Bolivia will be able to change its orientation will depend upon its ability to overcome this legacy of reliance on the external sector and the *Oriente* for economic growth.

This change-over will be further complicated by another legacy, that of the internal political economy that evolved from the historical development of the elite. The elite has had so much power and influence that government policies and decisions have been formulated to their favor in return for patronage. A consequence is that government economic decisions are often taken on political rather than economic grounds. This has become such an engrained *modus operendi* in Bolivian government that it stands in the way of sound and rational economic decisions.

Therefore, a key factor in predicting the long-run success of the Bolivian economy is the capacity and the will of the Bolivian people, and especially their government, to extricate themselves from the legacy of the past and undertake the tough reforms and policy changes that will enable Bolivia to proceed along the path that leads to economic development. Whenever the status quo is threatened by change, those who stand to lose resist. The above prescription calls for economic reforms and policies that eliminate many of the privileges, subsidies, and income transfers to which the elite have long become accustomed, a reallocation of resources from the richer to the poorer regions of the country, and substantial changes in the public sector and decentralized agencies that would threaten the bureaucracy and administrators. Moreover, increasing the terms of trade for agriculture will heavily impact on the urban sector and decreasing the external terms of trade will run counter to almost all sectors of society, and, therefore, encounter considerable opposition. In face of such opposition it will take a strong and popular government to make the necessary inroads. The next section examines whether the military government is likely to be up to the challenge.

THE FUTURE OF MILITARY GOVERNMENTS

The performance of the economy will be the principal factor that directly and indirectly determines the stability and longevity of Bolivian governments. Directly, favorable economic conditions will contribute to stability, whereas unfavorable conditions can be destabilizing as they create hardships and cause adjustments in policy that lead to dissension and dissatisfaction with the government.

In the shorter run, the most important factors will be the performance of the external sector. Given the extreme external dependence of the Bolivian economy, economic fluctuations and periodic crises can be expected. The depth of a crisis and the ability of a government to take remedial measures will impact on the stability of the government. In the longer run, the level of economic growth and the distribution of the associated changes in income and wealth will be the primary factors contributing to the level of satisfaction of the populace and, hence, government stability.

Indirectly, the performance of the economy will influence political movements, coalitions, and alliances which, in turn, will manifest as they impact upon governments. To the extent that economic policies of a government are commensurate with the interests of these movements, alliances and coalitions, the government will enjoy greater stability. If they are not, then conflict and dissension will emerge. The success of a government will depend upon its ability to respond to these changes.

The two-year attempt at redemocratization clearly demonstrates that a restructuring of political movements is taking place. In this period the restructuring was able to gain sufficient momentum that it is unlikely that the current bans on political activity will be able to suppress it. Indeed, they are likely to reinforce it.

The restructuring arises from the re-emergence of populism, as manifested in the leftist movement, which in turn has caused a strong reaction by the right and conservative elements. The result is a polarization of society. The process was abetted by the lessening ability of the National Revolutionary Movement Party (MNR) and other centrist political parties to serve as leavening elements. As a result, much of the former bulwark of the MNR support—the peasants, workers, and the middle class—became disaffected and shifted their alliances to the left. There is little prospect for the recovery of the MNR and its splinter parties. Their leadership now is of advanced age, having come mostly from the cadre that led the 1952 revolution and the MNR governments, and the ban on political parties and the closing of congress in the Banzer years did not allow another generation to develop. With the current bans there is scant training ground for new leadership. In contrast the leadership of both the left and the right is younger. The new structure means that future governments will tend to be either of the left or the right, with few prospects for viable middle-ground parties.

The current conservative military government is molded in the pattern of the Banzer government. It has established a coalition with the conservative right and has attempted to repress the populist elements and the left. If it continues to be structured in this pattern its economic programs and policies, like those of Banzer, likely will be inadequate to create the conditions for the long-term economic development of the economy. As elaborated above, the long-term development programs will require an inward-looking approach to supplement the external sector.

These domestically oriented policies, however, have a populist bias designed to create more economic opportunities for the peasants and working classes. Given the fear and antipathy of the conservative governments to the populist movement, they cannot be expected to wholeheartedly throw their support behind these populist measures. The result, as was the case under Banzer, will be inadequate attention directed to the domestic economy. If this occurs political instability will increase. The foreign sector will not be strong enough to carry the economy to long-run development and the periodic balance of payments crises will be destabilizing. Furthermore, the relative neglect of the populist elements will increase their resentment, which will also be destabilizing. The conservative military governments will be under pressure to hold elections.

It would be expected that the military will resist elections unless they foresee that a candidate friendly to their persuasion can win. The latter is unlikely because of the current trend of restructuring of the political movements. With the decline of the center, the leftist coalitions easily should gain a majority. Therefore, the conservative military can be expected to tenaciously want to avoid elections. Their tactics would be to promise to hold the election sometime in the future, but to find it convenient to postpone them until they considered the time propitious to their interests.

Meanwhile it is probable the threat from the left will increase. With the growing strength of the left and the demise of the MNR, the peasants and workers likely will not be as malleable nor as content to wait for their due progress as they have in the past. They will take heart from the leftists who are challenging military governments in other countries. The threat of this occurring in Bolivia will create a reaction by more moderate forces. Within the military the more liberal officers would want to modify the conservative rule by undertaking policies directed to help the populist sector, thereby decreasing instability and eventually holding elections. Whether or not this will occur will depend upon the degree of dissatisfaction with the military government and the resilience of the conservative military and their private sector coalition. If the conservatives fail, an alternative would be sought and the ruling coalition would weaken and bend, allowing new alliances to form. A logical outcome would be for the moderate military to form a coalition that would keep the armed forces in power but include centrist elements of both the right and left. If the moderate forces were to gain control the pressures leading to internal instability should lessen considerably. The moderate government's implementation of economic measures that benefit the populist forces and the domestic economy should lead Bolivia on the correct path to long-term development.

If the conservatives were to continue in power, the polarization of Bolivia would become greater over time as latent resentment builds up among those opposing the government. There would be pressure for elections, but, unless the conservative government should fail badly, elections likely will not be forthcoming. The potential for domestic instability will rise and the prospects for an eventual confrontation between the left and the right will increase. Were elections to occur and the left were to win, the conservative military likely would again intervene to prevent them from attaining power. In this manner the conservative rule would be perpetuated.

CONCLUSIONS

Since the 1952 revolution, Bolivia experienced considerable social change and economic growth. In the late 1970s, however, it became clear that the legacies of the MNR and military governments left Bolivia in a weak position to deal with current and future economic problems. The extreme dependence on the external sector made Bolivia subject to periodic balance of payments crises and did not provide a solid base for long-term economic development. The two-year attempt at redemocratization showed the weakness of the political system as well as the ultimate strength of the military.

By 1980 the combination of the economic crisis and struggles of the attempt at redemocratization placed Bolivia at a juncture that was critical for the nation's future. If the conservative military governments remain inflexible and do not take the necessary economic reforms and policies, including those that give opportunities to the working and peasant classes, the prospects for both economic development and political stability are quite unfavorable.

The burden is upon the military to recognize dangers in this strategy and make the necessary but major reforms and adjustments in economic policies. Given the entrenched interests and antipathy to the left by the conservative military and private sector interests who form the ruling elite, such reforms will be difficult. If, however, they are not undertaken, Bolivia will sacrifice immediate opportunities for long-term economic development and come closer to the time when its stock of non-renewable resources has declined and limits exports such that future efforts for development will be more difficult. Meanwhile domestic instability will rise and may reach the point where it would spill forth as an internal conflict. If this occurs Bolivia may experience another populist revolution to correct the failures of that of 1952.

ENDNOTE FOR CHAPTER XVII

1. "Cocaine Bankrolls Regime in Bolivia, Diplomats Maintain," *Arizona Republic* (Phoenix), September 14, 1980, p. AA-10.   This estimate was undoubtedly conservative.   The United Nations Narcotics Control Board estimated that Bolivian cocaine production was valued at 1.2 billion dollars in 1980 as reported in, "In Brief," *Latin American Weekly Report*, February 13, 1981, p. 11.

Epilogue

García Meza resigned the presidency on August 4, 1981. His administration's lack of success in correcting the economic crisis, the involvement of high-level military officers in narcotics trafficking, blatant and wide-spread corruption within the military with the cocaine-derived dollars and the failure to obtain normalized relations with the United States, principally due to the narcotics situation, had led to considerable disillusion among the populace as well as devisiveness within the military. Numerous coups were threatened over the course of his regime but the president successfully fended them. When it became abundantly clear that this regime was not leading Bolivia out of its crisis but, indeed, worsening it with the drug connections and corruption, the attempts to overthrow the government became more serious. There were four coups tried in June and July. Finally, two exiled moderate generals—Alberto Natusch Busch and Lucio Añez Riveras—were able to force a change in the government when they led troops that seized the Santa Cruz airport. From this position of strength, which was supported by many military commanders, they were able to force the resignation of the president and to have a strong influence upon who would eventually be his successor.

Initially, García Meza turned the government over to a three-man junta comprised of persons loyal to him: the Head of the Air Force, General Waldo Bernal; the Commander of the Navy, Admiral Oscar Pammo; and the Head of the Army, General Celso Torrelio. The linkages between the junta and García Meza plus the fact that the ex-president continued to live in the presidential residence, and even received the junta a few days after the changeover at a cocktail party in honor of his birthday, strongly suggested that the junta would be controlled by the ex-president. Bernal, who was closely tied to the ex-president, was the heir apparent. This was unacceptable to the rebels and many others. Finally, after a month of negotiations, on September 4 Torrelio was named president. He was a compromise selection. Although considered to be a García Meza loyalist, he had the fewest ties to the ex-president of the three members of the junta. He had not been implicated in drug trafficking and, moreover, represented the largest branch of the armed forces.

Shortly after assuming office Torrelio made positive moves in promising a return to democracy in three years and revealing general plans that called for a major restructuring of the economy with a greater role assigned to the private sector. Furthermore, he convinced the United States of his sincerity in cracking down on narcotics traffickers with the result that in November, the North American country normalized relations by placing Edwin Corr, a narcotics expert, as ambassador in La Paz.

In the meantime the economy continued to deteriorate. The IMF had imposed very stringent and harsh requirements to obtain their standby credit. Torrelio, realizing that compliance to meet these requirements would lead to considerable unrest and disturbances, proceeded cautiously. In February 1982 he devalued the Bolivian peso from 25 to 44 per U.S. dollar and raised import and export taxes.

These measures, however, fell short of the IMF requirements, which included the elimination of subsidies on basic food stuffs. Confidence in the peso continued to fall, such that within weeks it was trading at rates of exchange in excess of 100 per dollar in the parallel markets of La Paz. In March the government announced policies to eliminate consumer subsidies on some basic food items and to adopt a multiple exchange rate. Workers demonstrated in Cochabamba and six persons were killed and eleven wounded as police opened fire on the demonstrators.

The show of strength by populist forces caused the government to reassess its strategy. Immediately there was pressure to lift the repressive measures on political parties and to push for early elections. Torrelio, succumbing to this pressure, began to relent. In May he announced a general and unrestricted amnesty for political figures and the lifting of bans on political parties and organized labor. However, in order to maintain control over the process, he proposed a dialogue between the political parties and the military to chart the return to democracy. In response many of the political parties agreed to put aside their differences to interface with the government. Pressure was placed upon Torrelio to convene the congress that had been elected in 1980 to allow them to name a civilian president, presumably Siles Zuazo. Torrelio compromised and announced general elections for April 1983. In the meantime the military could try to reestablish its credibility.

The liberalization raised concern among the conservative military and private sector interests who feared losing control. The president's caving in to popular pressure plus his inability to manage the economy and secure IMF financing caused them considerable concern. Moreover, COB was increasing its pressure on the government by sponsoring a series of demonstrations and calling for an immediate end to military rule. The military had no choice. Torrelio had to go. On July 15 he announced his intention to resign. On July 21, after considerable infighting, the military named General Guido Vildoso Calderón to the presidency. The conservatives remained in power; Vildoso had been a strong supporter of the García Meza regime.

The pressure was now on Vildoso. The deteriorating economy was extremely onerous and Bolivia was on the verge of defaulting on its servicing of its foreign debt. Meanwhile, the peso further lost its value and traded higher than 300 per dollar on occasion. The resulting rampant inflation considerably lowered the real incomes of most families, a situation which was aggravated by shortages of bread, meat, and other staples as suppliers withheld their products from the market. Simultaneously, the new president was pressured for immediate elections by COB and to convene the 1980 congress by a number of the political parties.

The president had little choice but to act. On the political front, he held to the April election date but reestablished the 1965 electoral law, to replace that passed by congress in 1980, which would favor a government candidate. On the economic front, he courted the United

States by agreeing to implement measures to try to eradicate coca production in order to obtain a commitment of considerable foreign assistance. He undertook serious negotiations with the IMF, which implied that Bolivians would have to further tighten their belts with stringent austerity measures were IMF assistance to be forthcoming.

The reaction of the populace was overwhelming. Organized labor was pleased with neither the political nor the economic solution, both of which forebode difficulties for the working class. Their demonstrations continued. In early September the tin miners at the important Huanuni mine went on strike. Between September 7 and 17 COB orchestrated work stoppages and strikes took place over the whole country shutting down the mines, banks, and communications sectors. The final straw was a nationwide general strike and demonstrations. There was a portent of a genuine populist revolution.

It was clear that the Vildoso government would be unable to undertake the necessary economic measures if it were to remain in power. There was strong sentiment, even among many who had staunchly supported the military regimes of the past two years, for a change in government. On September 17 the military commanders met and decided that they had no alternative but to step down. They opted to convene the congress elected in 1980 and to turn the government over to the president that body would designate. A sense of normalcy returned as most Bolivians were relieved to be quit of the reign of the disappointing military governments and looked to give the new civilian government its turn to try to come to grips with the problems. The congress quickly named Hernán Siles Zuazo and Jaime Paz Zamora as president and vice-president and they assumed office on October 10.

In conclusion, the failure of the military governments, between 1980 and 1982, to come to grips with the increasing economic crisis in combination with their lack of strong leadership and blatant corruption, created a widespread lack of confidence in their ability to govern and forced them to turn the government over to civilian hands. Whether or not Siles Zuazo will be able to effectively govern is uncertain. Although political parties temporarily set aside their differences to name the new leaders, it is unlikely that all will be harmonious in the future, a factor that will be exacerbated by the fact that the UDP does not have a majority in the congress. Moreover, the new government will have to take a course of action that is acceptable to both the left and the military, a path that has numerous inherent conflicts. Although the latter was badly bruised by its failure to govern, a regrouping will take place and the armed forces will continue to pose a threat to civilian rule should it be unsuccessful in dealing with the economic crisis or threaten unpalatable reforms and policies.

The serious and deep contemporary economic problems likely will be destabilizing as they cause further political instability. Unless the Siles Zuazo government can obtain and maintain widespread support this will impose constraints on its latitude of action. If it is unsuccessful, a change in government will be forthcoming; it would not be surprising to see another military or civilian-military government come to power.

In the meantime, the internal problems and the need to try to resolve the current economic crisis will divert attention from the longer run. The measures required to place Bolivia on the path to economic development will go begging, postponing the time when Bolivia could become less dependent on the foreign trade sector by establishing a stronger and more viable domestic economy. It is clear that the cost of instability to Bolivia is indeed high, both in the short and long run. One would hope that Bolivia would be able to rid itself of instability. Unfortunately, the legacy of the past offers faint hope for the future.

Glossary of Acronyms

ABTN	Andean Brussels Trade Nomenclature
ADN	The National Democratic Action Party
AFIN	The Alliance of the National Leftist Forces Party
AID	The United States Agency for International Development
AIFLD	The American Institute for Free Labor Development
ALDE	Food for Development
ALIN	The National Alliance of the Left Party
APIN	The Popular Alliance for National Integration Party
APRA	The Popular Alliance of American Revolutionaries
BAB	The Bolivian Agricultural Bank
CBF	The Bolivian Development Corporation
CDF	The Forestry Development Center
CET	Common External Tariff
CIAT	The Tropical Agricultural Research Center
CIMA	The Center for Research and Improvement of Sugar Cane
CNECA	The National Commission for Sugar Cane Studies
CNRA	The National Land Reform Council
COB	The Bolivian Workers Central
COBOLCA	The Bolivian Coffee Committee
CODEBENI	The Development Corporation of The Beni
CODECH	The Development Corporation of Chuquisaca
CODETAR	The Development Corporation of Tarija
COFADENA	The Military Development Corporation
COMBOFLA	The Bolivian Wool Promotion Committee
COMIBOL	The Bolivian State Mining Company
CONADE	The National Committee to Defend Democracy
CONAMAR	The National Maritime Council
CONEPLAN	The Economic and Planning Council
CORDECO	The Development Corporation of Cochabamba
CORDECRUZ	The Development Corporation of Santa Cruz
CORDENO	The Regional Development Council of the Northwest
CORDEOR	The Development Corporation of Oruro
CORDEPAZ	The Development Corporation of La Paz
CORDEPO	The Development Corporation of Potosí
CORGEPAI	The Development Corporation of Abápo-Izozog Project
ECLA	The Economic Commission for Latin America
EEC	The European Economic Community
ENA	The National Rice Enterprise
ENAF	The National Smelting Company
FDR-NA	The New Alternative Democratic Revolutionary Front Party
FMNR-U	The Nationalist Revolutionary Movement Unity Front Party
FNP	The National Popular Front
FRA II	The Agricultural Refinancing Fund II
FRI	The Leftist Revolutionary Front Party
FSB	The Bolivian Socialist Falange Party
FSTMB	The Bolivian Federation of Miners Unions
GOB	The Bolivian Government
GSA	The United States General Service Administration
IBTA	The Bolivian Institute of Agricultural Technology
IDB	The Inter-American Development Bank
IMF	The International Monetary Fund
INALPRE	The National Institute for Pre-Investment
INC	The National Institute of Colonization

INDEF	The National Institute of Financing
INE	The National Institute of Statistics
INGAVI	The Ingavi Integral Development Project
INI	The National Institute of Investment
INT	The National Wheat Institute
ITA	The International Tin Agreement
ITB	The Bolivian Technology Institute
ITC	The International Tin Council
LAFTA	The Latin American Free Trade Association
MACA	The Ministry of Peasant Affairs and Agriculture
MIN	The Nationalist Movement of the Left Party
MIR	The Revolutionary Movement of the Left Party
MITKA	The Indian Movement Tupaj Katari Party
MITKA-1	The Indian Movement Tupaj Katari Party Number One
MNR	The National Revolutionary Movement Party
MNR-A	The National Revolutionary Movement Alliance Party
MNRH	The National Revolutionary Movement Historical Party
MRNI	The National Revolutionary Movement of the Left Party
OAS	The Organization of American States
PCB	The Bolivian Communist Party
PDC	The Christian Democratic Party
PIL	Milk Processing Plants
PIR	The Revolutionary Party of the Left
POR	The Revolutionary Workers Party
PRA	The Authentic Revolutionary Party
PRI	The Revolutionary Institutional Party
PRIN	The National Revolutionary Party of the Left
PRIN-A	The Leftist National Revolutionary Party Alliance
PS-1	The Number One Socialist Party
PUB	The Bolivian Union Party
SAI	The Interamerican Agricultural Service
SENARB	The National Service of Hoof and Mouth Disease Rabies and Brucelosis
SIDP	The Sectorial Industrial Development Program
SNDC	The National Community Development Service
SNMH	The National Meteorological and Hydrological Service
SSND	The Socio-economic Strategy for National Development
UDP	The Democratic Popular Coalition
VO	The Workers Vanguard Party
YPFB	The Bolivian State Petroleum Company

Index